Changing Rural Society

Aymara musician (Lauren Klein)

Changing Rural Society

A Study of Communities in Bolivia

WILLIAM J. McEWEN

*with the support of the
Bolivia Project Staff*

Published under the auspices of
the Research Institute for the Study of Man

OXFORD UNIVERSITY PRESS
New York London Toronto
1975

Originally presented in a report entitled *Changing Rural Bolivia*, issued by
the Research Institute for the Study of Man, the material in this volume
stemmed from research done under contract to the Peace Corps.

BOLIVIA PROJECT ADMINISTRATION

Vera Rubin
Lambros Comitas
William J. McEwen

SENIOR FIELD WORKERS

Katherine Barnes
Hans Buechler
Dwight Heath
Solomon Miller
Victor Novick
Eloy Robalino S.

SENIOR ANALYSTS

Adrienne Aron
Marta Callejo
Isabella Conti
Blanca Muratorio

The complete list of project personnel is given in Appendix I.

PREFACE

This volume is one product of a major research study carried out in Bolivia by the Research Institute for the Study of Man. At the request of and under contract to the Peace Corps, RISM designed and implemented a three-year program of anthropological and epidemiological research which had two major related objectives: the delineation of the characteristic social features of rural Bolivian communities in different ecological regions of the country, and the identification of the major problems of health and disease in these communities. Analyses of these sociocultural features and problems of health care were seen as fundamental to the planning of effective community development programs and to the work of Peace Corps Volunteers and other community-level workers.

When RISM was approached in 1963 to conduct the project for the Peace Corps in Bolivia, a primary concern in developing the research plan was to study the communities in relation to the national society and its distinctive ecological, ethnic, and political features; the striking contrasts in physical ecology; the very large Indian population, which is concentrated in the highlands; the political militance and power of the mining unions, with their large Indian membership; and the predominance of rural society (in rural-urban demographic comparison). Looming in the background of each of these features of contemporary Bolivia was the Revolution of 1952, which had clearly changed the salience of all these factors in the life of the nation. Thus the Revolution was a keystone in the research design.

An equally important general consideration was the development of a plan of research which would be useful to the Peace Corps. The first contingent of Peace Corps Volunteers was sent to Bolivia in 1962. By 1963 there were 152 Volunteers working throughout Bolivia, almost half of them in the public health and sanitation program. Previous research by and for the Peace Corps had been strongly psychological and oriented toward questions concerning the personal adjustment of Volunteers in alien settings. The RISM project was geared to focus on the situations in which Volunteers work and the sociocultural factors involved.

Since Bolivia is one of the least urbanized countries of Latin America, there was a compelling sociodemographic case to concentrate on the rural population. This was further reinforced by the dramatic impact of the Revolution on rural Bolivian society. A review of published reports revealed that little satisfactory information was available either on rural society or on its health problems. In 1964 Bolivia was still regarded as "practically terra incognita, as far as studies of the contemporary culture are concerned" [Strickon, 1964, p. 146]. Despite the passage of a decade, this is still substantially true, though the amount of research, at various stages of completion, has increased markedly.

As the rural community is an important component of developing societies, a focus of research in social anthropology, and the locus of Peace Corps Volunteer activity, it was selected as the unit of study, and research strategy was based on the comparison of contrasting communities. Comparison has generally been treated more in the abstract than substantively in social anthropological field research, particularly where individual field workers are involved. Its scientific value is unquestioned, however, and large-scale projects provide the opportunity for a broadened research design. The consequences and complications of this decision cannot be reviewed here in adequate detail, but a brief comment explaining the structure and roles of the Bolivia Project Staff and acknowledging their respective contributions is in order.

An initial comparative community study design was developed which concentrated on community social structure and problem-solving, especially in the area of health. It was further determined to provide basic medical data as a framework for the behavioral data on health, and an epidemiological survey, designed by Dr. Mahfouz Zaki, was added to the community studies. The anthropological research design focused on community politics and social stratification as the critical dimensions in community organization and problem solving to provide systematic data for a comparison of communities on these variables. Community selection thus became critical to the research, and the months of July through September 1964 were spent reconnoitering the three major ecological zones of Bolivia: western highlands, central valleys, and eastern lowlands. These community surveys were carried out by a team consisting of Dwight

Heath, William McEwen, and Victor Novick. Dr. Zaki found it impossible to meet the field schedule to survey the epidemiological study requirements, and he was replaced by Dr. Abdel Omran, who joined the reconnaissance team in Bolivia and subsequently revised and developed the epidemiological fieldwork plan. The results of the epidemiological surveys, augmented by some of the medical anthropological data, have been published by the Research Institute for the Study of Man [Omran, McEwen, and Zaki, 1967].

It was initially planned that two anthropological field teams would each study two sets of communities over a two-year period, while an epidemiological team would survey all four communities during a one-year period. Administrative and staffing problems encountered in the normal course of large-scale fieldwork make flexibility in planning field research an absolute necessity, which may turn out to be beneficial. As a result, six communities rather than four were studied for varying lengths of time at different periods between October 1964 and December 1966. Fieldwork in Reyes was carried out between October 1964 and September 1965, in Coroico between December 1964 and October 1965, in Compi between December 1964 and January 1966, in Villa Abecia between October 1965 and June 1966, in Sorata between November 1964 and February 1965 and again between July 1965 and September 1966, in San Miguel between April and September 1965 and between July and December 1966. A major effort was made to include both Bolivian as well as United States nationals in all the field teams.

Major credit for collecting the basic data analyzed in the present account is due to the anthropological field team. Each field team was headed by a senior anthropologist: Victor Novick in Reyes and Villa Abecia, Dwight Heath in Coroico, Solomon Miller in San Miguel, Hans Buechler in Compi, and William J. McEwen in Sorata. While the first four are not responsible for the present analysis, this book would not have been possible without their contribution. This holds true also for the other team members, both Bolivian and North American. All are identified in the personnel roster, but two must be singled out for their very considerable field assistance: Katherine Barnes von Marschall, who worked in Coroico, Villa Abecia, and Sorata; and Eloy Robaline S., who worked in Coroico and Sorata.

In order to coordinate the fieldwork and establish the bases for comparisons, an extended outline of research topics and questions was prepared for the guidance of the community study teams. During the course of the fieldwork, copies of the typed field notes were sent at monthly intervals from Bolivia to Berkeley, California, where a bilingual team coded and processed the data according to the community study outline. These topically organized and chronologically ordered notes provided an overview of fieldwork in progress in the communities and the development of categories for analysis. The processing, based on a complex coding scheme of the voluminous field notes, was an extremely arduous and demanding task. The final analysis and write-up depended on this work, and the coding team deserves a full measure of credit, especially Adrienne Aron, who completed by far the largest part of this task. Finally, several members of the Berkeley staff were recruited to undertake analyses of the processed field data, a task which they carried out with great skill. Special recognition must be given to Blanca Muratorio and Marta Callejo, who completed drafts for the analysis of Villa Abecia and Reyes, respectively; to Adrienne Aron and Isabella Conti, who completed drafts for some of the sections on Coroico and Sorata; and to Joan Medlin, who prepared a draft of the section on the San Miguel setting. These analyses greatly facilitated preparation of the present volume.

In addition to the focused ethnography, which employed traditional methods of participant observation, an interview survey was carried out in the six communities at the end of the community study fieldwork. The interview schedule was designed to cover the central topics being investigated by the anthropological field teams. This pretested schedule was administered to probability samples in the six communities. Two interviewing teams, one Spanish-speaking and the other Aymara-speaking, were recruited and trained for this work, partly from the anthropological teams which were then disbanding. Blanca Muratorio helped develop the interview schedule and directed the pretesting and final survey in Bolivia. She was assisted by Michael Pettitt, who headed the Aymara-speaking team. They and their team members, who are listed on the roster, deserve great credit for successfully carrying out an unusually difficult job. Anyone who has attempted a survey in rural Latin America will appreciate the magnitude of the problems they faced. The results of this work are expected in subsequent volumes.

Because of its size and complexity, this multidisciplinary field project involved considerable administrative responsibility, interlarded with the usual run of expectable but not predictable field crises. Day-to-day administrative responsibility was carried by the staff of the Research Institute for the Study of Man in New York. In order to minimize administrative costs, no central office was established in Bolivia. Once procedures and arrangements had been worked out for the project, each team leader was responsible for his own research administration, and each also assisted the epidemiological team, which drew on the expertise of the anthropological teams wherever possible. RISM oversaw the flow of epidemiological and anthropological supplies to Bolivia and the return of data to New York and on to Berkeley. The laboratory analysis of epidemiological samples and data processing also had to be organized. Among those at RISM who contributed to working out the myriad problems of administration at a distance are Carol Dickert, Dena Hirsh, June Murray Anderson, and Andrea Talbutt.

Beyond the day-to-day logistical work associated with keeping a large research project functioning, there is the vital administrative level of policy management. The planning, organization, and over-all direction of the study were the responsibility of the undersigned. Frequent meetings were held to discuss the progress of work and to make key decisions, and our correspondence was voluminous. Despite a variety of obligations, we coordinated our schedules so that, for example, when McEwen, the project research director, was not in Bolivia, either Comitas or Rubin could be there without any lengthy interludes.

A number of persons who assisted the project also should be mentioned. Among these are the staff of Peace Corps/Bolivia, Acting Peace Corps Representative (PCR) Daniel Sharp, PCR Jason Edwards, interim Peace Corps Director Richard A. Griscom, PCR Arthur Purcell, and their administrative assistants, all of whom helped with shipments of field notes, handled correspondence, and provided general logistical support for the project. We are also indebted to many Peace Corps Volunteers for their friendliness and assistance with difficult chores. Grateful acknowledgment is also due Juan Forster, Director of Caritas/Bolivia, Leon Shertler of Food for Peace, and the Bolivian Indianist Institute and its director, Dr. Oscar Arze Q., and his staff. We are most indebted to the Bolivian Ministry of Health and its professional staff for their collaboration in the epidemiological study and their continued cooperation during the course of the project.

In the earlier epidemiological and anthropological reports as well as in this publication, the contemporary names of the communities are employed. This has been dictated by epidemiological practice, in which the salience of the findings, and their verification or comparison, requires such specification. On the other hand, the names of all persons, except for national or historical figures, are fictitious. To these anonymous community residents the project owes the greatest debt. They permitted our entry, endured our continual questioning and observing, and provided many memorable personal experiences.

Mention should be made about funding. This study was carried out under Peace Corps Contract (PC(W)-397), which provided financial support for three years, commencing in August 1964. However, given the level of complexity of research and analysis, which was unanticipated at the planning stage, considerable supplementary support was necessary. Consequently, over a third of the total cost of the project came from the general funds of the Research Institute for the Study of Man, as a contribution to the productive application of social science to human problems.

We believe that the major objectives of the study were achieved and that the wide-ranging collaborative relations of a truly excellent project staff were successful. It is our hope that this volume, other publications of the Bolivia project, and those which are still forthcoming will contribute to our understanding of a most vital and pressing problem—the dynamics of rural community life and the directions of communal change not only in Bolivia, but in the developing world.

Vera Rubin
Lambros Comitas
William J. McEwen

CONTENTS

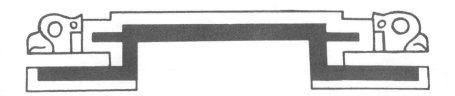

I

INTRODUCTION

BOLIVIA
Bolivia Project Study Communities

0   100   200   300
MILES

SOUTH
AMERICA

BRAZIL

PANDO

BENI

Reyes

PERU

Lake
Titicaca   Sorata
Compi
Coroico
LaPaz   Cochabamba   SANTA CRUZ

Oruro   Santa Cruz
San
Miguel

Pacific
Ocean   POTOSI

Villa Abecia

TARIJA   PARAGUAY

CHILE

ARGENTINA

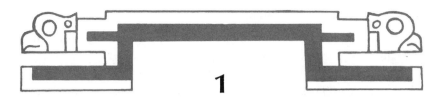

CHANGING
RURAL SOCIETY

Development, modernization, industrialization—whatever it is called, change has been the great preoccupation of underdeveloped societies throughout the world in recent decades. And in each case, attention has been concentrated on the conditions under which societal change occurs and the range of consequences that can be expected. Involved in the issue are political, sociocultural, economic, and many other dimensions, all forming an interconnecting web of forces whose complexity is matched only by the bewildering variety of changes that can actually be observed in the contemporary world.

In some nations, dimly perceived changes threaten to overwhelm the society; in others, ill-conceived changes produce unexpected and destructive consequences; in still others, resistance to change creates tensions and conflicts which grow increasingly costly.

But how do societies change? And how do changes in one sector or level of a society affect other sectors and levels? Unfortunately, our understanding of such processes and what their consequences will be is still far from comprehensive [Appelbaum, 1970, pp. 127-37]. Yet, given the swift pace of such change, and the violence which so often accompanies it, we would do well to direct our attention to these problems.

One promising approach is the study of strategic cases.

In order to find such cases, we turn to Latin America. There the rural population is in the majority in all but a few countries, and agriculture is the dominant sector, the leading source of jobs and income. In fact, in most of these countries, agriculture provides from 20 to 30 per cent or more of the gross national product [ECLA, 1970, pp. 18-19]. Beyond these demographic and economic indicators, there is an even more fundamental consideration. Beginning in colonial times, the rural societies of Latin America were organized around large agricultural estates, the great haciendas. These served to structure the power and status relations of rural life, and they also greatly influenced the same relations at the national level. Indeed, in all but the most industrialized, most urbanized, most modernized of the Latin American nations, this is still the case.

The countries of Latin America are often treated as a unit. Although they do share a number of important characteristics, they also differ from one another in equally important ways. For example, the Latin American nations are frequently regarded as bastions of tradition, with their social orders basically anchored in a colonial past which persists into the present [Pike, 1973, pp. 29-41]. This is true, in varying degrees, of many of these nations. However, there are several which depart markedly from this characterization. These are the countries which are going through change, and such countries present strategic opportunities to examine the processes and consequences of societal change.

Bolivia is a changing country.

Bolivia has a high birth rate (45 per 1000), high illiteracy (67.9 per cent), low per capita income ($122 per year), and a high proportion of the economically active employed in agriculture (63.3 per cent) [Lambert, 1969, pp. 26-27]. These are indices of what Lambert has called an "archaic social structure," whose special features include a predominantly Indian population bound by a way of life and a social organization that keeps it outside the mainstream of the national society. The result is a social and cultural dualism in which development processes affect only a very narrow spectrum of the urban population and do not affect the larger rural population at all. In turn, the urban social and economic elites wield overwhelming political influence, which is sustained by the lack of effective participation by rural populations in the political life of a national society alien to them [Lambert, 1969, pp. 23, 35-36].

Key factors which have produced and maintained these traditional social structures have been concentrated ownership of land, especially cultivated land, and the socioeconomic organization, the hacienda, which was developed to exploit such land control [Chevalier, 1963]. In this respect, too, Bolivia has been prototypical, with an estimated 95 per cent of all agricultural land, according to the last census (1950), held in the form of haciendas by only 4 per cent of all landowners [Garcia, 1964, p. 128]. Paralleling the economic dominance of the haciendas was a political dominance by hacendados of the rural countryside. As Hobsbawm [1967, p. 49] has described it:

> The political structure of the Latin American countryside was . . . that of formal or informal power exercised by local families of estate owners—sometimes in rivalry with others of their kind—each at the apex of a local pyramid of power and patronage; controlling, or seeking to control against local rivals, both the local parts of government administration and the local influence of the national government. . . . In so far as political "parties" existed, they were—and still to some extent are—merely labels tied on to local families and their clienteles, whose votes (if they had any) went, like their armed support and their loyalty in general, to their patron or lord. So far as the mass of the peasantry was concerned, there was no such thing as "national" politics, but only local politics which might or might not have national labels attached to the local persons of power.

The basic social, political, and economic institutions of Lambert's archaic social structures have shown a striking degree of strength, tenacity, and viability—to the despair of those concerned with national development. As Veliz [1967, p. 1] recently noted for all Latin America:

> Perhaps nowhere else and at no other time have so many governments, political parties, international agencies, and pressure groups with otherwise obviously conflicting interests publicly agreed so wholeheartedly on the desirability of a profound alteration of the institutional structure of society. At the same time, seldom have so many influential would-be improvers had so little to show for their efforts.

A partial exception to this generalization is Bolivia. While on many indices Bolivia still merits Lambert's archaic society label, it has also succeeded in achieving some of the basic institutional changes that are the necessary precursors of national development and modernization. In the present context the most important of these is the end of isolation of the rural agricultural population, primarily the Indian hacienda peons and independent Indian agriculturalists, and full participation in national, especially national political, society [Bendix, 1970, p. 271].

The turning point in initiating basic institutional change was the Revolution of 1952. Like other Latin American societies, Bolivia has experienced numerous revolutions of the classic type, in which changes in central government personnel took place without any substantial change in the distribution of power [see Kling, 1968]. The 1952 Revolution was a different kind, a political revolt that became a social revolution. How and why this occurred are still being debated [Malloy, 1968, Blasier, 1966-67, Patch, 1963]. What occurred is somewhat clearer. In the first months of the MNR government the major mining properties were nationalized and a series of labor welfare laws enacted. These measures affected primarily the urban labor force and more especially the highly organized, politicized, and powerful mining unions. Three other measures were more directly applicable to the rural, especially the peon, population. One was the agrarian reform program, which expropriated most of the land of the larger estates, depending on size and quality, distributed hacienda land to former peons, abolished hacienda labor obligations, and created peasant unions as corporate bodies to represent local peons in agrarian reform affairs. In fact, land agitation by peons preceded official agrarian reform, with peons driving landowners off and seizing entire estates. In other areas change occurred more slowly, and transfer of land took place legally, under the reform program. The various technical requirements of legal reform, such as land surveys, when coupled with shortages of technical personnel plus provisions made for appeal, slowed legal land transfer and stimulated both illegal seizure by peons on the one hand and continued dominance by hacendados on the other. If land reform has not proceeded smoothly and efficiently to reorder the agrarian economy, nevertheless it has largely destroyed the traditional hacienda system and with it the major institution of the rural Bolivian social structure.

An extremely important consequence of agrarian reform policy was the organization and spread of peasant sindicatos, or unions. Through these unions and their officers, hacienda peons negotiated with the agrarian reform courts and national officials, other national agencies conducting rural programs, local government officials, and, not least important, former hacienda patróns. The peasant unions, integrated into the national governmental system as traditional Indian government had never been, tended to incorporate and dominate the latter where it was still viable on the ex-haciendas. In addition, local unions were incorporated, in nesting fashion, into regional and national syndical structures which were closely linked at all levels to the MNR political party. It was through the peasant unions that Indian peons were integrated into the national society. It was the nationally defined political role of the peasant union which provided most Indian peons with their first opportunity and stimulus to participate in the wider sociopolitical arena of national affairs. Reinforcing this development was the MNR policy of restricting the strength of the national army and police forces, while arming civilian units to serve as militias for defense of the government. Most militia units were based on the labor unions, including the peasant unions.

A second major reform measure, one whose impact was proportionally greater on rural society, was electoral reform. One of the first acts of the new MNR government was to establish universal suffrage, abolishing sex, literacy, and income restrictions and making voting obligatory. By this act the various political underdogs of Bolivian society became full citizens, with a legally defined political role. Since the law in Latin America has achieved a certain notoriety by accenting form over substance [Lambert, 1969, pp. 115-26], a third major reform acquires strategic and developmental significance. This was the program to extend basic education in Bolivia, with special emphasis on improved rural education that would, among other things, transmit an understanding of citizenship rights and duties. There was an attempt at a complete reorganization of the Bolivian educational system, designed both to extend educational opportunity and to make education more relevant to the needs of the different sectors of the population and the changing needs of the country [Alexander, 1958, pp. 80-92]. Out of this effort came a special rural education program, administered by the Ministry of Rural Affairs rather than the Ministry of Education, which provided both elementary and adult education.

These and other reform measures set in motion a series of major changes in one of the most traditional, least modernized nations of Latin America. In such a country the reform program confronted monumental obstacles, and achievement has been very uneven [Osborne, 1964, pp. 69-81]. Moreover, the political framework underlying the reform programs gradually deteriorated, culminating in the military coup of 1964. This classic *golpe* dispossessed the MNR government, and the country has been ruled by army-dominated governments ever since [Malloy, 1971, pp. 138-53; Whitehead, 1972]. Nevertheless, it is questionable whether the far-reaching changes initiated in 1952 can be reversed, and thus Bolivia still constitutes one of the major tests in the Latin American context for understanding societal change. This was even more clearly the case when the research reported in this book was undertaken, between 1964 and 1966.

What happened to rural Bolivian society in the aftermath of revolution and reform? Beyond the rhetoric, the charges and countercharges, beyond the instant reports of spectacular progress and the equally insistent recountings of personal tragedies, how has rural social life actually been altered?

The answers to these questions were sought through detailed study of six rural communities. While rural Bolivian society includes more than its farm villages and market towns, these local communities do in fact contain a large fraction of the local population and, more importantly, represent significant centers of social organization and change. Furthermore, such communities are dependent parts of the larger society and can be expected to reflect in varying degrees the forces for change initiated by the Revolution of 1952. From this standpoint, the local community becomes the observable stage on which some of the critical social dramas of the society are enacted.

Local communities articulate with the larger society in several different ways and in turn are organized along different lines. Two forms of articulation and the resultant dimensions of community organization stand out in the Bolivian case and became the focus of community study. These were social stratification and politicization. Typically, in socially stratified communities members of one stratum differ from those of another in their style of life, their beliefs and values, and their forms of association, but, more especially, they differ in prestige, wealth, and power [Kahl, 1957, pp. 1-12]. While all communities exhibit differences in individual status associated with differences in prestige, power, and wealth, a stratified hierarchy is a structure of ranked groups invidiously distinguished and unequally sharing in the rewards and privileges of the community [Tumin, 1967, pp. 24-46]. The reality of a stratification order profoundly affects both the organization of local communities and how they function [Bell and Newby, 1972, pp. 82-185 *passim*].

Social stratification has been a key factor in the development of Bolivia. At least as early as the Inca penetration and conquest of what is now highland Bolivia, a stratified social system existed [Baudin, 1961, pp. 33-55]. Of greater contemporary relevance is the Spanish Conquest of the sixteenth century, which resulted in a variety of complex stratification orders. In subjugated areas with large Indian populations, such as Alto Peru, the system was organized around a ranking stratum of Spanish rulers to whom the Indians were subject. In the course of development, as a result of economic, political, and social processes, important intermediate strata began to appear, as well as further stratification along regional and rural-urban lines [Legters and Blanchard, 1963, pp. 107-31]. These added complexities have not blunted the sharp features of social stratification in the rural zones. However, rural communities do vary in the extent to which they are internally stratified. In many small villages there are differences in income, in material goods, in prestige, and in power, but these differences are relatively slight, and there are no distinguishable social strata. These are unstratified, or one-level, systems, in contrast to hierarchical systems. Two of the communities studied, San Miguel and Compi, are unstratified communities, while the other four are examples of hierarchical stratification in rural life.

The second dimension of community organization selected as critical to the Bolivian situation is politicization, or the intensification of political awareness and participation. This is a critical and protean factor of vital importance to the developing nations [Ilchman and Uphoff, 1969, pp. 30-32]. In most of these countries the population is predominantly rural and agriculturally based. These rural populations tend to be physically isolated from the politically active centers of the country as well as intellectually isolated due to lack of education and limited communication. Traditional status relations between landlords and their peasant agriculturalists and between town merchants and peasants have also depressed political participation. Finally, laws of citizenship have frequently excluded large categories of rural residents from political activity by applying restrictive qualifications of education, property ownership, and sex, among others [Cotler, 1970]. Decreasing physical isolation, increasing communication, rising immigration to urban centers, and economic trends which are straining traditional agricultural and mercantile patterns are eroding traditional political barriers and bonds of rural populations. Further, this population is becoming an increasingly important factor in national politics [Huntington, 1968, pp. 433-61]. In many it is the key to national political domination.

Bolivia illustrates how an obscure peasantry emerges as a dominant force in national, as well as regional and local, political affairs through a politicizing process. In Bolivia the rural peasantry is predominantly Indian. Although they constitute as much as two-thirds of the entire population, Indians were traditionally and systematically excluded from national politics. Illiterate, isolated from all but word-of-mouth communication, they were largely an inert political mass. From 1952 on, however, their situation was radically altered. The larger agricultural estates were seized for division among peasants; the peons were freed from feudalistic labor obligations; universal suffrage was enacted without regard to property, linguistic, or educational qualifications; campesino sindicatos, peasant unions, were established, some of them armed to serve as paramilitary units. One consequence of these measures was that the barriers which had isolated the rural peasant, especially the Indian, from the national society were breached. In the rhetoric of the Revolution, rural Indians became campesinos, "countrymen." The campesino sindicatos were drawn into the MNR government and party and were exhorted to take their place in the vanguard of the revolution. This politicization of the Bolivian rural population did not occur everywhere, or at least not with the same intensity. The communities studied here were selected to show the effects of variation in politicization as well as social stratification. Two of them, Villa Abecia and San Miguel, are only slightly politicized. Two others, Reyes and Compi, are moderately politicized, while Coroico and Sorata are highly politicized.

These six communities thus represent significant variations along the two organizational dimensions that appear central to understanding how the Revolution of 1952 has changed rural Bolivian society. How the communities vary in these two, as well as in other, related features is best seen by summarizing their salient characteristics. San Miguel and Compi are agricultural villages, the one oriented to subsistence agriculture, the other market-oriented. While the two villages share an Aymara Indian peasant culture, they contrast organizationally.

San Miguel is a so-called free Indian community, which is to say it survived the spread and domination of the hacienda system as a community in control of its own lands. As a corollary, it is a self-governing community within the larger national governmental structure. This local government is still largely traditional both in form and in function. In contrast, Compi, a market-oriented community, belonged to a hacienda —a difference which has made all the difference. Agrarian reform ignored the free Indian communities except to authorize them to reclaim land that had been taken from them subsequent to 1900. Since San Miguel had lost no lands, none were available, and while peasant union organization was not restricted to ex-hacienda peons, in practice this is where organization was likely to occur and be supported by the government.

In Compi, the hacienda government was overthrown soon after the Revolution and a union organized to obtain the various benefits of reform. There ensued a series of struggles between the hacienda peons and the hacendado family, hacienda peons and small pockets of free Indian comuneros who had survived in the area and now claimed parts of the hacienda, and hacienda peons and ex-peon émigrés who returned to claim their share of hacienda land. This development greatly weakened the internal social integration of the community, which can be seen in the splitting off of hacienda settlements and creation of their own small unions to represent them. A parallel and related change accompanying reform at Compi has been a shift of the ex-peon families from subsistence to cash-crop agriculture, involving specialization in onions for sale in urban markets.

The other four communities are market towns. Two are in former agricultural hacienda zones, and a third is in a cattle and marginal farming zone. Of them, more later. The fourth, Villa Abecia, is a minor market town, but, primarily, it is a small oasis of intensive irrigation viticulture surrounded by rather barren hills. This community, like the Indian community of San Miguel, has been little changed by the Revolution and largely for the same reason—that agrarian reform, as the linch pin of all the reform programs, had little impact because it was largely inapplicable—but in a different way. The lands lost by the patróns of Villa Abecia were large tracts of marginal agricultural and pasture land in the hills, never of great economic importance to them. The valuable land was the irrigated river-bottom land, but since most of this was held in small parcels of from one to ten acres, it was classified as small or medium holdings and not affected by reform legislation. And, while a peasant union was organized soon after the Revolution, it has been dominated by the Villa Abecia patrons and, in fact, was led by a son of one of the leading patrón families for much of its history. Consequently Villa Abecia is now, as it was in the past, a community composed of a small group of elite patrón families who dominate a much larger population of landless peons. Between these two traditional and defining social strata is a relatively small and changing stratum of small merchants, office and skilled workers, and craftsmen.

The other three towns are all in large hacienda areas and represent points on a continuum of increased change resulting from MNR reform. In Reyes, agrarian legislation did little to alter ownership of the cattle estancias, since the town lies in an area of low population density and large areas of unoccupied land whose economic development has been greatly restricted by transport limitations. However, the value of farm land as opposed to range land depends very much on accessibility to local markets and thus there has been a limited struggle for land proximate to towns. The agrarian reform also outlawed debt peonage, thus freeing most of the ranching labor force, many of whom tried their hand at farming, found it less profitable than they had anticipated, and drifted back to the ranches. The other two towns, Coroico and Sorata, were in classic agricultural hacienda zones. In both, the hacendado families that had dominated these towns have lost all or most of their lands and have either left the communities or remain with but a vestige of their former wealth. In Coroico a set of middlemen, drawn from all social strata, have emerged as the center of economic power in the community, while in Sorata there has been a great expansion in both the market orientation of ex-peon agricultural producers and in the network of middlemen, drawn both from town cholos and the Indian peons themselves, that transports produce to city markets, resulting in a diffusion of economic power. In both areas peasant unions are strong, active, and generally highly politicized. In Sorata they have succeeded in gaining control of the town and provincial government, whose offices are now filled with Aymara-speaking, peasant politicians.

These community summaries indicate that the MNR reforms were capable of producing profound institutional change in rural Bolivian society, but did so in varying degree, depending on a variety of factors. The major social and political effects have been a decline of the hacendado class following the weakening of their economic base; the disappearance or slackening of lines of control over hacienda peons; the organization of peasant unions as corporate interest associations having a variety of legal and political as well as economic and social responsibilities; the extension of a national political role for the peasants, extended throughout the countryside and organized both through the governmental political party and through the peasant unions; and the strengthening of old as well as the creation of new economic opportunities, especially for ex-hacienda peons—all of which effects have undermined the traditional social stratification.

In the following chapters, detailed characterizations are presented of each community, beginning with the hierarchically stratified communities and describing, first, the least politicized, then the moderately politicized, and, finally, the two highly politicized communities. Then the two unstratified communities, varying from little to moderately politicized, are presented. Each community is described separately in order to bring out the interconnections between the different features of each. In every case the central focus is on status and power, on social stratification and politicization. Particular attention is paid to community power, authority, leadership, political participation, community status, status groups, group membership, group leadership, and inter-group relations. Finally, in order to show how these elements of community social organization affect each other, one or more efforts at community problem-solving are described. Each of these communities tells us something of the character of rural society in what was one of the most traditional of the Latin American nations. Taken together, they also show how that rural society has been changed through sociopolitical revolution. The Revolution of 1952 ended many years ago, but its effects can still be observed. Where those effects occurred and the forms they took, as well as where they did not occur and how this was possible, can help us understand the meaning of social change and stability in the rural sectors of the developing nations.

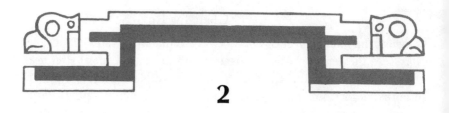

2

THE BOLIVIAN SETTING

Bolivia is the fifth largest country in South America, its area being 423,163 square miles, somewhat over half the size of Mexico and not quite twice the size of Texas. Within this moderately large country there exists a marked regionalism, the effect especially of geographic obstacles to communication and geographic imperatives in population distribution. All Bolivia is in three major ecological zones: high plateau, valleys, and lowlands [Osborne, 1964, pp. 7-34].

The high plateau (the altiplano) covers about one-fifth of the country, in the west and southwest. It is a series of large tablelands extending from north to south, walled off to the west by the Cordillera Occidental and to the east by the Cordillera Real, snow-capped chains of the Andes. Elevation varies from 12,000 to 13,000 feet above sea level, and the region is generally treeless and barren and tends to be cold, windy and arid. The flanking mountains rise to 23,000 feet, and in them are most of the mines and known mineral wealth of the country. On the altiplano live perhaps 70 per cent of Bolivia's people. Two of the communities of this study are in this ecological zone.

Compi is a community of the northern altiplano. It is situated beside Lake Titicaca, and consequently has slightly warmer weather, more reliable rainfall, and fewer hailstorms than other parts of the high plateau. South of Compi is San Miguel, in the central altiplano, a zone which is generally more arid, less fertile, and subjected to extremes of cold and wind.

Most of the eastern chain of the Andes, the Cordillera Real, is dry, stony, and sparsely populated. However, cutting through the eastern

La Paz market (Lambros Comitas)

Cordillera is another livable world, a complex belt of valleys that connects the altiplano to lower lands in the east. This valley region comprises about 10 per cent of the area of Bolivia but contains 20 per cent of her population. It is a fantastically convoluted region of jagged mountains that drop away into myriad canyons and valleys. Some canyons extend for miles, but are only a few hundred yards across. The considerably wider valleys sometimes offer a broad expanse of relatively flat land. Crossing the eastern Cordillera at altitudes of 15,000 to 16,000 feet, the canyons and valleys descend into another, main-valley area, which slips down from 10,000 to 2000 feet above sea level.

Two of the study communities are in upper, higher-altitude valleys. One of these, Sorata, is not far in an airline sense from either La Paz or Compi, but lies far over on the eastern side of the Cordillera Real and down at an elevation of 8000 feet. There are no broad valleys here, so much of the agriculture is practiced on steep hillsides. The climate of Sorata is markedly Mediterranean, with seasonal grasses, groves of eucalyptus, and large fields of maize.

The second of our communities in the upper valleys is Villa Abecia. It lies south, close to the Argentine border. Although it is only slightly lower in altitude than Sorata, Villa Abecia's climate and vegetation are very different, being affected by an immense, desert-like area—the Chaco, to the southeast—which covers most of northern Paraguay and part of southern Bolivia. Except for a brief period following the rainy season, most farmlands in the Villa Abecia area must be irrigated, which generally means river-bottom cultivation. Sparsely covered, steep mountainsides shed flash floods during the rainy season, and rising drafts in the heat of the summer often bring down destructive hailstorms. Floods and hail take an annual toll of crops. And because roads are continuously washed away, some part of what is left for harvest may go unmarketed.

As valley succeeds valley in the sometimes gradual, sometimes precipitous descent to the trans-Andean eastern lowlands, the Mediterranean climate of the upper valleys gives way to a semitropical environment. Much of the lower-valleys zone is accessible only on foot or on horseback. An exception is the zone known as the Yungas, in which lies the study community of Coroico. This is a zone of deep canyons, year-round rivers, and lush vegetation. It produces such semitropical crops as coffee, bananas, and citrus fruits, as well as coca (source of cocaine and chewed for its stimulant properties), all grown on carefully terraced hillsides. The Yungas has always been an important agricultural area in Bolivia.

The low hills of the lower valleys eventually give way to the Llanos del Oriente, an immense flat plain which stretches north and east to the Brazilian frontier and south to Paraguay. The Oriente is about 70 per cent of the total land area of Bolivia. It varies in altitude, from 300 to 1500 feet, and is hot and wet. Heavy seasonal rains inundate great expanses for weeks at a time. Over this great flat area tropical jungle alternates with open forests and savannah grasslands, and though it is rich in plant and animal growth, it contains no more than about 15 per cent of Bolivia's population. In this area of generally small and widely separated settlements is the sixth study community, Reyes. It lies in grassland but not far from forest, near the western edge of the northern part of the Oriente.

The three major regions of Bolivia differ greatly in accessibility. The lowland Oriente region is the most isolated, though it has recently been penetrated by one of the few paved roads in Bolivia, a highway which carries traffic between Cochabamba and Santa Cruz. Two rail lines also run from Santa Cruz, one to the Brazilian border in the east and the other to Argentina in the south. But these facilities still leave most of the Oriente without road or rail transport. Travel is by foot, horseback, canoe, or small boat, except that important towns such as Reyes—and even some unimportant ones—are served by the national airlines.

The generally flat terrain and the great distances make air transport an ideal though expensive form of rapid transport in the Oriente. In the valleys region, terrain rules out aircraft; while on the altiplano, it is more a matter of being financially out of range for small farm villages. The terrain in the valleys region is also inhospitable to railroads, so most traffic moves over raw roads that generally have been bulldozed out of the mountainsides and are subject to continual erosion and destruction. The three valleys communities of this study are reached by such roads.

A rail line traverses the length of the altiplano but has little impact on most of the communities in this region, for it serves few cities, and is mainly an export carrier of mined minerals. Few communities have airline service, and the road network is poor. Nevertheless, goods and people do move, for most of the altiplano is level, dry, and hard, and heavy-duty trucks can reach most communities without any road at all. At times, it is only necessary to point the vehicle in the right direction and follow the landmarks and the stars. This is the case with travel to San

Miguel, except during the rainy season, when it is quite inaccessible by vehicle.

National census data are far from reliable. The 1950 census gave the proportion of rural residents as 66.1 per cent, but since all administrative centers, regardless of region, were counted as urban, this figure is very likely an underestimate [Lyle and Calman, 1966, p. 14, Table 7]. The National Planning Council estimated the rural population in 1960 as 71 per cent [Junta Nacional de Planeamiento, 1961]. Other data give the proportion of residents of localities of over 100,000 persons in 1957 as 10.2 per cent, which would mean that 89.8 per cent were in rural communities [Lyle and Calman, 1966, p. 15, Table 8].

About 70 per cent of the labor force is engaged in one or another of the agricultural occupations [Zondag, 1966, p. 18], which accounted for approximately one-third of the gross national product in Bolivia in 1964 [Zondag, 1966, p. 202, Table 15]. On the other hand, 40 per cent of Bolivia's imports in approximately the same period were foodstuffs, which the country itself theoretically could produce, while 95 per cent of the value of all exports came not from the sale of agricultural products, but of minerals [Zondag, 1966, p. 177]. In short, this predominantly agricultural population does not produce enough food to meet its needs, but feeds itself in part through its mineral exports.

Each of the six communities of this study is within the agricultural sector of the Bolivian economy. In them we shall find some of the problems and prospects of the whole agricultural sector as seen at the local level. As a set, they represent the major regional variations that occur in Bolivia in terms of distinctive physical ecologies, some peculiarities of microenvironments and microclimates excepted. They typify some of the most important farm and market communities of the country.

SOCIETY AND GOVERNMENT

Just as the research communities exhibit environmental and economic variations encountered in rural Bolivia, so they reflect some of the major forms and variations in social and political organization. According to the National Planning Agency, the Bolivian population is 52.9 per cent Indian, 32 per cent cholo (mixed descent), 14.8 per cent white, and 0.3 per cent other races [Osborne, 1964, p. 106]. In fact, this is more a distribution of cultural types than a racial distribution. There are few whites in Bolivia who have no Indian ancestry, while the definition of a cholo depends on cultural criteria of language and manners more than anything else. Further, these figures probably greatly overestimate the proportion of whites and underestimate that of Indians.

Whether thought of as fundamentally racial or ethnic groupings, this way of categorizing the national population has had an important influence on Bolivian society ever since the early decades following the Spanish conquest, and it still affects its social stratification. At the time of the conquest, as at present, the Indian population was concentrated on the altiplano. Within a few years most of the Indians were not only under Spanish administrative control but also under the economic control of individual Spaniards, through repartimiento and encomienda grants that gave the conquerors legal right to Indian tribute and labor. Such grants, and the legal theory behind them, went through tortuous development during the colonial period, but in time they enabled the Spanish minority to amass large agricultural estates to which Indians were bound by feudalistic obligations. Then as now, agricultural labor was supplied chiefly by Indians. Up to the Revolution of 1952, hacienda labor was performed as a complex set of specific work obligations in exchange for the use of a small subsistence plot of land on the hacienda. Compi is an example of this type of community.

In some parts of the altiplano the frigid climate, infertile, rocky land, and relative inaccessibility lowered the potentialities of labor exploitation and marginal agriculture. As a consequence, haciendas were never established, and the Indians were allowed to retain their land and live in what have been termed "free" communities. The number of such communities today is something under 5000, though the size of the "free" population is unknown [Urquidi, 1966, p. 211]. Such communities have experienced a quite different course of development, making for differences in their relations with the national government and the blancos, the governing class. San Miguel is an example of a free Indian community and illustrates some of these differences.

Following the Spanish conquest, a number of towns were established throughout the country as governmental and marketing centers. Coroico and Sorata are examples. Other communities, because of similarly strategic geo-economic location, ultimately developed into such towns, which were generally populated by Spaniards and mestizos, with a minority of Indians. Examples of this development are Reyes and Villa Abecia.

In the eastern lowlands and the southern valleys, the much smaller Indian population was rapidly reduced and today survives as a distinct segment of the population, mainly in small nomadic bands in the more isolated jungle zones of the lowlands. A major consequence of this for social relations in the towns of these regions can be seen by contrasting them with Coroico and Sorata and their environs. Before 1952, caste-like social strata in these communities were rigidly defined in terms of race (indio, cholo, mestizo, blanco), even though the distinctions between strata were largely cultural differences in language, dress, and manners. In contrast, not only has racial distinctiveness disappeared to a great extent in Reyes and Villa Abecia, but cultural distinctiveness has similarly declined. In these communities stratification is more directly a matter of power and wealth. Four of the communities of this study illustrate different ways in which cultural traditions have been combined with economic and political power in rural Bolivia to produce a strongly hierarchical stratification order. San Miguel and Compi, on the other hand, are communities of Indian agriculturalists, fundamentally unstratified.

Bolivia has a highly centralized national government, in which the decisive power is in the hands of the President. Down from the national level, the country is divided into departamentos, provincias, and cantons. Domination by the central executive over the regional and local levels of government is ensured because their key officers are appointed from the top [Leonard, 1952, p. 189ff].

In contrast to most rural communities, all but one of the study communities are exceptional in that they have regional governmental importance. Coroico, Sorata, Reyes, and Villa Abecia are all capitals of provincias. Each, therefore, has a set of appointed officials who direct province affairs, in addition to another appointed set who direct town affairs. San Miguel is the capital of a canton, also a regional unit of government. Compi is not exceptional in this regard, since it forms only part of a canton and is not a regional capital.

Study of the six communities reveals an often wide gap between legal rules, written in the national capital, and actual local practice. This vexing problem has a number of antecedents, which will be discussed in later chapters. A question of not least importance is whether local government as it functions today is viable. Bolivia has had a number of national constitutional revisions, the latest in 1967, altering some aspects of local government, but always central control has been maintained at the expense of local responsibility.

Since the early years after Bolivia's independence in 1828, contests for control of the national government have generally been conducted in a nominally political party context. Because constitutional literacy and income requirements disenfranchised well over 90 per cent of the population, such contests were mainly between urban elite groups. Even among these, party personalism dominated party organization and programs. As a consequence, until the rise of the leftist parties and, later, the MNR, political parties as such had little structural substance. This was even more true in the rural towns and villages, and even today in the rural zones political parties are often marginal, weak, unstable organizations.

There are three political parties of national importance. The Movimiento Nacionalista Revolucionario (MNR) is the radical reform party that came to power in 1952 and governed Bolivia continuously until 1964. The Falange Socialista Boliviana (FSB) is the party of conservative interests in Bolivia and the main opposition to the government. The Movimiento Popular Cristiano (MPC) is the new government party. It has continued to support most of the reform programs of the MNR, but with increasing, even drastic, attention to economic solvency. There are many other parties, but these are the three that had national as well as local importance during the period of this study.

1952, THE YEAR OF REVOLUTION

The most decisive event in recent Bolivian history was the seizure of the national government by the MNR in 1952. Bolivia has experienced frequent violent changes of government, but the rise to power of the MNR was the first change that had wide popular support, that was not merely a palace revolution. The crisis out of which the MNR emerged had been developing over a period of years and was compounded of disparate but interrelated factors. Among the most important of these were stagnation and imbalance in the national economy; inadequate tax revenue; an increasingly inept national administration; the growing organization and militancy of labor groups, especially miners; and the spreading dissatisfaction in the politically critical urban populations [Malloy, 1968].

The MNR did not suddenly appear with a well-developed set of solutions to Bolivia's national problems. The forces pressing for radical reform had built up over a long period, and the MNR emerged out of a tortuous history primarily as the organizational framework through which a variety of groups and interests pressing for change could combine forces. The MNR was far from being a monolithic party. Its initial executive and programatic actions depended very much on tactical considerations and the balance of competing pressures that existed at any given moment. However, how and why certain reforms came to be supported by the MNR is not so important in the present context as the fact that reforms were in fact enacted, and that there were widespread local repercussions. [See Alexander, 1958, for a discussion of the rise and early years of the MNR government.]

Within months of taking over the national government, the MNR adopted labor legislation and social security measures and nationalized the major mining properties. These acts had only an indirect effect, if any, on rural populations. The degree of effect depended very much on the position of a rural community in the governmental system, on its social character, and especially on the relevance of specific reform legislation to its economic character.

The agrarian reform that the MNR instituted had radical consequences for many areas of life [Patch, 1963]. This act largely destroyed the feudalistic hacienda system. The extent of concentration of land ownership under the hacienda system had been revealed by the 1950 census. The data of that census showed that 3.8 per cent of private land holdings constituted 81.8 per cent of agricultural property [Lyle and Calman, 1966, pp. 60-61, Table 37].

The dissatisfaction of the Indian peons on the haciendas had become intense in some areas even before the formal inauguration of agrarian reform in August of 1953. On some haciendas, especially in Cochabamba, Indians refused to work. Some hacienda owners were driven off and their lands were seized. In other areas, changes occurred more slowly, and Indian occupancy of hacienda land took place legally, under the reform program.

Most of the agrarian reform program went through rapidly and thoroughly, though problems involving the assignment of formal land titles have still not been completely resolved. Hacienda labor obligations ceased and landlords were forbidden to exact work without payment of wages, unless under a harvest-sharing arrangement. The Indian peons were the primary beneficiaries. In general, peons kept as their own the subsistence plots that they had been working on the haciendas. Depending on the size and quality of the land, peons in many cases took over a major part of the land that the hacendado had formerly reserved for himself. In some cases the Indians got it all. Political considerations as well as sheer force were important in the division of land of the hacienda proper.

An extremely important consequence of agrarian reform was the organization and proliferation of peasant sindicatos. Through these unions the peons negotiated with the agrarian reform courts and other reform agencies, and dealt with their patróns. The sindicatos enabled them to make collective decisions, to select persons to represent them and to control hacienda-wide affairs. On many haciendas local government evolved from these sindicatos. Equally important, they were the instrument for integrating the rural Indian peons into the national society. It was through the sindicato that most peons for the first time had an opportunity to participate in the wider sociopolitical arena of national affairs. Strengthening this development was the MNR's policy of decreasing the strength of the national army and national police forces, while arming civilian militia units for national defense. These units were mainly the sindicatos—not only the urban labor unions, but also the campesino sindicatos. Further, campesino sindicato officials became the local representatives and spokesmen for the MNR as a political force.

As it developed, the various parts of the agrarian reform program were to have a variety of social, economic, and political effects on the rural countryside and rural communities. The program had more relevance to some areas than to others, and its effects were frequently uneven. Where it was relevant, its effects were radical, and this can be seen by comparing the study communities. Compi was a hacienda community, while Coroico and Sorata were market towns, serving a hacienda countryside. All three have experienced major changes since 1952. Villa Abecia and Reyes are towns that were closely linked to hacienda-type economies, but the special character of those economies blunted the application of reform in their areas and they experienced much less change. San Miguel is a free Indian community in an area without haciendas. The agrarian reform program did not apply to such areas, and therefore it, too, felt little change.

The first radical measure of the MNR program that had full impact on the rural population was electoral reform, an act which enfranchised the Indians. Before 1952 eligibility to vote had been restricted to men who were eighteen or older, if married, or twenty-one or older, if single, who were literate, and who had a cash income of 200 bolivianos ($4.00) per year or more or were property owners [Leonard, 1952, pp. 189ff].

(This may seem a modest sum, but most Indians had no cash income; like the equally modest poll tax in the U.S. South, it did not have to be large to be effective.) In July of 1952, within four months of the Revolution, the new MNR government established universal suffrage, abolishing the sex, literacy, and income restrictions on eligibility to vote, and making voting obligatory. The consequences were dramatic. In the presidential election before the Revolution, 126,125 votes were cast. In the first presidential election after the Revolution, there were 931,888, and in the presidential election of 1964 there were 1,294,000 votes cast [Legters and Blanchard, 1963, p. 358], a more than tenfold increase, largely from having drawn rural Indians into the national political process. The development of a new political status for these peasants was brought about by the MNR mainly through the new sindicato structure. The new status has its symbol in the MNR policy of referring to Indians as "campesinos" in all official statements, which had the effect of removing the term "indio" from most ordinary discourse except as a pejorative.

While the new national politics under the MNR required that the numerically preponderant Indian population be immediately advanced to full citizenship regardless of literacy, the fact of illiteracy remained a major obstacle to the improvement of the Indian's social, economic, and political position. Before the Revolution there were very few schools on haciendas, so it is not surprising that most Indian peons were illiterate. To give special recognition to the desperate educational need in the rural countryside, the MNR separated rural education from urban education and assigned this responsibility to the new Ministerio de Asuntos Campesinos, which was exclusively concerned with the affairs of the rural population. By 1965 the new ministry estimated that there were 7000 teachers in rural zones. While many of these were not adequately prepared, schools are still understaffed and ill-equipped, and the entire rural educational program is plagued with a variety of serious problems, the extension of education has been a major reform [Comitas, 1968].

1964: THE OVERTHROW OF THE MNR

Where, how, and what changes took place in Bolivia's rural communities as a result of the MNR reform programs is what a comparison of the six study communities tells. San Miguel and Villa Abecia have been little affected by the Revolution, and they illustrate traditional forms of rural community organization. In contrast, the other four communities exhibit various consequences of impact.

The studies were carried out over a period of approximately three years. During this time, in November 1964, the MNR government was overthrown by the army, and the government was run by military dictatorship until July 1966. For a brief period the sindicatos were outlawed, and their officials were removed from other posts of influence; but soon the sindicatos were restored and many of the old leaders returned. Then a new national political party was formed (the MPC) and preparations for national elections were begun. Significantly, the military coup d'état period was referred to by the new government as the "Restored Revolution." The fallen MNR was accused of corruption and terroristic activities, but its agrarian, political, and educational reforms were reaffirmed. Many campesino sindicato leaders and ex-hacendados had expected a reversal of MNR policies, but this did not in fact occur at the time. The MPC directed its efforts at a strengthening of the national economy. National elections were held in July of 1966, and the military leader of the interim government, General René Barrientos, was elected to a four-year term as President.

Many of the events of this period and the effects they created are reflected in the community studies. However, these studies were not all done simultaneously. As a result, the analyses reveal not only differences between types of communities, but also differences in what each community was reacting to at the time it was studied. In some instances it has been possible to fill in the gaps of time by reconstructing a critical episode that was reported, though not in fact observed. In other cases this was not possible, which explains, for example, why only three of the community analyses refer to the election of 1966, for only three were studied at that time.

Although some of the events that occurred during the research were somewhat unsettling to the research itself, they reaffirm a basic point: that even small rural communities have important connections to the outside world, but that these vary and so must be considered a problematic feature of any rural community. National developments frequently stimulated local developments, and the ways in which the different communities reacted are reported. Reactions to such national developments emphasize the necessity of defining the larger regional and national contexts in which small communities function, as a basis for understanding the internal workings of these communities.

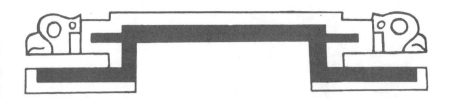

II

VILLA ABECIA
A Complex Traditional
Community

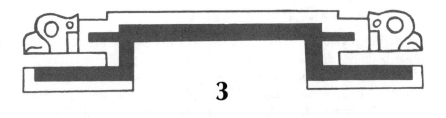

3

THE SETTING

Villa Abecia is a small town of only a few more than a hundred houses in the valleys region of Southern Bolivia, about 7500 feet above sea level, an area of ravines and canyons that links the altiplano in the west to tropical lowlands in the east. The country is dry and barren, except for those valley bottoms in which rivers and streams provide a year-round source of water. Villa Abecia is at the southern end of Cinti Valley, which is broad and hilly within itself, and well known in Bolivia for its grapes and wine. Approached from the north, the town appears as an oasis, as a cluster of white buildings on a small hill, surrounded by green vineyards which soon give way to the dry earth and rock of the mountainsides.

The main source of water for the Cinti Valley, the Rio Grande River, turns east well before Villa Abecia is reached, so here the vineyards must depend instead on the Rio Chico, a small mountain stream. A complex network of big and little ditches carries water to the 270 acres or so that are all of Villa Abecia's irrigable land. Opposite the town, on the other side of the river, are the intensely cultivated vineyards of an area known as La Banda. Dotted among the vineyards of La Banda is an occasional large house belonging to a vineyard owner, while scattered throughout these properties, but more difficult to see because of their small size, are the houses of peasant field workers.

The town is laid out in an irregular grid pattern around a small plaza. Most of the streets are cobbled. The houses, of two to four rooms, are made of adobe, mostly single-storied, with cane roofs. In the back yards are bread ovens and sheds for animals. Fronting on the plaza, which is the commercial and social center of town, are the church, the priest's house, the government offices and two country hotels. In most of the other buildings on the plaza are small stores, and pensiones rather like coffee houses, where people meet to eat and drink and talk, and play dice or cards. The only important buildings not on the plaza are the hospital and the Internado, the orphanage. The hospital, built in 1942, has nine beds but is not much used, only now and then for some minor medical problem. The Internado is used by the parish priest for child care, education, and social programs. A small primary school is just off the plaza, behind the church, but there is no secondary school.

THE PEOPLE

In 1965, according to the census carried out by the project, there were 622 people living in Villa Abecia, but the number at home varies with the seasons. There were 118 households, with an average of five members. More than 70 per cent of the people were born either in the town or within a radius of thirty miles. The dominant language of the population is Spanish. Even the peons of the area, who are not Indians, as on the altiplano or northern valleys, speak Spanish. On the other hand, most of the merchants, known as Vitichis, from the town of Vitichi, only forty-five miles from Villa Abecia but high up near Potosí, speak Quechua as well.

The climate of Villa Abecia is temperate throughout the year, generally sunny and dry. The summers are moderately hot, and even in winter the days are warm, though the nights are likely to be cold. The seasonal rains of spring and summer begin in November or December and last until February or March. During the rainy season the area is subject to hailstorms. A series of these in the summer of 1965, during the study, destroyed most of the crops.

Villa Abecia changes markedly with the seasons—in appearance, in numbers of people, and in movement. Summertime, green and bright and flowering, is the season of much activity and many people. Students are back from school and migrant workers have returned from the zafra (harvest) in the Argentine sugar fields. Everybody has money, and the plaza stores and the plaza itself are crowded, busy with buying and social gathering. There are no modern recreation facilities. The chief recreation is standing around the plaza, at food and beverage stands, or, for the more affluent, sitting for hours at the pensiones or dancing away whole afternoons and evenings at many parties in private homes.

Come winter, the plaza is empty a good deal of the time. By seven or eight o'clock at night the streets are dark and deserted, and only the flickering light of candles and kerosene wicks—in this unelectrified town —can be seen in the once busy shops. Only some national celebration or holiday brightens the winter months, as at the Fiesta of San Juan—then both town and countryside build bonfires, and friends and relatives gather round for wine and cinnamon tea.

OUTSIDE COMMUNICATIONS

An all-weather dirt road, a section of the still far from finished Pan-American Highway, ties the Cinti Valley to Potosí, La Paz, and Sucre in the north and Tarija in the south. This road runs through Villa Abecia, along the eastern side of the plaza. Several flotas (fleets) of buses transport people and goods to the larger near-by towns and the more distant centers of trade and government. The trip to La Paz takes two days; one stops at night to rest in a crude country lodge. The journey is a long, dusty, tiring bone-shaker, but the buses are generally filled and frequently turn people away.

There are also rough roads and trails running east and west from town. One of the most important of these, a footpath out of Villa Abecia which soon becomes a cobblestone road, is the way to Jailia, a village about seven miles southwest. Known as the Old Spanish Road, it was probably built by the Spaniards during colonial days. Villa Abecia people own property in Jailia, mainly vineyards.

The wait for the bus is information-exchanging time. Buses rarely arrive on schedule. For the relatives and friends of coming and going travelers, and townspeople who have come to collect their bus-borne mail, packages, and newspapers, the later the arrival the more time there is for gossip, for chatting and strolling. Villa Abecia's sources of outside information are the mail, which comes only on Saturday, incoming travelers, newspapers from La Paz, the Spanish edition of the *Reader's Digest*, and a few radios. There is also a telephone connection with the telegraph office at Tupiza, a mining town on the altiplano, about thirty miles southwest of Villa Abecia.

Trucks on the relatively busy north-south road are an auxiliary way to travel and ship goods to near-by cities. The drivers can even be prevailed upon to carry small packages and personal messages. Many people in Villa Abecia thus keep in close touch with Sucre and Potosí in the north and, especially, the departmental capital of Tarija, only four or five hours to the south.

IN TIME

Throughout the colonial period, Villa Abecia's closest ties were with Sucre, to the north, then the capital of Bolivia and the most important city in the region. The Spanish founded Sucre early in the sixteenth century; they were attracted by its fertile lands and mild climate. It grew rapidly in prominence as a base area for the gold and silver mine enterprises in the cold arid zones of the altiplano, and as the site of the Audiencia Real (Royal Court) and of one of the early universities of South America, Universidad de San Xavier, founded in 1624. Many men who had decisive roles in the Wars of Independence at the beginning of the nineteenth century studied at this university.

For centuries, the important Spanish families living in Sucre held large properties throughout the Cinti Valley. Ruins of their large homes on these fincas (estates or ranches) can still be found around Villa Abecia. An historical document of 1796 concerns one of these fincas. It is an inventory of its assets set down by a crown agent who was sent to investigate because the owner had not paid the decimo tax—one-tenth of his annual profit—to the Hacienda Real (Royal Treasury). The inventory lists large vineyards, a wine distillery, and 300 head of cattle, an extremely large herd compared with the number of animals found around the town today.

Before the arrival of the Spanish, the whole area, one of small, scattered settlements, was under the influence of the Incas. Arrowheads, pottery, stone tools, and chulpas (graves) are the surface evidence of earlier cultures. Many artifacts have been dug up by townspeople in search of hidden treasure.

Many Villa Abecians believe their town was on a caravan route from the gold and silver mines, and there are tales of tapados, of hidden wealth, buried by the Spaniards because of the death of transport animals or attack by the Indians. There are several men in town who have had unusual quantities of ready money, and these, some say, found Spanish treasure.

In 1944 Cinti Province was split, and the southern part became independent and was named Sud Cinti, with Villa Abecia as its capital. This was the outcome of a long struggle by the landowners for local autonomy and for a way to avoid long and tiring trips to Camargo for documentation of their legal affairs and commercial transactions.

The sharp break with the past that occurred in some parts of Bolivia with the Revolution of 1952 did not occur in Villa Abecia. Southern Bolivia is distant and relatively isolated from the mainstream of national affairs. The centers of revolutionary thinking and action were in the north, in Cochabamba and La Paz. In the Villa Abecia area there were no large masses of peasants who could be organized into a revolutionary force, for most fincas had only a handful of peons and were too small for practical expropriation. During the early years of the Revolution, only one peasant leader, Chumacero, aggressively agitated for radical measures, and he was a former miner from the altiplano. From his headquarters in Culpina, a small town to the south, he attempted to organize sindicatos in the Villa Abecia area. The patróns vigorously opposed him and succeeded in keeping many of their peons from even non-violent action.

The high point of agitation under Chumacero was reached when he led two mounted columns of peasants through the streets of Villa Abecia. This show of strength was sufficient to frighten the patróns and force them to forgo some of their feudalistic claims on peon labor. Shortly afterward, Chumacero was murdered, and there were no more demonstrations in Villa Abecia.

Villa Abecia has changed only slightly over the years. Little of even this moderate change was a result of the 1952 Revolution. Very likely the eradication of malaria some years earlier was a more important factor. What is more striking is the evidence of continuity. Villa Abecia is still basically a society of the patrón and his peons—a community of relatively undisturbed tradition.

TOWN ECONOMY

The juice of the grape is the lifeblood of Villa Abecia. There is almost no one in the community who is not dependent on it. The whole Cinti

Valley, indeed, is famous throughout Bolivia for wines and singani, a grape brandy. Other products of commercial importance to the valley are figs, peaches, cherries, and apples, grown at somewhat higher altitudes and where water is less abundant. Maize, wheat, tomatoes, and green vegetables are grown for local consumption and for barter with neighboring villages. Sheep and goats are raised on the now state-owned grazing pasture lands in the area, and the meat, cheese, and dung are marketed locally. Woollen blankets, sacks, and other articles are woven solely for household use.

Work in the vineyards goes on throughout the year. The summer months of February and March are especially busy with the harvest. During June and July the soil is turned and fertilized, and the plants are sprayed to protect them against insects and diseases. August and September are given to preparing the land for planting and to pruning and tending the vines.

Most of the properties around Villa Abecia are small or medium holdings, as defined by the Agrarian Reform Law. They vary from one acre or less to a maximum of twenty-five. Any farm of more than five acres is considered large. By inheritance or by purchase, many people have several small plots, scattered around the town and in the near-by villages of Jailia, Taraya, Tarcana, La Cueva, and others.

Twelve acres of irrigated land produce about five tons of grapes, locally considered to be a very good crop. Good yields notwithstanding, there are economic pressures. Viticulture demands skilled labor and intensive care. Not inconsiderable sums go for labor, fertilizers, insecticides, and wooden posts to support the vines. And besides, there are natural disasters. Small proprietors frequently are unable to invest in land improvement or to pay for insurance against hailstorms. A branch of the National Agricultural Bank at Camargo grants agricultural loans repayable at harvest time; but in Villa Abecia landowners protest that interest rates are too high and the time for repayment too short. Only those with large properties, with influence at the bank, can get loans for periods of five to eight years. And even these must run the gauntlet of complex regulations, of harassing paperwork and costly delays. Some rules eliminate potential borrowers for no relevant reasons. For example, there is a rule that bank engineers who appraise property must travel by jeep. But many loan-worthy properties cannot be reached by jeep. No jeep, no appraisers; no appraisers, no loans. The bank is also of little help when natural disaster strikes, for it is more likely to be worried about the soundness of its investments than concerned with the landowners' urgent needs. Thus, despite the government's income from high taxes on wine production, little assistance comes back in the form of loans, or even technical information or materials for improving that production.

IRRIGATION

Irrigation is essential to the production of good grapes in Cinti Valley. Water taken from the river and distributed through a system of ditches would be sufficient to irrigate all the land presently under cultivation if it were apportioned according to need. It is not so apportioned, however, since rights to the use of river water are privately owned. Water rights are a separate part of land titles, and must be separately negotiated in acquiring a piece of land. As property has changed hands over the generations, inequities of water rights have been written into contracts. Theoretically, these inequities were abolished by the Agrarian Reform Law, but the law has never been fully enforced in Villa Abecia. Under agrarian reform, the selling of water by one landowner to another also was made illegal, but this still goes on. One of the responsibilities of the agrarian judge, who was stationed in Villa Abecia until 1964, was to enforce a proportional distribution of irrigation water and to act on complaints; but there is no evidence that he had much success.

In Villa Abecia, the right to water means the right to draw from the irrigation ditches. In present practice, property owners in the irrigation zone draw water only during certain hours on certain days. A comprehensive schedule exists, specifying the turno, the time period when water may be turned onto a given property. Traditionally, this schedule has been controlled by the property owners, without any government regulations, and so it is still, despite agrarian reform.

The right to irrigation water obligates a landowner to assign one of his peons to clean and repair the ditches for every day that he takes water. In addition, his peons must guard the ditches to see that no neighbors divert water to their own property out of turn. Some owners pay an extra wage for this patrol work, which goes on night and day, while others give their peons some additional fruit trees or a little more land. During the rainy season the schedule of turnos is not in effect. Indeed, there is an overabundance of water, but the cleaning and repairing of ditches must go on.

THE LABOR FORCE

Now, as in the past, the burden of cultivation in Villa Abecia is borne by peons. To appreciate how little the traditional agricultural system has been changed by the Revolution it is useful to compare the pre-agrarian reform system with that of the present. Before 1952, a small, culturally homogeneous group of patróns owned all the land in the area. This was classified in three types. The most important was the irrigated acres around Villa Abecia. Then there was the land that was too high and lacked sufficient water for growing grapes, and this was planted with potatoes, corn, wheat, and fruit. The third type was pasture, on the surrounding hills and mountains, rented for sheep and goat grazing. The rent for this grazing land was generally paid in dung for fertilizer and in wooden posts, both needed in the vineyards.

Only a very small amount of land, generally the more isolated and less productive, was owned by free peasants. Most peasants were landless and worked as peons. Two types of peons developed in this system, the arrenderos and the viñateros. The arrenderos worked the higher altitude lands of the patróns, and in turn were allowed to use a small plot, generally not larger than one hectare (2.47 acres), for their own subsistence. In addition, they were required to work in their patrón's vineyard for a period of forty to fifty days, depending on the size and quality of the plot they held in arriendo. For additional work they received a small daily wage. In the Villa Abecia area the largest landowners had as many as fifty arrenderos.

The viñateros lived near the vineyards of their patróns and were required to give most of their time to the demanding work of caring for the grapes. For this they received a small daily wage, a small part of the fruit crop, and small plots in the vineyards for their own use. Occasionally they were also given the use of a plot in higher valleys.

Both arrenderos and viñateros had yet another labor duty to their patróns. On Sundays, before their weekly wages were entered in the account books, they were required to work without pay until noon, either in the vineyards or at any other task specified by the patrón. This Sunday faena was required by all patróns. If a peon refused, his wages were reduced.

In addition to their work obligations, most peons acquired debt obligations to their patrón. He was generally the only source of extra food, money, legal advice, and medical care. Emergency borrowings for food or medicines over periods of years mounted beyond possibility of repayment and tied the peon to his patrón at a cost of whatever freedom was left to him.

In the years immediately following the Revolution of 1952, when the local peasant sindicato was better organized and more militant than it was subsequently, the peons of Villa Abecia were able to force some changes in their work situation. The Agrarian Reform Law eliminated the faena. The patróns now had to pay higher wages to the viñateros, as well as daily wages for all work done by the arrenderos in the vineyards.

The viñateros received no land under agrarian reform and continued to work in the vineyards in the traditional way, with a right to a small plot of ground for themselves and a part of the fruit harvest. Unpaid labor by peons has decreased considerably but has not been abolished. Some patróns have replaced the traditional verbal work agreement with a written contract, as required by law, but the new contracts include few improvements for the peon. The average daily wage paid to the viñatero is three to four pesos (24 to 32 U.S. cents).

The arrenderos, though lacking legal title to their plots in most cases, work them now as their own. More importantly, they no longer feel obliged to give forty to fifty days of work to the patrón and will work in the vineyards only for wages. Today peons work without wages only in their own cooperative work parties, still called the faena. Peasants who own land, or who have use rights to land, help each other with difficult agricultural work, especially at planting time. They move in groups from plot to plot to help in the sowing. The peasant who is helped provides food and drink for all, and the day generally ends in music and dancing.

Work in the vineyards is done almost exclusively by men. With few exceptions, patróns are in the vineyards too, working or supervising. Meanwhile, the peasant women are working for their households, collecting firewood, carrying water from the ditches, spinning wool, weaving and making clothes, and caring for the animals. Some women, however, still feel obliged to work without pay in the patrón's household, washing clothes or preparing food.

A change in the labor scene comes with an annual winter migration of some peons. They go off to work in Santa Cruz or Argentina from May to November. Most of them prefer the sugar plantations in Argentina because of better working conditions and better wages. The Argentine plantations send trucks to take them to the border. From there, after a medical examination, they are sent on by train to the sugar fields, where they work as cane cutters.

The migrants from Villa Abecia try to remain together, to work and live together on the plantations. For a few months they are better off in some ways than they are at home. They are better housed and better fed. They get meat and milk regularly and are cared for medically. However, the work is very hard, made more difficult by a humid climate and insects, and is not without hazard of accidental injury. But, recently, the sugar corporations have begun to pay indemnities for work-related accidents. For most migrants, the disadvantages are offset by their wages, which average 4000 pesos ($320) for the season.

Some Villa Abecia workers have been going to Argentina for the cane harvest for almost twenty years. Those who return regularly, thus acquiring skills, and particularly those with some ability to read and write, are likely to get better jobs. In any case, the migrants can make more money in six or seven months in the sugar fields than they could make in a year in the vineyards of Villa Abecia. Most cane workers end the season with relatively large sums of ready cash, some of which they spend in Argentina on such things as bicycles, sewing machines and radios; but much comes home to Villa Abecia to be invested in land and houses. Some even lend their money to local landowners. These migrants are a minority of the peons of Villa Abecia. Their work and its effect on their lives clearly separate them from the local viñateros and most arrenderos.

FRUIT AND WINE MARKETS

At harvest time the peons gather the grapes in large baskets and load them onto trucks for the market. The bulk of the harvest goes to the wine presses. Some is sold as table fruit, mostly locally. Some of it goes to the distillation of singani (brandy). The larger landowners, with better grapes and larger quantities, sell to big buyers from La Paz and Potosí, but the smaller growers usually sell to the wineries in Villa Abecia. A few growers make raisins of white grapes, and these are sold mainly in the Tarija and Sucre markets. Most growers who make wine produce both red and white and make singani as well. For most of them, wine making is a family tradition. Equipment is simple and the process is elementary. The result is a great unevenness of product, comparing one producer with another and the product of one year with that of another.

They enter their wines in national competitions annually, and a few can boast of awards. None admits to producing any but the purest, finest wine. In fact, adulteration with sugar and water is common, for wine made only of the juice of the grape cannot be sold very profitably.

Singani distilling in Villa Abecia (William McEwen)

Tax regulations prescribe the production of not less than 1000 liters of wine at a time. When harvests are good this is easy, but when crops are poor wine makers may have to combine their production to make up the required quantity. Wine is also made in smaller quantities, and there is strong social pressure against denouncing this illegal production.

The biggest winery in Villa Abecia is a cooperative, founded by a small group of the bigger landowners who obtained a loan of about 40,000 pesos ($3200) from the National Agricultural Bank. The cooperative now has fourteen members, each of whom sells part of his crop to the cooperative. A few of the members are paid to run the group's winery and distillery, and profits are shared among the members in proportion to the quantities of grapes they provide. The cooperative has a rudimentary bottling plant operated by two girls. The members complain of the need for improved bottling facilities and for canning machinery, for much of the wine must now be stored and fruit is wasted for lack of immediate markets. Not all local wine makers are in the cooperative or want to be. They say that sales sometimes depend on quick decisions, impossible in the cooperative, which requires that members meet to discuss such matters.

Some producers sell their wine in markets as distant as Santa Cruz and Oruro, but the smaller ones cannot afford to pay the required taxes and costs of transportation to these markets. Some local winemakers sell to agents or distributors in the larger cities, but here, too, there are difficulties, because agents frequently fail to pay regularly for the wines they sell, and besides, they charge for their services.

The market for fruits other than grapes is primarily local, and the form of exchange is frequently barter. Villa Abecia merchants travel to Jailia and to other near-by villages to trade cloth and other merchandise for dried fruit. In turn, the people of Jailia exchange grapes and dried fruit for meat in Culpina. In general, the flow of bartered goods consists of fruit and singani moving from the lower valleys to the colder, higher valleys, in exchange for potatoes, beans, and meat.

The position of Villa Abecia in regional commerce corresponds closely to the road pattern discussed earlier. The main commercial stream is north and south between Tarija and Potosí. Villa Abecia is in this stream, contributes to it, and is able to take advantage of it to keep its own economy moving. Most of the wine made in Villa Abecia goes out over this north-south line, and the products moving along this line from other towns come in. Radiating in a more complex pattern, though mainly east and west, is the foot and mule traffic in products in and out of Villa Abecia within a more concentrated area. The fact that transactions in the north-south pattern are carried out in cash, while those in the east-west directions are often carried out in the form of barter, suggests the intermediate economic development position of this community in contemporary Bolivia.

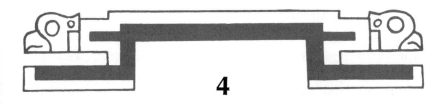

4

POWER AND
AUTHORITY

The fundamental arrangements by which one person or group is subordinated to another are essential to an understanding of how communities function as organized sets of relations between people. This is especially so where relations between groups are characterized by conflicts of interest. Despite the potential for change created by the Revolution of 1952, the social power structure of Villa Abecia is relatively simple in comparison with those of the other communities of this study, in that it is essentially a matter of relations between two status positions, that of the patrón and that of the peon. The essence of these relations is expressed in three forms of power: economic power, traditional authority, and political power.

ECONOMIC POWER

Economic power in Villa Abecia, today as in the past, is derived from control of land, water, and labor by a small group of patróns. This power is exerted in several ways. The patrón is the source of almost all means of existence. In time of need it is the patrón who can assist—if he will. In the absence of an effective sindicato, a viñatero may be dismissed with little or nothing to show for years of work. Similarly, the patrón may cancel a tenancy contract and force an arrendero off the land, though this power has become less effective in recent years.

The Agrarian Reform Law of 1953 declared all latifundia, large estates, to be illegal, but the owners of small or medium holdings and of some larger mechanized farms were permitted to retain all or part of their lands, though they were required to apply for new titles. Land held in excess of limits set for each type of terrain was subject to expropriation. Pasture land was nationalized and campesinos were granted free and unrestricted use of it. Campesinos who had held use rights were to be given title to such plots if they had been obliged to give free labor to their patrón. Other provisions of the law required that all campesinos engaged to work on the land be given wages on written contract terms and be freed of all labor obligations. Serfdom was thus abolished, without exception.

Agrarian courts consisting of a judge, a secretary, and a topographer were created in all important towns. Such courts were empowered to adjudicate land claims brought by either a patrón or a peon. The peasant sindicatos played an important part in the work of these courts in most areas. An office of work inspector was also established in the important towns, to ensure the legality of labor contracts.

The patróns of Villa Abecia were largely unaffected by reforms. Many of the irrigated holdings are small properties (three hectares or less), not subject to expropriation under any condition. All of the other irrigated holdings were medium properties under the law (three to twenty-four hectares). Legally, the peons who worked usufructuary plots on these medium properties could gain title to their plots; however, in most cases the patróns avoided even these losses. By 1964 there were twenty-four patróns in Villa Abecia who had obtained new titles to their land, but only one peon had been able to secure a land title. Thus, while they lost large tracts of pasture through agrarian reform, most patróns still have their valuable properties intact.

The success of the patróns in keeping title to their lands did not come without effort. Most of them joined the ruling MNR party and worked from within to influence the application of reform law. To prevent peons from acquiring land and contesting their power, the patróns gained control of the local Agrarian Reform Court and held it from 1955 to 1964. They maneuvered one of their own group into the office of the agrarian reform judge and controlled him through bribery or political pressure. Another factor in their success was the absence in Villa Abecia of a militant sindicato, which could have challenged patrón and judge and vigorously defended the interests of the peons. In other towns in the area, where sindicatos were strong, as in Jailia, Achuma, Camargo, and Culpina, patróns lost land and campesinos gained legal land titles.

The patróns of Villa Abecia circumvented the Agrarian Reform Law and prevented their arrenderos from obtaining title to their plots by arguing before the agrarian court, which they controlled, that the arrenderos were not serfs, because they worked on a wage basis. This was true only in that the arrenderos were not obliged to provide the variety of free services characteristic of haciendas in the north or on the altiplano, and were paid a daily wage for the days spent working in the vineyards beyond the obligatory forty to fifty days—plus faena time—for which they were not paid.

In response to the pressure of agrarian reform there is a pronounced tendency among the patróns to minimize the size of their properties. If asked how much land they own, the typical answers are, "I have a small chacrita (plot)," or, "only a few hectares." The chacritas frequently are several rich, irrigated acres. Further, patróns own land against which claims could be made, and are very careful to avoid calling attention to it.

While some claims before the agrarian court have been pending since 1962, and only one peon has secured a land title since 1953, the patróns of Villa Abecia have been able to secure their rights easily and speedily. This is illustrated in a comment by one of the major landowners:

Ah! It was the will of God that I didn't lose anything—without lifting a finger to defend myself! I didn't have one lawyer or anything, and I was able to keep my properties. Mine was the first name to come up in court. I went before the police chief [in 1953] and the agrarian judge, but I told them not to make a big noise, to simply review the facts, talk to my workers, and then decide. After that I didn't do anything, just complied with what they said. One day Diego Agote was going to La Paz. I yelled out, "Hey, Diego, bring back my titles with you." And sure enough, he later came back with them. They were sitting in the agrarian judge's office! I hadn't paid anything—only about 3000 bolivianos for Diego to get them out of hock.

While the patrón in this case laid it to the "will of God" that his property remained intact, the facts are that the peons did not oppose him, and that Diego Agote is the sub-prefect of the province and a close friend. According to one of the former agrarian judges, this patrón received titles to properties larger than the law allowed. Some of this land is now being sold by the patrón—legally—to arrenderos who had prior legal claim to it.

Some redistribution of land from patrón to peon has occurred, but mostly in the less productive hill areas, through private sale or uncontested peon occupancy. While few arrenderos have succeeded in obtaining legal title to the plots they have traditionally cultivated, they continue to work these plots for themselves and regard them as their own. Equally important, many of the arrenderos no longer work in the vineyards of the patróns in return for the land they use, which they claim was one of the feudalistic labor obligations abolished by agrarian reform. Patróns, on the other hand, argue that this labor was in lieu of cash rental for their plots and that rental in some form should continue. Nevertheless, the patróns are constrained from taking legal action in these cases because they prefer not to stir enquiry into the ambiguous legal position of the arrendero under the Agrarian Reform Law, and because of their own frequently illegal possession of properties in the higher valleys. This explains the willingness of the patróns to sell plots of land to the occupying arrenderos, even making generous long-term payment arrangements. Patróns with new titles can sell their land as they please, but sales of land by those who do not hold new titles are illegal. Significantly, local judges have been honoring these sales without questioning the legality of titles. The arrenderos, generally uninformed about the law and their legal rights, accept whatever arrangements are offered them.

In most recent land disputes between peon and patrón, the posture of the peon is that of a person reluctant to antagonize or disturb a patrón, of a man who has no alternative and no resources, ignorant and afraid. Two peons who offered to buy a small piece of abandoned and almost worthless land from their patrón were asked to pay an outrageous price. Reluctant to take the case to the agrarian judge in Camargo for fear of losing their jobs as viñateros, they agreed. In this and similar cases, the peon continues to exhibit the traditional patterns of servility.

In this arid region, to have control of an abundance of water is to have economic power. Control of water, like control of land, gives control over people. In any transfer of land, irrigation water is a separate negotiable item. Over the generations, rights to river water have become very unequally apportioned to the lands around Villa Abecia. Agrarian reform law says each property must receive a quantity of water proportionate to its size; but in this reform as in others, customary practice prevails.

In the Villa Abecia irrigation system, those who have water rights take turns in drawing from a highly complex network of ditches in accordance with rules laid down in many conventions and informal arrangements. Even some patróns do not fully understand what is going on. Only the peons, working directly with the system, have been able to master all its regulatory intricacies.

It should not be astonishing that imprecise claims to water so precisely needed give rise to competitive conflict. Such conflict occurs between patróns and between peons and between patrón and peon. It is this last form of conflict that is most relevant to this study, for it is another means by which the patróns strengthen their position in relation to peons. Needless to say, the patrón comes out on top.

Important conflict occurs when the patrón causes an extra burden to fall on the peon. For example, the number of peons each patrón must assign to clean the irrigation ditches and the amount of work each peon must do are determined by the hours of water consumed, and if a patrón sends fewer peons than are required for the job, those who do go work harder and longer. The peons are aware that even trivial matters result in a short-handed ditch gang, and they get no extra pay for the extra work. Their complaints—if they dare complain—are ignored.

Conflict between patrón and peon occurs when a patrón informally arranges to divert part of his turno to another patrón. A patrón rarely does this if water is needed for his own lands; but when he does make these arrangements the viñateros go short, because they can irrigate their own plots only during the turno of their patrón. Without legal rights to land or water, the viñateros are in no position to protest. They complain only to each other, though occasionally one will talk to his own uninvolved patrón, in the hope that he will have some effect on those who break the traditional rules. Unfortunately, the big patróns are—as one peon put it—above the rules:

Diego Agote is the owner of the water in La Banda. He gives water to whomever he wishes. We, the peons, do not say a word. How are we going to say anything if even the other owners keep their mouths shut? We are the peons, we cannot do anything, even if we would complain and shout.

The cohesion of the patrón stratum expresses itself in another type of conflict between patrón and peon. In this type the issue is in fact between two patróns. When a conflict develops, but they are otherwise on good terms, they will frequently fight it out through their peons. For instance: Francisco Campos, a peon of Marta Torres, was irrigating her vineyards. Diego Agote sent one of his peons to divert the Torres water to the Agote fields. The two peons fought over who should have the water. Later, Agote's peon reported the fight to his patrón, and he in turn confronted Marta. Rather than antagonize Agote by defending her peon, she acknowledged that he was to blame. Agote then sent for Campos and gave him a tongue-lashing. Campos took it, but later complained of Señora Torres:

And my own patrón, that old fool, instead of being on my side, she turns against me. What else does she want? I was concerned about taking care of her property and that's how she repays me. I am not going to let myself be beaten and outraged, if on top of all that she lets me down.

TRADITIONAL AUTHORITY

It would be misleading to suggest that coercion through economic power is the only device for maintaining the power of the patrón in Villa Abecia. There is a second basis, which makes active coercion largely superfluous. This is the system of traditional authority, in which there is universal agreement about who is to command, who must obey. Traditional authority defines the separate rights and reciprocal responsibilities of patrón and peon, and continuing acceptance gives the system a legitimacy that reduces the need for correction or coercion.

Despite the reformist nature of the Revolution, most members of the community are still guided in their everyday actions by their common understanding of all that is implicit in the traditional distinction between patróns and peons. The Revolution has produced some changes in economic relations and social beliefs, but the traditional authority system in Villa Abecia is largely undisturbed.

Landowner Maria Santana, called Marequita, is the grand symbol of traditional society in Villa Abecia. She is known to all. Her large holdings give her power and prestige. She defines and reinforces the norms of the community and punishes those who deviate. She represents in her own person the patrón stratum. To understand her social position, her outlook, her actions, is to understand the traditional authority system of the community.

Marequita has lived in Villa Abecia for about forty years. Her father, descendant of a very important family in Sucre, died when she was very young, and she was left without close relatives. When she came of age and took charge of her inheritance, she found herself possessed of several properties with almost one hundred peons. She directly supervised their agricultural work, an unusual role for a woman at that time. Characteristically, she became active politically in 1940 and has served as alcalde (mayor).

Her house just off the plaza is a hive of activity, an information exchange to which all her female friends bring the news and gossip of the town. Almost every night her closest friends meet there to play cards. In this group are four of the major landowners and several other important people. They are all very close friends among themselves, and frequently aid and influence one another. Marequita bosses them all, calling everybody hijo (son) except Diego Agote, whom she treats more as an equal. The near-by plaza is another center of her activities. There she can be found in daily chat, expounding on the important issues, even international politics. She is an intelligent, forceful person, a skillful leader, and clearly enjoys being the outstanding citizen. To the other patróns she is a "correct patrón," one who serves as the standard of patrón conduct. To the peons she is the "good, paternalistic patrón," the definer of proper patrón-peon relations.

The right to command, to obedience without question, is based on a shared understanding of correct conduct appropriate to different social positions. In Villa Abecia the conception of the correct patrón is one who is condescending, benevolent, and indulgent toward the less-privileged peon. Social relations with the peon should be familiar, expressed by the use of intimate forms of address. The patrón should accept, even encourage, some forms of social connection quite aside from strictly work relations, such as becoming a compadre (co-parent). The patrón should be willing to do favors for his peons, feel responsible for them, and be a source of advice and confidence. The patrón is expected to feel that paternalistic conduct establishes his greater social worth and that he should take pride in the moral correctness of his position.

But these are ideal standards. Few patróns, with the possible exception of Marequita, come close to fulfilling them. This is not to say that they fail to think of themselves as the obliging nobles of noblesse oblige, chiefly because Marequita exerts a potent force upon them through her own exemplary conduct toward her peons. She addresses her peons as hijito (little son) or papito (little daddy). They call her La Niña (the girl), she who never married; though her house servants call her mamita (mommy) and behave toward her with ease and familiarity. That she swears a great deal and constantly orders them around does not bother them, for she behaves in the same manner with patróns.

Marequita holds it the duty of the patrón to educate his peons in a virtuous way of life. If peons drink too much on work days, she regards this as a fault of the patrón. She permits no drinking on the job among her own. She is very aware that her peons are dependent upon her and is eager that it be known that she treats them well. She is also aware that it is easier to deal with a single complaining peon than with a sindicato official.

For years she has kept an account book in which she records the wages of each peon, his purchases from her, his loans, and all other material obligations. Every Sunday Marequita's peons come to her house for an updating of the book. She keeps a detailed account of wage credits and debts, and when the harvest is in she balances the two. She willingly provides (within reason) whatever her peons want, recording it and asking them to write it down in a book of their own, all the while coaxing them to work harder. She clearly enjoys the relationship and deals with them in a friendly, open manner. Responding to her familiarity, they feel at ease, speak up to her, and disagree on occasion. In establishing a personal relationship with each peon, she reinforces their identification with her, and their chronic indebtedness further binds them. In general, they feel obligated to her "for all she has done for us in the past."

Marequita believes it to be the paternalistic responsibility of the patrón to provide "the extra things." Among these are medicines and funerals. Being a madrina (godmother) of peon children is another "extra." She is proud of having the largest number of such compadrazgo relations in the community. Their more than symbolic value is suggested in one patrón's wishful comment:

I should like to be their compadre; it would help a lot. I am not, and it has to be of their choosing. I couldn't obligate them to want me for a compadre. No, but it would help, for compadrazgo creates a certain level of familiarity between people. Between patrón and his peons, it is then no longer simply professional, but more personal and familiar. There is more affection, and both parties benefit. I would like to be in that position, so as to coax them to work better and able to tell them I'd lend them money if they need it. But you can't make them your compadre; it has to be a thing of free will.

This patrón is a forastero, an outsider, not of the town, and of marginal social status because he was once a taxi driver.

In his turn, the ideally correct peon would be obedient, unassuming, unaggressive, and a hard worker, a man who knows the obligations of his status, and who would derive his self-esteem from his conforming to these criteria. As with patróns, so with peons: not all of them conform. But the level of conformity among peons is undoubtedly higher than it is with patróns. Some peons are thoroughly convinced of the correctness of traditional ways. Others conform because they see no realistic alternative, and others because of the risks of non-conformity. In some cases, conformity is reinforced by the debts of close kin. One of the more radical migrant peons explains his loyalty to his patrón in terms of the obligations created by his wife's being reared in the patrón's house and by a wedding party that the patrón held for him, which in fact the peon paid for. Significantly, most of the peasants in Villa Abecia refer to themselves as "peons," not as "campesinos," the title sanctioned by the Revolution for all peasant laborers.

POLITICAL POWER: PARTY POLITICS

In addition to the threat to their economic domination posed by the Agrarian Reform Law, after the Revolution the patróns were confronted with a second significant challenge to their power. This came from the new enfranchising laws, which gave the right to vote to all adults of both sexes, without educational, economic, or other restrictive qualifications. In general, the sindicatos have been the primary vehicles for effecting change in the political status of the campesinos, for achieving their new rights and freeing them of traditional obligations, for bringing about a shift in the balance of power.

In areas where the sindicatos were strong much political power, including control of both party politics and local government, often shifted to them; but in Villa Abecia the patróns were able to contain the local sindicato, partly through their being able to control local party politics. Most of the leading patróns quickly joined the new governing party, the MNR. Their economic strength and their traditional authority enabled the patrón group to dominate the local MNR, and the close connections between party and peasant sindicato made it possible for the patróns to control the latter organization as well.

The participation of large landowners in a political party espousing land reform and peasant rights is not the contradiction that it may appear. Political parties naturally seek political power, sometimes for what power can effect; but most political parties in Bolivia seek nothing else. Party programs and party ideology are for the most part empty rhetoric.

Though this is markedly less true in the case of the MNR, political parties are usually so weak in the rural areas that the ideological differences between them have had but little effect. Consequently, a Villa Abecia patrón in the MNR sees no moral or ideological dilemma in his position, no conflict between his own interests and party principles. Nor does a Villa Abecia patrón in the MNR have a more radical view of agrarian problems than a patrón who is a member of one of the more conservative parties. The patróns in Villa Abecia did not join the MNR to carry out reform, but to curtail it.

In the years since 1952, three patróns have held the major government offices. Diego Agote was sub-prefect, the head of provincial government, from 1952 to 1964; Andres Mardueño was the alcalde from 1952 to 1954; and since 1954, Jose Madrigal has headed the town government. Throughout this period these same three men at different times held the key position in the local MNR of jefe de comando (party coordinator). In the nine years from 1952 to 1961, when Villa Abecia had an agrarian judge, the post was filled by two local patróns who also belonged to the MNR.

During the period of MNR rule in Bolivia (1952-1964), there was almost no political opposition in town. A few patróns belonged to other parties, but they were too few to be effective. In the 1962 senatorial election 98 per cent of the valid votes (this excludes the blank votes and those ruled invalid) were for the MNR and 2 per cent (four votes) for the PRA, a party formed by a splinter group from the MNR. In near-by Jailia, all the valid votes were for the MNR. In the 1964 presidential election 99 per cent of the valid votes in Villa Abecia were for the MNR and 1 per cent (two votes) for the PRA. Again in Jailia, all the votes were for the MNR. In 1964 the representatives of the other parties made no attempt to qualify for a position on the ballot.

The dominance of the MNR in Villa Abecia should not be taken as a sign of party fervor. Voting is not only an adult right, but a legal obligation, and most adults in Villa Abecia do turn out. Nevertheless, except among people like Marequita, the local doctor, the local judge, and other government officials—those who keep up with political affairs—politics of any kind do not often enter conversation. The alcalde, Sr. Madrigal, said:

This town is a dead town. Here people only know about politics from what they hear on the radio. They do not make politics something really alive in town. They are apathetic.

In recent years the political scene in Villa Abecia, as elsewhere in Bolivia, has become confused. The ruling MNR broke into factions, and then was overthrown in the coup of 1964. Finally, new parties and coalitions formed as the presidential election of 1966 approached. Following the coup of 1964 many local government offices changed hands throughout Bolivia. But the changes often had little significance except for the persons involved. Ignacio Martinez replaced Diego Agote as sub-prefect, but both are large landowners; the alcalde, Sr. Madrigal, stayed on as the chief executive of Villa Abecia.

With a new party in power, the MNR put up no candidates in Villa Abecia for the 1966 national election, so the MPC—the party of the de facto government in La Paz—won easily. A few MNR ballots were cast, but they were judged invalid. The patróns again had taken the lead and their peons followed. It was said that all the peons of the sub-prefect switched from MNR to MPC without knowing anything about the new party, just to please their patrón.

The confidence of the patróns in their political future is based on their success in maintaining control of the local political scene, especially of the campesino sindicato. The kind of orientation provided by the patróns when they gained control after the murder of Chumacero, the militant peasant organizer, is suggested in the following statement from a speech by Diego Agote, who was sub-prefect at the time:

This centrale (regional sindicato federation) will be one of the strongest bastions of the Revolution and of our cooperation. For the Revolution, we must work without class distinctions, so that one day we get benefits for the country, the government, the patróns, and the peon. We must also fight against Communism, a party that would never lead us to save our homes nor our lands.

To further their control the patróns managed to have a member of their own group, Miguel Montes, elected secretary-general of the centrale. According to Montes, later agrarian judge, his task was to put a brake on sindicato reform activity, which was being rekindled by sindicato leaders from outside the area.

The effect of patrón influence has been to weaken and demoralize the local sindicato. Most peons in Villa Abecia were passive sindicato members at best. They attended meetings infrequently, and neither asked for nor received much help. Most of them are poorly informed about the Agrarian Reform Law and have only a vague impression that—somehow

—the sindicato is supposed to defend the poor. The older campesinos who knew Chumacero agree that he was the only leader who explained the meaning of agrarian reform. The younger peons, who did not know Chumacero, have little interest in political action.

GOVERNMENT AUTHORITY

Some of the characteristics of government in Bolivia have produced conditions and consequences that cannot be predicted from the other parts of the power system.

Villa Abecia, as the capital of the Province of Sud Cinti, is the seat of both a town government and a regional government. The latter is headed by a sub-prefect, appointed by the prefect (head) of the Department of Chuquisaca in Sucre, who has authority over the entire population of the province. The sub-prefect is primarily concerned with enforcement of the law in the province. He is assisted in this by a provincial chief of police, appointed from Sucre but responsible to the sub-prefect. In each provincial community—including Villa Abecia—the sub-prefect is represented by a corregidor, whom he appoints.

The town government of Villa Abecia is headed by an alcalde, who is assisted by an official mayor (deputy alcalde) and an intendente municipal, the supervisor of public works and facilities. The responsibilities of the alcalde include the maintenance of streets, plaza, public buildings, and sanitary facilities of the town, as well as the regulation of public water, and the levying of municipal taxes. He is supposed to keep the public informed of town problems and of the management of public funds.

Ideally, the alcalde and sub-prefect are selected by the prefect in Sucre from a slate of three nominees for each position put forward in an open meeting in Villa Abecia. In practice, there are many variations on this pattern: the "open" meeting may not be open; the nominating procedures may be strictly controlled by local politicians and others influential in the community; and finally, the prefect may reject the entire slate and substitute any person of his choice, including non-residents.

Other offices in Villa Abecia include a unit of the lowest level of the national court system, a court of first jurisdiction, staffed by a judge and a secretary, in which initial proceedings in most civil and criminal cases are heard. There are, also, an official notary, who is head of the Registro

Civil (office of Public Records); a tax agent, who collects levies on wine, commerce, and property; administrators of the post and telegraph offices; the director of the public primary school, and the physician who directs the local public hospital. There is also a branch of the federal highway agency (Servicio de Caminos), whose job is to maintain the north-south highway leading to Potosí and Tarija. Excepting the subprefect and the alcalde, none of the occupants of these offices wields authority beyond the narrowly interpreted limits of his official duties. Some even lack authority in the performance of their work and depend more on their extra-official status to carry out their duties, as in the case of the doctor, who is a large landholder and whose occupation carries considerable prestige.

One other office, public but not official, is that of the local priest. Since he is German and regarded as an outsider, neither his cassock nor his person has given him any large measure of power in the community. He remains rather aloof, but many consider him a good priest precisely because he does not meddle in local affairs. He devotes considerable time to the campesinos in the surrounding area, but has not been very successful in persuading them to participate in church activities. He commands most respect among the women, but his influence is largely in religious affairs.

This sketch of officialdom is an outline of local government as it is locally defined. In actual operation, however, local government rarely conforms to the definitions. Responsibilities and jurisdictions overlap to such an extent that correct procedure is never clear. A consequence of this overlap is constant conflict between officials. In any given instance, justice may be dispensed by the sub-prefect, the alcalde, the judge, the chief of police, or even some other—or all of them may get involved. Officeholders frequently lack relevant qualifications. In some cases adequate qualifications are not specified, and in others they may be but are ignored. Tenure is likely to be uncertain at the local level, so there are few who resemble a career official. Rather, there is likely to be a shuttling back and forth between private enterprise and public office, though indeed it may be hard to distinguish between the two positions. A patrón does not sell his land because he has been appointed to an office, nor does anyone expect him to. Public servants typically lay as much emphasis on the private gains extractable from an official position as they do on the duties they are theoretically expected to perform. Graft and corruption are all but synonymous with public office.

The result of all this is a great reduction of effectiveness in local government. Yet the responsibilities of maintaining order, dispensing justice, and providing basic public services are carried out, though often to only a very limited extent. Some officials may become effective because of their high status in the community and the far-flung social relationships from which they draw support. This is the sub-prefect's method of accommodation. He devotes himself to the surrounding villages, leaving the town to the alcalde. In the villages he deals with campesinos as a large landowner, as patrón to peon. In Jailia, where he has compadrazgo relations with numerous peons, he is recognized as a socially superior person, though he does not assert himself among them. He acts correctly, a condescending and paternalistic patrón. He even delivers their babies without charge, since there is no midwife in Jailia and he happens to have some experience in this work. He is generally treated with traditional deference, and he is frequently sought out for legal advice and to settle disputes.

Another effective form of accommodation within the confusion of local government is to rely on one's own force of character, personal resources, and abilities—essentially a personalistic method. The incumbent alcalde, Jose Madrigal, says he is effective because of his personalidad, his force of person. What he means by personalidad is that he speaks effectively in public, handles difficult situations without getting rattled, and is able to convince and persuade others. His general policy is to seek national governmental rather than local support for all local public projects. For example, a crisis developed when a severe hailstorm damaged the public water system, interrupting the flow into town. Madrigal proposed a request for federal aid, but many residents said the seriousness of the matter would not wait on time-consuming negotiations. Under considerable pressure, he was forced to call an open meeting to discuss his proposal, but he so intimidated the people that no one was willing to stand up and oppose his position. He contained the opposition and then sought a way to resolve the problem as he worked. In the course of the discussion the priest made a suggestion in accord with the alcalde's policy, and this he seized on. Exploiting the respect held for the priest, he brought the suggestion to a vote, announced it as accepted without a tally, and was able to close in his own favor what had begun as a hostile meeting.

There is a third form of accommodation to political office, not so important in Villa Abecia, but it stands out in some of the other communities. This is accommodation through inaction. When officials lack personal skills or superior status, they are left with few means within government to accomplish anything. And that is what many accomplish: nothing.

The police of Villa Abecia are the most corrupt and abusive of all public authorities. Local people lay the blame on national officials. They say the less competent, poor performers among the police are sent to the provinces. But perhaps a more important factor is a regulation requiring the appointment of police to areas with which they are not acquainted and for limited periods of time. The justification for this rule is that it lessens the probability of personal and social involvement that could compromise the exercise of official duties. In fact, the opposite effect would be preferable, since one of the great constraining forces on local officials is their social involvement, their need to protect their status in the community. The policeman, a stranger on the scene for but a short time, is free of almost all restraints in pursuit of his private interests.

It is the peons who feel the rub. The patróns and the better educated members of the community fight back. If a police official makes himself obnoxious they are likely to telegraph to his superiors in Sucre, demanding his replacement. And if the demand is insistent enough they get action. The peons, on the other hand, feel impotent when faced with officials, including the police. Take the following exchange between Marequita and one of her peons:

> *Marequita* What happened with the police?
> *Peon* He made me pay twenty pesos [$1.60].
> *Marequita* Ah, hija, I told you not to go in there.
> *Peon* But Mamita, what could I do?
> *Marequita* Nothing, I guess, but you knew he'd collect a fine.

Police and government what they are, it is not surprising that most people avoid the procedures of formal justice and seek solutions to their problems through informal and traditional means. Patróns negotiate directly with each other. Peons turn to their patróns to decide their disputes.

There are no trained lawyers in Villa Abecia. For legal aid, peons go to the tinterillos, two self-tutored, self-styled lawyers with no legal training. The important people consult professional lawyers in the cities. The town judge is respected because of his profession, because he is a patrón, and because he belongs to a family socially prominent in the history of Sucre. However, he is old and thought to be a bit senile. His knowledge of the law is disputed by everyone, and he has been accused of causing delays and perplexing complications through errors of procedure.

A DISPUTE BETWEEN PATRÓN AND PEON

The social structure of even a relatively simply organized community reflects a complex interplay of powers. These constitute a system which operates as a unity and is so experienced. This unity of interwoven powers is well illustrated in an instance of conflict within the fundamental relationship on which the social structure of Villa Abecia rests—that of patrón to peon.

Faustino Medina worked for thirteen years on the lands of Victoria Santana. During this time, while she lived in distant Sucre, he supervised the work in her vineyards. In all these years he received no wages. As is usual, he cultivated a plot of her land for himself, and it was his understanding, partly based on assurances from Ignacio Martinez, patrón and sub-prefect, that eventually he would be paid for his work.

But when Doña Victoria returned to Villa Abecia in 1965 she refused to acknowledge the work that Faustino had done and denied his claim for back wages. Counterattacking, she accused him of misappropriating part of her land and tried to have him thrown off. Faustino asked the sindicato to intercede. An ad hoc sindicato commission was elected and went to Doña Victoria to explain Faustino's rights. Under the Agrarian Reform Law, they said, she could not fire him before the end of the harvest. The commission assured Faustino that they would support him, but took no further action.

Though Faustino sought aid from the sindicato, it seems clear that he felt dependent on the patrón. She continued to give him orders and he continued his work, behaving in a subservient manner and appearing to be somewhat bewildered by her hostility. Doña Victoria finally agreed to let Faustino stay on until the end of the harvest, but only if he would not seek back wages or further involve the sindicato. It was widely agreed that Doña Victoria would lose the argument were it carried to court. Nevertheless, Doña Victoria's other peons came forward to lay blame on Faustino. The following comment summarizes their criticism:

He was cutting her wood to build his house, and telling us we'd be fools if we didn't do the same. When the patrón came to town, he wanted us to sign a paper to sue her because of his back wages. We didn't know anything. We are very grateful to the lady, because we are living on her land, satisfied and happy, and we have nothing to say, only that Faustino was bad. He bossed us even worse than the patrón, and was abusive.

There is no doubt that the patrón herself prompted the peons in this testimony. Nonetheless, the criticisms suggest that in their eyes Faustino had violated his proper responsibilities as a peon by having cultivated land to which he was not entitled, and in asserting authority over the other peons.

In the midst of the dispute Doña Victoria's son-in-law, a lawyer from Sucre, arrived in town and persuaded Faustino to accompany him to the sub-prefect's office to work out a settlement. Out of this came a formal contract, in which Doña Victoria agreed to Faustino's working until the completion of the harvest. This was the finale in a series of acts in which the power of the patrón was marshaled to contain a challenge. The work contract prepared by the lawyer and signed by Faustino restates the traditional positions of patrón and peon:

I, Victoria Santana, . . . had realized that Faustino Medina . . . , without my permission, was using the land of my vineyards. But out of my own generosity, I relinquish my rights to collect the value of the trees he felled for his own profit. . . . And to protect him from any harm, I allow him to stay until the harvest is over. . . .

I, Faustino Medina, . . . accept all the previous statement, and testify that I do not have any more claims or complaints against that lady. And, that the suit I made before was the result of deceitful counsels, which I received from persons who wanted to cause trouble, where there are no problems. Therefore, I desist from that action, because it has no valid grounds whatsoever.

Both parties agree that now they are in perfect harmony. From now on, all work will be paid for, according to the customs of the place. . . .

The viñatero, Faustino, will collaborate in all work, with eager interest and respect for the landowner.

Faustino's agreement to an unfavorable and highly impermanent settlement, when the facts of the case appeared to point to victory for him, can be understood only in terms of pressures generated by the dispute and his inability to counter them.

The portrait of the generous patrón, the emphasis on the weakness and the obligations of the peon, and the exhortations to work hard reflect central values of the contemporary social order in Villa Abecia. Faustino overreached his position and has now been corrected. The patrón showed an excess of choler, but criticism from the other patróns will perhaps restrain her. Most importantly, such conflicts as this case illustrates are shown to be still easily managed within the traditional social system of the community, and their resolution sustains the dominance of patróns over peons.

Maria Santana, the Marequita of earlier mention, is the sister-in-law of Doña Victoria, and though their personal relations are very strained, she also became involved in this case as a leading patrón and important figure. The local power system is revealed in her discussion of the case:

Hijito, you know, that was really something! Here Doña Victoria thought she could fire someone just like that, regardless of the reform. She thought she was God Almighty. Well, the compadre [Faustino] came to me and I told him to get the help of the sindicato. He said they had done nothing, and what should he do? Well, Hijito, I told him to go and talk to Doña Victoria and straighten it out. He began to cry here, saying that she wouldn't even let him within spitting distance of her house, screaming out "indio" and all types of dirty things. But, papito, his own men fried him! Well, then the son-in-law of Doña Victoria came to see me. He told me that in any court Doña Victoria would lose, but that he wanted to resolve this without fuss. He asked me what should be done, and I told him that, in my opinion, they should keep Faustino on until the harvest and then see what happens. At that time, and Faustino knows this, they can take his lands, his house, his pastures, all.

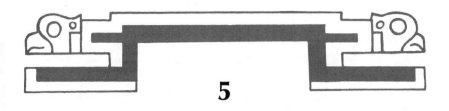

5

SOCIAL STRATIFICATION

The ranking of social positions in a stratification system rests primarily on differences of power, wealth and prestige. Stratification by wealth and power creates in Villa Abecia two main strata: patrón and peon. Differences in prestige rest on several other criteria and create a more complex stratification system around that of patrón and peon.

One basis of prestige is race as socially defined. Terms such as blanco, mestizo, cholo, and indio are heard in everyday conversations. Blanco means white; mestizo and cholo mean "mixed-blood"; indio means Indian. These terms are not used simply to denote biological race, but are used principally to indicate either the social status of a person or a social stratum of the community. The word blanco can mean either light-skinned or of European descent. There are few people in Villa Abecia whose skin pigmentation is literally what would generally be recognized as blanco, and fewer who can claim European descent. But the word is there and has come to mean a member of the gente decente (decent people), the top social stratum of the community. A person may have dark skin and be descended from Indians, but if he has money, is educated and lives in the manner of the patrón, he is a blanco, a decente.

If the word indio is defined as a distinctive racial or sociocultural group, then there are no Indians in Villa Abecia. Most persons recognize that racially the population is mestizo. Indio is a word infrequently heard. Its primary meaning is now derogatory, used of a person whose conduct is reprehensible. The more frequently used terms for agricultural workers are peon or campesino, status terms in which the implication of race is largely absent.

Over the whole reach of the hierarchy the strata are also distinguished by the quality of deference shown to one in comparison with another. From this perspective there are four strata, rather than two. In referring to the top stratum, people frequently use the terms gente decente or gente buena (good people) instead of patrón. The next stratum is comprised of a few merchants (most of whom are known as Vitichis) plus some clerks, office workers and specialists. A very small third stratum is distinguished as campesinos civilizados, made up of the migratory campesinos who go to the sugar plantations and of some of the less skilled craftsmen and day laborers and house servants. Finally, the fourth and lowest stratum is comprised of the peons, sometimes referred to as campesinos.

The epitome of the decente is the patrón. However, land ownership, with its implied wealth, is not the only qualification for membership here. Proper style of life, level of "culture," moral behavior, lineage, and local origin are also counted, singly and in combination, in assigning a person to a particular prestige stratum. All the wealthy patróns are decente, but even relatively impoverished patróns are decente if they qualify by lineage and "cultural" and moral behavior. On the other hand, wealthy Vitichis are not decentes, because their origin, style of life, and Quechua speech disqualify them.

As is frequently the case with a traditional elite, which has most to lose in terms of privileges, the decentes show more concern than the other prestige strata for precise prestige assignment. Among themselves they distinguish a sub-class of marginal decentes, comprised of persons and families whose prestige qualifications are tainted. Examples are sons of old decente families who have married campesino women and live somewhat like campesinos, or who have become very heavy drinkers and are regarded as shiftless and irresponsible.

The Vitichis are a separate prestige stratum below the decentes, to which can be added a small number of civil servants and skilled workers whose prestige standing is approximately equal. This class is dominated by the Vitichis, exclusively tradesmen. They own the important stores in town, except for three owned by landowners. The townspeople consider them outsiders, and so do the Vitichis themselves. They are in Villa Abecia to make money, and will then go back to their homes in Vitichi. Their women chew coca and wear polleras, the many-skirted costume of the chola. In other parts of Bolivia the Vitichis would be called cholos. Like cholos, they are bilingual (in Quechua and Spanish).

They tend to trade in the cheaper goods and are more likely to extend credit, so most of their customers are campesinos from the surrounding villages. They are a serious people, put much emphasis on industriousness, and think the patróns of Villa Abecia are a lazy lot. As one of them said:

We are outsiders, and it is better not to pay attention to those people [decentes]. Those from the town are lazy people. There is no reason why a person with money should be lazy. These people and their rich sons should work. Instead, they play, and think the world owes them something. We are from outside and we are workers, that's why we are here. But the rest don't like us because we work.

As a general category, the campesinos comprise the most numerous group. The majority conform to the classic, pre-revolutionary pattern, that of the deferential, illiterate peon, resigned for generations to an impoverished and precarious existence, living in crude huts in the vineyards and fields, dressed in homespun and working long hours.

But since the 1940's, a new type of campesino, the campesino civilizado, has appeared in Villa Abecia. These are the peasants who go off to work in the sugar fields for high seasonal pay. Some have received land under the agrarian reform, and some are arrenderos who have bought land or otherwise have control of a farm plot. In all cases these are individuals who no longer have to work in the vineyards of the patróns for a meagre living. These zafra (sugar harvest) workers spend the other half of their lives back in Villa Abecia as shoe repairers, bricklayers, butchers, and so on. Zafreros with large families must spend most of their earnings on food and rent, but the younger, unmarried zafreros build comfortable houses and have beds, tables and chairs, bicycles and radios. They spend considerable time among themselves at parties and athletics, activities for which the peons have neither leisure nor money.

Affluence sets the zafreros apart. Travel, association with people of different backgrounds, and comparative wealth have given these campesinos a great measure of self-assurance. They are no longer diffident and humble peons, but are inclined to be independent and to speak up for their rights. They resent the traditional status system in Villa Abecia, and though they are still a small group, they constitute the most serious challenge to that system.

Domestics and foster children occupy somewhat special status positions linked to the lowest stratum. These have a mobility potential and are not always easy to place in the prestige hierarchy. The first of these special positions is that of the imillas, or emilias, the women who work as maids in decente homes. All of them come from peasant families, and those recently recruited, still wearing polleras and chewing coca, cannot be distinguished from campesino women. Their fashion of life has undergone a quick change, for they live in the homes of the decentes and eat from their kitchens. In time, they stop chewing coca, abandon the pollera for *de vestido*—Western-style dress—cut their braids off, learn to speak better Spanish and otherwise attempt to emulate their employers. Some aspire to even better things, dream of going off to Tarija or Sucre, or even Argentina, where they can make more than an equivalent of $4.00 a month, their average wage in Villa Abecia.

Social ambition for many imillas is not so much to become more like decentes, but to become less like campesinos. This is suggested in the comment of an imilla who has lived with a decente family since she was a young girl:

Sometimes I have thought of wearing polleras, but more and more the servants are no longer wearing them, but changing for fine vestidos. They want to be like their patróns, and they don't even want to greet older people any more. By wearing vestidos they have become spoiled. I wear vestidos, but my patróns have taught me how we ought to behave. Besides, when the llocallas [young campesinos] see one of us with polleras, they annoy her and make shameful propositions to her. On the contrary, if we wear vestido, we are respected, and we can even have proper boy friends.

On the other hand, some imillas wear vestidos when they visit Tarija and other cities, but change into the pollera when they return to Villa Abecia. These still have strong campesino ties, and are sensitive to criticism that they are "trying to put on airs" and are "not good enough to wear vestidos."

Imillas may hold their special place in society, somewhat above campesinos, for several years, but it is usually a temporary status, changing when the girls marry. As a group they are isolated and turn to each other for companionship and recreation. It is also a vulnerable status, and some imillas become prostitutes in town, not only for the llocallas but also for the decentes.

The second special position is that of the hijo de crianza, the foster child. These are usually children of poor peons, given to decente families and raised by them. They may be treated as servants. If so, their status may be even lower than that of a servant, for they receive no wages. Sometimes the child is reared as a member of the family and may achieve near-decente status, but there is social pressure against this among the decentes.

Villa Abecia is too small to have socially distinctive residential districts, but there is a segregation effect. The best houses are concentrated around the plaza and the rest diminish in quality with distance from the center. Except for some large homes on the surrounding fincas, the far outlying people live in crude huts. Patróns and the better off Vitichis live in the houses around the plaza. Marginal decentes, smaller merchants, and skilled workers live nearer the periphery. Most campesinos have their houses in the surrounding fields. Segregation by status most sharply meets the eye in public settings. In earlier years campesinos were not permitted to sit on plaza benches. Now they sit along the east and west sides, where often a campesina sells food or chicha, a fermented maize drink. These sides are primarily campesino territory, while the north side is where decente men congregate.

Marequita Santana has an honored claim on the southeast corner of the plaza near her house. There, usually joined by members of her family and her close friends, she passes part of each day. One day she found young campesinos sitting on the bench in that place. "I am sorry, hijitos," she said, "this is my bench." They stood up without a word and left. This form of status separation also occurs at town meetings and fiestas.

At large private decente parties an hijo de crianza may be accepted, but when a peon has been asked to attend—this being a birthday or a wedding in a patrón family—he is no less a social inferior and is expected to show proper subordination and deference. He is there only to pay his respects, and then remain apart or quickly leave. In contrast, patróns who attend parties given by their peons, thus honoring them, are no less paternalistic and condescending. No change occurs in status barrier, either way.

Traditional quasi-religious fiestas often bring members of the different prestige strata together, but their interaction is again circumscribed by status. The Taripacu is a campesino fiesta given in honor of a compadre. Campesinos troop through the streets carrying baskets filled with cakes and gifts and dancing to the traditional music of the now-vanished Chapaco Indians until they arrive at the compadre's house, where the fiesta ends in drinking and dancing. In this, and in street fiestas, the greatest being the Carnaval before Lent, it is usual for decentes to join campesinos in singing and dancing. Decente girls take part, but are very careful not to join hands with campesinos. When dancing is in couples, rather than in rounds, campesinos never dance with decente girls, but decente young men dance with servant and campesino girls.

There is also a stratification effect in moral standards; but there the license is in favor of the campesino. The decentes believe themselves to have a stronger sense of honor, responsibility, and family loyalty. These traits, as well as the sense of virtue felt in the cultivating of one's superior endowments and the importance of one's cultural tradition, are held to be decente characteristics, but are regarded as unusual in a campesino or even a Vitichi. Campesinos are not expected to adhere to these values. Public opinion is harsher and social pressure is much more severe, therefore, on the moral transgressions of decentes than on those of campesinos.

Theft, habitual drunkenness, premarital pregnancies, and physical fighting provoke strong sanctions against decentes, but are considered normal in campesinos. The decentes think campesinos care little whether the girl they marry is a virgin, whereas a decente girl known to have had sexual relations may not find a proper husband. Campesino tradition supports decente suspicion in this particular. A customary practice among the campesinos is amañarse, in which a couple live together for a year or more before marrying. This has the consent of all parents, with the understanding that it will terminate in marriage if they are compatible. To the decente, accepting differences of moral standards is a method of underlining the correctness of the social stratification system. Where belief and practice of separate strata are identical, the implicit challenge to the stratification order is resolved by labeling it exceptional.

Education is another basis for prestige assignment. All decente children go to primary school and almost all continue to secondary school. Many go on to universities in Tarija, Sucre, Oruro, Potosí, or La Paz. Vitichis also make an effort to put their children through secondary as well as primary schools. The campesinos are beginning to attach value to an education, but they still have serious economic problems in obtaining even a primary education.

Many campesinos, but more the older ones, are illiterate. Others have had but one or two years of primary education. Adult education and improved primary education were two objectives of the revolutionary MNR party, specifically to raise the campesinos; but the adult literacy program never got started in Villa Abecia. Further, the established obstacles to a peon child's attending the local primary school remain. Some patróns oblige peon children to work along with their parents on the fincas when they could be in school. The local primary school charges no tuition, but many campesinos cannot afford to buy notebooks and pencils, much less the customary uniform. Others are ashamed to send their children bare-foot in rags. Still, by and large, younger campesinos are getting more edu-cation than their parents did.

One of the more critical features of social mobility, the shifting of people from level to level in the stratification system, tells a great deal about how the system functions and maintains itself. Since the bases of status in Villa Abecia—wealth, power, and prestige—are so completely monopolized by the patróns, there should be relatively little shifting. It is clear that social mobility requires a source of wealth outside Villa Abe-cia, and that wealth alone is not sufficient. These points can be illus-trated by two instances, one a successful shift, the other not.

Vidal Naranjo, an altiplano Indian who, by hard work, ability, and some luck became a truck driver and later a transportista (an independ-ent trucker) in Tarija, is the one who failed. About 1950 he sold his house and truck in Tarija and moved to Villa Abecia to work as a truck driver for Andres Mardueño, one of the biggest patróns. After a few years Naranjo invested his savings in a large vineyard. Employing sev-eral peons, he made enough money to buy a house on the plaza and open a general store, which is run by his wife.

Naranjo is respected as a good, hardworking man, but is regarded by others and by himself as an outsider and is socially isolated. He is ad-dressed as maestro, a term widely applied to persons holding skilled or semi-skilled jobs. The term is inappropriate for a landowner and is there-fore a constant reminder of his inferior social position. He does not at-tend public meetings, nor is he invited to parties or other social activities of the decente. His wife still wears traditional campesino dress and he still chews coca occasionally.

Naranjo admits to not a single friend in Villa Abecia, but explains that this is because he does not drink. He seems to take pride in not be-ing a "drunken indio." In this and other respects he identifies with the decente, though sobriety is not invariable even among them. His ambigu-ous social status as a rich Indian patrón makes life very difficult. He says he intends to leave soon for Potosí, where some of his children are in school. There he intends to buy a store for his wife and a taxi for himself and return to his earlier occupation of chauffeur.

Carlos Preciado had more in his favor, and he succeeded. He was born in Villa Abecia, the illegitimate son of a decente father who never recognized him. As a young man he worked as a tailor, but on his return from the Chaco War he opened a hotel with his savings. He married a girl whose father was a well-to-do cholo, and who inherited his money. Preciado is highly regarded in the community, both for the money he controls and because he is a responsible, serious, moral person. The Preciados are accepted as decente, but this is somewhat qualified by the cholo background of Señora Preciado. That she has great social ambitions for herself and for her family annoys other decente families. It was, for instance, something of a tragedy to Sra. Preciado, but a satisfaction to some of the decentes, when she failed to break into the tightly closed aristocratic circles of Sucre.

Most of the conditions that affect social status combine in Villa Abecia to restrict mobility. No opportunities for new wealth have appeared in the community, and old wealth is carefully husbanded by a small number of patróns. Thus, the material conditions of mobility lie almost entirely outside the community.

Downward mobility is as important as upward, but no cases appeared that would illustrate it. There are two instances of members of decente families whose conduct is regarded as so outrageous that they are widely criticized and generally avoided by other decentes. Both are serious problem-drinkers. Since both are partially supported and protected by their families, it is too early to tell whether they or their children will lose status permanently in the community.

The social stratification system in Villa Abecia has undergone some minor but no major changes because of the Revolution of 1952. Today, as for prior generations, this system consists basically of a small landowning elite over a larger land-working population. Most of the town's wealth, power, and prestige are reserved to its elite, while the privileges of the peasantry are few. This is a type of status order that was widely prevalent throughout Bolivia before 1952.

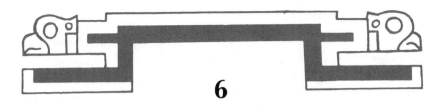

6

GROUPS AND ORGANIZATIONS

Since Villa Abecia has a small and relatively stable population, there are few persons in the town who are not acquainted with everyone, but in this situation acquaintance is not a step toward friendship. Friendship is strongly conditioned by status, so most good friends are social equals. Most campesinos think that friendship between persons of different prestige strata is almost impossible. Some decentes think so too, but assert that status differences should not influence friendship; or they say that persons of different status can be friends if the status differences are "not essential." It is the campesinos who are more realistic. They do not mistake paternalism for friendship.

At all levels of society, membership in groups of friends and family and compadre relationships reinforce mutual assistance and obligations. The ties are especially important among the decentes for maintaining status interests and influencing community action. The collective relationship around Marequita Santana presents a good example.

Marequita is the indisputable leader and uniting force of two friendship groups, a group of old maids and the loba (a card game) group. Postmistress Marta Torres, Teresa Arellano, Paz Duran, and Marequita are the old maids. They gather at Marequita's house, at the post office, or at Marequita's plaza bench, mainly to gossip. They also attend mass together occasionally.

The loba group includes the old maids and Andres Mardueño and Diego Agote. All own land in Villa Abecia; all are decentes. These members of Marequita's clique have affection for each other, hold each other in esteem and assist and protect each other's interests. When Mardueño was unable to sell his grapes after a December hailstorm, Marequita sold them for him as if they were her own, without profit, "as a favor to him because he is my friend." In turn, Mardueño is always willing to let the others use his distillery.

But family ties transcend all others. In Villa Abecia Marequita has two nephews with wives and children; an unmarried nephew; Victoria Santana, widow of her brother; and Marta Torres, a distant relative. Marequita stands at the head, a spinster matriarch, and all except her sister-in-law treat her with affection and respect.

To be taken to the heart of such a family, however, relationship by birth or marriage alone is not always enough. For example, Marequita does not consider that Marta Torres is up to Santana standards in household manners and interpersonal etiquette, and this she frequently deplores; but she keeps her in the family group because of their long and close friendship, bad manners and impoliteness notwithstanding. Marequita is forceful and demanding—the expected role of the head of the family in Villa Abecia—no matter that she is not a man. In turn, the members receive her unconditional loyalty, constant moral support, and generous economic assistance, and they are loyal to her and assist her whenever they can. All have their own primary economic interests; all but one are landowners. Consequently, the economic impact of the group on its members is somewhat marginal.

More typically, family groups have related economic interests. An example is the Preciado family—mother, father, and six children—each of whom has an economic role in the family wine enterprise. Two of the children, Alfredo and Lydia, live with their parents, and the other four, David, Elva, Patricia, and Tomas, either work or go to school in Oruro. Alfredo supervises his father's vineyards and works beside the peons. His sister Lydia tends the family store throughout the day, every day of the week, accepting this as a family duty. Alfredo occasionally rebels against what he says is too much labor for too little reward, but there has never been a breach of cooperation. The eldest son represents the family business in Oruro, acting as intermediary between his father and the distributing agent for the family's wine and sangani products. One of his sisters works as secretary and accountant for the same distributor. The father writes twice a week and parcels are always on the move between the two branches of the family.

In general, relations between members of a family are relaxed and affectionate. The father is the family authority, but the austere aloofness noted in men in other Latin American communities—which accounts for the real influence of mothers elsewhere, a countervailing influence—is less marked in Villa Abecia. Here the father is more approachable—at the center of everyday family affairs. Mother shares with father the direction of the family, though she is subordinate.

Sex roles become sharply distinguished in the family. Girls learn their household duties at an early age, and boys start young as well, working alongside their fathers, though this is less true of sons of higher status, who will spend longer years in school and possibly go on to a different occupation or a profession. As boys grow older they are supervised less and less, but girls who have sexually matured are closely guarded by parents and brothers as well, especially among the decentes. And yet, the meeting of the sexes appears to be more open and friendly in Villa Abecia than in many Latin American communities, the young men here seeming to be less intensely engrossed with machismo, their maleness.

One of the most important of social ties in Villa Abecia is compadrazgo, the tie of fictive kin relationships. Compadrazgo establishes obligations not only between a padrino (godparent) and ahijado (godchild), but also among the compadres, the godparent and his godchild's parents. These obligations frequently are of great importance in everyday life. Baptismal compradazgo, ritually established by Catholicism, is the most important, for here the rights and obligations are formally associated with strong social, moral, and spiritual values. Closely related to baptismal compadrazgo are compadrazgo de agua bendita (blessed water) and compadrazgo de misa de salud (health mass). These are baptisms performed by the godparent himself when there is fear that the child may suddenly die and are the same in their significance, the difference being that a mass is later celebrated in one but not the other.

Other forms of compadrazgo are similarly associated with church ceremony and belief. These are at the first communion, at confirmation, and at marriage. A variant which is almost exclusively campesino is the compadrazgo de mortaja (shroud), in which a person becomes the godparent of a dead child and is obliged to provide the shroud and oversee the funeral.

One form of compadrazgo found in Villa Abecia is disapproved of by the priest, but without marked effect. This is the bond of guaguas de pan (babies of bread) which is entered into by women and is comparable to the compadrazgo de amistad (friendship) among men. To become comadres de guagua de pan two women carry out a ceremony consisting in a mock baptism of a baby doll made of bread, which is soaked in wine after the baptism and eaten.

Wealth, power, and prestige have an important influence on the selection of compadres. Compadrazgo involves real obligations and some of these can be expensive. It also brings advantages, and few persons are unmoved by these potentials when selecting a compadre. For the patrón it is another means of influencing his peon. Campesinos frequently must refuse to become godparents because of the cost in baptismal fees and clothes for the child and other gifts, but they seek patróns as compadres because of possible favoritism and economic benefit. The Vitichis seek social advantage in their compadres. For example, Manuel Frias, a Vitichi merchant, chose as compadres of marriage for his daughter, Diego Agote, Carlos Preciado, and three members of the Mardueño family, all important decentes. He explained his choices this way:

In looking for the right persons one takes into account how they behave socially, or if they excel socially or culturally. Then, one tries to have certain relationships with them. I found all these characteristics in the persons I named as godparents for my daughter. Relationship becomes more intimate. There is social, cultural and economic advantage. Compadrazgo strengthens the friendship link, and through it one is able to move upward socially.

In Villa Abecia, where social relationships are little affected by formal organization but are mainly personal, the flexibility of compadrazgo in establishing mutual obligations has transformed it into a key feature of society. Its utility in obtaining personal advantage, which often means limiting some other person's advantage, is perhaps most important of all. It is exploited to obtain more regular work, credit in a store, loans of money, help during the harvest, more water for irrigation, better deals in land, assistance with the children's education, moral support, and advice in time of need. In the traditional society of Villa Abecia the system of compadrazgo has become an important adaptive mechanism.

FORMAL ORGANIZATION

Formal groups and organizations are few and tend to be unstable. National political parties become active only with elections, but at other times are very nebulous organizations. The Veterans of the Chaco War has very few active members and no regular meetings. There are forty to fifty veterans in town, including campesinos, but few think it worthwhile to pay their monthly dues because, they say, membership tax exemption benefits are never available and the officers are chronically dishonest.

The most viable and important of the few formal organizations is the wine cooperative. Founded in 1964, it has approximately fifteen members, all vineyard owners. Some of its members are residents of Carreras, Taraya, and Sucre, but are all related to important patróns in town. Although some small property owners have become members, the big owners thus far have dominated the cooperative. Ignacio Martinez is general president and Andres Mardueño is his deputy. Prudencio Rioja is treasurer, and Rosendo Maldonado is general secretary. All are important landowners. Maldonado has studied wine making and claims charge of wine production. These four have discussed the possibility of ousting the others on the ground that it was their property that was put up as security for loans from the Agricultural Bank, and, since they assume all the risks, they should receive the benefits without sharing.

Only two of the large landowners are not members of the cooperative. One is Marequita Santana, who does not produce her own wine, and the other is Carlos Preciado, who prefers to produce independently because he thinks the rules and procedures reduce profit-making opportunities. Membership has also been restricted because vineyard owners join mainly to borrow money, and the loans from the Agricultural Bank are not large enough even to cover the needs of present members.

Another grouping of some importance is that of the sports clubs, although typically they have a short and unstable life. Since their membership is drawn primarily from young adults, they become active only when the students return from the cities and the zafreros come back from Argentina and Santa Cruz. Four sports groups have been active in recent years. Two draw their members, both males and females, from decente families. In one the age range is from sixteen to about thirty; in the other, from eleven to fifteen. Both groups play basketball and soccer, but the most popular activity of the older group is dancing in the homes of the girl members. Married men usually are excluded because the girls believe they are inclined to drink too much and thus spoil the fun and games.

The two other groups draw their members from zafreros and lower status Vitichi families and, to a lesser extent, from peons. Sport is taken more seriously in these two clubs, and competitive matches are arranged with teams from near-by towns as well as with the older decente club.

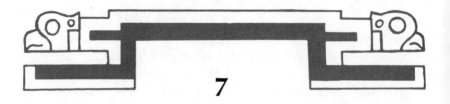

7

COMMUNITY ACTION

Contaminated drinking water, inadequate public sanitation, scant means of communication, lack of electricity and poor school facilities are some of the more insistent problems in Villa Abecia.

It has been usual for local government to appeal to the central government for technical aid and especially money whenever problems come up, but this is risky business because the central government never has enough of either, especially money. Success in this approach depends heavily on the political connections, on the influence local officials have in national circles. The alcalde, Jose Madrigal, has had an impressive record of success, but his influence in La Paz may be waning. Between his appointment to office by an MNR regime in 1961 and the end of 1964 he got central government funds through his party friends for the improvement of the local primary school building, for concrete sidewalks and benches around the plaza, for a government office building and for other public works. His successes greatly enhanced his prestige. He could boast of "good contacts" in La Paz, of being a devoted public official and the only citizen really concerned with the welfare of the town. The extent of his popularity was demonstrated after the change of government in 1964. Though MNR officials in other towns were immediately thrown out by local citizens, or soon were to be unseated, the townspeople in Villa Abecia successfully petitioned the central government to continue Madrigal in office. But his MNR friends are gone, and since 1964 the alcalde has had to depend increasingly on local resources for local projects. However, the old pattern of reliance on the central government and the alcalde's personal interest and influence in previous successes have had a spoiling effect; but quite aside from this there is an even more important factor impeding any effective shift to basically local support in getting anything done. The campesinos, who comprise the majority of the population, are not regarded by town officials, decentes, or Vitichis as full citizens, despite their legal claim to this status since the Revolution, and for this reason it is difficult, if not impossible, for them to cooperate in community affairs. The decente belief that campesinos are ignorant, lazy, and irresponsible provides a more than adequate rationale for excluding them from the discussions and planning that must precede collective effort, and their social segregation prevents the opening of the channels of communication that would be necessary for informed campesino action. The sindicato seems to have served this purpose in the mid-1950's, but in recent years it has become an ineffectual organization. It is indicative of the current situation of the campesinos that when representatives of a national Catholic aid organization arrived to estimate emergency needs following hailstorm disaster, they were content to inquire only among the patróns about the needs of the peons.

The campesinos are neither assisted nor encouraged in accepting community responsibility. Further, they would run the risk of seeing the benefits of their efforts accrue mainly to others, primarily the decentes. Improvement of the school building would benefit the town, but many campesinos find it impossible to send their children to school. Thus, any appeal to campesino self-interest cannot but fall on skeptical ears.

The hard-working, educated Vitichis offer comparatively far greater immediate potential for developing community cooperation. Yet this potential must be severely qualified. Many Vitichis regard themselves as transients who will one day return to their native town. They have no long-range commitment to Villa Abecia. Moreover, the decentes consider the Vitichis to be outsiders, not really of the place, which further tends to isolate them from participation in community affairs.

The only major segment of the population remaining, the one most crucial to action, are the decentes. But though they feel a strong sense of community loyalty and responsibility, in some ways they think they *are* the community, and constantly equate the interests of the town only with their own interest. Marequita Santana, for instance, reacts to the proposed electric light project by saying: "¿Qué me importa?"—"What do I care? I have my lantern." The absense of electric lighting raises no problem for her because she can afford lanterns and oil to fuel them. The many families who live in flickering candlelight simply do not count. On top of all this there is mutual distrust between government officials and the citizens of the town. The officials are skeptical of the possibility of assistance from the population, whether in work, money, or even ideas. The people, in turn, suspect the motives of their officials and especially their honesty in handling money. The affair of the plaza illustrates this conflict.

The appearance of the plaza is criticized by everyone, but when the alcalde has attempted to improve it he has generally received little co-operation and sometimes has been charged with having made it worse. When he imposed water rationing so that he would have enough to keep plaza plants and grass alive, there was widespread complaining and people violated the order, watering their gardens anyway. When he was offered free plants in Tarija to improve the plaza, people said he put off picking them up so that he might charge the town for them, but keep the money for himself. On his part, the alcalde pleads that he can do little to improve the plaza if townspeople refuse to pay taxes intended for public works.

The decentes avoid public affairs. To them, the problems of local government are peripheral problems, not worth the attention of decentes, and concern about them only invites their ridicule. In this unpromising setting collective action is nevertheless not completely impossible. On the night of December 29, 1965, a furious hailstorm hit the town and surrounding countryside, destroying grape and other crops. A second hailstorm occurred two days later. Torrential rains followed. The river overflowed and flash floods came down through the ravines above the town. The racing flood waters carried tons of mud, sand, gravel, and huge boulders onto the properties below. Some properties virtually disappeared beneath the debris, while on others only barren rock remained.

Property owners met the next day and dispatched telegrams to central government officials, La Paz newspapers and the La Paz radio. When it was suggested that campesinos should also sign the telegrams, the sub-prefect signed for the sindicato on his own authority. At a second meeting three days later it was decided to send a commission to seek aid from President Barrientos, the American Embassy, and any other likely source. The commission included the alcalde, the sub-prefect, two of the largest landowners, and two or three other persons to represent near-by villages and the campesinos. It was decided that each landowner would contribute a sum proportional to the size of his property to pay the expenses of the commission. Two patróns volunteered to collect this money, but it was more than a week before they had enough to send the commission on its way.

Work party on the altiplano (Lambros Comitas)

When the commission got back, a special meeting was called to hear its report. Some members boasted of having had great success. The property owners among them had obtained an extension of eight years on their loans from the Agricultural Bank. The American Embassy had promised some pipe for the flood-damaged water system, and seeds and a few tools for the campesinos. There was talk in town that commission members had exerted themselves primarily for their own benefit. Some said they pocketed money donated by the president, though no evidence was adduced.

The immediate problem caused by the hailstorm was the interruption of the public water supply. Water for household use is piped into Villa Abecia from a cement storage tank in the hills north of the town. An open stream fed by a spring is the source of this water, and while the tank was not damaged, the stream was diverted from its course by flood debris, and tons of deposited rock broke the pipeline running out of the tank. On the day after the first storm the alcalde and others inspected the water system to assess the damage. They found that it was extensive, and decided that it would be wise to relocate the pipeline to a safer position. This report heightened the general concern. There was no water coming from household faucets, and neither was there any available from the near-by irrigation ditches because these were full of mud and rocks. Water was to be had from the river, but only insufficient quantities could be carried. Most households had small gardens of vegetables and fruits, and these would soon die without water. There was also worry that an epidemic might develop from drinking contaminated water.

At the second public meeting, on January 3, when the commission was formed, various arguments for urgent action were put forward. The majority favored direct local action. But the alcalde argued that the town must wait for the government engineers and for government assistance in rebuilding the water system. He supported his position by pointing out that the municipal treasury lacked adequate funds to undertake expensive repairs, that emergency repairs would represent money thrown away, since the system had to be redesigned, and that any stop-gap repairs would weaken the position of the town in seeking government assistance to reconstruct the water system. No one at the meeting was willing to challenge the alcalde directly, to initiate any action that he opposed, so the meeting ended with the alcalde's policy in effect adopted.

In the week following the January 3 meeting, dissatisfaction with the alcalde's position increased. Still, no one attempted to organize opinion against him. In this situation, the anthropologist associated with this study, interested and sympathetic, became a focus for direct action. The handful of citizens in somewhat active opposition to the alcalde sought to reverse his policy through another public meeting, which was called on January 10, but they were routed again by the alcalde's rhetoric. With many still dissatisfied, several—including one of the project field workers —confronted the alcalde with a firm decision: they and other members of the community were going to do something about the water problem whether he liked it or not. The next morning this small group, including the sub-prefect and two of the project field workers, discovered that the tank and the feeder stream were intact, requiring only cleaning, and that only fifty yards of pipe, not the 300 of the alcalde's estimate, had been buried and might require excavating. Part of the group was immediately sent to town to get help, tools, and food, and the others set to work dredging mud with their hands. In less than an hour water was flowing into the tank and on into the pipeline. As the hours passed, more and more people arrived from town to join in the work. Men and women, adults and children, patróns and peons, all pitched in to do what they could. Even the alcalde arrived, but only to give orders. By nightfall the town had water.

This may be an impressive success story, but its implications are largely negative. Up to the day of activity, attitudes conformed exactly with the Villa Abecian pattern. A solution to a community problem is sought through the central government, and this mode of solution is most particularly favored by the person most visibly charged with public responsibility, the alcalde. The leading patróns and the decentes in general may criticize, but they do nothing. The peons are not supposed to have a voice in public affairs and are not heard. The difference in this case is that even patróns need water. They did not take charge, but it was clear that they were in disagreement with the alcalde, and also that something had to be done. Energetic intervention by members of the study staff doubtless disturbed the pattern somewhat, making it difficult to guess what might have happened if they had not been present.

Crisis makes possible arrangements and activities that are otherwise difficult, if not impossible, to evoke. In Villa Abecia the patterns of social relations and social belief otherwise tend to prevent collective activity. Local government officials and many decentes refer to the town as apathetic. Apathy appears less important in preventing community action in Villa Abecia than the traditional structure of power, status, and social obligations. Realistically, it is among the decentes that the greatest possibilities for community action lie. Clarification of the limitations of

local government and local government responsibilities vis-à-vis the decentes immediately become issues of importance from this viewpoint.
Increasing community participation by the patróns must raise the issue of who benefits. For communities like Villa Abecia such issues must
temper optimism concerning their capacity for collective self-help.

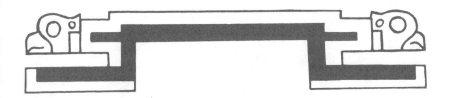

III

REYES
A Complex
Stable Community

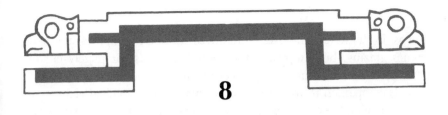

8

THE SETTING

The town of Reyes is near the western edge of the vast lowland plain of the Beni in Eastern Bolivia. This is an area of few people and much land, with huge natural pastures alternating with tropical forests. The town sits on a low rise in the plain, approximately 700 feet above sea level, from which the grasslands extend on all sides beyond sight, so flat that it fills with water during the rainy season and remains under several inches of it for several months. Three sides of the town are bounded by the curiche, a U-shaped moat dug long ago to protect the place from Indians. Just beyond the curiche is the Lechería, a stream that flows only during the rainy season but which is a year-round source of reservoir water.

Within the old moat the town is laid out in a regular grid pattern of more than fifty blocks, except on the periphery where settlement is sparse, the streets become paths, and there is heavy vegetation. The town gives the impression of spaciousness. The streets are wide, and there are many scattered vacant lots. The houses are far apart, and the properties are either fenced with wire or have no fence at all—they are not shut in by the traditional high adobe walls. Almost all the houses are of one story, with two or three rooms, occasionally four or five, and are made of a variety of materials—adobe, mud-plastered adobe, cement-coated adobe, wooden poles, or simply palm leaves. Almost every household has a garden with some fruit trees, including avocado and citrus fruits. A few people have their own wells and neighbors draw from these or go to the curiche.

There are two plazas in Reyes, after the pattern of Spanish Colonial towns. Both are unattractive, unimproved. In one the odd horse or cow comes grazing, but the other, the central plaza, is completely cut off from use by a wire fence. At a corner of this plaza are a wooden church and its companion rectory, and behind them is the parochial elementary school. Facing the church on the other side of the plaza is a small adobe public high school. One block in back of this is the public elementary school. In one of the larger houses on the central plaza local government is run from a rented room.

THE PEOPLE AND THEIR ACTIVITY

In 1965 the project census counted 2129 persons in Reyes, distributed among 322 households, one-quarter of which were of more than eight persons. All the townspeople speak Spanish, but one-quarter also speak one of several Indian languages—Quechua, Aymara, or a language of the lowlands, such as Reyesano.

Throughout most of the year the climate is humid and hot, the temperature usually ranging between 97° and 61° Fahrenheit. The rainy season, at its wettest in December and January, varies in length and in rainfall. The average is 70 inches a year. During the rains the dirt streets are transformed into mud sloughs and at times into rivers.

On an ordinary weekday activity starts early. The butchers open shop at the slaughterhouse at four a.m., but a queue forms well before that. The general stores are open by seven o'clock or earlier, and the women begin their chores and the children are at play. As the morning progresses the streets gradually fill with chatting, bustling people, but at noon all stops, the stores are closed, the streets are deserted, the doors and shutters of the houses are shut. This is the time of greatest heat, of mid-day meal and siesta. At two thirty the stores open again and the town returns to life. Chatter and bustle reach a high point at dusk at the street intersection one block south of the central plaza, where a movie theatre stands on one corner and an open-air coffee and beer kiosk on another. At eleven o'clock the few street lights are turned off and most people go home. But at the coffee and beer cantinas and kiosks the men are at cards and dice by lantern light, and their games and talk may go on beyond midnight.

OUTSIDE CONTACTS

Throughout much of its history Reyes has been in comparative isolation. There are no railroads or highways through the Beni, not even unimproved roads, for the yearly flooding would make roads difficult to build and costly to maintain. But horses, and carts with large wooden wheels drawn by oxen, travel the flat terrain throughout the year over a tangle of crossing trails. Within the town a few trucks, a jeep, and a couple of tractors provide transport, and recently some cattlemen have taken to the range on lightweight motorcycles.

The remoteness of centuries was broken for Reyes in 1946 with the construction of an airfield by the Corporación Boliviana de Fomento (Bolivian Development Corporation), a federal agency whose chief local function is increased production and improvement of the quality of Beni cattle. The CBF, with headquarters in Reyes, established breeding farms stocked with imported Cebu and Santa Gertrudis bulls. CBF planes now carry dressed beef directly from Reyes to La Paz and return with goods for local merchants. Weekly flights out of Trinidad, the departmental capital, touch down at Reyes and three or four other towns. There are also irregularly scheduled direct flights between Reyes and La Paz, sometimes as often as once a week, for the transport of goods. All flights are subject to weather, the dirt landing field being usable only when dry. Mail is carried by plane. The state operates a radio-telegraph office at Reyes, but heavy rains interrupt even radio communications, isolating the town completely.

IN TIME

A large part of the central Beni as far west as Reyes was known to the early Spanish explorers as Moxos, after the name of an Indian tribe of the region. Rumors of great wealth in this back country prompted several expeditions to set out from Lima, Asunción, and Cochabamba between 1539 and 1630. In fact, the area was lightly populated by small bands of semi-nomadic Indians who had little gold for the Spaniards.

At the end of the seventeenth century, before the imposition of Spanish military or administrative authority, the Jesuits founded a mission in the Moxos country and attempted to create a simple utopian society. At

Loading beef at Reyes airport (William McEwen)

mission stations, two Jesuits were assigned as physicians, teachers, and inspectors of work. An Indian civil administration was set up to govern over the newly congregated and resettled Indians. The Indians elected from their own numbers a corregidor, several regidores, alcaldes, and a council, and the communities settled down to farming and craftwork, taught and supervised by the priests. No one received a salary, nor was there any type of money in use. Each member of a community received what he needed out of the collective production. The mission stations rapidly extended their control over the Indian population of the Moxos, and to prevent despoilment of the Indians the Jesuits barred Spanish colonists from mission territory. But colonists still came in search of riches and to seize Indians to work as serfs on plantations in the south. The Jesuits eventually prevailed in this conflict and the King of Spain dispatched a Royal Letter forbidding the entry of colonists into the mission area.

Reyes was the tenth Jesuit mission founded in Moxos, sometime between 1700 and 1710. It was situated on the Rio Beni, just west of where the town now lies. A half-century later, in 1767, with all the governments of Europe aligned against their order, Spain expelled the Jesuits from her South American dominions and Reyes, with all the rest, passed from church to civil control. With the departure of the Jesuits traders came, offering attractive goods on terms little understood by the Indians, and quickly swindled them of their animals and land. His possessions gone, the Indian himself became security for his debts, and he was thus forced to involuntary labor. The superficial legality of these transactions put the power and prestige of the colonial government behind the merchants. Under the law, the Indian could in effect be bought by anyone who would pay his debt, thereby enslaving him to a new creditor—for few Indians ever were able to pay their debts. By the nineteenth century the Moxos had become a region of colonial estates with large herds of cattle and horses. Many of these merchant landlords were "turcos"—traders from the eastern Mediterranean. During the nineteenth century Spaniards came to Reyes in increasing numbers as governmental officials, merchants, workers, and adventurers, lured by economic booms in quinine and rubber.

In the 1850's an intense demand for quinine developed on the world market. The cinchona bark found in the forests of the Beni was the best in Bolivia, and the people of Reyes set to work collecting it. The labor ranks were swelled by people from near-by villages as well as from distant parts of the country. Requiring little investment, profits could be made by all. Then the British planted the cinchona tree in India and Malaya, and by 1870 their more efficient plantation production and shorter trade routes destroyed the demand for Bolivian bark.

Hardly was the quinine boom over when the search for natural rubber began, in 1874, and Reyes had another economic upsurge. This, as it turned out, was an accident of geographic ignorance. Rubber collected in the western Beni was brought up-river to Puerto Salinas, west of Reyes on the Rio Beni, and over the few miles to Reyes, then overland in a long trek to Santa Ana, where it was reloaded and sent down the Rio Mamore into Brazil. Reyes became a land trans-shipment center because no one knew that the Rio Beni joins the Rio Mamore at the Brazilian border, and that the rubber need never have been unloaded.

Two or three very large firms and many small ones were established to handle the rubber trade, and they were soon dealing in other merchandise up and down the rivers and along the trade routes. In 1880 the true course of the Rio Beni was found and the overland rubber route through Reyes lost its purpose. A sharp decline in commerce took place, but Reyes continued to profit from the rubber boom until after the turn of the century.

Cattle which the Jesuits had introduced in the 1600's had by now multiplied on the virgin pasturelands from a few hundred to many thousands of head. There was no control of breeding and great wild herds had grown up. At the same time, merchants and other men of means were taking over the large tracts of land that were to become cattle estancias. For a time after the Corporación Boliviana de Fomento had come in to improve cattle production, Reyes was the only community with air transportation within hundreds of miles, so it became a central cattle market and shipping point. But now every important town of the region has its airfield. Further, reckless exploitation of the cattle herds in recent decades and unchecked diseases in the animals have greatly diminished their numbers. Meat was flown out of Reyes daily in the early 1950's, but now only once or twice a week.

Reyes, which had been made a provincial capital in 1939, had a change of local government officials after the Revolution of 1952, but little else changed. There was no hostility, none of the fighting between peons and patróns that occurred in other areas. The relation of land to labor that contributed to the Revolution of 1952, as seen in the other towns studied, did not exist in Reyes.

Boys and bullocks in Reyes (William McEwen)

TOWN ECONOMY

In cattle raising lies the greatest concentration of wealth in the community, despite earlier unrestrained slaughter and epizootics of rabies and hoof and mouth disease. Threatened with the destruction of the herds, most cattle growers are adopting remedies. Estancias are being fenced to control breeding and new breeds have been introduced. More herds are being vaccinated, and there are efforts to produce disease-resistant strains.

Cattle are tended more closely, moved to high ground during the rainy season and to water sources during the dry, so that good physical condition can be maintained and the loss of animals minimized, but these measures have made cattle raising more costly. Most cattlemen today own no more than a few hundred head. A few have herds of one to two thousand, but none is greater than 5000. The small breeder, hardest hit by increasing costs, is least able to get bank loans, for the Banco Agrícola requires that the assets of the borrower be three times greater than his loan. Even so, loans are for short periods and interest is high.

Most of the cattle in the Reyes area are sold to a middleman who has them butchered in Reyes and ships the carcasses by air to La Paz. Cattlemen can make a greater profit by shipping the meat themselves, but they risk a considerable loss since there are no local refrigeration facilities and bad weather may halt air traffic. Under these circumstances the meat must be processed locally as charqui (dried, salted meat), for which cattlemen get about half the fresh meat sales price.

To reduce the cost of air shipment, most of the local meat dealers arrange to have the meat planes return with goods for resale in Reyes. This provides the town with an important, though expensive, source of trade goods. A direct but not very profitable by-product of cattle raising is the local work in leather. A small tannery near town employs several men, and more make leather goods in their homes. Saddles and other leather articles required by cowpunchers, and shoes and sandals, are the principal types of leatherwork. They are produced for local consumption only, and demand is light and uneven.

Another significant group in terms of concentrated wealth and importance in the local economy are the retail merchants. While dozens of people in town sell goods, especially as a part-time activity, three or four merchants dominate retail trade. Their stores carry the greatest quantities and largest assortments of merchandise. Almost all household needs can be obtained in any one of these stores, much of it brought in from La Paz. The larger merchants are also moneylenders, to whom small farmers pledge their harvests for loans and credit, an arrangement very favorable to the merchants.

Reyes is now in another of its periods of economic decline, this time through the loss of its position as the only shipping point of beef for a large area. The CBF, which once had a work force of more than 200, now has only thirty people on its payroll, though it continues to provide work to a substantial number by contracting for specific tasks such as posts for range fences. There is no other source of employment that compares with the CBF. The estancias have work crews, but each one employs no more than a handful of vaqueros. The stores and other businesses in town employ even fewer persons. Men who have few skills or almost none find a living at odd jobs, and many families depend entirely on small game and fish and what they can raise in their own gardens and on their chacos, their small subsistence plots of farmland beyond the town. Nearly every family raises poultry and pigs. Lack of work and short-term employment are causes of much complaint.

The full-time farmers, over 25 per cent of the male labor force, raise cash crops, but primarily for the local market. Rice, maize, yucca, and guineo (a variety of banana) are the most common crops. Tobacco, sugar cane, and coffee are also cultivated, but to a lesser extent. No fertilizers are used. Depleted soil is simply abandoned. Neither are insecticides used. Only the montes, the woodlands cleared long ago, are available for farming. The pampas are entirely in the hands of the cattlemen.

Independent agricultural work was the goal of many of the mozos, the peons of the cattle ranchers who were freed of their debts by the Agrarian Reform Law. While still working as mozos, many had cultivated a small chaco on the patrón's estancia. Then they received a few acres of land under agrarian law, but many have now returned to the cattle estancias to work for wages. Their farms yielded very small profits at best in the limited Reyes market, and it was not unusual for these men to discover by harvest time that they owed more than the value of their crops.

The area around Reyes offers a number of other means of livelihood. Though none of these provides full-time work for anyone, they are important economic supplements. Rubber is still produced on a very small scale, and many varieties of trees in the nearby forests are cut for house construction, furniture, light poles, roofing material, and other uses. Wild cats and jaguars are hunted for their fur, small animals and fowl are hunted for their meat, and fish are abundant but are caught only for home consumption.

Money for most families seems constantly in short supply. There is continual borrowing and chronic indebtedness. Workers regularly seek advances on their wages. Most retail stores sell on credit and make direct loans. Interest varies widely, depending on the amount of the loan and its duration. Debt peonage became illegal under the Agrarian Reform Law, and all pre-1952 farm worker debts were voided, but mozos still become indebted to their patróns and others, and local authorities are inclined to support the patrón when he demands that the mozo work off his debt.

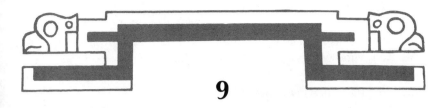

9

POWER AND
AUTHORITY

Reyes is a larger, more heterogeneous community than Villa Abecia. Its cycles of economic boom and recession have favored various segments of the population, and have not permitted the continuity of control that is such a prominent characteristic of Villa Abecia. On the other hand, the Revolution of 1952 did nothing to Reyes in any truly revolutionary sense, though significant changes were greater than in Villa Abecia. It was the same Revolution, but with differing effects, the social structure of Reyes being relatively less stable and of greater complexity.

LOCUS OF POWER

The most important form of exploitable wealth in Reyes today is meat. The ganaderos, the cattlemen, are therefore pre-eminent in the community power system. The pampas of the Beni favor the raising of cattle and have been an important part of the Reyes scene ever since its founding. With the development of air transport they became the one valuable commodity with a market in the world outside, but not all ganaderos possess important wealth. Some have as few as 100 or even only 50 head, but they are important because their group holds the greatest power, most of it concentrated in those with herds of 1000 to 5000.

The cattle estancias of even the biggest ganaderos came through the Revolution almost unchanged, chiefly because the Agrarian Reform Law acknowledged that cattle raising requires broad expanses of land. Besides, large tracts of unused land, especially in forest, were available for allocation to peons. There was almost no expropriation under the law, and even when confiscation is alleged to have taken place it was often of land that had been abandoned, land that had become the property of the state under the new national law.

The economic dominance of the ganaderos has been threatened less by agrarian reform than by poor technical management and the forces of nature. Neglect during periods of heavy rain or intense heat causes heavy losses among cattle. Worse still, rampant diseases have destroyed entire herds. Not a few prosperous ganaderos were wiped out in a single attack in the days before the now widespread use of vaccines.

Ganaderos of once great power and prestige are now but shadows of a former prominence based on large holdings. Others have fallen from the ganaderos class altogether, and have been forced into unskilled work to make a living. The effect has been a hindrance to the continuity of dominance by this group and to the development of an elitist tradition, such as that among the patróns of Villa Abecia.

The power of the ganaderos over their workers traditionally took the form of debt peonage. Workers were forced to pay very high prices for the goods they needed and high interest rates for essential money, but their wages would rarely permit repayment. Further profits were made out of their ignorance, through easy falsification of accounts. By such means the mozos became hopelessly indebted, and their debts in time were inherited by their children. The effect was a stable supply of cheap, controlled labor. Agrarian reform crippled this traditional peonage system by abolishing all debts contracted by agricultural laborers prior to the Revolution, and by requiring formal work contracts which must specify the rights and wages, as well as the obligations of the worker, and also the rights and obligations of the employer. Nevertheless, mozos must still depend on patróns for work and patróns still make loans of goods or money to their mozos. These debts can no longer be inherited, but they are certainly collectible so long as the patrón can force the mozo to work and local authorities support his doing so. Here, too, the Revolution wrought a change. The public floggings to which mozos traditionally were subjected are now prohibited. In this and other ways, agrarian reform has greatly restrained the once almost unlimited power that the patrón in Reyes had over the peon. The peon of today is less deferential, more independent in outlook and action. Still, he must eat, and this sustains the power of the ganadero, for the smaller estancias employ no more than three to four vaqueros, the larger ones usually no more than ten to fifteen. Demand for labor being low, profits from independent farming being not high enough for a decent living, it is easy for the cattle estancias to recruit mozos on the boss's terms.

Yet another source of ganadero power is his well-established reputation for violence. Before 1939, before its becoming a provincial capital, Reyes had no formal local government, no policemen. Isolated, at a great distance from formal authority, the town conducted itself according to the classic frontier rule of force. The history of Reyes is full of tales of gunfights, atrocious assaults, and assassinations. Prudence dictated only that murder be done with as little risk as possible. The shot was fired from a concealed position, from a dark doorway.

Today, ganaderos are more likely to hire a killer or have indebted henchmen do the job. One local ganadero recently was accused of having used his men to commit several murders. The evidence against this cattleman was inconclusive, but most people consider the charges true. Furthermore, the ganadero can usually count on the cooperation of the authorities. When these affairs get beyond local jurisdiction he can generally avoid difficulty by letting the prima facie killers face the charges, which is possibly a part of what they have been paid to do. Though quality of law and order probably has improved considerably in the past decade, the old pattern of terror and violence has not been completely erased.

Two of the most talked of assassination incidents of recent years concerned two MNR families, people of the Revolution, who had come to town to represent the new political order. The first MNR family—a large one—arrived in 1953 and were active in organizing a local branch of the MNR party. Through their political connections they took a strong lead in town affairs, in efforts to develop the party's economic interests. A dispute arose between the family and the director of the CBF over a debt. This progressed from an exchange of messages to an exchange of words to an exchange of blows. At this point the CBF director armed some of his men and drove into town to settle the quarrel. He also picked up several of the ganaderos who were becoming increasingly antagonistic toward the family because of their growing power, their open hostility to the ganaderos, and their favoring the peons. The CBF director and his gang fired on the houses and buildings of this large family, killing several of them. The others fled. The CBF director promptly left town, but members of the family later returned and killed one of the ganaderos—then retired from Reyes for good. No investigation, no arrest, no further action occurred.

The second MNR family arrived in Reyes in 1954. One member had been appointed alcalde, and his brother had been named head of the local federation of sindicatos. Both brothers were militant MNR officials and quickly made many enemies among the ganaderos. Not long after their arrival the brother who headed the Centrál was accused of raping a townswoman whose husband was away from home. The husband returned, sought out the brother and shot him dead. People on the side of the peons say that the woman's accusation of rape was planned by the ganaderos as a pretext for getting rid of a threat to their way of life.

Shortly thereafter an investigation commission arrived from La Paz to examine charges of corruption against the other brother, the alcalde. He, too, had drawn the ire of the ganaderos for promoting the interests of the peons and protecting their rights. For example, instead of allowing ganaderos who had physically abused their peons to get off with a fine, he would jail them for a day or two. The arrival of the investigators brought armed groups of opposed ganaderos and peons into town. With that, the commission decided to interrogate the alcalde in La Paz, though the peons had to be persuaded to allow him to leave. He did not return to Reyes. He was jailed in La Paz and subsequently disappeared from view.

The activities of these two families were the high point of the only serious, organized challenge to the dominant power position of the ganaderos under the MNR government. In both cases violence played an important part of the maintenance of ganadero power. It was the only time that persons of importance took the part of the peons. In Reyes, as in Villa Abecia, the patróns were able to find a modus vivendi with the new national government that enabled them to survive with much of their power intact.

Two ganaderos are especially prominent today in town affairs. They represent the two styles employed by most ganaderos in their exercise of power, the elitist style and the activist. Luis Regla typifies the elitist style, the pretense of unobtrusiveness. He seldom goes to public meetings, regardless of their importance, and when he does he seldom participates, even when asked to. But he takes part by proxy, having someone there who is a known associate. As one of the wealthiest ganaderos he is frequently invited to form or serve on a committee, generally in the hope that he will make a large financial contribution to its work. He is not a frequent collaborator in voluntary community projects and has even gone so far as to refuse to pay his cattle taxes, on the grounds that the money is misused. On the other hand, he has donated a large sum to remodel the central plaza.

The other ganadero, Abel Zarco, is a model activist. This is a style that is especially congenial to politicians and government officials, as Zarco once was. He came to Reyes as sub-prefect, but married into a wealthy cattle family and became a ganadero. He attends all public meetings and holds offices in many different groups. He talks more at meetings and contributes more ideas than others. He is inclined to direct these meetings in an autocratic manner, and even if not allowed to take over he is sufficiently skillful in debate to get what he wants with considerable frequency. Elitists like Regla try to avoid open struggles, try instead for private settlements, from which decisions can be implemented without fanfare.

While one form of violence has been a source of strength to the ganaderos, another form has weakened their class position. Discord and conflict occur frequently among them. There are lawsuits over inheritance rights and suits occur between relatives as well as other ganaderos over cattle agreements. They are forever seeking allies from among themselves to attack yet another of their group as opportunity presents itself.

An instance of dissension among the ganaderos occurred in 1965 when it appeared that Luis Regla might be appointed to replace the alcalde, who was accused of incompetence and at a public meeting had been asked to resign. It was suggested that Regla be appointed because he had offered money to complete the remodeling of the central plaza. This proposal split the ganaderos, one side supporting Regla and the other rallying around sub-prefect Abel Zarco, friend of the alcalde.

The core of Regla's supporters, mostly wealthy ganaderos, were card-playing companions at a drinking and gaming cantina, and the alcalde's backers were ganaderos and a few officials who regularly gathered at the Azcui kiosk, another place for cards, coffee, and beer. The alcalde finally resigned, followed by Zarco, who quit in protest against what he called irresponsible criticism, but he was also losing a pliable alcalde, a loss through which his position as sub-prefect became less attractive. Zarco then attempted with the support of his faction to force Regla to sign a statement that he would complete the remodeling of the central plaza on becoming alcalde, using his own funds if necessary. Regla refused to accept the office under this condition, and eventually a new alcalde and sub-prefect were appointed from La Paz.

This incident should not suggest that the ganaderos are organized in two stable groups of rival card players. Most ganaderos freely move from one gathering place to the other. Ties of kinship and friendship, recreational association, personal and economic interests, and various animosities create a complex web of crosscutting interconnections among the ganaderos and their families. There are constantly shifting alliances formed to meet a specific situation. Such alliances exploit whatever part of the network is useful to the occasion. Other problems and other occasions bring about new alliances.

Despite internal factionalism and conflict, the ganaderos are aware of their common interests and of their power to influence community decisions in favor of those interests. However, in contrast to the leaders of Villa Abecia, they have not been able, except for a relatively short period between 1930 and 1952, to monopolize all power in the community. There are several subsidiary groups with whom they must share control. The most important of these are the comerciantes, the merchants, some of whom have amassed considerable wealth. They can buy immunity from the law, and all else that money affords. They are issuers of credit and lenders of cash, on whom laborers and farmers depend for everyday necessities. Many of their debtors never completely pay off, and from these the merchants expect deference and can exact subservience. The creditor merchant is in a position to influence a relatively large proportion of the population.

A somewhat tangential power is held by the small sindicatos scattered over the countryside, and especially by the secretary general of the local federation of sindicatos. The sindicatos are not usually involved in community affairs, but are likely to be approached to supply peons when a town project requires a labor force. The leader of the sindicatos at these times becomes a person to be reckoned with. In the Reyes area the sindicatos were never the militant units that arose in other parts of Bolivia. Since the fall of the MNR in 1964, the local sindicatos have become even more timorous. They represent no threat to the power of the ganaderos and the merchants.

Another minor center of power is the Church, meaning the bishop and Padre Lorenzo, his chief assistant. Padre Lorenzo is an official in several groups, a member of various committees, and directs a soccer team. He frequently directs his sermons to discussions of community action.

Finally, two organizations must be mentioned in speaking of power in the community. One is the ever-present Association of Veterans of the Chaco War. Typically, in Bolivia, this organization has little or no say in community affairs. The difference in Reyes is that it has a reputation for having important political contacts in La Paz. There is no evidence for this except some instances when local officials have been replaced without explanation, but this in itself is not an unusual occurrence. Nevertheless, a reputation for power is itself a source of power, so the president of this organization is generally included whenever the important people of the community assemble.

The second organization is the Amigos del Progreso, the Friends of Progress, a civic improvement association which will be discussed later. Its members are the important vecinos (residents) of the town. It is a force in the community because the collective power of its members is considerable. Among these are the ganaderos, merchants, CBF officials, the bishop and priest, the doctor, local government officials, and a few others. The Amigos del Progreso unites most of the facets of power in Reyes. It is a new organization that has become very prominent in community action.

GOVERNMENT AUTHORITY

Before 1939 Reyes had a corregidor, an official appointed by the provincial sub-prefect as the sole authority. This period of government is referred to as a time of open corruption and dictatorial force. The corregidor supported the ganaderos completely and in turn was allowed to exploit his office for personal profit. It was a time when a complaint from a ganadero brought immediate flogging of the offending mozo by the corregidor's men.

In 1939 Reyes became the capital of the province and received a full set of local officials. Chief among these are the sub-prefect, the alcalde and the intendente. The sub-prefect is administratively responsible for the entire province, while the alcalde has similar responsibility for the town. Other important settlements in the province, the cantons, are governed by corregidores appointed by the sub-prefect, but the surrounding countryside is governed by a cacique appointed by the alcalde. The intendente is responsible for enforcing the regulations covering public services. Private activity under public regulation, such as retail selling, is under the authority of the alcalde. There is also a small police force.

Even though the legal jurisdiction of the alcalde is broad and inclusive, the actual definition of his responsibilities is typically narrow. Aside from upholding the laws, a task largely delegated to others, the office is mostly concerned with cattle slaughtering, public lighting, sanitation, and civic celebrations. New or chronic community problems rarely receive more than passing notice. The public elementary school building fell into decay before a substitute was found. The central plaza is an overgrown, virtually abandoned plot. There has been much criticism, but government has taken no action. There are no sidewalks, and during the rainy season the streets are under water or are rivers of mud.

The response of all alcaldes to the need for action is that there are no funds in the municipal treasury. And it is true that Reyes suffers from inadequate revenue. Its most important income is from the tax on meat shipped from town, but the yield is very irregular. Reyes has had no officials who have been able to get that extra financial assistance from the national government, not even on a modest scale, that distinguishes the performance of a successful local politician.

In Reyes the proper concerns and responsibilities of local officials are ambiguously defined, leading to overlapping jurisdictions. Rare is the officeholder who has a clear conception of what his office entails. This is partly due to the lack of professional cadres of officials, to poor education, and to little, if any, relevant experience. There is essential unreality in there being elaborate legal specifications for local government but no means to make this government-on-paper viable.

The uninformed and misinformed official wonders whether he may appoint a subordinate, whether he ought to submit a list of candidates to La Paz, or must simply wait for La Paz to do something. Typically, he resolves the problem by not resolving anything, lest his decision turn out to be a wrong one. Overlapping jurisdictions leave the citizen not knowing where to go for help. Minor judicial matters are summarily handled by the sub-prefect, the alcalde, and the intendente. This overlapping creates a potentially competitive situation by bringing the influence of personality rather than official office to the fore. The two most important local officials, the sub-prefect and the alcalde, both have a claim to primary authority over the town. Given a forceful sub-prefect,

he tends to eclipse the alcalde. Given another, less aggressive and dominating, and the alcalde gains some of his earlier responsibilities, such as
presiding at public meetings and receiving town committees and delegations.

Another obstacle to effective government is the way offices are obtained and kept. Local residence qualifications, education, or experience
are not important. Officials frequently are appointed from outside the
town. One of the work inspectors was illiterate and one of the agrarian
judges was neither a lawyer nor acquainted with the Agrarian Reform
Law. Honesty or ability is not decisive. Lack of good character may
rouse criticism, but no one seems to have been barred from office by such
limitations. No Indian or campesino holds office, but they lack so many
of the apparently important qualifications that nothing can be concluded
from this.

Political affiliation is of considerable importance in acquiring official
position. It was even more important during the period of MNR rule,
when party membership was necessary. The uncertain situation following the overthrow of the MNR government in 1964 enabled conservative
parties to promote their interests more aggressively. Persons who took
office immediately following the 1964 coup were either members of the
conservative FSB party or of unknown affiliation. As the political situation became clarified, and a new government party took shape, these
men were replaced by others who were assumed to be loyal to the new
government.

Of transcendent importance in obtaining office is tener muñeca, "to
have connections." A common topic of gossip in Reyes is that someone
has gone to La Paz to obtain some official appointment or that someone
is threatening to go to La Paz to obtain an official job now held by another person. There is much boasting of valuable connections with important officials of the central government, but no one publicly offers
intimate details of these connections. The "connections" have many
different roots. Kinship, compadrazgo, friendship, money, political following, any or all may be the nature of them. Different appointments
can be traced to different networks. Though the routes frequently are
complex and hidden from view, all involve "connections."

The liabilities of public office being well known, there is little competition for most government jobs, especially the executive ones. Many
local offices are minor bureaucratic positions for which the pay is small
but sufficient, or sufficiently elastic, to be attractive, such as the offices

of tax collector and of the various inspectors of slaughterhouses, of forests, of public work contracts, and of agrarian work. These offices are the local outposts of national agencies, to which they are directly responsible. In the same bureaucratic category are two jobs for which there is intense competition. These are the office of the agrarian judge, who has jurisdiction over land disputes and allocations of land under the Agrarian Reform Law, and that of surveyor, who does the land surveys. The pay is low, but the extra fees run high. Land surveys are required in all distribution and claims cases, and fees must be paid by the litigants. There are great potentials in these two jobs, in both fees and bribes.

The workings of muñeca cut short many a career. Appointments are often for unspecified periods; but even in those for which periods are fixed, few officeholders complete the course. The job of intendente changed hands three times in 1958; that of sub-prefect, three times in 1960 and four times in 1964; that of alcalde, four times in 1964. Sometimes rumors of change circulate beforehand. Other times, the first notice is the official document in which the name of the new man is announced. The most popular topic of that day is speculation about how he got his appointment.

A branch of the lowest level of the national courts system, the Corte de Primera Instancia, sits in Reyes, presided over by a judge, the juez instructór. Usually these judges have had legal training, but the law is not the paramount factor in the disposition of the case. Indians and campesinos get short shrift, blunt and hostile. Mozos and laborers barely come off any better. They get no legal assistance, their ignorance is openly taken as an advantage, and penalties are harsh. Judgments are handed down in favor of the man with connections, and the process is notoriously eased through bribery.

The office of agrarian judge is open to the same persuasive influences. Only the heads of the sindicatos, with relevant experience and an organization behind them, have had any success in defending campesino interests. Since mid-1965 there has been no agrarian judge in Reyes. The area is now served by the departmental capital. Nor is it in the agrarian courts alone that the spirit of reform has been subverted. Inspectors were appointed by the MNR government to enforce new labor laws requiring formal contracts to protect workers in town and country against traditional abuses. In Reyes, claims and complaints by workers or peasants have been rare. Most actions are initiated by patróns. These offices have, in fact, become a new means for employers to collect on the debts of their workers.

To the extent of its functioning at all, government in Reyes is in the hands of the ganaderos and large merchants, as can be seen in the events following the downfall of the MNR government in the autumn of 1964. On the day following radio news of the coup d'état, it was announced over the loudspeaker at the outdoor cinema that there would be a meeting of the people of the town that afternoon at the police station. The stated purpose was to form a new local government. Relatively few people responded. The sub-prefect, the alcalde, the intendente, and other officials were present. The town's only physician was chosen to be chairman and proceeded to supervise the election of a temporary, three-man governing council. A minor professional of a high social status was elected president, and the members were the president of the Chaco veterans and a schoolteacher. Someone suggested that a representative of the peasants should be appointed, but the idea was ignored. The meeting then proceeded to the election of provisional officials. A cattle owner was elected alcalde and a business entrepreneur became sub-prefect. MNR officials and militants were passed over. Throughout the discussion, the selection of candidates, and their election, the meeting was dominated by one of the important ganaderos.

The conduct and outcome of this open meeting in the community reveals one of the primary conditions of local government. This is the restricted segment of the community that considers itself to be the public of local government and to which local officials restrict their responsiveness. In a community of more than 300 household heads alone, there were not more than fifty persons of all ages, both sexes and all propertied levels at this public meeting. No craftsmen, no laborers, no peasants attended. This was an assembly of vecinos, which in this context does not mean "neighbors," but residents of importance and prestige. Significantly, the old officials said little, and agreed without protest to hand over their offices to the persons selected at this meeting.

Local government appears to get along only by sufferance of ganaderos and merchants. This is especially apparent in its effort to collect taxes. The alcalde frequently acts as if the taxpayer were doing him a special favor. He calls a ganadero to his office, explains the financial problems of the town, sometimes has to tell specifically how the money is to be used, and occasionally ends up by reducing the tax to get any payment at all. To collect the tax on the local general stores the alcalde called a meeting of the merchants at his office. When they balked he offered to reduce the tax. He explained that the money was needed for the reconstruction of the primary school, a very pressing problem. The merchants countered by pointing out that some of the men engaged in the reconstruction owed them money, and suggested that their wages be applied against these debts. The alcalde accepted the proposal.

Rarely is the alcalde ready to provoke a confrontation on the tax payment issue. The only instance in recent times involved a rich ganadero who owed a considerable sum in taxes and refused to pay, on the ground that nothing useful would be done with his money. After long, unyielding negotiation, the alcalde finally forbade him to ship cattle from the Reyes landing strip. This brought down considerable criticism on the alcalde. He was accused of making enemies unnecessarily. He was also accused of contributing to further economic recession, since this ganadero probably would ship his cattle from the air strip at Santa Rosa, a small town east of Reyes. In fact, the ganadero solved his problem by shipping through a middleman in Reyes. The controversy continued for several months more, until the ganadero at last agreed to pay part of his taxes.

POLITICAL POWER

After the Revolution of 1952 the MNR government party achieved an importance at national and local levels that no party had ever had before. It organized and directed mass participation. It trained government leaders and established a communication network throughout the country at all levels. It became an important source of favor from above and applied its influence locally under central direction. Since the fall of the MNR government the party at the local level has become but one of several poorly organized associations.

Most of the major parties have supporters in Reyes. Before the 1964 coup the majority of Reyesanos supported the MNR and the FSB was second. After 1964, many MNR supporters shifted to the new MPC. There are also small numbers who favor the PRA, the PURS, the Communist Party, and the old Liberal Party. Political parties form and die at a high rate. A number of them are little more than paper organizations, with a directorate but few members. Political parties, as they function in the small towns and villages, frequently constitute no more than unstable cliques.

For even the major political parties it is often difficult to see a distinctive, ideological orientation; this is not for lack of pronouncements of policy, of which there is a great deal for all parties. The problem is that the rhetoric of party pronouncements, like the legal basis of local government, has slight relevance to the everyday world of Bolivians, including the politicians. If there exists any working ideology, it seems to be one of expediency in maintaining power. In Reyes, as elsewhere, politics are a favorite topic of conversation, but there is little talk of principles, issues, or programs. Discussion centers on the criticism, on the dishonesty, culpability, immorality of officials and politicians, and on why it is important that the party of the speaker come to power. Party functionaries, in fact, are frequently unacquainted with the official position of their party on various issues.

From statements by party members in Reyes it is possible to draw only some inferences about party differences on national issues. MNR members feel more sympathetic toward the peasants. They frequently cite injustices committed before 1952 and the measures taken by the MNR government to redress the peasant situation. They rely on the campesinos to return the MNR to power in Reyes, undoubtedly a factor in their pro-campesino utterances. In contrast, most FSB activists deplore the agrarian reform and complain that the campesinos no longer work hard now that they have land. They are strong supporters of law and order, and feel that MNR reform measures are making the campesino population ungovernable.

The MPC, organized in 1965 as the new government party, presents itself in Reyes as a continuation of the MNR. Locally it was announced that the MPC would follow the same economic and political policies, but without the corruption and abuses associated with the MNR. The most intensely ideological are the Communist activists, who impute all of the problems of the Beni region, as well as of Bolivia as a whole, to the United States.

The major political parties have had a largely symbolic significance. Only since the MNR and changes in the franchise have political parties acquired some organizational importance, even locally, and not many parties have adapted to the changing situation. Large numbers of Reyesanos have no involvement at all in political affairs. For those who are involved, political conviction plays a small part, political opportunism a great one. The only objective of many in supporting a party is to obtain some public office or official favor. Others, who fear that their party has little chance of coming to power, readily change their allegiance. As one Reyesano commented:

In the late 1940's when the PURS came to power, every Reyesano became a Republican. Then when the MNR came into power, everyone became a Movimientista. Now everybody is MPC.

Campesinos alone appear to be different. There is widespread sympathy among them for the MNR. This explains the stress placed by MPC organizers on their party as a continuation of the MNR. Despite this, many campesinos in the Reyes area refused to change their party membership. They said they would support the MPC at the elections only if the MNR would not put up candidates.

Opportunism is recognized by Reyesanos as a prime mover in political activity, so much so that a person's expressed party preference is ignored, and clues to political allegiance are found in the company a man keeps, the persons who are his friends, and in what he has to say on specific issues. In effect, secrecy surrounds political affiliation. This is true even of some of the most politically active persons, including a recent subprefect, a phenomenon that underscores the ambiguity of party politics as a source of power in the community. But, despite the dictates of opportunism, there are some differences of social composition among the several political parties, yet here the true opportunist is found on the membership rosters of two parties.

A number of MNR members, especially town workers, joined because of their jobs, and in the CBF all employees were required to belong to the MNR, though many of these people had no political interests—or may even have been opposed to the MNR. When the MPC became the party in power, the first to switch membership were CBF officials, who explained that it was really the same party and so involved no real change. Since they were government employees, no one really expected anything else of them. Indeed, CBF officials became the most active MPC recruiters among the campesinos. It is difficult to know how many persons have shifted to the MPC, because the MNR reorganized after a period of inactivity following the coup of 1964, and many who had affiliated with the MPC began again to attend MNR meetings.

The Falangistas of the FSB are mainly town dwellers—store owners, traders, craftsmen, some schoolteachers, some ganaderos. Some members felt that the FSB was receiving increasing support from workers and campesinos, but others complained that it would never come to power, "because we are like a caste, we have no members among the workers." A small number of ganaderos, some craftsmen and campesinos, and one professional comprise the local Communist party. Those still loyal to the old Liberal party are a few wealthy ganaderos and a lawyer. Too few persons belong to the other parties to establish the character of their membership.

Considering that the three wealthiest occupations—ganaderos, merchants, and professionals—function as quasi-groups in the community, there is rather little political homogeneity. Some ganaderos support the MNR, others the FSB; but those who are most active in politics and community affairs support no party openly, stimulating much conjecture about their political allegiance. Similarly, merchants support both the MNR and the FSB. The MNR "connections" of some of them are said to have been an important factor in their prosperity. As for the professionals, they may be the true eclectics, for their affiliations are spread from the ancient Liberals to the Communists.

Only the MNR, during its period of control from 1952 to 1964, can be said to have had important political functions. It was a highly articulated organization, geographically comprehensive and practically coincident with the structure of government. At both department and provincial levels there existed comandos zonales, regional commands, for implementing party policy; but the MNR was weakly organized in the Reyes area. A regional command there was, but it was never very active. The party was successful, however, in organizing sindicatos in the rural zone, and these constituted the main source of its strength in Reyes, though many were not strong and some had virtually ceased to exist by 1964.

A year after the military coup of 1964 a group of army officers arrived to organize the new government MPC party, but they soon departed, having created little more than a skeletal structure that had only one official charged with the registering of new members.

The FSB was in an even more disorganized condition, holding only one meeting during the period of the study to choose representatives to a national convention in La Paz, while other parties do not really exist as organizations at all.

The local Communist party is in a somewhat special situation because of the secrecy with which it surrounds itself, probably accounting in part for the rather widespread anticommunist fear and hostility in the towns-people. There was much gossiping about the Communists, but few facts were available. Their meetings were small and brief. They generally included both townspeople and campesinos, but the party appeared to have little support in either town or country, perhaps as a consequence of their preoccupation with international issues.

Local political parties at best are amorphous organizations, consisting of but one or two officials who have a roster of presumed members or sympathizers. Only under the stimulus of an important national event, an election, or party convention, is there anything like political action. A national political figure may show up for a harangue, but the enthusiasm he generates is generally very short-lived.

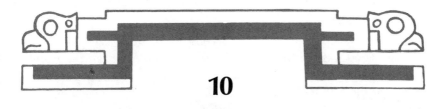

SOCIAL STRATIFICATION

Conditions peculiar to eastern Bolivia disrupted and distorted the growth of a classic colonial stratification order. First, the Indian population was comparatively thin and was rapidly reduced by epidemics of introduced diseases, leaving no appreciable numbers for economic exploitation. Second, the relatively simple political organization of the Indian tribes of the Beni made them less tractable to the Spanish forced labor system. Third, the series of economic booms and recessions in northeastern Bolivia caused ups and downs of individual social status as fortunes were rapidly won and lost. Within this highly mobile society there was extensive intermarriage between small populations of blancos and indios, and since the proportion of blancos to indios was not as unbalanced as in the valleys and the highlands of Bolivia, the result was a relatively fast erosion of the racial basis of status. The bulk of the population became mestizo. Nevertheless, racial terms like "blanco" continued as a means of denoting social status.

As the possibilities for easy wealth became fewer and cattle became the greatest form of wealth, social mobility decreased and strata lines began to harden. This was a period that apparently reached its peak in the 1920's, when "everybody knew his place and nobody tried to mix with people of other classes." It was a time when strict status etiquette was observed. No mestizo or Indian would sit down in the presence of a blanco unless he were asked to.

Recent events again weakened the rigidity of social stratification. Of critical importance was the Chaco War of 1932-35, in which blanco prestige suffered heavily from ineffectual handling of the army and the disastrous losses of the war. The second major historical event of the recent period was the MNR Revolution of 1952. Although the Revolution did not greatly affect the wealth and power of the local elite in Reyes, it did free the campesinos from some economic and status obligations and promoted somewhat more equalitarian social relations.

The initial conditions and the changes over the years have given the Reyes region a complex stratification order. It is sharply bounded at the extremes, but has a very extensive and convoluted middle section whose boundaries are quite indistinct. At the top are the gente buena (or gente decente), the good, the decent people. At the bottom are the campesinos, the peasants. In the middle are the mestizos. Blanco is a synonym for gente buena, but is used infrequently. Campesino has become almost synonymous with indio, but the latter term is far more frequently applied to the remnants of the old tribes.

Of the classic terms of racial distinction only mestizo has survived to denote a major social stratum. The status implications of race that a term like mestizo evokes, as blanco and indio once did, is still a part of Reyesano thinking. Blancos are always gente buena, while mestizos are never gente buena, say the Reyesanos. However, there are few persons in Reyes—notwithstanding blanco status—who can claim only European ancestry. Rather it is wealth, occupation, comportment, and family membership that in fact determine status.

THE SOCIAL STRATA

In the Reyesano status order the gente buena and the campesinos are clear-cut high and low prestige strata. The gente buena are the ganaderos, the bigger merchants, the professionals—the doctor, the lawyer. They have wealth, live in houses of four or five rooms with brick floors and tile roofs, have ample furniture and cabinets for china and glassware. Their houses generally have electric lights, and a privy and a well in the back yard.

Gente buena men wear suits on important occasions. Their trousers and shirt of everyday wear are clean and carefully ironed. They, especially the ganaderos, wear felt hats, imported from Brazil; and they wear shoes or boots, always kept polished, though the streets are either muddy or dusty. Gente buena women wear knee-length dresses of expensive cloth. Their hair is cut short or at medium length and is artificially waved. Clothing and shoes distinguish the gente buena from all those engaged in manual work.

Most gente buena have had at least several years of primary school and attach much importance to advanced education. Most of their children go to secondary school and some to the university at La Paz. Some go to the capital even for primary schooling. Gente buena speak Spanish exclusively, although a few also know another non-Indian language.

At the other end are the campesinos, peasant farmers who live on small subsistence chacos in the surrounding countryside. Some are able to sell a small part of what they raise to merchants in town. Families of five or six are crowded into a one-room or two-room house of pole walls, palm roof, dirt floor. There may be a crude table or a chair. They sleep on the ground. They have no electricity, no well. Water is carried from the river or the moat. Earth is their latrine.

The campesino's trousers and shirt are usually homemade, patched and ragged, unironed, and not often very clean. He wears a straw hat and either goes barefoot or wears sandals. The dress of campesino women varies with age. Older women usually wear the traditional tipoy, a straight dress down to their ankles, and their long hair is usually braided. Young girls wear knee-length dresses of sateen or flowered cotton and often cut their hair.

The Indian languages are gradually dying among the campesinos and Spanish is now universally spoken, though for many of the older ones it is a second language. Most campesinos have had no education. At best a campesino gets one or two years of primary school, but most have no schooling. Few can read or write.

Occupying most of the middle ground are the mestizos. They are the CBF contractors, the technicians, clerks, craftsmen, skilled workers, and semiskilled laborers who—with their families—make up two-thirds of the population of the town. The distinctive character of this stratum is the very considerable range of prestige positions within it. But these are merely the gross differentiations. There are even further sub-differences to consider. The CBF contractor who occasionally provides material for fence construction is a modest workingman. But the regular CBF contractors who are builders as well as suppliers of wire and wood play cards with the gente buena. There is a similar ordering of craftsmen, from those who have a regular clientele and are the most skillful and charge higher prices for their work, to those whose skills and prices are measurably lower, down to the craftsman whose product is poor and whose sales are few. Skilled workers—carpenters, adobe makers, and the like—are sharply distinguished from laborers. They are paid by the job, while laborers receive a daily wage.

All mestizos speak Spanish, few speak any other language. Most of them have had some primary education, and in this and their dress and social conduct they are closer to the gente buena than to campesinos. Their houses are likely to be in between, to have two or three rooms, roofs of palm leaves, and floors of packed dirt, usually no electricity, and no well of their own. Most mestizos dig holes in the yard for disposal of excreta and sometimes enclose them.

Between the mestizo and the true campesino there is the town campesino, a man of ambiguous status. He was once a dirt peasant in the surrounding campo. He still has a chaco to raise food for his family, but is trying to make a living doing odd jobs or assisting a craftsman. In contrast with his country cousin, he is fairly at ease among strangers and retains few distinctive campesino customs. His wife may take in washing, while his son gets some primary schooling. He is considered a low mestizo on one occasion but still campesino on another, depending on which of his conflicting status characteristics is seen as relevant to the occasion.

The wide range of mestizo prestige has important implications for this stratum. There is almost as much difference between mestizos of the upper reaches of the stratum and those of the bottom as there is between those of the bottom and the adjoining town campesinos, or those at the top and the adjoining gente. This reflects the considerable instability of the status order through past generations, and the considerable amount of movement up and down that has taken place. It also reflects the considerable homogeneity of race and language that has facilitated mobility. It is important to the mestizo stratum that its limits tend to be blurred. Town campesinos are characterized by an inconsistency of status-defining elements, which means that they share some of those elements with the mestizos above them. The same is true at the other end of the scale. The existence of such a situation, of course, further facilitates over-all status mobility.

One stratum remains to be identified—that of the marginal gente buena. They are the smaller merchants and minor professionals, teachers, and top CBF contractors. They are also gente buena families whose fortunes have been waning for some time, as well as the most successful mestizos who are on the way up, most of whom are clearly not working people. They are generally moderately well-educated by town standards and deport themselves in gente fashion, but are not accorded the prestige of the solid gente buena.

SOCIAL EFFECTS OF STRATIFICATION

Public social affairs, semi-public recreation, and private parties are all occasions that show the effects of social stratification, but they vary in their sensitivity. The street corner, the church, and the outdoor cinema are settings for the open interaction of all members of the community. They are least sensitive to stratification effects, but nevertheless reveal them.

Reyes is a town of much street activity, but at two corners the action is at its highest and most gossipy. At one of these corners is a general store patronized by mestizos and campesinos, and here they congregate. At the second corner, opposite the cinema, is the most prestigious gaming and drinking kiosk, where mainly gente buena men and youths congregate.

Reyesano men spend considerable time in kiosks and cantinas. The Azcui kiosk and the Pelayo cantina are places where gente buena predominate. Wagers at cards in these two recreation centers are often as much as a laborer makes in a week. Ganaderos have lost herds and estancias in a single night. Two other cantinas are patronized mostly by mestizos, small merchants, skilled workers, a few CBF cowboys, a barber, a school janitor, day laborers, and a few who are unemployed, as well as by the campesinos when they come to town.

In church and cinema there are no formal rules about segregated seating, but most people know their place. For example, two lines of men form in the church for confession, one of gente buena and the other campesinos. Even though the line of campesinos may be very much the longer, no campesino will move over to the other line. Often the circumstances and setting of a public activity, such as civic processions, church functions, and entertainments, force division into two parts. In such situations the mestizo stratum itself divides, the upper part joining the gente buena and the lower part the campesinos.

Almost any event in Reyes—a christening, a wedding, a birthday, a graduation, an arrival, a departure, a victory by a soccer team—is sufficient reason for having a party. The private party is the setting of greatest social intimacy and is most sensitive to status interests. For the gente buena, to invite a person to a party is to accept him as a status equal. Those who do not qualify are carefully excluded. Gossip reinforces this segregation effect, for news of who attended what party soon gets about and is eagerly discussed. Even when an exception is made, and a person of lower status is invited to a gente buena party, the status consciousness of the guests may cancel the intentions of the host. At one gente buena party a popular mestizo was stopped by one of the guests and asked whether he was there to serve. The mestizo replied that he had been invited, but he left immediately.

Regularly at the larger gente buena parties the common folk and their children gather at the doors and windows to gape. This contributes to the showcase effect of these affairs, for which hostesses have gone to considerable expense to uphold or enhance their reputations.

The young of the gente buena are the most status-conscious of all. Invitations to their parties are most rigidly controlled, and here the aspiring lad of questionable status faces the acerbic test. Will he be accepted by the young girls as an equal? Frequently they refuse to dance with boys whom they consider unqualified. Some young men of ambiguous status attend these gente buena parties but ask no girl to dance for fear of being rejected.

Mestizo parties are modest and comparatively simple. Instead of cocktails, straight alcohol is mixed with water or fruit juice; though passed around in water glasses, the quantities are small. The parties of the town campesinos are called "burys" and also feature the use of straight alcohol and music from discs or radio. Lower status mestizos may be invited to the burys. While campesino men prefer to dance in groups the girls enjoy dancing with partners, so the mestizos receive a good welcome. Young gente buena men come uninvited to burys, with the young girls and casual sexual encounter in mind. These young men are admitted, but their campesino hosts may warn them not to abuse their positions as guests. In recent years the mestizos and town campesinos have become more actively intolerant of these gente buena intrusions.

RELATIONS BETWEEN STRATA

Relations between the different social strata are strongly revealed in the beliefs held by the members of one stratum concerning the other. The gente buena say campesinos are childlike, ignorant, and lazy. Common remarks are: "Campesinos have no idea of what to do with their money. They spend it quickly on whatever takes their fancy." "Campesinos are lazy and produce only what is barely necessary to survive." To the gente buena, these imputed traits explain the poverty of the campesinos. They mock the speech, social manners, and moral conduct of campesinos. "He [a town campesino] may come to town and wear shoes, he may learn manners, but he remains an indio." Intermarriage would be unthinkable. On the other hand, campesinos recognize the virtues of wealth, education, and social grandeur in the gente buena, and even vaguely sense a racial superiority. On their part, campesinos think of intermarriage only as most unlikely to happen, the more so because they are fully aware that enduring extramarital unions of gente buena men and campesino women are not uncommon. The gente buena man is privileged, so much so that his raping a country campesino woman does not even provoke discussion. Deference to gente buena even extends to the country campesino's marriage bed. While he would almost certainly assault and perhaps murder a fellow campesino for having seduced his wife, he is unlikely to do anything if the man is a gente buena. Town campesinos, in contrast, have become less docile. They permit gente buena men to attend their dances, but often will not allow them to take campesino girls away from the party. Gente buena sexual adventurers recently have been followed and beaten by town campesinos.

Having to bow to the superiority of the gente buena, campesinos and mestizos try to ease their own situation by establishing ties of mutual obligation between themselves and gente buena in the traditional ways, as they do in Villa Abecia, though there are fewer variations in the ties. Here, as elsewhere in Latin America, the most important of these ties are those of compadrazgo. Campesinos and mestizos try to find gente buena to be padrinos for their children, thus acquiring compadres for themselves. Church precept exerts pressure on gente buena to accept the relationship, though it may be declined. The padrino in Reyes obligates himself to certain duties toward his ahijado, for example, to give him presents on his birthday and to be responsible for him on the death of his parents. He is also expected to be favorably disposed to his new compadre, the child's parent. Despite the fact that gente buena padrinos do not always fulfill their obligations, there is a decided tendency for lower status persons to seek higher status individuals as a form of security for both child and parent. In contrast, the gente buena select padrinos from their own stratum. If the chosen gente buena is not at hand, a campesino can act as proxy in the ceremony.

Through the growth of sindicatos the subservient position of the campesino in his relations with gente buena and even mestizos has undergone a change. Before the Revolution of 1952, when large numbers of campesinos were required for some collective or community enterprise, the ganaderos ordered out their mozos. Today most ganaderos employ fewer mozos and their conditions of work less often permit their use in such projects. Now larger numbers of campesinos are independent farmers, organized in sindicatos, and the gente buena are confronted by men who have been freed of many of their traditional obligations. Under these conditions the gente buena find that campesinos must be persuaded that their participation in a community project is in their own best interests. Such organized bargaining takes place, however, only under rather special conditions, the wider possibilities of collective campesino effort having not yet been realized or even attempted. In general, the relations between strata are still those of deference on the one side and privilege on the other. It is a status system, however, in which the dividing lines are wavering, and the movement between strata is considerable.

STATUS MOBILITY

Compared with Villa Abecia, the status system of Reyes is open and social mobility is much greater. The criteria of status that are relatively immutable—such as place of birth, membership in the prestigious family, language, and especially race—are not of great importance in Reyes. Race is a concept defined mainly by social and economic criteria; wealth, occupation, manners, and style of life are the most important status definers.

Most of the instances of recent upward status movement have occurred through changes in wealth, inheritance, insurance benefits, indemnifications, and so on, enabling the fortunate recipient to open a tienda, a shop, or set up another form of business. New wealth can raise the lowly people at least as high as the top ranks of the mestizos, and possibly even as high as the marginal gente buena. They find themselves being addressed in a different way. Instead of being called by their first or last name unadorned by title, they are addressed as señora or doña or don. Gente buena accept invitations to their parties. They are likely to be asked to serve as padrino of a club or a public event. This is accepted as a way of being asked to make a donation to the organization or event, but it also suggests that wealth has endowed new qualities and manners in the man, and that he would honor the club by his attendance.

Not infrequently, newly acquired wealth runs into disaster because of lack of business experience. The decline in status is just as sudden. Respectful forms of address are heard no more. The higher status townspeople no longer recognize the poor fellow. He is never again invited to sponsor anything. But for those who are able at least to keep their new wealth, if not increase it, the next step is often marriage into a gente buena family and elevation to that status. The very next step is to disown all poor relatives. One newly elevated gente buena collared his poor, uneducated father at the Reyes landing strip and put him right back on the plane without allowing him into town. He appears to have been well advised. An important store owner lost prestige and was ridiculed after her sister came for a visit, because the sister had very dark skin and spoke faulty Spanish.

The established gente buena deplore the importance of money and status grading. One of them stated:

An Indian or a mestizo tries to overcome his humble position, and he finally introduces himself among gente buena. I find this good. If he is well-bred and polite, he should be considered as one considers gente buena. What makes me mad is that mestizos and Indians should be accepted for their money, because as soon as they have a little money they think themselves better than gente buena.

Recognizing that fortunes may suddenly turn, gente buena simultaneously emphasize manners, which serve to protect their own status by making it less accessible to others.

Education is also important to social mobility, and in two different ways. One of them is to provide the basis for the manners thought of so highly by gente buena. More generally, education provides the verbal and intellectual skills that are useful to gente buena activities. In fact, there are not great differences in the educational attainment of the different strata in Reyes. Segments of all strata have had no education at all, while most have had some years of primary school. Mestizos drop out of formal education earlier than gente buena, and campesinos earlier still. Some gente buena have finished secondary school and a few have had some university training. What appears more important in distinguishing the strata is not the difference in years of schooling so much as differences in the opportunities to apply their education. The gente buena have more need to use words and figures in their work and other activities, while mestizos and especially campesinos forget what they have learned from lack of use. The other importance of education is to equip a person for a better occupation. Campesinos are particularly conscious of this possibility and make every effort to send their children to school. Gente buena also recognize the importance of education and regularly send their children to elementary as well as advanced schools. Among the gente buena this is almost a matter of course, while campesinos and poorer mestizos often reveal a fervor to have children succeed in school and thus advance themselves.

Downward mobility has always been an important social phenomenon in Reyes. The principal cause of downward social movement is loss of wealth. The economic recessions of the past claimed many victims. More recently, mismanagement of cattle and loss of whole herds through disease have caused the social decline of many persons. Severe losses in gambling and inferior marriages have also had unfortunate effects on status.

The decline of gente buena families through loss of wealth usually proceeds slowly over several generations. Their high status often lingers as long as appropriate occupation, manners, and style of life continue. There are relatively impoverished ganaderos in the community who are still treated as ganaderos, not as the poor people they actually are. They are addressed respectfully and continue to associate intimately with gente buena. But once they deviate from the manners and morals of their high status, their claims are likely to be challenged. In the crisis of their decline these deviations occur. In the long run they are not able to provide their children with an adequate education or place them in occupations that qualify them as gente buena. While the father may have been able to retain much of his status, the children may not.

THE MODIFIED STATUS OF CAMPESINOS

Most of the social mobility in Reyes concerns individuals or families rather than entire strata. The one partial exception is the campesino.

The Revolution produced no radical changes for the campesinos of Reyes and its environs, but did bring on some important ones. Their initial release from debt peonage and their acquisition of land did not greatly affect the other strata, but the campesinos ever since have been more independent. They have acquired a bit of economic strength and rather better living conditions. These have been important gains, raising their status in Reyes society. Something of the character of this change can be seen in the following incident.

A campesino who had been drinking and playing cards at one of the mestizo cantinas entered the Azcui kiosk, where a group of ganaderos were drinking and gambling. He was well-dressed, in new trousers, new white shirt, new shoes, but he wore no socks and his teeth were decayed. As one of the ganaderos shook the dice, the campesino, shy and a little drunk, put ten pesos on the table—the day's wages of a laborer. A ganadero who was watching the game said to the players: "Look who's going to win the game. That money on the table will make you lose." He was laughing at the campesino who had dared to bet against a ganadero. In response, the campesino asked in an almost inaudible voice, "Why, can't I play?" The ganadero who had been joking said: "Of course you can't, camba de mierda. If Gilberto [the ganadero rolling the dice] loses, I'll whip you." The ganaderos were amused at the uncomfortable situation in which the campesino had put himself. He did not take his money off the table. He drew it a little closer, but left the bet in place. The ganadero threw the dice and lost. The ganadero who had been watching and joking then said: "I told you I was going to whip you, but I will give you a chance to escape the kicks. You can leave now so I won't have to knock you about." Though ill at ease, the campesino did not leave.

The ganadero who had been joking took the dice and prepared to throw. The campesino again put ten pesos on the table, and the ganadero said: "If I don't win, I believe I will have to carry out my threat." He threw and the campesino won again. Now the ganadero made no more jokes. The ganadero prepared to throw the dice again, but now he put a fifty-peso bet on the table. The campesino put down another ten pesos. "This time," said the ganadero, "put up twenty or leave." The ganadero threw and lost again. The campesino took the twenty pesos he had won and laughed loudly. The ganadero he had been playing against said, "This camba de mierda is lucky, but I will carry out what I have promised. I want him to win these fifty pesos and then I will teach him not to mix with gente buena." Without a word, the campesino turned and left, leaving the ganadero humiliated and angry. The ganadero called after him: "I'll whip you, dirty camba, wherever I find you."

This incident illustrates both the continuity and the change in the status of the campesino in the Reyes status order. There is still deference but there is also greater independence. The campesino had obviously been drinking, which probably helped him to face the hostility that he knew he would encounter in the Azcui kiosk. He never once attempted to sit down, but played while standing beside the table. Although the butt of jokes and insulted, he never once responded. However, he did go into this game room, which he would never have done before 1952. He also played on equal terms with the ganaderos and continued even when pressed to withdraw. And, though he was threatened for his impertinence, nothing was done to force him to leave, even after he had bested two of the ganaderos. Before 1952 he would have been thrown out and probably beaten.

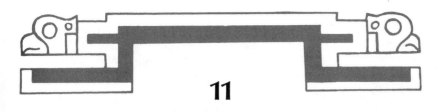

11

GROUPS AND ORGANIZATIONS

Crosscutting the power and status hierarchies of Reyes are a large number of overlapping groups and organizations. Most Reyesanos are members of several of these social units, establishing a complex network of reciprocal bonds. The most important are those of family and friends.

FAMILY TIES AND KINSHIP

The average age at marriage is twenty-five for women and thirty-four for men. The average household contains six persons, but there are many with more than ten. Most households contain a simple nuclear family. However, many families adopt an hijo de crianza, a foster child, generally of a poor family or the child of a dead relative. In some households grandmothers, uncles, and other kin who have no place of their own are included.

Older children of gente buena families, boys particularly, go off to La Paz for advanced schooling, but are home during vacation. Many of these are likely to stay in the city after graduation because of lack of opportunity in Reyes, a condition which affects young mestizos and town campesinos as well. When mestizo young men leave home they seek work in the larger towns of the Beni or in the department capital towns of Santa Cruz and La Paz. A few daughters also leave Reyes, either to work in La Paz or to marry into a family in one of the nearest towns.

Marriage may be either civil, or religious, or both. The gente buena may marry either way or both. Concubinato, the consensual union, is very common among campesinos, town campesinos, and lower status mestizos. Some gente buena men who have legitimate families in town also have concubines and illegitimate children in the countryside. The status of the children of these unions depends largely on the attitude of the father. If he recognizes them they may inherit property and may even be granted a large measure of his social status. Unrecognized children of the less stable unions are considered the children only of the mother and seldom benefit by the status of the father.

Divorce is common, especially among mestizos and town campesinos, many of whom have been married two or more times. It occurs with less frequency among the gente buena. In lower strata there are unmarried women who have had children by different men, some of whom bear the surname of the mother, some that of the father. Concupiscence is a primary cause of family instability. Either the husband falls in love with another woman or the wife has been unfaithful. Occasionally, drunkenness is the issue. When divorce takes place children generally remain with the mother.

Beyond the nuclear family, ties of kinship have no fixed value. Second-degree relatives—grandparents, uncles, and first cousins, even married sisters and brothers—may be treated with respect, with feelings of warmth, with a sense of obligation, or may be treated casually, ignored, even regarded with hostility. Beyond these close kin of the nuclear family is a much larger set, referred to as parientes. These are the distant relatives, such as third and fourth cousins and great-aunts and -uncles. To many families, the exact kin relationship of these parientes is vague or unknown. Nevertheless, their social importance is not always different from that of close kin. They are another set of persons with whom close social ties can be established.

It is primarily within the nuclear family that kinship ties have an established significance. Such ties are defined in terms of the central concerns that distinguish adults from children and males from females. Most wives are primarily responsible for the maintenance of the house and the care of children. This requires their presence at home for most of each day, but many wives of town campesinos and lower status mestizos work as washerwomen, cooks, or maids, which takes them out of the house for at least part of the day. A few higher status mestizo wives work as teachers or nurses, and those with families that own stores frequently work in them.

With few exceptions, married women do not participate in voluntary groups or organizations, and even less frequently do they hold office in any of them. Except for a small group of gente buena wives who play cards regularly and a larger group of gente buena girls who play basketball, women have no organized recreation. Married women spend a good part of their free time visiting with friends or sitting in front of the house to catch a bit of gossip.

Married men spend almost all their leisure hours on the street corners and in the cantinas and kiosks. The ganaderos, who have considerable leisure time at different periods of the year, spend a good part of both day and night at a kiosk playing card and dice games. Husbands keep their own counsel about their outside activities and most wives are careful not to enquire, lest they be sharply reminded of their proper place. One woman insulted a man with whom her husband had been fighting a few minutes earlier. The husband told her to mind her own business and sent her into the house. Husbands and wives rarely go out together. Even on the few occasions when they are invited to private parties, it is expected that they will not associate with each other.

The wife generally has undisputed responsibility for the routine activities of house and children, but when problems arise the husband's authority is paramount. Though absent a good deal, the husband takes an active interest in family affairs and does not hesitate to intervene. The older the son, the more the father is concerned that he exhibit the desired general traits of manliness and capability, while the mother generally attempts to ease these increasing pressures. In families without adult males, young sons help out by getting work of some kind. Adult sons are expected to turn in the greater part of their income.

Girls in all families are introduced to the routine of household work at an early age. Fathers show a casual though warm interest in their daughters until they mature sexually, then they become increasingly concerned and keep a wary eye on all the young men. Brothers, and sometimes other close male relatives, also mount hymeneal guard over the girl's social activities. Brothers usually learn about boy friends before the father and may be the first to take protective measures. One young man who informed a brother that he was a girl's boy friend was curtly told, "Don't ever make that joke again." Despite family surveillance, girls manage to meet boys surreptitiously. When sexual adventures become known in the family, attempts are made to force a marriage—especially if the young man is viewed as a qualified suitor. The protectiveness of brothers is not without its tyranny. They order their sisters to perform small services for them, such as to wash a shirt or iron a pair of trousers.

In the conflict between the men of the family and daughters, the mother will frequently take the daughter's side. In one case a young man was disapproved by the men of the family, but after persistent effort he was able to win over the mother, who permitted him to see the daughter without revealing this to the men in the family and even permitted him to open the question of possible marriage. On the other hand, mothers characteristically seek the assistance of fathers in maintaining parental authority over the children. A complaint to the father that a child is not obeying is generally sufficient to cause him to intervene effectively.

Establishing a new family is a serious step, not only for the couple involved but also for the two parental families. Parents want their daughters to marry responsible, hard working, and morally respectable young men. Extremes of gambling or drinking are frequent disqualifiers. Some parents also oppose divorced men. Young people themselves play the major role in selecting future partners, but few can escape the screening process of parents and other close relatives.

The most generally prominent criterion is social status. Both sets of parents as well as the focal parties themselves tend to seek persons of equivalent status, either deliberately or by utilizing the built-in social restrictions of the community. The protective family tries to prevent inter-status contacts. And the higher the status, the greater the effort. Thus, the careful screening of those invited to gente buena parties has the additional consequence of shielding marriageable girls from those of lower status.

When a flirtation between a gente buena girl and a mestizo boy becomes known, active opposition is mobilized by the girl's family. If the situation looks serious she may be sent to another town to stay with relatives. But if not, and the lovers are persistent in the face of opposition, not infrequently the family will consent rather than take the risk of their running away. The adamant opposition of a girl's parents is easily sustained by outraged friends and relatives, but if some relatives favor the match the parents are more likely to yield. In opposing marriages across strata, Reyesanos commonly express their opposition in terms of race. The anger and resistance is against a blanco's marrying a mestizo, or against a mestizo's marrying an indio.

The extension of kinship ties through compadrazgo is also prominent in Reyes. Compadrazgo relationships include the many varieties that are sanctioned by the Church, but the important ones are first communion, confirmation, marriage, and especially baptism. The padrinos of baptism accept the most serious obligations, and this establishes the strongest ties of compadrazgo. Friends and relatives are the primary candidates in Reyes. Compadrazgo is a way of transforming a mere pariente into a close and more dependable relative, or a casual friend into a close one. Most often this occurs when close ties are forming and compadrazgo is a way to speed the process.

There is also a tendency for families of lower social status to select those of higher status. The gente buena, however, are less affected by feudalistic economic interests than the patróns of Villa Abecia and therefore have little reason to encourage compadrazgo relationships with workmen. This is not the case, however, on the cattle estancias, where the vaqueros and mozos still seek the ganadero patrón as compadre and where mutual interest supports the bond.

FRIENDSHIP GROUPS

A second important relationship binding members of the community is friendship. One is obligated to respect and assist a close friend almost as much as a close relative, in some cases even more so. Close friends are common to both sexes and to all ages. The network of dyadic ties that are formed by friendships have varied effects—provide an outlet for family tension, a channel of communication between families and a basis of extrafamily social support, all of which add to the resilience of the social structure. Friendship also gives rise to two different social groups.

Among the boys and young men of Reyes are groups referred to as cuerdas, cliques. Persons joining these groups vary in age from around thirteen, or post-elementary school, to those in their late twenties and early thirties. The cuerdas tend to be similar in age and in social status. For girls there is nothing of this sort.

The cuerdas play a central part in the lives of their members and must be counted as important groups in the community. Membership is not uniformly clear-cut in all cuerdas. Some have a name, and only a recognized member is permitted to call himself by that name. Others use a distinctive signaling whistle that identifies them as accepted members.

The character of the cuerda is best brought out by examining one, a cuerda about a year-and-a-half old. Some of the members knew each other in the local primary school and have been acquainted since childhood, but they had never formed a group. All of the members are sons of gente buena families. The cuerda in this case has no membership identification mark or signal. It regularly attempts to eliminate certain persons, boys of lower social status, before embarking on group activities. One method of elimination is to pretend that no activities are in the offing and more or less ignore the non-members until they go away.

The eight regular members of this cuerda meet every evening around eight o'clock, at a street corner. There they may stand for a considerable time, or they stroll the streets, smoking, chatting, and planning their activities for the night. Typically, they will go to a movie, or go buy ice cream, or attend a party. For more serious affairs, like stealing chickens or sexual adventures, the group will generally break into pairs. Some members have closer ties with some than with other members, but to outsiders they are all friends.

The cuerdas in this age range tend to be more active and, in turn, more cohesive than the cliques of older youths. These boys have no regular jobs and consequently have more free time to spend together. The boys firmly state that no member dominates the group, but in fact one member, the oldest, regularly makes more suggestions than the others and his advice is generally accepted.

The cohesion of this cuerda is evident in affairs between members and their girl friends. They act as go-betweens for each other and as sentinels. They will all attend a movie, not because anyone wants to see it but because one of the members can use it as an opportunity to visit with his girl friend. They are very close in their feelings, attitudes, and interests. The cuerdas are seldom aggressive, but if a member is involved in a fight his opponent will very probably have to fight separately each of the other members of the cuerda in addition.

Cuerdas last from a year to several years. Boys do not change cuerdas as they change in age, but rather advance in age within their cuerda. The cuerdas occasionally break up because of internal friction. They also disband when their members leave to work or go to school in another town or to go out to work on the estancias. The cuerdas of the older youths most often lose their members through marriage, and this destroys them. Newly married men, unlike other adult men, spend much of their free time at home. They are often subjected to ribald criticism, but this does not prevent them from breaking off from the cuerda and spending little time on the streets. The cuerda being discussed is far from this point and represents the cuerda at a period of maximum importance.

In a community with very little recreational facilities, an important effect of the cuerda is that it organizes and regulates the leisure time of a segment of the population that has little but time on its hands. The cuerda is a context for training in independence, for the boys are out of the household and on their own most of the time. It is an important bridge between living with their parents and having a family of their own. A girl met in the cuerda period will probably become a wife.

The other important friendship groups, more loosely organized than the cuerdas, are those of the kiosks. While young men meet on the street corners, older men gather at the kiosk or cantina. Gente buena men have much free time, especially the ganaderos, and this is spent in the kiosks. A consequence of making the kiosks rather than homes their headquarters has been the development of a number of relatively stable, gente buena kiosk friendship groups. Examples are the two groups that frequent the Azcui kiosk.

One group clusters around Luis Regla, one of the greatest ganaderos in the area. Two of the other members are also ganaderos, but neither possesses more than a hundred head of cattle. One was formerly a major cattle owner, but he lost most of his animals to disease in the 1950's. All three support the MNR. A fourth member is a cantina owner who temporarily occupied a series of local government offices following the coup of 1964. All in this group supported Regla in his effort to become alcalde. The economic position of Regla is very much superior to that of the other members in the group. They share a limited political interest, but, particularly, share an enthusiasm for card playing.

The other group consists of four to five ganaderos, none of whom is especially wealthy. One member supports the MNR, but the others are members of the FSB. No one member stands out authoritatively or in any other way in this group, but all are eager card players and share a dislike for Regla.

The opposition between these two groups stems from an intrafamily quarrel over an inheritance which was finally contested in court. One of two sisters emerged the winner, and she is the wife of Regla. The husband of the sister who lost is a member of the second group. When the kiosk is full the two groups can be seen as distinct clusters in the gathering, but when there are few customers the two brothers-in-law and their friends do not hesitate to sit at the same table and play, the game transcending animosity.

Almost all of the regulars at the Azcui kiosk are gente buena. Most are ganaderos, but there are also some store owners and professionals. The majority are married, ranging from thirty to fifty-six years of age. This kiosk is a place where important and influential men come to talk, gamble, drink, and observe the street activities. An important feature of this kiosk is its construction and location. It sits on one of the corners of the most socially active street intersections of the town. It is the major street corner for the gente buena cuerdas and a vantage point on much of the town's comings and goings. Since the major portion of the kiosk has no walls, all of this scene is open to the men at the tables.

Conversation is constant at and around the tables, even during the games. Many conversations concern the games, the runs of luck, and the possibilities of cheating. Fights, shootings, and cattle rustling are discussed in the greatest detail. Sexual adventures are recounted with gusto. Political conversations also run high, along with the problem of the mines and the foreign relations of Bolivia. Many of the regulars at the kiosk are important sources of information and sufficiently important in themselves to be newsworthy. Thus, this rather unimposing place with its thatch roof is in fact quite important in providing a setting for the regular contact of persons with status and power in the community, where issues are discussed and opinions are shaped. Other kiosks and cantinas have their regular customers and small friendship groups, but they do not have the wider importance of the Azcui kiosk.

The cuerdas and kiosk groups are important in the maintenance of a stable and viable social order in a community like Reyes. They are the means for linking persons in mutual obligations and provide a basis for organizing their activities.

FORMAL GROUPS AND ORGANIZATIONS

There are more than twenty special interest groups and associations in Reyes, and they tap all sectors of the population for members. One of these, formed in separate units, is the Catholic Church's Legion de Maria. One of its affiliates is the Legion de Señora del Carmen, which has branches in the rural countryside. Its members—all males—are mestizos and town campesinos. The organization works for moral improvement, gives assistance to the sick and needy, and spreads anticommunist propaganda.

A second unit is the Reina del Santo Rosario, whose members are the young girls of the parochial school. This is a private primary school run by nuns, mainly serving gente buena girls. It also is concerned with moral improvement and charitable work, but charity is regarded as an individual responsibility, in contrast to the collective efforts of the men. The meetings of this organization are taken up with prayer and reports of each member's acts of charity, which consist mainly of visits to the sick and intercession with the deity for their recovery. A third unit is the Sagrado Corazon de Jesus. Its members are the married women of gente buena families. Their only obligation of membership is to attend mass on the first Friday of each month.

The population overwhelmingly professes Catholicism, but most men take little part in church-sponsored activities, except as they may have bearing on status and economic reward. For example, men who join the Legion de Señora del Carmen, which stresses self-sacrifice, discipline, and hard work, gain a reputation as responsible and diligent workers, no small asset in a town with limited employment opportunities. More directly, membership in the legion can lead to employment on church projects.

Prominent among special interest organizations in Reyes are the sport clubs, chiefly soccer teams, all loosely tied within an athletic league which is responsible for the scheduling of matches and tournaments, for arbitration of disputes, and, especially, for enforcement of rules. One team is made up of students, mainly sons of gente buena families, a second of CBF employees, and a third of town campesinos. Soccer is the most popular sports activity in Reyes, and during the season there are matches every Sunday afternoon, well-attended by cheering throngs. All teams select madrinas, godmothers, who provide uniforms, equipment and refreshments. A soccer player of unusual skill may be invited into higher social circles. One outstanding mestizo player was frequently invited to the parties of the younger gente buena. Aside from this, fame sometimes promotes economic fortune by bringing a player to the attention of employers.

Soccer and the soccer teams are one of the few topics of common interest in Reyes and consequently are a force for general cohesion in the community. This is furthered by the ceremonies that inaugurate the soccer season each year in which the madrinas all appear, the bands play, and trophy badges are displayed to the appreciative audience of townspeople. Cohesion is also advanced by the inter-town matches that polarize the townspeople against the outside opponent. This is one of the few occasions when it is possible for the league to enforce training discipline, for the appeal to the players is that the prestige of the community is at stake.

Organizing for economic advantage has met with no success. A few years ago the ganaderos organized a cooperative to advance their interests, but personal disagreements and rivalry and the traditional suspicion of officials who handle money led to its early dissolution. None of the craft or other sindicatos are present in Reyes, and those of campesinos in the surrounding countryside have no direct impact on the town.

The priest has started a savings and loan cooperative within the overall socioeconomic program of the Catholic Church in Bolivia. Membership in the cooperative is open to all for a fee. The purpose of the program is to provide loans at less than excessive interest. Those joining are primarily workers who hope to free themselves of their dependence on merchant usurers. This cooperative is still recruiting members and has yet to make a loan or pay a savings dividend, but if it ever gets going it may very well collide with the merchants.

The rank and file of the Veterans of the Chaco War are workers and town campesinos who look to that organization for the paltry benefits that come from the national treasury. Its limited success in this has seriously weakened most of the local units. The organization avoids involvement in sectarian political activity, but its president is active in community affairs. During the political uncertainty that followed the coup of 1964, the military team that came to Reyes delegated to the Chaco Veterans responsibility for maintaining order in the community, but the organization did not seriously attempt this. Nevertheless, the Veterans have a reputation for influence with national government officials and for having used it on occasion to oust local officials.

The Amigos del Progreso, an organization with a thoroughly civic outlook, was formed in June 1965 by a small group of gente buena to consider the pressing problems of the community and do something about them. By their second meeting the membership roster included most of the important people of the town, the big cattle owners, the larger merchants, the top officials of the CBF, town government officials, the bishop, and the important professionals. An effort was made to bring in all parts of the community, even the sindicatos, but the organization has remained essentially gente buena.

During the period of this study the Amigos rapidly became important. They tackled the school building problem energetically and soon became an alternative center of community leadership. The plight of local government is, indeed, clearly revealed in the rise of the Amigos. The authorities soon wanted the Amigos to take responsibility for civic programs. Even when the activities of the Amigos clearly overlapped government responsibility, the authorities preferred that the Amigos act on their own. When the Amigos asked for a tax levy in aid of their community work, the town officials suggested that the Amigos request permission of the national government to collect the taxes themselves. The methods of this group will be examined further in the discussion of community action. As a group of persons of similar status and known to each other, many of them having ties of kinship and friendship, the Amigos del Progreso is a type of organization common to the larger rural towns.

The kinship, friendship, and special interest groupings among the Reyes population are social clusters, complexly interrelated through common membership and common interests, and tied together vertically through power and status relations. Compared with Villa Abecia, this three-dimensional web is more complex, but looser. The webbing of the Reyes social order is more elastic than that of Villa Abecia, allowing for a social system more tolerant of individuality.

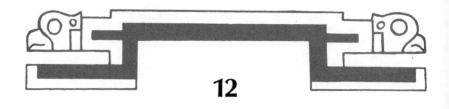

12

COMMUNITY ACTION

Despite its status as a provincial capital, Reyes has difficulty in satisfying valid public needs for education, uncontaminated water, a sewerage system, roads, markets, and law enforcement. Bolivian communities are in a quandary because public organizations responsible for public problems exist, but only rarely are they either active or effective. Occasionally a community receives special attention from an outside agency. This has been the case in Reyes with the CBF, and in recent years the town has benefited from the presence of Peace Corps Volunteers. However, the community cannot rely on outside assistance, which is often quixotic and undependable, nor can it depend upon the government. There do exist some alternative organizational means for dealing with these problems. The voluntary committee is one of the most important of these.

Committees are formed for very specific ends, such as to obtain playground equipment or provide a library for the public elementary school. Once the specific task is done, they disband; though they are as likely to fall apart with the task still undone. At the time of this study there were committees for schools and cathedral construction, plaza improvement, and civic celebrations. The committee for school construction is the most revealing of community action by committee.

THE ADOBE SCHOOLHOUSE—A COMMITTEE PROJECT

The public elementary school occupies temporary quarters in a building one block off the central plaza. The school was once in permanent quarters that are remembered as having been fairly satisfactory, but sometime around 1951, according to townspeople, the director of the local CBF project offered to make some improvements as a gesture of good will toward the community. His project engineer examined the building and recommended that the roofing tiles be removed and reset. A considerable number were broken in the process, and before new tiles could be found—and the roof replaced—heavy rains struck and the exposed adobe walls became sodden and crumbled. The director of the CBF called a meeting of the important people to decide whether to repair the damage or construct a new building. The sub-prefect favored repair, but a majority was opposed. The CBF supplied men and a tractor, tore the place down and sold all salvageable materials. According to the former sub-prefect, the CBF kept the salvage money and did nothing further. It must be remembered that the CBF was a very large, important operation at that time, its director a man of power.

About two years later a CBF engineer became interested in the problem and organized a committee of prominent townspeople, mainly ganaderos, who contributed funds for the work. Somehow, it is said, the money disappeared. A few years later a third committee was organized by a wealthy Reyesano who was one of the major contractors for the CBF, and a number of people offered money and materials. A brick foundation for a new building was laid but nothing else was accomplished. As before, there were accusations of skullduggery.

In 1963 a fourth committee was constituted. After somewhat more than a year of effort it could point to considerable accomplishment. Of the two sections planned for the new school building, one had been completed except for minor interior work, and about half the wall of the second section was up. Then, in November of 1964 an influential member of the committee resigned, and a month later one of the two most dedicated members left town. Then the other one moved away in April and committee action declined. In September of 1965 the building was still unfinished.

The fourth committee accomplished much more than any of the previous ones, but it was not an unqualified success. Among its members were the priest, the local doctor, the sub-prefect, two schoolteachers, a wife of one of the wealthiest ganaderos, a judge's secretary, and the CBF administrator. Associated with the committee was a Peace Corps Volunteer. It was a group of considerable prestige as well as power in the community. All members but one were gente buena. Public committees in Reyes are not organized to be representative of the population, but rather on an elite basis, on the assumption that this will inspire confidence and cooperation.

Two members, the doctor and the Peace Corps Volunteer, were certainly the hardest workers. Committee members may put in several hours in discussion and planning at meetings, but they do not expect to have to work very hard, least of all do any physical work. The doctor, but especially the Peace Corps Volunteer, participated actively in the construction work, but complained constantly that Reyesanos simply would not help, that neither example nor exhortation could persuade them.

Only when a crisis threatened was it possible to move the committee members themselves into action. When the contractor, for example, announced that he had to have money to pay his workmen or he would have to stop the work, the committee stirred itself and raised the money. Another time, a Peace Corps Volunteer got funds from the Alliance for Progress for materials that were not locally available, but he soon had to point out that, though the terms of the donation required that construction be completed within 180 days, they had now been at it for more than twelve months and were in danger of losing these funds. Under this threat the committee took another step forward.

The committee's problems were not all internal. It enlisted the sub-prefect as a member in the hope that he could be counted on to supply crucial funds to cover current small debts and otherwise support the project through his office, but he could do this only in a rather tortuous manner. He knew, for instance, that an inheritance tax was about to be collected, and he set this aside for the school. Some national taxes had recently been collected, and he requested of the national government that he be allowed to use these. Again, every able-bodied male citizen is obliged to give three days of work annually to the local government or to pay a stipulated sum for the hiring of another man to replace him. The sub-prefect earmarked the payments on a number of these obligations, called prestación vial, for the school. However, local officials can be arbitrarily changed. The sub-prefect and alcalde were replaced, and the new administration told the committee:

We have other expenses. We want to dedicate ourselves to other works besides the school. We have other projects, such as the plaza, the meat market. The streets need repair before the rains. The cemetery needs cleaning. We have many things to do. On the other hand, the alcaldía does not have any income, for the cattle are lean and sick in this season.

This ended the modest support from the local government. Earlier, the sub-prefect and the supervisor of rural schools had gone to La Paz to appeal to the Minister of Education and the President of the Republic, but they came back empty-handed. The committee also sought aid from other organizations in town. Some committee members who were members of the Amigos del Progreso approached that organization for help, but the Amigos were giving their attention to a road construction project and turned the committee down. But then the Amigos discovered that the funds they expected from the Alliance for Progress would be available for roads only on completion of the school and they became interested.

The Amigos called an open meeting to which they invited the teachers because, they said, teachers should be more active in the project. At this meeting the former sub-prefect summarized the problems. A large sum of money was needed, he said, but nothing was coming from the local government because people would not pay their taxes. He warned of their losing Alliance for Progress support because of delay in completing the work. He then lashed out at the whole population, but especially at the teachers:

The Alliance will take away the funds they have promised us and give them to another town more genuinely interested in progressing. Thus, we have to hurry. The town must live up to its side of the contracts by supplying money for salaries, by providing all materials, at the site, ready for use. Jorge Jones [a Peace Corps Volunteer] has bought the materials for the school and they are in La Paz, ready to come down when we are ready here. Now I don't want to throw the blame on the teachers, but it must be said in all truth that they have been no more than spectators, sitting on the fence and laughing. The problem does not lie with the committee of four people. It is you the teachers, the directors, the students, and the town who must see the work through. And the teachers must be a driving force, leading and guiding the town. It is criminal not to have done anything, just to have sat and laughed at the efforts of others.

The response of the teachers to this attack was immediate. One said that every teacher had contributed money to the school construction project and that the teachers as a group had organized a series of fund-raising carnivals, held every Sunday some months earlier. When it was suggested that the teachers could organize a carnival for a coming holiday, another teacher said this was already planned. It was clear that the committee's relations with the teachers had been autocratic and distant.

General community interest was low and suspicion high. According to the contractor in charge of the school construction work, when people in town heard that an effort was going to be made to collect more funds for the school, the most frequent comment was, "Oh, no, not again." Few people offered money, materials, or time. Most argued that they had helped before and nothing had come of it. The seriousness of the situation came out at one of the committee meetings:

We have a deficit of 156 pesos [approximately $13.00] and we still lack materials to finish the building. This time you must do all you can to obtain funds. We never thought that we would have to buy all the materials. Before starting our work, we thought that they would be donated, since this is a project that will benefit all the town. It has been very painful to see that we are doing the best we can and have obtained so little collaboration from the town.

Unfortunately, the committee had a long legacy of failure and corruption to live down. Reyesanos distrust anyone who is handling public money. Everyone could cite examples of mismanagement, graft, pilfering, and the mysterious disappearance of a treasury. One committee member suggested, "The best thing to do is to form a committee of women to ask for the money. People trust the women more." The suggestion was adopted, and one of the women on the committee undertook the task. But this did not work either, leading another committeeman to lament:

I wish that at this point we could stop all the criticism that has been going around about the committee and to this end I intend to post tomorrow in the street an account of all its financial operations.

It is equally difficult to get townspeople to volunteer their labor for community projects. Two male Peace Corps Volunteers who were successively involved in the school project helped with construction work on the school as an example to the community. Both commented that they often had an audience, but that few ever stepped forward to lend a hand.

BUILDING A ROAD TO THE RIVER— AMIGOS DEL PROGRESO

In addition to the voluntary committee, the second device for taking action on local problems is the civic association. While a few of the founding members of the Amigos del Progreso saw it as a social club, it was soon guided by the more prominent members to confront community problems. It never had more than twenty-five really active participants, but this is not reflected in the scope of its projects. The construction of a road from Reyes to the Rio Beni at Puerto Salinas captured the quickest interest of the Amigos. It is the only project of considerable value to the community that was brought to a successful conclusion by a group of townspeople.

This road, one of the early projects of the CBF soon after it was established in Reyes, is an opening to river trade. Part of the town's food supply comes in over it. It enables campesinos with chacos near the river to ship their produce to market. However, it was not constructed to withstand either torrential rains or the heavy use to which it is subjected.

The country between Reyes and Puerto Salinas is flat and very low, with year-round standing water at many places. Nowhere are there any materials that would provide a solid foundation for this road. It has been created by piling dirt to a level slightly above that of flanking swamp and flooded lowlands. Rapidly growing tropical brush and trees nearer the river shade the road from the sun and keep it wet. Heavily laden two-wheeled carts pulled by oxen gouge deep ruts in the soft stretches of the road. The rains pour down and the ruts grow deeper, and soon the road is impassable for motor traffic. Each year the washouts and ruts need filling and the vegetation must be cut back. The CBF then puts its men to work so that its trucks may move again.

The Amigos del Progreso became involved in the Puerto Salinas road project by way of a casual conversation between the manager of the CBF and the sub-prefect at an Amigos meeting. The CBF had begun its yearly repair of the road, and the manager was discussing with the sub-prefect what could be done to keep the two-wheeled carts off it until it would be thoroughly dry. Other Amigos overheard, and the informal chat became a formal discussion. Talk broadened to the possibility of so repairing the road that it would not be subject to serious yearly damage and interruption. Before the meeting ended the road had become the first major activity of the association. A committee of volunteers agreed to inspect the most vulnerable sections of the road, determine the number of days each section would have to be closed following a rain, and to mark the routes of detours around these sections to enable carts to reach town. Materials, machinery, and money would be needed to make substantial improvements. Outside assistance was suggested: bor-

row road-building equipment from the not too distant Alto Beni colonization zone; ask the national government for permission to use locally
collected national taxes; look for Alliance for Progress funds. As for possible United States financial aid, the Peace Corps Volunteer was asked
to investigate. The CBF had a tractor and a grader and there was certainly a labor pool potentially available.

The Amigos sought labor from a number of sources. One three-mile
stretch of road near the campesino estancias of Guaguauno and San Jose
had to be closed for repairs, so a committee went to the estancias and
spoke to the members of their sindicatos. The advantages of an improved road and their responsibilities as citizens were stressed and both
sindicatos agreed to cooperate. The president of the Legion de Maria
offered a band of his men. The commander of an army detachment biv-
ouacked near Reyes also agreed to cooperate. Even some of the Amigos
offered to work on the road to show the community, especially the campesinos, that they were not asking of others what they were not ready to
give of themselves. When it came down to the actual job, however, labor's ranks were thin.

A half-dozen or so campesinos from the two sindicatos appeared on
the day assigned, but they left one-quarter of their task unfinished. Furthermore, they said they would not return to finish the work because
their fellows from the sindicatos had not shown up at all. The next day
the sub-prefect went to the estancias and forced a number of campesinos to return with him to work on the road under their prestación
vial obligation. The Legion de Maria volunteers never appeared, because
they demanded that all their meals be served on the project, a condition
which the Amigos would not accept. Neither did any Amigos show up,
those who had pledged themselves sending paid laborers instead. A reas-
sessment now took place, and there came a rather quick shift from
voluntary to obligatory and paid labor, the bulk of it performed by campesinos who were forced to work off their prestación vial obligations. A
wealthy ganadero and the Amigos provided food on the job and fuel for
the CBF road machines. Under CBF supervision, the work gangs raised
the level of the road, reinforced a bridge and opened up a number of detours for two-wheeled carts during muddy periods.

While pushing ahead with local materials and manpower, the Amigos
sought outside support. The Peace Corps Volunteer was appointed to
negotiate with the AID in Bolivia. He visited officials of the AID Community Development Program in La Paz and returned with the message

that, if the community was serious about its road project, the Program would cover half the cost. Further, AID was sending an engineer to look things over and give a cost estimate. The Amigos were very pleased with this news and were confident that the work already done would cover their half of the expenses.

When the AID engineer arrived, the CBF manager outlined the work already done, paying particular attention to the fact that the community was required to supply 50 per cent of the cost of any project:

About half of the work is being done by the Proyecto Ganadero de Reyes [CBF] and the other half by the people from town, mostly those that you see here now. The work being done by the Proyecto Ganadero is almost all out of my own pocket, since we had no funds available for this sort of work. Our machines are for work with cattle. We thus ask that these factors be taken into account. So far we have done about eleven miles, lacking only three miles or so more to arrive at the river. Just now the tractors are clearing all the way to the river. So, we ask for your collaboration, that you advise us and guide us, tell us if it is well done or not. We have never had a plan of an engineer, only the good judgment of the tractor drivers.

With the requirements of the AID projects in mind, the CBF manager greatly amplified the contribution of the community. Actually most of the work on the road was being done by the CBF itself with its machines.

The AID engineer found technical weaknesses in the project. He tried to soften the blow by praising the great amount of work that had been done, the clearing of underbrush and the filling in of ruts. But these improvements, he said, could only be regarded as temporary. They had moved dirt around and piled it up to make the road higher, but with the coming of heavy rains erosion would begin again and soon the road would be in ruins. This work, he said, could not be counted against the costs of the project. The Amigos took his report soberly and set up a committee to find out how much would be needed to do the job properly—the amount of labor, the number of tractors, the quantity of gravel for the road foundation.

Without gravel or additional tractors, they pushed ahead with what was on hand and at last the road came to the Rio Beni. On September 2, after three months of work, the new road was officially inaugurated. Impassable muddy stretches there will still be. Nevertheless, this road has been a major accomplishment.

That so much was done is attributable in part to the character of the

Amigos del Progreso as a civic body. Its members are men of power and status in the community, and their coming together was an expression of their status obligations, their sense of responsibility for the community. Collectively they assumed powers of leadership over local government itself, and proceeded as if the town's affairs were their very own, making whatever decisions they felt were necessary. When something was needed, local officials were informed, as when the sub-prefect was told how many campesinos were wanted to do a particular job.

Not even with the campesinos could the Amigos be so peremptory. Those who were sent to persuade the campesinos to give voluntary labor were very carefully chosen. They were picked for their influence—the bishop, the supervisor of rural schools, the doctor, the alcalde and the CBF manager. The campesinos generally assented to these requests, but not enthusiastically. One of them told the committee that he and his fellows wanted to be sure that the road was to be completed as far as the river, for the CBF had promised this many times. Now and again Amigos complained that the campesinos were not cooperating wholeheartedly, and the commanding officer of the soldiers who were working on the road accused campesinos of having refused to sell him rice to feed his men. There is some suspicion that he was refused because no payment for the rice was intended. In any case, the peasants made it clear that they could no longer be manipulated as arbitrarily as they had been before the Revolution. The gente buena still have much power. Means were found to enforce campesino participation in the road project. But absolute dominance over them has clearly dwindled.

UNDERPINNINGS OF COMMUNITY ACTION

The relative success of the Amigos on the one hand, and the failure of the school committee on the other, make it possible by analysis of what made the difference to evaluate the prospects for community action in this town. There are several basic weaknesses in both organizations. One is the exclusivity of membership. In Reyes, there is a tradition of community responsibility among the decentes that encourages participation in civic organizations. Unfortunately, the counterpart of this is a belief that this responsibility is a prerogative only of decentes, and none of the egalitarian ethic of the Revolution has shaken this notion. While others in the community, who constitute by far the majority, are frequently asked to make a contribution to community work, they contribute as outsiders in an enterprise clearly run by a privileged sector.

Another common trait is the short staying power of most decente volunteers. Their sense of obligation will bring many out for initial meetings, and some can always be counted on to give some of their time on a more or less regular basis, but none will persist over the long haul if attracted only by a sense of communal responsibility. Another marked characteristic is that few are willing to make any great sacrifice, especially a material one, for a community project. This is neither unusual nor unreasonable; but since most projects face costly obstacles, it introduces a major impediment to sustained voluntary action.

Two other linked features are the importance of outsiders and a lack of local technical competence. Projects in Reyes are dependent on the "enlightened" stranger, often a professional person temporarily resident in the community. The education, quasi-public position, and dependence of such persons on the community all facilitate their involvement in community projects. However, despite the participation of relatively highly educated persons, there is often little interest—and less specific competence—in the technical requirements of a project, often with discouraging or disastrous consequences. For example, a veterinarian is not by the fact of his profession competent to direct the construction of an all-weather road.

Inadequacies of all sorts played parts in the two projects discussed. Both were hampered by the narrow base of their support and by material obstacles. The school committee gradually faded away, especially when the key outsiders left the community, though the staying power of the Amigos was not really tested, since its activities were concluded rather quickly. The question of why interest fades introduces two other matters.

First, successful efforts are usually those in which key participants are attracted by a large measure of self-interest. Second, they often involve at least a few powerful residents, who control important resources. The school required supplies that had to be purchased and skilled labor that had to be paid. With no really important persons pushing this project and raising funds critical to success, it foundered. The road project, on the other hand, required mainly machines and unskilled labor. The CBF administrator, greatly interested in the road for his own activities, had the machines and was more than willing to supply them. It was also

relatively easy to secure the labor through the sub-prefect and the prestación vial. The drawback to this "successful" project was that the lack of
awareness of technical problems meant that the completed road will
soon again be rutted and washed away.

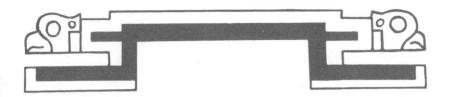

IV

COROICO
A Complex, Radically
Changed Community

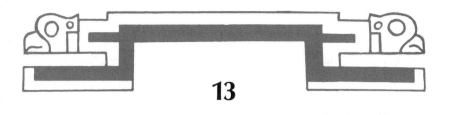

13

THE SETTING

Coroico lies about 6000 feet above sea level in the Yungas, a part of the valleys region formed by a slope of the Andes east of La Paz. It is a region of harshly broken terrain, of sharp ridges and deep, narrow valleys. In the upper reaches of the Yungas the air is thin and cold and vegetation is slight, but at the level of Coroico the climate is semitropical and vegetation is lush.

The town is perched on a narrow promontory several hundred feet above the Rio Coroico. In the distance, looming high above the town, snow-topped Mount Uchumachi is visible. So uneven is the land that there is a difference of 400 feet between the highest and lowest parts of this town, barely greater than four blocks by five in size. The population of Coroico was 2147 in the project census of 1964. There were 513 households with an average of four persons. About 68 per cent of the people are native to the town; 47 per cent speak both Spanish and Aymara; 30 per cent speak only Spanish, and 15 per cent only Aymara.

The town is a picture of aged, settled density. Its narrow cobblestoned streets are lined with two-story buildings of plastered adobe with tile roofs and iron balconies. Most of its buildings are old, somewhat gaudy, and in disrepair. There is but one plaza, shaded by huge, old palm trees. Along the whole of one side are only the church and the offices of the town government. To the right and left and across from the church are branch offices of national agencies, provincial government quarters, private homes, and places of business. One block off the plaza is the mercado, the marketplace, a paved rectangle bounded by small merchants' stalls.

Before and after the rainy season the climate of Coroico is warm, pleasant, though sometimes humid. During the winter months it is cold, damp and frequently foggy. Rains generally begin sporadically in September and increase in frequency until they occur daily between December and February and then taper off in April or May. At the height of the rains the mountain roads are turned to mud and subject to frequent landslides. This is the season of least movement. Few people are in the streets, except for the weekend market and an occasional fiesta.

A paucity of people contributes to the generally slow pace in town. Many of the large old homes shelter but remnants of formerly extensive households. Campesinos of the town are away all day, at work on their lands. Some live on their plots in the campo for several days at a time. Other campesinos in the surrounding rural area own houses in town which they use only on weekends when they come to market. Many doors for many days are locked up tight. Even time seems to hesitate. Few people keep to their appointments, and there are always some who never arrive and some meetings that never begin.

OUTSIDE COMMUNICATION

Before the Revolution of 1952 Coroico was the trade center for very productive haciendas worked by a large Indian population. Radiating from the town are paths and dirt roads to the nearby hacienda communities. One of these roads connects Coroico to three other important towns in the Yungas, which lie almost in a straight line southeast of Coroico on widely separated mountain ridges.

The agricultural prosperity of the Yungas has always been dependent on the markets of the altiplano, especially La Paz. Until the twentieth century coca and other agricultural products were carried out by mule caravan over well-worn trails. Even before the turn of the century a road was begun from the La Paz side, financed partly by foreign interests, but the going was tediously slow because the Andean slopes are deep in shale and subject to frequent slides. The broken terrain made construction difficult and expensive. Not until 1936 did a road adequate for motorized transport reach Coroico. It is a narrow road of extreme grades, unpaved and full of hairpin curves. Were it not for landslides it would be passable throughout the year, and it carries a great quantity of goods in and out of the Yungas. It once took mule caravans three days to reach La Paz, but a loaded truck now covers the sixty-two miles in seven hours and a private vehicle does it in four. By 1960 the La Paz road into the Yungas had been further extended by a spur section which bypassed Coroico and went on for another sixty miles or so to Caranavi, once a small Indian hamlet in virgin territory, but today a boom town larger than Coroico.

Yungas road to Coroico (Lambros Comitas)

Before the turn of the century, work was begun on a railroad into the Yungas from La Paz. The technical difficulties of railroad construction in the Andes consumed considerable foreign capital before a narrow-gauge line was laid between La Paz and Hichuloma in 1924. Prohibitive costs blocked its completion twenty-three miles short of Coroico, so passengers and freight had to be carried by bus and truck to the terminus. High freight rates, slow speed, erratic schedules, featherbedding, the inconvenience and cost of having to load and reload goods in and out of

Coroico, and competitive truck traffic ran the railroad deeply into debt, and it finally closed in 1965. This presented no serious problem to campesinos and merchants, but it did cause problems for people who wanted to travel to La Paz without having to ride on top of a heavily loaded truck. Today a La Paz bus line runs a regular service of one round trip each week.

The town is liveliest on Saturday and Sunday, when campesinos come in from the countryside to buy and sell and the market is full of merchants and townspeople. In the plaza people gather to chat. On one of the government buildings beside the church is a bulletin board where notices of public interest are posted. There is also a public address system which blares out an occasional important announcement. Besides gossip, the bulletin board, and the loudspeaker, there are radio broadcasts and newspapers from La Paz; and for quick private communication with the world there is a telegraph office—service subject to interruption. Postal communication, because of unsteady road conditions and inefficient administration, is unreliable.

IN TIME

This part of the Yungas was conquered by the Spanish in 1538 and by 1591 lands in the area of Coroico had been granted by royal decree to soldiers and courtiers. As Villa San Pedro, Coroico was established in the sixteenth century as a trade and administrative center. It flourished in periods of gold and rubber booms in the region, and in 1903 Villa San Pedro was elevated to the administrative status of a city and changed its name to Coroico, from the Aymara word korihuaico, meaning golden partridge.

In the past ten to twenty years the importance of Coroico has diminished. The new road into Caranavi and a great increase in truck transport throughout all of the Yungas has established competing commercial centers. Many products that used to be made by Coroico artisans can now be had more cheaply in La Paz. Agricultural produce of the once all but inaccessible Caranavi area now compete with local products in the Coroico market.

Coroico has also been seriously affected by political changes in Bolivia following the Revolution of 1952. Since the colonial era the rich agricultural lands of the Yungas have been held by a small Spanish aristocracy.

In the early years of Spanish rule large numbers of Aymara Indians were forcibly transported to the Yungas to work the haciendas. The hacendados and their families spent part of their time on their estates and part in their town houses in Coroico. A few of the wealthiest also had homes in La Paz. The proximity of the Yungas to La Paz, its large Indian population, and its agricultural wealth made it an early target for agrarian reform following the Revolution, and MNR officials soon entered the Yungas to organize campesino sindicatos and to expropriate the land holdings.

But the Spanish aristocracy in the Coroico area had been leaving since the late 1940's, when it appeared that a fundamental revolution was imminent. While there was little physical violence here in 1952, most of the still resident hacendados either left discreetly or were forced to leave. The majority went on to La Paz. The few who remained in Coroico were able to salvage very little, either of their goods or of their land.

In 1952 the Indians of the countryside, for generations in peonage, found themselves free and equal citizens of Bolivia. As in Villa Abecia, Reyes, and everywhere else, they were given the franchise and the right to organize. Unionism was actively fostered by the government, and in 1953 they received the expropriated lands.

The impact on the town was profound. Indian producers entered directly into buying and selling in the Coroico market and their purchasing power increased, to be diverted considerably in recent years from Coroico to La Paz. Freed from the haciendas, many campesinos moved into the towns like Coroico, where living conditions are better and where their children can get an education. Some campesinos spend long hours traveling daily to and from their plots. Others have given up agriculture altogether. Many have become unskilled laborers, some have learned a craft, and a few have become merchants. These town campesinos make up 15 to 20 per cent of the population of the town.

Still, Coroico remains a mestizo town, its cultural and social life more Spanish than Indian. The mestizos are the majority. They fill the better jobs, run the better businesses, and control the town. The effect is that town and country are against each other. To the mestizo townspeople the campesinos are ignorant Indians who have been unfairly rewarded by the Revolution, while the campesinos see the town and its people as a continuing source of discrimination, mistreatment, and fraud.

Economic and political changes have greatly reduced the former eminence of Coroico but have not totally eclipsed it. It is still a provincial capital and, therefore, a center for regional governmental and judicial offices. It is also the headquarters of a Catholic diocese. And it is the biggest and most accessible marketplace for a still large area. It also produces craft products of everyday necessity.

TOWN ECONOMY

The rich farmland yields a variety of crops, including corn, potatoes, peanuts, chili peppers, avocados, dates, several varieties of bananas, citrus fruits, coffee, and coca. The important cash crops of the area are coffee, oranges, limes, tangerines, and, to a lesser extent, coca. Climate and altitude provide ideal conditions for coffee growing, and a high and steady demand makes it a very profitable crop. The majority of campesinos cultivate coffee as their major crop and produce bananas in considerable quantities because the trees provide necessary shade for young coffee plants. Other crops are raised in smaller quantities, some only for household consumption.

Coffee production around Coroico has increased in importance over the years and coca production has steadily declined because land and climate farther south and southeast are more favorable to it. Similarly, banana sales have fallen off in competition with the new banana-producing lands of the Alto Beni zone around Caranavi. The economics of coffee reflect the radical impact of the Revolution on this community. There are no large-scale producers around Coroico, for there are no large production units. In Reyes the large cattle estancia is run by the ganadero and his mozos, and in Villa Abecia the much smaller but economically overwhelming grape finca is run by the patrón and his peons, but the big haciendas and hacendados of Coroico are gone. Most of the hacienda land was broken into farms of less than ten acres and is now in the hands of the campesinos who had worked it as peons. Not all of them as yet hold legal title to their land, but they exercise effective control. Any disliked ex-patrón who ventures onto his old lands risks verbal abuse and physical assault.

The wealth of the land has not been shifted intact from the hands of the elite to the hands of their former peons. The quantity of coffee produced on some of the old haciendas, and the managerial experience and sales connections of hacienda owners, generally enabled some, though not all, to deal directly with large coffee processors in La Paz. The proportionately small production and the parochial marketing abilities of the campesinos discourage direct selling. One result of land reform has been the rise to prominence of the coffee rescatador, the middleman, who buys from many small producers and sells in bulk in La Paz.

The importance of the rescatador to the coffee business is not restricted to his intermediary marketing function, but is also closely related to his role as a creditor. Coffee is harvested and sold from April to September, and during these months most campesinos have money in their pockets. But very few have other sources of income and their cash from coffee sales is generally exhausted long before the next harvest. During the six months of the off season most rescatadors make loans to campesinos against the next crop. This involves very little risk for the lender, since there is little possibility of crop failure. The rescatadors do not forthrightly ask for interest on their loans because, they say, the concept of interest is incomprehensible to campesinos. Since most of the coffee-growing campesinos borrow and all the rescatadors make loans, a system has been developed in which loan charges are absorbed by the profits that exist in the buying and selling of the coffee.

This is how the system works. A campesino who is short of cash by October borrows, for example, $100 from a rescatador and promises to repay the loan within six months, by which time he will be harvesting his coffee again. The agreement calls for a repayment of the $100 or an equivalent value in coffee. At harvest time the campesino sells his crop to his creditor, the rescatador. The rescatador subtracts the value of the loan, $100, and gives the balance to the campesino. Now the profit to the rescatador in this "free" lending of money comes in three ways. The local rescatador buys at a lower price than the buyer in La Paz. Part of this difference, subtracting transportation and overhead charges, will contribute to profits. The rescatador also takes a quantity of coffee in excess of true measure. The units of measure for the purchase of coffee are the arroba, which is equal to twenty-five pounds, and the quintal, which is four arrobas. However, in Coroico the quintal at the time of the study was defined as equivalent to 110 pounds, while out in the countryside it was 120 pounds. These differences are known to all and are the customary allowance for the work of collecting and moving the coffee to market. The greater the distance from the La Paz market, the bigger the allowance. These differences in weight contribute to the profit of the rescatador. Finally, most rescatadors give themselves a small bonus of coffee with each purchase. After the weighing they add a few extra handfuls to their purchase, called the yapa, the "extra," a customary practice.

These practices in the buying of coffee may be worth as much as half the value of the loan. This explains how townspeople could lose ownership of the surrounding land but still retain a significant portion of the profits from that land. It is the rescatador who takes a major share of the existing profits in coffee under the present system. The campesino in fact frequently does not repay his loan. His need of cash and the low price he receives for his crop will make it necessary to defer repayment. This suits the rescatador. A campesino may sell his coffee to anyone, but it is understood that a campesino in debt to a rescatador will sell his coffee only to his creditor.

The rescatadors do not set prices or change weights in a capricious or arbitrary manner. The determining factors are the market price of coffee in La Paz, which sets their lower limit of profit, and the campesino's inability to sell his coffee in La Paz himself. The campesino is at a disadvantage in several ways. His production is small and he is unacquainted with La Paz buyers. His ways are rustic and his Spanish is poor. The rescatadors set prices that will give them a good profit, but they are constrained from pushing prices too low lest they reach a point at which the campesino would be compelled to stop producing or to market the coffee himself. Since campesinos are already selling other produce in La Paz markets, this is not a remote possibility.

Campesinos are aware of the ways in which the rescatador cuts into their profits, but thus far they have had little success in breaking the system. In 1965 they tried through the sindicatos to restore the countryside arroba to its traditional La Paz value of twenty-five pounds. At a regional meeting of sindicatos it was announced that members intended to sell only by the twenty-five-pound arroba measure and that campesinos who disregarded this resolution would be fined. This action encountered unshakeable resistance from the rescatadors. Although campesinos threatened to sell elsewhere, for most of them there was no alternative. A group of campesinos loaded their coffee on mules and trudged for twelve hours to the village of Suapi, only to find that Suapi rescatadors were using the same arroba weight as those in Coroico.

Today it is the big rescatadors who have become the economic elite of Coroico. Some are ex-patróns, some are merchants, some are former campesinos, others have always been rescatadors. Their economic hold on the campesinos is reinforced by the nature of the coffee plant. It requires attention throughout the year, making it impossible for the campesino to seek work elsewhere between harvests to keep himself from debt. Some of the bigger merchants also lend money to campesinos against the coffee harvest. These loans are sometimes repaid in cash but more frequently by a portion of the crop, and there is always an understanding that the debtor will deal only with his creditor. Most comerciantes, who form the largest occupational group in town, have no money to lend and operate on the narrowest of margins. Their stock is often pitifully small, a few pieces of fruit and some rolls, and many are women.

Next in numerical importance in Coroico are the craftsmen and skilled workers, who comprise approximately one-third of the labor force. These are the shoemakers, hatmakers, tailors, jewelers, carpenters, masons, truck drivers, bakers, blacksmiths, and butchers, all of substantial numbers. Some of these occupations—the blacksmiths and the carpenters, the forgers of tools and builders of equipment, the truck drivers—also derive their livelihood from the campesino's coffee.

For artisans and craftsmen, times are changing. Their work is considered old-fashioned and too expensive. The hand-made ceramic tile of Coroico, still to be seen on many of the old buildings, has been supplanted by less expensive corrugated metal. Rich and poor alike increasingly prefer factory clothing.

The town also gives a livelihood to a small number of professionals and semiprofessionals. There are a doctor, a dentist, two lawyers, two judges, and three pharmacists in Coroico, and more than twenty school teachers, most of whom are women. The majority of these professionals spend as much time as possible away from the community and leave as soon as they can secure a post in a city. At the other end of the occupational scale are the unskilled laborers and servants. Most are campesinos seeking a better future away from the land. The women work as maids, cooks, or laundresses. The men assist with building construction or repair work, or get jobs as porters or watchmen. Others find work as assistants to craftsmen or skilled workers, which pays very little, but holds the promise that the worker will learn a skill and become an independent artisan.

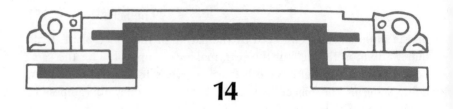

14

POWER AND
AUTHORITY

In contrast to Villa Abecia and Reyes, Coroico felt the full force of the Revolution of 1952. Here the Revolution has produced upheaval in the social order. A once important hacendado now waits on customers in his dingy little bar. One of the richest men in town is an Indian. And government officials court the favor of campesino sindicatos. In the following account we will discuss the economic basis of power and related matters, and then we will shift our attention to government and politics, which is where the campesinos have most sharply contested the old and new elites of the town.

ECONOMIC POWER

One of the most radical consequences of the Revolution for Coroico was the destruction of the economic elite of the community, the hacendados. Until that time the town had existed to service the great haciendas. The small number of families who owned these properties, large in size and in Indian manpower, controlled an extreme concentration of wealth. With homes both in town and on their haciendas, these landlords and their families dominated both town and countryside. Shopkeepers, craftsmen, and skilled workers were dependent on their good will. Town officials were often related to hacendado families, but, whether they were or not, remained in office at their pleasure.

On the hacienda the economic power of the patrón was augmented by traditional authority. Peons who did not fulfill their assigned work could expect swift punishment, a fine or a lashing. Many haciendas had small windowless huts for summary incarceration and trivial theft brought three days of confinement.

At the outbreak of revolution in 1952 terrifying stories of pillaging and armed attack came from the altiplano and Cochabamba, and hacendados around Coroico fled, leaving the Indians in possession of the land. While most hacendados have a legal right to a small part of their former properties, many are too fearful of their former peons ever to return. Others with more aggressiveness or less cause for concern did claim their portions, but found that none of their former peons would work for them, even for daily wages, and they were forced to sell out.

A few ex-hacendados have remained in Coroico. Most are no longer wealthy, many are quite impoverished. Some live in their large town houses, now falling into disrepair. They eke out a living by renting rooms to schoolteachers, by selling or renting what remains of their movable property, and by the odd minor business deal. A few hope for a return of their properties and have kept this idea alive in their children. In 1965 campesinos came on the son of Lorenzo Montes, a landless hacendado still living in Coroico, while he was picking fruit on one of his father's former haciendas and they angrily chased him off. Puzzled and irate, the son complained:

Yesterday in town I saw one of the campesinos who came after me. I asked him why they did it, what I had done, and he just said that we bother them too much, that we should keep away. But it's our property. No one ever paid us for it. Yet we can't do anything about it! Does that seem like justice?

However, the traditional authority of the patrón is no more, except in the imagination of some ex-hacendados. But despite loss of property and wealth, within Coroico there is still a faded measure of respect for the Diaz, Pineda, Uribe, Vasquez, and other old, important families. They are asked to serve on civic committees and are given places of honor at public affairs. But it is a hollow, wavering respect. Aristocracy is no longer a force in the community. In its place is the new elite, that of the rescatadors who have profited handsomely out of the need of a fragmented agricultural economy to adjust itself to a market system designed for large-scale production. While rescatadors are not as rich as hacendados once were, they hold a large share of the wealth of the town. Some own one or more trucks, used to transport coffee to La Paz and for general haulage. Some also own retail stores and all are money lenders.

In contrast to the patróns of Villa Abecia and the ganaderos of Reyes, the rescatadors of Coroico do not constitute a social group. They are too heterogeneous to have developed social solidarity. A few are ex-hacendados, but many more were once poor merchants. Others were traveling merchants or muleteers. A few were even campesinos. All speak Aymara, but some speak only broken Spanish. Some have had a few years of secondary school, others no more than a year or two of any schooling at all.

Since the claim of the rescatador to power is purely economic, to gain any direct social or political power in the community he would have to sacrifice some of his wealth to buy these other forms of power. A few are therefore content not to be invited to serve on civic committees, content to be considered of little importance and to have little influence on community affairs. Most of them, however, are able to maintain and, in fact, reinforce their economic power through political and social means. It is mainly these rescatadors who run the community. In addition to the economic elite (the rescatadors and the big shopkeepers), the professionals (the doctor, the dentist, the pharmacists, the lawyers, and the tinterillos—the untrained, self-appointed lawyers) also have a measure of power, not through their wealth, but because they are in a position to influence others. In short, there is no organized power structure in the town. Categories of workmen, merchants as well, are represented by sindicatos in Bolivia and there are several different sindicatos for merchants. But in Coroico they disappeared or were severely crippled in the coup d'état of 1964. In any case, the craftsmen and skilled workers live in a precarious market, and for this reason the sindicatos have never flourished among them.

The church in Coroico, with its well-maintained buildings, its well-appointed living quarters for priests and nuns, its big new school building, and its vehicles, stands out as economically well-supported, but much of this support comes from the United States. Most of the priests are American Franciscans, sponsored by the Catholic diocese of St. Louis, Missouri. The relative affluence of the local church rouses envy, but it is not a basis for power. The policy of the bishop is to restrict himself to religious matters and not become involved in other aspects of community life. This does not always hold for individual priests.

POLITICAL POWER

Before 1952 no campesinos of the Coroico area and relatively few townspeople took part in politics. Until that time political activity was a privilege of the educated, economic elite. Offices in the local political parties and the local government were all filled by members of the important families. Now, all adult citizens without exception are required to vote in national elections. But though Coroiqueños dutifully turn out, effective political activity in town has changed little since 1952. Most unskilled laborers, skilled workers, craftsmen, and small merchants still do not concern themselves with politics. They leave the uncertain world of government to the economic and status elite, the big rescatadors, the merchants, and the professionals.

On the other hand, the town elite is no longer as solid as it once appeared to be. The social and cultural diversity of today's economic elite and the relative rapidity of its formation have impeded the development of a united political force in the community. Before the Revolution the old elite had their Sociedad de Proprietarios de Yungas (Society of Yungas Landholders). This is gone, an anachronism disbanded by official decree, and while no decree prevents the ex-hacendados or the rescatadors from organizing themselves now, that initial action of the Revolutionary government still deters the growth of such groups.

Political office is won competitively, that is to say, usually through having superior competitive muñeca with higher officials in La Paz. But, without ties of economic interest, kinship, friendship, and cultural tradition, without the union of wealth and status, or common interest, the town elite is divided by politics. Besides, the campesino sindicatos in the countryside have developed as a political force, competing with the town for strategic resources.

As a rich agricultural zone with a large campesino population, the Yungas received early attention in the agrarian reform program. Most haciendas were of medium size (eleven to 150 hectares) and subject to reallocation. The central government representatives who helped the peons organize sindicatos on the haciendas were MNR activists. Legal action in taking over the lands was initiated in the collective name of the peons of each hacienda, or of several if they were small, and the sindicato was the means by which they took collective decisions. The agrarian reform program was completely identified with the MNR government, and no opportunity was lost to remind the campesinos that they owed their new rights and advantages to President Paz Estenssoro. Campesinos were expected or ordered to vote MNR, and almost always did.

Bolivia's population being predominantly rural, the entry of the campesinos into politics drastically altered local and national politics. In

Coroico, this took the form of increasing campesino influence on the prefectural and national governments at the expense of the town, whose appointed officials are still mestizo residents. The failure of campesinos to obtain political control of Coroico does not represent an unqualified victory of townspeople over them. As sindicatos have gained experience in political affairs and sindicato leadership has matured, Yungas campesinos have become more insistent and effective in pursuing their interests. This has been facilitated by the formation, immediately after the Revolution, of the Ministerio de Asuntos Campesinos—exclusively concerned with campesino matters—which has provided the campesinos with a channel of access to national decision-making. Sindicatos of the Coroico area have sought national government funds for schools, better water supplies, electricity, and other improvements. This has placed the town itself in competition with surrounding sindicato communities for the same limited funds, and the town has frequently been the loser. The campesinos are no longer totally dependent on the town government of Coroico. However, this is not a total disadvantage to the town, because it has enabled it to manage its own affairs even in the face of a new and important source of regional political power.

Throughout the 1920's and 1930's the important local parties were the Liberals and the Republicans. By the 1940's the MNR and the FSB, the Falange, had become the major local parties. Throughout all these years the workers and small shopkeepers of the town participated little in political activity and the campesinos not at all. Through the 1950's up to now the MNR and FSB have continued as the major parties in Coroico, though as many as ten other parties have minor representation. Since 1952 the FSB, a right-wing party modeled on the Spanish Falange, has been the rallying point for those opposed to MNR social and political policies. Although without victory in twelve years, and with little hope of electoral success because of solid campesino support for the MNR, FSB members in Coroico have loyally waited their chance. The confusion in the days following the overthrow of the MNR gave them their opportunity, and the way they used it provides a case study in the workings of local politics.

On November 3, 1964, Alcalde Jesus Cuevas boasted to a friend that the MNR would govern for another one hundred years. The friend recalls what happened on the following day:

Jesus and I were out taking a walk together when the news of Paz Estenssoro's fall came to us. Jesus Cuevas almost dropped dead. He insisted that he was not going to hand over the alcalde's office. I told him, "Look, you've got to hand it over decently. You've got to do it because the party's fallen." I kept insisting until he finally assented.

As the news spread, FSB leaders called an open meeting to select new town officials. However, it appears they intended the meeting to be a sounding board only for Falangistas, or so it seemed to one of their opponents:

There was an open meeting, but it was closed to dissenting voices. There were only sixty or seventy people, and the only ones allowed to speak were their supporters. There was chaos throughout the nation, and no one knew quite what to do. This was the situation these men took advantage of. When chaos broke out in La Paz and Jesus Cuevas found out there was a change of government he abandoned his office. What he should have done was to have awaited instructions, or to have said, "I will remain to hand over this office to the legally elected representative of the people of Coroico." Instead, he bolted. It was his stupidity. Well, those men took over immediately. They seized the opportunity.

Although General Barrientos, the leader of the coup, spoke of correcting the abuses of the MNR regime, people in Coroico and elsewhere differed about what the abuses were. The general was not a member of the FSB, but the local Falangistas hoped he meant, among other things, that land confiscation had been one of the abuses. In any case, it was clear to them that if national MNR officials had to be replaced, so did local MNR officials. And who but themselves were qualified?

The Falangistas selected Pablo Jimenez as alcalde and the MNR government walked out without a struggle. Four days later the FSB deputy alcalde announced over the public address system that he and his party colleagues had been recognized by the "Supreme Government of the Revolution of Restoration of the Country." The FSB had succeeded, but that their own future might also be uncertain was suggested at the time by an MNR supporter:

The authorities of Coroico are Falangistas who came in with the tide of November fourth. Who can oust them? Nobody! Right now it's impossible to think of getting rid of them. The Falangistas are very sectarian. They have hopes of returning to the way of life that existed before the Revolution of April 9, 1952, but they'll never get away with it. The campesinos will see to that.

The new alcalde, a man in his early forties, was generally well thought of in the community. He lived with his widowed mother, who helped him with his coffee business. The positive regard for him was partly due to discontent. Although Cuevas had been alcalde only a short time, it was rumored that he had already embezzled more than $2000.

Jimenez and his associates were in office hardly a month when General Barrientos came for a short visit. A crowd of about 800 assembled in the plaza to see and hear the general, but they first had to listen to the alcalde, the deputy alcalde, and the sub-prefect—all Falangistas—praise the general and damn the MNR. In turn, the general praised the people of Coroico and also recited the evils of the earlier government. But he very pointedly affirmed his support of the agrarian reform policy of the MNR government. A month later the prefect of the department arrived to discuss community problems and he promised to contribute a small sum (one million bolivianos, equivalent to $83.33) to improve the water system.

Another month went by, and General Barrientos came back for a second public visit. This time he spoke of the nonpartisan nature of his government, of the importance of national unity and development, and of community projects. At this point the Franciscan priest who led the campaign to improve the water system announced to the crowd that the prefect of the department had contributed to the project and he asked for a proportionately large contribution from the general. Barrientos quickly offered two million and was roundly cheered. About three weeks later the alcalde and his official fellows received telegrams from La Paz, thanking them for their services and saying that a new alcalde would arrive shortly. Before that could happen Jimenez went to La Paz to see if he could reverse the decision. Meanwhile, some said this was the work of Cuevas, the former MNR alcalde. Some said the campesino sindicatos were being listened to again in La Paz. Others said Jimenez brought it on himself when he permitted the priest to embarrass the general by publicly asking for money. Confounding all of them, Jimenez returned in a few days with an order reinstating him and all his associates.

By June the position of the alcalde truly worsened. He had been in office for seven months but had done nothing to improve the plaza or keep the railroad from shutting down. No one could see that anything had been done, but what was happening to local tax monies? Over all this muttering, General Barrientos announced the formation of a new party, the Popular Christian Movement (MPC), and since all the town's officials were well-known militant Falangistas, there was doubt whether they would be allowed to remain in office.

In September a prominent merchant who had been active with all the parties, but not strongly identified with any, was seen conferring with a group of campesinos, and when he was asked what was going on he said the campesinos of Cruz Loma were planning to take over. This was a gross exaggeration, probably not intended to be taken seriously. Cruz Loma was a focal point of sindicato activity. The truth was that Mateo Angula, a tinterillo not identified with any party, was approached by campesinos from Cruz Loma and asked to be a candidate for alcalde. He declined, but in a later discussion revealed that a change was indeed coming:

I'll tell you something entirely off the record. Last week the Ministry of Government issued a statement that the alcalde of Coroico would be changed. But I told them I would not campaign. I don't want to do that. I feel I could improve Coroico, make it a working, integrated, autonomous town. But I will not go to the people for that, especially since the proclamation for change hasn't been made public. That might provoke something.

Soon it was made public. The Ministry of Government announced that a new alcalde would be appointed from a list of three names submitted from the town. The three persons named were Mateo Angulo, Torribio Uribe, the head of the newly formed Coroico MPC, and a finca owner named Campos. A few days later Uribe was named alcalde.

The campesino sindicatos in the Yungas have been an important factor in town politics since the Revolution, though their power is not overt. As one Coroiqueño put it:

The campesinos are powerful in that in all Bolivia they have the influence and pure numbers to call the plays, to elect the President. They don't operate directly in town, but through the proper channels.

Their channels are the national ministries in La Paz, especially the Ministerio de Asuntos Campesinos, and the office of the President itself. Jesus Cuevas, the former MNR alcalde, said of the former peons:

All the campesinos around Coroico are organized. They are the ones who choose the leaders in Coroico. Look at the history of the MNR here—the campesinos held the strings. What they do is go directly to the Ministry of Government in La Paz, and because the government listens to these guys, they have their way. Beforehand, they go around to likely people in town and ask them if they would like to be alcalde.

Another important feature of local politics that this episode reveals is the dominant role of political opportunism. The MPC did not draw unengaged townspeople into political affairs, but attracted FSB and MNR activists. This further weakened the position of the FSB alcalde. It also brought back several MNR politicians who had gone into semiretirement after the 1964 coup. With Barrientos an almost certain winner of the coming presidential election, the MPC was obviously the way to political advantage, and there were many willing converts. As the Coroiqueños say, "They blew with the wind." Jimenez recalled that he had become alcalde with the solid backing of the FSB, "but it seems that now we are a little fragmented." Shortly before this, Uribe had formed a local branch of the MPC. He was known to have supported the campesino request for a reduction of produce taxes. As a leader of the new party in Coroico and a supporter of campesino interests, it is not surprising that his visit to La Paz paid off with the selection of himself as the new alcalde.

The change from Cuevas to Jimenez to Uribe in less than a year took place within the context of local political party activity, which is a more prominent feature of the Coroico community than of Villa Abecia and Reyes. In Coroico the community meetings, community projects, civic rallies, and committees are much more politically partisan in character than in the other two towns. Almost all such activities are sponsored and organized either by a political party or the local government. Since the latter is generally identified with a particular political party, local government sponsorship is also partisan. As an example, Jimenez, as alcalde, ordered that the interiors of all public buildings on the plaza be painted as part of his town improvement program. The work was carried out and it did improve the appearance of the buildings. But the completed work also served to advertise the FSB party, for he had had all the rooms of the buildings painted in the color of his party, light blue.

Most campesinos hold membership in the sindicatos formed on the haciendas. During the years of MNR government the sindicatos were units of the MNR. After the formation of a new government party many switched to the MPC to be on the winning side, although it was clear in many areas that campesinos continued to favor MNR policies and that they were confused about the relation of the MPC to the MNR.

That sindicato activities are political, the only effective means of obtaining a variety of aids and services from the national government, and that to be effective the members must be partisan, many campesinos now know. They resent the time required of them to participate in political rallies, and the money it takes to entertain visiting politicians, but many have also come to appreciate the advantages of political organization and strength. The value of political activism is illustrated in the following two incidents. The first is told by a Coroico truck driver:

One day a committee of Falangistas came to call on me and they asked me to join their party. I told them that I was very busy with my work and that I didn't care much for politics. I said I was awfully sorry, but I wasn't interested and didn't see that I'd gain much by joining. Well, after that I sure got it in the teeth. When they see Lara's truck coming, three or four town employees get prepared to slap a tax on me. Once the chief of police came to my store to ask me to donate two sacks of cement for that wall they're constructing in front of the post office. Well, to avoid trouble, I gave them two sacks. Later he got hold of my son and told him, "Look, Lara, you'd better go get me two loads of sand or stone." Then my son, who's a real rebel, talked back to him. The chief called my son names and tore his shirt because he wouldn't obey him. He told my son that if he didn't bring in two truckloads he'd find his truck out on the street, easy prey for anyone who wanted to strip it.

The next incident is related by a jeweler:

Some years ago I went to La Paz to see about getting a scholarship for one of my sons. It didn't matter much which son got it. I have eight sons. But I ended up spending money and getting no results. When one of my sons graduated in agronomy, I again went to La Paz. I visited the Minister of Agriculture and some other government offices, this time with the hope of securing a job for my son, but again I got nothing. They asked to see my party identification card, and when I told them I didn't belong to the MNR, they offered to sign me up, telling me that once I was a member I would see results. But I didn't join, and so all my efforts were in vain. I ended up with nothing. My son had to abandon his profession. Today he works as a clerk in a general store.

The subversion of politics for personal advantage by a privileged few is roundly denounced by the commonfolk. Here are five statements:

Those of us who live from our work don't want anything to do with parties. All they do is cheat you.

I am tired of all this political trickery. That's why I have no confidence in any political party—they're all alike.

In my opinion, none of the political parties is worth joining. From my experience I have found that political life is a sham.

I don't like to have much to do with politicos. I don't have respect for men like that, for they don't make their money honestly or by their own sweat.

I can't support any candidate, because nearly all of them are charlatans, liars, and cheaters.

The overriding concern of political parties with providing profit and privilege to their activists explains a number of characteristics of local parties that are otherwise anomalous. One is the irrelevance of political ideology. The political parties contain ideological labels in their names and political literature, and political speeches are generally couched in ideological terms. Most parties have borrowed their ideologies from European models. The MNR pictures itself as a revolutionary party and a proponent of radical economic and social programs. In these cases a political form is adopted locally, without any intention of implementing its substance. The need to serve political principles or ideological tenets can be equally as costly to party activists as to the general populace. Such a position makes no sense in Bolivian political life, where one becomes active in politics in order only to profit rather than to serve. Thus there is really no dilemma among the patróns of Villa Abecia who have joined the MNR, nor among the ex-hacendados of Coroico who are activists in the MNR.

Pablo Jimenez and his FSB associates stayed with the FSB for twelve years under MNR governments because they expected to have a chance to govern the town themselves someday and saw little chance of becoming influential in the MNR party in the face of the head start and advantages that others had over them. Had General Barrientos decided to take over the FSB and develop it as the new governing party, Jimenez and his associates would still be in office in Coroico.

The dominance of self-interest over public issues in Bolivian political parties is also seen in the relative absence of antagonism between local parties and their activists. During the years of MNR domination in Coroico, FSB leaders on occasion found themselves jailed or fined on one pretext or another, but these as often represented clashes of personalities as much as political clashes. In August of 1965, Torribio Uribe and a friend were beaten up by a group of Falangistas while they were distributing MPC literature. Significantly, almost all known incidents of political conflict in the community have involved townspeople, never townspeople against campesinos, as occurred in other areas.

But friendly accommodation is much more typical of political antagonists than any form of conflict. Jesus Cuevas, MNR ex-alcalde, has congenial relations with the FSB officials who replaced him. Ignacio Espinosa, the FSB sub-prefect in 1965, was a regular drinking companion of Torribio Uribe, and he continued to be even after Uribe became head of the local MPC and began to work to oust Espinosa's associate, Pablo Jimenez. José Pineda, head of the local FSB, plays cards several nights a week with Luis Vasquez, head of the local MNR. In one prominent family four of the brothers are active in the FSB, two support the MNR, and one is inactive politically. The brothers report no partisan quarreling.

GOVERNMENT AUTHORITY

Although within the space of a year three separate political parties were able to place their men in local offices, there were few politically relevant differences between these men. All were townspeople. All came from the higher social and economic strata. This is a large number of changes, but in the past decade it was not unusual for local officials to be changed at least once a year. Such a high rate of turnover would seem likely to produce an erratic, inefficient, and ineffective local government. While each new set of officials undoubtedly did bring some changes to local government, the basic elements in the pattern of local government continued.

Coroico, like Villa Abecia and Reyes, is a provincial capital. The ranking officials are the sub-prefect, who is the chief officer for the province, and the alcalde. The sub-prefect is responsible for public affairs throughout the province, while the alcalde's responsibilities are limited to community services. The structure of each of the administrations, provincial and local, is much as it is in Reyes.

Most townspeople have little to do with local government officials. Only when crises occur, as with the water supply in Villa Abecia, are citizens and officials moved to action. In Coroico, as in Reyes, drinking water is polluted, but no official seems able or even willing to do anything about it. This inaction may in part be attributable, here as in the other towns, to the limitations of local government. One limitation is overlapping and ambiguous jurisdiction. For example, a person who suspects he has been cheated by dishonest scales in the market ought to complain to the market inspector. But if he cannot find him, or does not like him, or is a good friend of the sub-prefect, he can take his complaint to his friend, or to a judge, or to the intendente, who oversees public works. Almost all officials are happy to receive complaints that may involve a fine. Fines are good for the municipal treasury and the official. Every official considers himself empowered to hear any issue or dispute and enforce a decision. No one official takes on all the jobs of the others all the time, only because the other officials are there to compete, but when they are absent this is exactly what happens.

Each official plays his role by ear, responding to requests from above and below as he sees fit. And, after all, he may be gone tomorrow. All official positions, here as elsewhere, are held at the pleasure of superiors. None of the important officials in Coroico has had any special training for his job and few have had more than a primary education. None has a trained staff. There are few fixed terms of office and no seniority rights. No one thinks of government as a career. The alcalde says he is a merchant, the deputy mayor that he is a pharmacist, the sub-prefect that he is a carpenter. Public office is only an interruption. Indeed, many carry on at their regular jobs, after a fashion, even while holding public office. The principal exceptions to the rule are judges and police officials, usually career men with formal training.

This foundation of government is further weakened by lack of money and the misuse of what there is. As in the other two towns, government in Coroico is seriously underfinanced. The sub-prefect, the highest ranking official in the province, has no budget for his office, his own very modest salary excepted. The major sources of public income, the taxes on wine in Villa Abecia, on cattle in Reyes, and on coffee in Coroico, are tapped by the national government, except for part of the shipping tax on cattle in Reyes. Officials work without supplies, equipment, or adequate assistance. Some do not have an office. The ones who do are housed in a government building with a collapsing wall.

As an important town in an important zone, close to La Paz, Coroico could normally expect to receive central government funds from time to time for municipal projects. Villa Abecia does, even though irregularly. That Coroico has received very little assistance in the past thirteen years is perhaps not so much to be attributed to an unfailing ineffectiveness in her local officials as to the rising power of the campesinos. While the townspeople would once have been the favored population of the area, the campesino sindicatos are now preferred. Their communities get the money for schools, roads, water, and electricity.

The corollary of underfinancing is low salaries. From the lowest local official to the highest, salaries range from approximately $5 to $35 a month. Some, such as the notaries, live on a part of the fees they charge, getting no salary. These incomes are inadequate to supply food and shelter for even a small family at a very modest level, and cause irresistible pressure to find other sources of money.

Most officials have no fixed hours of work. If a particular one must be seen it is generally necessary to search through the town. If he is not tending to personal business he may be at home, or at a local bar, or visiting a friend, but he is rarely in his office. Many give far more time and much greater attention to private work than they give to public duties, though sometimes the two are gainfully joined; for example, there was the alcalde's remedy for a sudden shortage of flour in town. After trucking his coffee to La Paz he returned with 1700 pounds of flour which he sold at low but profitable prices out of the government office building, "as a public service." Then there is the judge who occasionally serves as counsel to clients in his own court. Even to Coroiqueños whose cynicism is high this is too much. Public offices become private dwellings, used postage stamps are re-issued as new, books are sold out of the small public library, and small tax revenues disappear. But the biggest private profits from public office are from fees, fines, and bribes.

Almost every public service has its price, and the distinction between a fee, a fine, and a bribe is arbitrary. There are fixed fees for marriage licenses and copies of birth certificates, but if for any reason a citizen wishes to correct or alter the form the fee will be higher. If you want the intendente to get after your neighbor who throws his garbage in the street beside your house, he will act faster if he is given a small gift for his trouble. The dumping of garbage in the street is a violation, and your neighbor may be fined by the intendente, but he also may have the fine reduced or possibly forgotten if the intendente gets a small sum. The merchant pays a fee for marketplace stalls. He can get a better spot for a little something extra. Even within the awesome precincts of law and order, justice is for those who can afford it. This situation is openly acknowledged in the community. The DIC (Direccion de Investigacion Criminal) agent explains this vividly:

Let's say your brother is murdered. You come to Coroico for justice. I'm interested and sympathetic, but I have no transportation and no allowance for travel. So, if you want me to go investigate you have to pay my way, with meals, and pay for the travel and meals of another policeman who comes as my helper. And you have to provide lodging for us as long as we're investigating. Well then, suppose we're lucky and find the guilty party within a few days. We still have to bring him back to Coroico. So you, as the interested party, have to pay his transportation as well as ours. Then, when he's in jail here, you have to have his food brought in. Then you have to pay for his trip to La Paz and for the trip of his escort, a policeman who has to eat and have lodging for a few days in La Paz before you pay his expenses back to Coroico where he is stationed. All this the interested party alone has to pay. We have no funds. So justice is expensive, and many people let things go because they can't afford such costs. It's a shame, but there's no remedy.

Then there was the Campos case, one of accidental homicide, from which nothing ensued. Raul Campos, an ex-hacendado and former president of the Veterans of the Chaco War, got into an argument in 1964 with a fellow rescatador over the weighing of a quintal of coffee. Campos drew his pistol, fired a shot into the air and killed a woman who was passing by. Campos was arrested, but soon was released and that was the end of the case. The DIC agent commented on the Campos case, which he knew only from police records and secondhand comment, since he did not arrive in Coroico until 1965, as follows:

I wasn't here then, but I have heard the story. They say Campos was transporting a bag of something for Diaz, and the two of them got into a fight. Campos fired a shot and killed a woman. They took him to jail, but he paid them off and got out. That's the way it is here in Coroico. In all Bolivia, for that matter. You pay and you go free. In this case, there were no members of the family pressing for justice. It was one of those cases of manslaughter, unpremeditated, and the family didn't press charges. But I was not here, so I don't know all the facts.

Most Coroiqueños understand that legal protection is bought and that punishment is avoided by bribery. "They decide," said an ex-hacendado, "in favor of the fellow who brings them the biggest chicken." The man who has least suffers most from the workings of the law. As a person of no education, little money and few friends, the campesino is a ready victim for official exploitation. Before the Revolution he could count on his hacendado to protect him, but today the only organization that could defend him, his sindicato, is in the countryside, not in town, and there are as yet no sindicato tentacles that could reach so far on behalf of a persecuted member. But the sindicato had sufficient power to influence the selection of the alcalde in Coroico, and this is sufficient to have made local officials rather careful in their handling of campesinos in town. When campesinos are jailed, fined, or required to pay a fee, there is al-

ways a regulation at hand to justify the action. Ironically, the big rescatadors and merchants, some of whom are ex-hacendados, are most willing
and able to help campesinos who are facing legal charges. They pay fines
and bribes and intercede personally. This serves to increase the indebtedness of the campesino and bind him more tightly as a client.

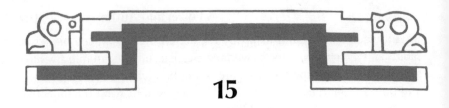

15

SOCIAL
STRATIFICATION

From the division of the haciendas among the former peons and their being freed from bondage flowed a series of further changes: the rise of the rescatadors, the partial movement of campesinos to town, and especially the entry of campesinos into new occupations. In the post-Revolutionary years the campesino sindicato became a force to be reckoned with, and in some areas it was more than able to redress the old imbalance of power between peon and patrón. The sindicatos in the Coroico area acquired sufficient influence with the national government to obtain a number of advantages for their members, including schools. But the improvement of the position of the campesino envisioned by the MNR fell short because the Revolutionary planners did not foresee that the fractionating of the concentrated economic power of haciendas would leave the individual campesino in a relatively weak bargaining position in the marketplace, and that a good share of the hacendados' economic power would flow to the rescatador. Further, the sindicatos themselves failed to use their new political power to bring about any basic changes in town and regional government. Despite their acknowledged ability to influence the selection of major governmental officials, local offices are still held by a privileged few for the benefit of a privileged few, to the disadvantage of the greater population and especially the campesinos.

The basic changes, muted changes, and aborted changes subsequent to 1952 are evident in the status structure of Coroico. Before the Revolution the community's society was sharply divided in a stratified hierarchy ruled by those decentes most eminent for traditional prestige and wealth. These were the hacendados, the race-proud families of Spanish descent who carefully controlled the marriage of their children to other decentes. These families were educated and polished, dressed in the European fashion, spoke only Spanish in polite conversation, and gave their lives to the cultivation of leisure.

Considerably below the decentes in social status, and also only a small part of the population, were the mestizos, most of whom are the mixed offspring of decente males. They were often responsibly accepted and given at least a primary education and a chance to learn Spanish. With these advantages they became merchants, government officials, clerks, and hacienda administrators. They dressed and spoke like decentes and emulated their manners and style of living just as far as their resources permitted. They had to work, but it was gentle work. Some learned to speak Aymara, which was useful in their jobs, and while they would perhaps wish to marry decentes, they took easily to marriage with Indians.

Only slightly lower than the mestizos in the social scale were the cholos, the culturally distinct, racially mixed stratum that appeared early in the colonial period. Until recent years they monopolized small-scale commerce and skilled work in the towns and countryside. Their hybrid origin and colonial cultural heritage are reflected in physical appearance and speech. They speak Aymara before Spanish, and affect a distinctive mode of dress, their women, the pollera and the derby hat, and their men a rather old-fashioned European dress. For the most part they married among themselves.

Far below the cholos in social status were the indios, the descendants of the indigenous people. This stratum made up the larger part of the population of the region, but a minority of the town. They had equally distinctive cultural traditions and social characteristics, received little or no formal education, spoke only Aymara, and got their living from unskilled, manual labor. Sharing approximately the same social status, though socially segregated from the indio, were perhaps a thousand Negroes scattered in isolated hamlets throughout the Yungas.

There was also a sub-category of indios, the free indios, culturally not different, but whose status was somewhat higher than that of the general Indian population. The free indio, who owned his own small plot of land or did unskilled work in town, was not a peon, not subject to the traditional authority of the decentes, and was relatively free to move as he pleased and work as he chose.

The traditional status hierarchy of the Coroico region developed early in the colonial era. It rested on the hacienda system of economy, for although mining has been important to the Bolivian national economy, the Bolivian population is overwhelmingly agricultural. Haciendas varied in size from a few hundred to many hundred hectares (one hectare = 2.47 acres), and they flourished on the labor of peons. In the Yungas peons were obliged to give four days each week to the patrón and in return were permitted to farm a small plot on the hacienda for themselves. Their hacienda work days were thirteen hours long, and on some haciendas the peons and their wives were obliged to work in the master's house for one-week periods, in rotation. Peons were occasionally required to care for hacienda animals, and if an animal appeared to have died before its natural time they had to reimburse the hacienda for the loss. Peons who did not meet their work obligations were fined, and on repeated failure were beaten. Beyond their specific work obligations, the peons and their families were in general subject to the authority of the hacendados and their families. Dependent on the hacienda for their livelihood, bound to it by indebtedness, and with no place to go except another hacienda, the peon learned that an hacendado's wishes were virtual commands and that any form of disobedience would be met by swift punishment.

OLD DECENTES AND NEW VECINOS: CHANGING SOCIAL STRATA

Somewhat more than a decade after the Revolution, the status order of Coroico is no longer a hierarchy of unambiguous strata. Today some of the old decente families live an economically precarious existence and have little, if any, political power. Other families of little prestige, cholos and even indios, have prospered in transport and trade. More townspeople speak Aymara and many indios now speak Spanish. European-style dress is becoming increasingly prevalent in all strata, and even the old pattern of residential segregation, in which families of higher status lived closer to the central plaza, has disintegrated. The bases of the traditional stratification order no longer support that order. Before the Revolution, race was a fundamental criterion of status. Today the flight of the hacendados has left few blanco families in Coroico. The influx of indios into town and their economic prosperity has promoted their intermarriage with cholos, mestizos, and even blancos, further blurring racial differences.

The result is an increasingly mixed population and an increasingly unstable racial criterion of status. Mestizos call themselves blancos, cholos dress in western style, and some indios, having become prosperous townsmen, have taken on many of the characteristics of the townsman in the process. Caucasian characteristics still lay claim to higher status, and status inequality is still justified in terms of racial differences, but in everyday life racial differences no longer guide social relations. Occupation, similarly, has become an uncertain basis of social status. Since 1952, the occupation of rescatador has become the most important and lucrative, and decentes now must share this position, if they hold it, with mestizos, cholos, and even indios. Trucking is another occupation that has risen in economic importance and become a new source of wealth. Its status was never high, for it was traditionally identified with cholos. Today it is lower still, for many campesinos have become truckers.

Not only have many of the criteria of status ceased to identify unambiguously discrete social strata, but there is no longer any consensus on what expressions properly describe the various strata of the community. "Decente" may refer to race, to having a Spanish name, to refined social manners, to membership in an old family, to some grouping of these characteristics, or to all of them. The same person may use the term decente in one of these meanings in one instance and one of the other meanings in another. One Coroiqueño gave four different meanings for the word decente: an honest person, a person with good manners, a person with a prestigious (meaning old Spanish) name, or a wealthy person. One person in town is considered to be a decente by some, a respectable mestizo by others, a rich cholo by still others, and a few consider him to be nothing but an Indian. This suggests the depth of the uncertainty now surrounding the assignment of social status in Coroico.

Rapid and extensive changes in the foundations of social status have affected both the character and correlates of social status. The most appropriate, best-fitting term for the top stratum in Coroico society today is vecino. Vecino means "neighbor" and is widely used in this sense. On occasion it is also used to refer collectively to all residents of the town, particularly when distinguishing them from outsiders. In an old variation on this latter usage, the word identifies a special category of townsmen. In this sense, vecino refers to residents of substantial economic and social importance. Thus, when vecinos were called to open town meetings in earlier times this was not an invitation to all residents of the town, but only to those property owners who represented the social elite of the community.

Elderly decentes in La Paz (Lambros Comitas)

But the term vecino defies precise definition now because the bases and characteristics of status have become mixed throughout the population. The vecino stratum is internally heterogeneous. With the breakup of the decente ranks and the emergence of mestizos as big rescatadors, a blurring has occurred in which the two are no longer consistently distinguished from each other, but are collectively referred to as vecino. This does not mean that decentes are never distinguished from mestizos, for they are. Not surprisingly, it is the old decente families who are most conscious of the distinction. They will employ expressions like "vecino nuevo" or "vecino de fuera" to distinguish social and geographic new-comers with claims to vecino status from old decentes like themselves. Even they do not use these terms consistently.

Vecinos have turned to status characteristics less amenable to change as the basis for asserting their own claim to high status. Occupation and even race no longer serve this purpose. With rich cholos and campesinos in town, neither does money. One that remains is education. Since one of the major programs of the MNR government was to provide educational opportunities to the campesino population and large numbers are now receiving some formal education, this might appear to be a questionable basis for establishing exclusive claims to high status. But the education to which vecinos attach importance is not formal schooling. What they mean is good breeding, proper manners, and refined comportment, forms of behavior that one learns in "refined, civilized" homes and that cannot be taught easily in public schools. Such a concept refers to earlier days, when Coroiqueños formed theatrical and musical groups for their own amusement and edification, brought in pianos from La Paz on the backs of peons so that the ladies of the house could learn and practice their music, and supported a local printing press that published a newspaper and pamphlets written by the local gentry. Unfortunately, today few vecinos have either the time or means for such pursuits, and the concept is anachronistic in relation to the actual way of life of these families. However, such special educational characteristics do disqualify cholo and campesino families, but they are increasingly unrealistic also for most vecinos.

It is taken for granted that vecino children will attend primary school and, if inclined, go on to the university, especially the boys. However, there is none of the intense preoccupation with education so characteristic of many campesinos. The special adult literacy classes that were set up under public school auspices after 1952 were attended by few illiterate vecinos. Partly, they were embarrassed, disinclined to reveal an inadequacy in common with campesinos. Others felt it was not important. On the other hand, more and more vecinos recognize the threat to their own status in the increasing number of campesinos and cholos who are getting a primary school education and even going on to secondary schools. As one vecino put it:

I do not agree with educational reform insofar as the government gives the Indians opportunities to study five or six years in primary school, then secondary school, and then even the university. That is inconceivable. For the campesino it is enough to give them two or three years of primary school and nothing else. If they go to the university, who is going to work the fields? They would have to leave the country and go to the cities, as is happening now. This is shameless. There should not be so many advantages for the campesinos, for soon they are going to dominate the country, they are going to be superior to the blancos.

While the mestizos have merged with a few remaining decentes to form the vecinos, the cholos have remained much as they were, except that they are more prosperous than ever. They continue to occupy the large middle ground between vecinos and campesinos. Since they were not subject to the legal, traditional, and economic restraints imposed on peons, the legal, political, and economic reforms of the MNR government had little direct effect on them, but their economic position has improved because of the considerable growth in micro-commerce that followed the dividing of the haciendas among the peons.

The trucking industry has become vital to Yungas agriculture, and cholos have been very prominent in its growth. Their willingness and ability to seize on new economic opportunities have also enabled some cholos to become important rescatadors. However, they have not merged like the mestizos with the decentes to become vecinos. To the old decentés the cholo is unmistakable, a lower order of person, not to be admitted into vecino circles. The cholos remain bilingual, speaking both Spanish and Aymara, but their Spanish tends to be more colloquial and the women speak rapidly and with a high-pitched whine that is very distinctive. While cholo men wear European-style dress that is not substantially different from that of vecinos, the women still wear the distinctive pollera, derby hat, and shawl.

The criticism and continued rejection of cholos by vecinos works against assimilation, but economic success is more important to the cholo than social acceptance, as indicated in this statement, made by a cholo woman:

I don't care if I am called a chola, because what is important for me is to know•how to work in order to have money. I am not going to live on the "good names" of the people of "blue blood." Their good names don't feed me. They may say what they want. I don't care as long as I have money and can educate my children. That's what I am concerned about.

The growing wealth and economic power of the cholos has made vecinos increasingly hostile toward them. On the other side, the cholos are threatened by the liberated campesinos. The peon who moves to town does not dress differently than nor does he often appear to be very different from the cholo. When he learns Spanish he no longer speaks differently, and when he becomes a skilled worker he competes with cholos. Similarly, when his wife wears the pollera and a derby hat and shoes, she too can look like a chola. Thus, while successful cholos do not become vecinos, successful campesinos do become cholos, so there are now old and new cholos, and, just as vecinos, and especially the decentes, emphasize lineage and family name as the only legitimate basis of vecino status, members of old cholo families emphasize lineage as the basis for distinguishing themselves from the newcomers. They stress the affluence and especially the refinement in manners of the old cholos, just as the old decentes do. Refined ways, say the old decentes and old cholos, cannot be bought or easily learned. This preserves, at least temporarily, a certain status exclusiveness in an otherwise changing and mixed situation.

Although the campesino's social status has improved since the Revolution, he is still on the low rung of the ladder—a foothold now ambiguous. On the one hand, the MNR government and sindicato leadership have proclaimed for over a decade that campesinos are legally, politically, and socially equal with all Bolivians, and at various times they have been urged to refuse the deference traditionally shown toward vecinos and to assert their rights of equality; but, on the other hand, both resident and visiting campesinos are constantly reminded in town that they are not the equals of cholos, and even more inferior with respect to vecinos.

In dress the campesino is frequently not distinguishable from a cholo, though some campesino men and women still do not wear shoes. Their houses in town cover almost the same range of size and age as others in the community, though more of them are smaller, with but one or two rooms. Their diet has improved; it does not differ greatly from that of cholo families. Set off against these improvements is the dependence of campesinos on local merchants and rescatadors. For the current generation of campesino adults who have not received the new advantage of formal schooling, this dependence can also lead to abuse, as noted by a chola shopkeeper:

There is an art of buying coffee from campesinos. You strike up a conversation with them and make a few jokes, and while they're engaged in talk, you quickly weigh the coffee they've brought in. They don't know how much they've brought, so if they have twenty pounds, I pay them for less. Some campesinos are so dumb that they never even count the money I give them.

Negroes constitute a separate segment of Coroico society, distinct from the campesinos and yet with approximately the same status. The history of Negroes in the Yungas has been closely linked with that of the Indians, but they are a relatively closed society, living by themselves in separate, rural villages. There have been Negroes in Coroico since shortly after the Spaniards arrived, but never more than a few families. Most of them live on Calle Ayacucho, which is a campesino street, and go from there to their fields to work. They dress like campesinos, but speak Spanish rather than Aymara, though some are bilingual. The stereotype that the vecino has of the Negro is similar to the one he holds of the Indian, that they are lazy, thieving, dirty, bad actors and not "civilized." There is little overt discrimination against them, but intermarriage is strongly condemned by all other strata and occurs infrequently.

STRATA INTERRELATIONS

The extensive change in the character of the stratification order in Coroico has introduced considerable tension. While cholos and campesinos stand around to chat in cholo shops, many vecinos walk in and out with only enough time spent and words used to obtain their purchases. A number of old vecino families are rarely seen in public. They stay home to avoid having to mix with those of lower social status. The intensity of this avoidance is illustrated by the vecino mother who refuses to send her child even to the parochial school, because the school admits campesinos and "she will never be educated there, with all those dumb, stupid indios."

Vecinos still honor traditional status obligations, such as those of compadrazgo, but even here avoidance appears. Vecinos accept requests to become padrinos to cholo children, for example, but they do not attend the parties that follow the religious ceremony and do not drink with their new cholo compadres. This avoidance is rationalized by stereotypic assertions that cholos are sneaky, untrustworthy, scheming, and aggressive, and that campesinos are dirty, lazy, ignorant, animal-like. Among vecinos the word cholo is used not only to refer to a social stratum, but as a term of derogation in which the stereotype meaning is intended. In the word campesino, the intent is not as clear-cut. When vecinos want to make sure that it is the stereotype that is understood, they will use the term indio. The cholos, whose specialization in small-scale commerce and trade brings them into contact with many people from both town and country, cannot afford to practice avoidance. Even though there is some exploitation of campesinos, the relations of cholos to campesinos are friendly. Their reaction to the hostility of the vecinos on the one side, and the invasion of their status by increasing numbers of campesinos on the other, has reaffirmed their own distinctive identity. As one old cholo woman says, "We don't try to hide the fact that we are cholitas. We wear polleras and these hats, we work in the market or around it, and all our friends are cholitas." For the most part the cholos keep any negative feelings they may have toward vecinos and campesinos well under control. It is when they are drunk that they express their feelings of insecurity and resentment.

The ambiguity of the campesino's status creates uncertainties that range from the important problems of his life, such as to whom to sell his coffee, to the everyday question of how to address a vecino. Before the Revolution it was mandatory for a campesino to address any vecino he encountered. This was a stylized exchange in which the campesino would approach the vecino, but not too closely, remove his hat, greet him as "tata," father, and then ask about his health and the health of all members of his family. In the immediate aftermath of the Revolution, when campesinos were being incited to eject the hacendados from the land, campesinos stopped greeting vecinos, even when spoken to, seldom used the deferential "tata," and even refused vecinos the right of way in the street. In town, at least, these expressions of open hostility have disappeared and campesinos and vecinos again greet each other. But it is not the old order that has returned. Vecinos now receive a casual "good morning" or "good morning, señor" with no use of deferential titles, while the campesinos are greeted in the same terms, except for the "señor." A few campesinos still use more deferential forms of greeting, and some vary the expression of deference with what they take to be the status of the person. However, a person's status is no longer easily apparent, and this makes the etiquette of greeting somewhat perplexing.

SOCIAL MOBILITY

The mestizos who emerged as the new economic elite were in a position to profit from a decline of the decentes, and few people in Coroico any longer distinguish between the two, but group them together as vecinos.

Many persons are aware that vecino ancestry is not so pure, that many have had chola mothers, but in the confused and changing status order of Coroico this is not a difference that counts for much any more.

The movement of social strata since the Revolution has obliterated one stratum and narrowed the differences between all of them, and this simplification has been furthered by extensive individual mobility. A sufficient number of years has elapsed since the Revolution to show that mobility occurs during a person's own life as well as from one generation to the next. In most of the cases of upward mobility the means has been money. An ex-campesino describes how he moved out of his father's stratum:

Before, the campesino was deceived. My father was a campesino and that's how I know. It isn't any good for a campesino to be looked down upon by others. I had a truck that my father bought me so that I would no longer be a campesino like him. With that truck I make trips to La Paz to sell various products. Little by little the people didn't look at me any more as the son of a campesino, but told me I was good and generous. Afterwards, I bought a house in town, and then I was not considered a campesino any more. Even though later on I sold my truck, nobody looks at me as an indio now. Now there are no longer any marked differences.

This man, a successful cattle merchant, has become a new cholo, despite his campesino parentage. Others have not found it quite as easy.

For example, Juan Mamani was an hacienda peon who, after the Revolution, left agriculture and with his two brothers bought a truck. By hard work he was able to expand his business and today is hauling produce for merchants of all the near-by towns to and from La Paz. He is considered a clever businessman, but is generally referred to as an indio, only infrequently as a cholo trucker. A chola in town says this is due to envy:

They call him an indio. He is, but he is civilized. He is nice, he tries to please, he is friendly and responsible. The people say bad things about him just because he is an indio, and he has had to take all sorts of opposition just on this account. People are envious because they cannot be as successful as he is. They won't work. He works, and that's why I'll buy from him and not from another. He works, and the others just think they own the world.

While Mamani is called an indio, his children will undoubtedly be new cholos, for already some vecinos and cholos do not treat him as an indio.

In contrast, one of the wealthiest men in town is an Indian whose name is Conde, the hispanicized version of Condori. He owns valuable property in Coroico and La Paz, lives modestly, dresses inconspicuously and associates with few people. His godson calls him a miser, but no one calls him an indio. He is referred to as a rich cholo.

It is quite possible that the children of well-to-do lower status families who will have had the advantages of education and will have acquired "civilized" manners may move as adults into the ranks of the vecino. There has been too little time for this to occur. As on most questions of status, opinions vary and agreement is small on such matters, reflecting the state of flux and the resulting lack of clarity in the system. For most campesinos, anyone with money is a decente. For many cholos it is education and proper conduct that make one decente. For most decentes, you have to be born one.

Many decentes are no longer able to afford the style of life that once set the standard for their stratum, but they strongly resist redefinition of their status. As one decente explained:

Pure blancos, as long as they are blancos, are accepted. But take an indio, for instance, and give him wealth. The people are still going to say he is an indio. You can't buy blood. Of course, this is changing more and more. Before, the families that were in top social positions were there due to name and wealth. Usually the two went hand in hand. Wealth was coffee. Now everyone meddles in coffee, and it is the only way to riches. And so people can earn more easily and they can gain position, but they don't have the other things the people formerly had: culture and higher style of living.

Here the importance of wealth is recognized, but it is subordinated to what money cannot buy or cannot buy easily—proper ancestors and proper ways. In time the extension of elementary and higher educational opportunities to cholos and campesinos may diffuse the higher style of life just as occupation and wealth have already crossed old status barriers. However, local public education is not really adequate and it is also too early to assess its impact on mobility and social status.

The stress of decentes on immutable criteria of status leads them to insist that a decente can never cease being one. Given the extensive changes that have occurred among the decentes, this would be surprising if true, but it is not. Though infrequently discussed, there have been a number of decentes who have fallen all the way to the bottom of the social hierarchy in Coroico, have, in fact, quite passed out of sight. Having lost their possessions in the Revolution and having no ability for other work, estranged from relatives or having none, they ended up on a little plot of land. Several of them married campesino girls, and their way of life is indistinguishable from that of any other poor campesino. At least two decente women have married campesinos and are now "wives of indios."

In Coroico, as in Villa Abecia and Reyes, marriage can be an important factor in precipitating or reinforcing social mobility. However, since social status itself is ambiguous in Coroico, it is not always clear when an inter-strata marriage has occurred, and many marriages only compound existing status ambiguity. On the other hand, where the status differences are considerable, it does affect the status of both partners. Because many vecino boys go away to school or to work and never return, vecino girls increasingly must either seek a partner in the cities or accept marriage with persons of lower status. This presents an advantageous situation to the ambitious and successful cholo boy. Among the inter-strata marriages that have occurred there is one which is especially well known in the community and which reflects many of the developments in Coroico since the Revolution. For this reason it is worth presenting in some detail.

THE MONTES FAMILY

Lorenzo Montes is the son and grandson of hacendados. The four haciendas that belonged to him at the time of the Revolution had been in his family for more than 160 years. They extended over 450 hectares, or a little over 1100 acres, and produced coffee, coca, bananas, and oranges. Montes recalls that he had many peons and had a generous income.

In 1922, at the age of twenty-eight, Lorenzo married a daughter of the locally distinguished Diaz family. They were married eleven years and had two children. In 1933 Montes divorced his wife and scandalized the community by marrying Julia Cerezo, a campesina from one of his haciendas. The marriage shocked local society. Lorenzo was strongly criticized, but life went on. Though now the wife of a wealthy hacendado and mistress of his big house, Señora Montes never appeared as the gracious hostess. When Lorenzo entertained he dined with his equals, while his wife ate in the kitchen. A priest who was a frequent visitor to the

Montes home said, "It would have been an insult to the other guests to have an indio at the table."

In 1953 Montes was thrown off his hacienda by his own peons and he, his wife, and the five children she had borne him moved to town. Montes still cannot understand why this happened to him. He recalls that he was always generous and concerned for his campesinos:

The Law for Instruction of the Campesinos was passed in 1936. That meant that every hacienda had to construct a school, and each one brought teachers from the altiplano. But then, in 1938, a new law said that if an hacienda was less than three kilometers from town the campesino children would have to go to the public school. We were less than three kilometers from town, but even so I built a school for my people. I didn't have to do it, but I did.

The campesinos on the Montes haciendas saw the situation rather differently. Asked what working for Montes was like, a former peon replied:

Very difficult. The campesino had to work three days for the patrón and so did their women. Yes, that's three days from a family and that's too much. Besides that, we had to give them our produce. That's why we threw them out when the reforms came. All of us had arms and we made Montes leave. [A woman standing beside the campesino exclaimed at this point: "Him they hate!"]

In the complaint proceedings of 1955 before the Agrarian Reform Court, in which the campesinos applied for legal title to their share of the Montes property, Montes was accused of a variety of abuses. He was charged with having forced his peons to live in unhygienic housing, with having exploited their labor without compensation, and with having exposed them to the danger of death by making them cross the river to his properties during the rainy season, when many would be swept away and drowned. Today Montes complains:

Nobody in Coroico is sympathetic. They listen and then they say, "That's the way it goes." I had to put up with a lot. They took all I had after the reform. And because my wife is, really, of a different race, the adjustment has been hard. They resent her for being my wife and consequently they resent me. I don't get fair treatment from any quarter—none at all, not even from my family. Look at me, picking up trash in the street! Ay, times are hard now. I'm not used to things like this. When I was growing up I had all the servants I needed and they showed me respect. Now I am nothing. Even in my house you see me doing this sort of thing, when it should be done by the women and children. I have to clean up the street, do work around here, and my family doesn't think anything of it.

One of his vecino nephews says, "Since he married the servant, thirty years or so ago, we've had nothing to do with them"; but other relatives have been kinder. Another nephew explains why he helps his uncle:

Lorenzo comes to visit me a lot. And he knows that if there is no noon meal at his house, for instance, he can come here and eat with us, even on the spur of the moment. And I know that I can go to their house. We don't have any business activities together, but he does come to me for help on all these legal matters that he has pending. [Montes seeks reparations from the government for his expropriated properties, and the nephew is the notary public.] And, being a relative, and knowing that he does not have one cent, I write up the papers for him free. His condition is very serious, I would say, and this comes from his having married that younger woman. They have about ten kids now, and that means they have to get money from somewhere.

The nephew very discreetly avoids the status problem of his uncle's wife and concentrates on their economic problems, but his economic situation is not as serious as the nephew suggests. If today Montes is poor, he is poor only in relation to his former wealth, for in comparison with really poor families the Montes family lives rather well. His wife, Julia, takes the brunt of contempt and hostility. From all sides she draws disapproval: "Oh, that fatso, she's just an india"; "She is just a chola, and has mountains of children." A chola sums it up:

She thinks she is refined because she has picked up a lot of Spanish from the old man. But, she was just his servant, and even lived with him before they were married. She is nothing but a chola and she puts on so many airs. She is a real sinner, señorita. They never set foot in church, and she was just his mistress. Everyone hates her, even her own mother. Oh, they're bad people. She looks just like a chola, doesn't she, with that hat sitting on her head? Just because she speaks Spanish she thinks she is something pretty special.

When Julia is called an india it is clear that the speakers are using this term as a pejorative, for even her enemies grudgingly acknowledge her chola status. If Lorenzo has come down in the social world of Coroico, his wife has very definitely come up. And if Lorenzo is no longer considered by some to be a decente, few would challenge his status as a vecino.

The social status of the Montes children is quite ambiguous. They are thought to be ill-bred and are disliked by most of their neighbors. One person says, "Lorenzo Montes is a vecino, and therefore his children are too." But another says, "He took his servant as his mistress, and all those children of theirs are just campesinos because they've got no education or culture." If the children had been carefully reared according to the old decente model, it is probable that they would be considered vecinos by everybody. It is the mother, however, who has had the active role in rearing the children. She is not in a position to teach them to become vecinos; in fact, she seems quite insensitive about it. It is clear that she would rather have her children make money in the cholo fashion than try to become vecinos.

Sra. Montes works hard herself and sees to it that all the children do. She supervises the several economic enterprises of the family, including one of the seven commercial ovens in town. She rents out rooms, runs a small retail store, buys and sells flour and quina, runs a small bar, sells firewood, and oversees the cultivation of a small parcel of land that is all that remains from the Montes haciendas. These activities are not making them rich, but they do provide them with a living sufficiently good to evoke envy among their neighbors. Lorenzo is seventy-three, but he waits on customers in the family's bar. Each of the children has specific tasks in one or more of the family businesses, but none of them is paid wages. The girls buy groceries, prepare bread, cook and look after the two little boys. The oldest boy at home, in his early twenties, brings fruit and firewood from their land. The little boys sweep up and care for the rented rooms. Hired workers operate the oven. In addition to supervising all the different projects, Sra. Montes makes frequent trips to other towns to buy flour and bring supplies to be sold in the family store. Since most of the businesses, including the oven, are in their house, the family members, with the exception of the mother, spend most of their time at home.

Indicative of the values of Sra. Montes is the scholastic situation of her children. Of the three Montes children of school age in 1965, none was in school. Two boys had failed so many subjects in primary school that they had dropped out until the next term, when they would repeat the grade they had failed. The girl in high school wanted very much to continue, but her parents refused to buy the required uniform. When asked what her parents thought about her not going to school, she replied:

They know. They don't care. I talked with my mother last night and told her why I was not going to school and she didn't say anything. She just agreed with me that I was not going. My father is too old. He can't work, and therefore he doesn't have any money. My mother has it.

He could ask her for the money but he doesn't want to. He doesn't care. He says it is better that girls go to work. They both want money, that's all. They don't care. My mother is a real bad one, isn't she, señorita? We have no time, no place to study, no light at night. If we try to study, she comes in and says, "What do you study for? It won't do you any good." And she makes fun of us. So we don't do well in our courses.

Six months later this girl moved to La Paz, found a job, and enrolled in night school.

Since Sra. Montes is willing to work hard and assume responsibility for the family economy, the father, who is old and tires easily, is content to remain on the sidelines and let his wife run things. Her values dominate the household. A daughter who spends her days in school and her evenings studying means one less person to provide free labor to make the family businesses a success. While the mother moves from one task to another throughout the day, the father passes much of his time reading the La Paz newspapers. Around him are the shabby remnants of the expensive Victorian furniture that once graced his home, from which he also saved an old photograph of Julia. The portrait was almost unrecognizable. She was dressed in western style, not in the pollera and derby hat and with the braids she wears today. It is a picture of the status she could not attain.

The Montes family reminds the town of the fall of the hacendados, the rise of campesinos to cholo status, and, especially, the mixing of social strata. As one old decente observed, "It's no longer possible to maintain one's prestige as a vecino. Today everyone mixes with everyone else and people aren't separated the way they used to be." And another adds: "Only thirty years ago there were still pure people in Coroico. But vecinos are taking Indian women, as Lorenzo Montes did, and vecino blood is getting mixed with that of cholos and campesinos."

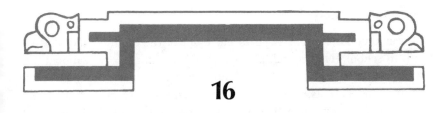

16

GROUPS AND ORGANIZATIONS

Coroico, like Reyes, is a community with a variety of groups and organizations in which overlapping membership should provide an important basis for community cohesion. In fact, little cohesion results from this pattern because membership in many of the groups and organizations is small. Membership turnover is high, and the attraction of members to their groups is not strong. In this situation the family is the one group in which durable relations are found, but even here strain and deep change have occurred in the past decade.

A large proportion of Coroico households contain few persons. In Coroico, 25.9 per cent of the households contain two persons or one, and 58.8 per cent contain four or fewer, while in Reyes the comparable proportions are 7.8 per cent and 28 per cent, and in Villa Abecia, 17 per cent and 38.2 per cent. Among these very small households are both very new and very old families, and there are many families that consist of an aged couple living by themselves or an elderly person and an adult child. In Coroico, 12.9 per cent of the population are fifty years old or older, while in Reyes only 8.6 per cent, and in Villa Abecia only 8 per cent are in that age range, in great part because older children and young adults leave the community. Because of limited secondary school facilities in Coroico, and the proximity of La Paz, many vecino families send their children, especially their boys, to secondary school in the capital, so vecino children often begin to move out of the family while they are still in school. The capital, along with the booming colonization town of Caranavi, is also a mecca for ambitious cholo young men, and even campesinos. Parents, especially elderly parents, complain of their loneliness and isolation when their children leave, but most of them accept the situation, if, indeed, they do not encourage their children to leave for the cities, where the weight of the past will not bear so heavily on them.

Another factor contributing to small size, and even more importantly to the composition of the family, is the frequent absence of the father in cholo and campesino families. Cholos and campesinos dominate the trucking business and many are home only one or two nights out of the week. Others go to the gold fields, the oil fields, or any other place in Bolivia where there is more economic activity, and may be away for several months to a year at a time. The wives do not follow, for the work may be temporary and the future uncertain, or they stay in Coroico because they have a business of their own, a small tienda or a stall in the marketplace, or they make bread for sale. Absent husbands often provide little support, so the mother must work to keep the family alive.

The separate business activities of cholas make them much less dependent on their husbands than either town campesino or vecino women are. There is frequently no pooling of earnings. The husband will give his wife the funds he thinks she requires to the extent that he is able, while the wife uses her earnings not only for her own and family expenses but may invest them in economic ventures of the husband, and she is often more successful. In contrast, vecino wives seldom work, their accepted place being at home. Some town campesinas work as servants or cooks, but, generally, they are not economic rivals of their husbands. Cholo wives, and to a lesser extent town campesino wives, are independent in the very form of marriage so usual among them. Vecino wives choose to marry under both civil and religious law, but many of the cholas and most of the campesinas are living in consensual unions, bound by no formal tie. Although some prestige is attached to formal marriage, many cholas point to the liability of having to give up their freedom and in having to accede to the demands of the husband.

Economic poverty, inferior education, sex adventuring, and an endemic addiction to alcohol appear to be the principal influences undermining family stability. Many families live from day to day on the slenderest of resources, from which, however, men and women manage to eke out enough to drown their problems in alcohol. Men and women, old and young, everybody drinks. Asked why there was so much drinking in town, an elderly vecino merchant said:

It is because practically everything one does is done with a drink, whether selecting a compadre, thanking a compadre, celebrating a birth, celebrating a marriage, making a business deal, celebrating the purchase of a new car or house or what have you, to create friendships, or just to drink with friends. People drink to mark their success and also their poverty and grief, they drink for a dead person, for having received an inheritance, at fiestas, at civic celebrations. In sum, one drinks for everything. There is no way to escape alcohol. In spite of the fact that today liquor is expensive, I think it is safe to say that more is consumed now than before.

Probably more men drink more alcohol on more occasions, but the women are not far behind, and when husbands and wives get drunk they fight, sometimes brutally. The squandering of money on alcohol, and drunken physical assault, cause most separations and divorces among cholos and town campesinos, the extramarital activity being common to both sexes. If there is no legal or religious bond, there is no formal obstacle to separation; but even when marriage has been formalized, the man who finds another woman more to his liking often simply leaves his family and sets up house with his new choice. Though vecino husbands drink as much and have greater means and presumably more choices in venery, their families are more easily spared the knowledge, and what their wives see they studiously ignore.

In most families older children are expected to get a job and the younger children to work in the house. The work demanded of vecino children may be relatively light, especially in the case of boys, for they are expected to attend to their studies, but cholo and town campesino boys start early as helpers to their fathers. Cholo and campesino girls learn domestic skills at their mother's side in the kitchen, but vecino girls in growing numbers are sent to secondary school in La Paz for some form of business training.

The young man marries when he can afford it, usually in his early twenties, and his wife is but a few years younger. Vecino men marry somewhat later because they remain in school longer. Most vecinos of the older generation married townspeople, but now their sons and daughters are going to school in the cities and often remain to work after graduation, and many are therefore marrying into distant families. Even those vecino girls who remain at home are inclined to look to the cities,

View from Coroico (Lambros Comitas)

especially to La Paz, for good husbands. They are often coached in their pursuit by parents who see few worthwhile prospects in Coroico and, consequently, a danger of their daughter's marrying into a lower social stratum. What happens when danger impends is recounted by a chola shopkeeper:

Two or three years ago Jorge fell in love with a young girl who lives near the padre's house. When he went to talk to the girl's mother she told him there was no need for him to fall in love with her daughter, who happens to be attending secondary school in La Paz. She told him, "You disgraceful cholo, bothering my daughter, why don't you look for a chola like yourself?" Later he was attracted to another young girl and the same thing happened. For that reason, he won't bother with these girls who walk around well dressed but who have nothing inside them.

Many town campesinos came alone from the campo as far away as the altiplano and have few or no relatives in town. Many have never returned to their native communities and have seen nothing more of their parents or siblings. Many report their fathers dead, either from what their mothers told them or because they do not know who their fathers are. Others know neither parent, because both father and mother ran off and they were given to other relatives or to a cholo or vecino family as criados, as foster-child servants. In other cases the mother may never have been married and may have had each of her children by a different man. With limited or no inheritance, most campesino youngsters are forced out of the home to seek work as best they can, and are scattered throughout the country. In these circumstances few town campesinos are able to claim more than a wife and their own children, maybe a mother and an occasional sibling.

In the following statement a young vecino, who has worked as a rescatador and also a public employee but now makes shoes, reveals his own range of family ties and tells of the disrupting effect of differences of wealth in families:

To me, family means only my parents, my brothers and sisters and my grandparents. The rest are kin, but distant kin with whom one has occasional relations. They don't come to visit us and we don't go to see them. The persons that I am close to are my father and my brothers, but I have more to do with relatives in Coroico than with relatives who don't live in town. The latter one forgets and others can't travel here. Among my relatives, those that have money are very proud and at times they put you down. More than that, they say they aren't relatives. Why? Because you don't have money like them. Only when it is convenient for them do they call you a relative. That's not worth the bother. For example, this José Pineda, the tinterillo, occasionally says we are relatives and other times says we are not. His wife is my father's sister.

The value of close kin is that they can be counted on in emergencies, do favors, advance loans, provide social support, and in general be counted on for aid, advice, and encouragement.

In Coroico, as in the other communities, compadrazgo takes a number of different forms, but again the important ones are baptism, marriage, first communion, and confirmation, in that order. Especially prominent in Coroico is the extreme secularization of compadrazgo as a means of raising money and goods for worthy causes or even for rather narrowly partisan activities. Older students are particularly adept at using compadrazgo to solicit support for recreation and school activities. A soccer team that needs to be outfitted solicits padrinos for shoes, shorts, shirts, and balls. People who cannot afford contributions are not approached, but it is shameful to refuse when the request is obviously within the person's means.

Vecinos today, as before, select their compadres from among their own kin and other vecinos, and for all the usual reasons, and compadrazgo ties are important to the rescatadors for their commercial value. For many vecinos, however, the obligations of compadrazgo have become too expensive, the compensations too small. Campesino compadres coming into town on market day expect a meal and perhaps even lodging, but with their haciendas gone, they have little to do with agriculture and no need for close relations with campesinos. Now, too, gifts from campesino compadres have become fewer and smaller. Whereas before the Revolution a campesino brought his vecino compadre several chickens, one or two dozen eggs or several bunches of bananas, now he brings one or two eggs, or a couple of bananas, and frequently nothing at all.

Among town campesinos, ties of compadrazgo have become attenuated through both family instability and geographic distances. It is not surprising that those who cannot name their fathers also cannot name a padrino. In some cases they never had any because they were not baptized. In other cases, the family broke up or the family of the padrino broke up, and one or more members moved away, so that a child never came to know his padrino. Similarly, the campesinos who have moved to Coroico frequently have little contact with their ahijados. One fifty-nine-year-old mason from an Indian community on the altiplano has more than sixty ahijados in his home town and in La Paz, but has seen none of them in the sixteen years since he moved to Coroico. His comment indicates that even among the Indians the obligations of compadrazgo can be a strain:

With the number of ahijados and compadres that I had in Tihuanaco and La Paz, we had many celebrations, many drunken parties. That's the way we lived. For that reason I am content not to have compadres or ahijados to bother me. I am tired of attending to so many compadres.

The social importance of compadrazgo is not in the gifts that it produces but in the relations of assistance and support which it establishes. These are very similar to the relations between close kin. The relations between padrino and ahijado are more formal, which is consistent with the age difference between the persons involved. Compadres should respect each other, do each other favors, lend money or foodstuffs, give counsel when asked, and aid each other. This is the ideal, but there are many exceptions, as a town campesino who works as a tailor attests:

Once I had an urgent problem and went to Don Ignacio [a well-to-do cholo shopkeeper] to ask him to lend me 50,000 bolivianos [$4.00]. Do you know what he said? "Look, ahijado, I would be pleased to make you a loan, but now we are poor because my wife has just bought things for the store that cost a lot of money. Ay, any other time I would make my godson a loan." You know why he wouldn't lend me the money? Because he had no confidence in me. If I had said, "Lend me 50,000 bolivianos and I will leave my sewing machine with you as security," he would have lent me the money in a flash. But I couldn't do that, because without the machine I cannot work.

Here in this town there are good compadres, who help, support one, who think well of a person, who respect a person, but at the same time there are some who are not worth anything, who are rich and right away forget the poor. It is three months since I have visited my padrino, Don Ignacio. What's the point of visiting someone who never will do a favor? I send one of my nephews to buy things from the store of Don Ignacio, like vanilla, noodles, rice, sugar, salt, candles, flour, and so on, but never is he man enough to give a gift, to say, "Take this little something to my ahijado."

To many persons compadrazgo means only "a mountain of obligation." One shopkeeper avoids it by saying she was not married in church and therefore the priests will not allow her to become a madrina. To make sure they get the message, she adds that she does not think much of those American priests and has poor relations with them.

FRIENDSHIP

There is a feeling in Coroico that friendships are not what they used to be. Old friends were scattered in the shattering of the old order and the town now seems too full of strangers and too full of neighbors not worth bothering with. For most people a friend is a person with whom they pass the time gossiping. There are visits between families, invitations to parties, drinking companions in the cantinas; but friendships are different. As a tailor tells it, "Since I am a tailor by profession, there are always a lot of people coming to my house. With all the people of the town and the estancias, I am amigo de boca [casual friend], nothing more."

Close friendships have survived for some vecinos, but for cholos, rejected by vecinos and economically threatened by town campesinos, close friendships are too great a burden. For their part, town campesinos find the idea unrealistic, though they say they had close friends in their native villages. According to a town campesino barber:

Amigos de confianza don't exist any more. I have a lot of friends, but not intimate friends. Where are you going to find intimate friends in this day and age? It is impossible to confide in friends. You can't tell a person here anything about your problems without his leaving shortly and telling the whole town or having him make a joke of your problems. Anyone who thinks he can have intimate friends is a fool.

The rapid changes in the social order have produced unusual numbers who are socially isolated. These persons are mainly at the extremes of the status order, such as elderly vecinos and town campesinos, people with few or no relatives and no close friends, who prefer to remain on the margins of the social life of the town. Many are not absolutely alone, for they may have a spouse or a child, and some may be members and even officers of voluntary organizations and take part in civic affairs, but otherwise have almost no social relations. This is a striking thing in a community so small.

FORMAL ASSOCIATIONS

Coroico, though a small town, has a wide variety of voluntary associations—the fraternal Veterans of the Chaco War; educational organizations, such as the Padres de Familia; several religious groups; many sports clubs; labor organizations and the several political parties—but these organizations have contributed little to the social cohesion of the community. Over half the adults belong to none, and those who join do so for narrowly perceived, short-range personal advantage. Few are willing to work for organizations as a means of collective power. As members find that an organization is unable to satisfy their specific interests they drop out, perhaps to join another seemingly more to their purposes. "Everyone who joins a group is looking out for his personal interests. It's all very individualistic."

The Veterans of the Chaco War has perhaps eighty members, but probably no more than fifteen are active and most of these are campesinos, though the leaders are vecino, given to much squabbling but not to beneficial action. One veteran says, "It is a stupidity. The only thing it gets us is wasted time. The government hasn't come through with any effective help [meaning pensions]."

The Mutual Aid Society is an insurance-type association to help pay for medical and burial expenses. It has about seventy-five dues-paying members, but it suffers from misunderstandings among its members about the categories of aid for which they are eligible and the rules under which aid is made available. And it suffers further because of suspicion about the handling of considerable sums of money collected from its vecino and prosperous cholo members.

The religious associations are mostly for women, small, close-knit groups, but even so their membership turnover is very high. They receive religious instruction and are involved in the promotion of Church policy. They would like to see more people at mass more regularly and fewer concubines and unbaptized children. The young girls, particularly, join church groups as a way to get out of the house for a time. In general, the nuns who direct and counsel these females are quite discouraged.

The sports groups take only soccer seriously. The clubs frequently start out with ambitious plans for intellectual self-improvement and dedication to civic projects, but they end up playing ball. Members jump from one club to another, and few engage in serious practice. As in Reyes, membership is strongly governed by social status, but in contrast to Reyes, there is a tendency in some clubs to take on a political coloring. The Uchumachi Club was reputed to be a Falangista stronghold.

While campesinos sindicatos have emerged as centers of power in the countryside, there are many other sindicatos of little national importance. In Coroico, there are sindicatos of local truck drivers, butchers, and small-scale wholesale merchants who take farm produce to La Paz. These sindicatos regulate prices and work standards, adjudicate disputes between members and those who deal with them, and may have some control over jobs; in short, they have a narrow trade-union orientation. Most of Coroico's organizations are tombs of apathy, carnivals of turnover and bedlams of distrust, torn by factionalism and bickering.

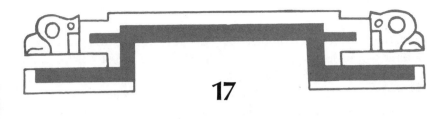

17

COMMUNITY ACTION

There is a pattern of action common to many towns of intermediate importance in Bolivia whenever a move is made to improve or provide facilities that affect its living conditions, such as the building of a public market or the repair of a water system. Municipal projects are the responsibility of local government, but local governments lack means, and cannot float a municipal bond issue, but can only seek the aid of the prefectural government or the national agencies. These are the only sources of sufficient revenue to finance municipal projects, the only possessors of the technical staffs necessary for their planning and construction. Local officials may divert some of their own limited funds and also attempt to stir local support by organizing committees and delegations to impress upon higher officials that the townspeople are committed to action, but the important thing is muñeca, the influence that local officials have at higher levels and the interest that one or more higher officials may have in the particular local officials. This makes for erratic development at the local level, but it does provide a means for redirecting at least a part of tax revenues to some communities.

THE POTABLE WATER PROJECT

Coroico has been one of the towns that has profited from outside aid. It was given funds around 1920 to purchase an electric generator, around 1930 it received funds to build a hydroelectric plant on the Coroico river, and in 1940 it got money for a limited sewer system. Major aid came through the Zuazo brothers, natives of the Yungas who became important figures in the MNR. Julio Zuazo Cuenca was a senator, and, later, in the mid-1940's, a prefect of the Department of La Paz during the first MNR regime. With his support, the town built a new primary school building and a large hotel, and got money for a hospital. Through his brother Eduardo, smaller sums were made available for improving the plaza and the streets around it.

These and other public projects were made possible because prefectural and national officials were interested. After the opening of the all-weather road to La Paz in 1936 many officials spent a pleasant weekend in Coroico, enjoying the warm climate, so different from the rarified cold of La Paz. However, after the Revolution of 1952 Coroico was displaced from its favored political position. While prefectural and national funds were being channeled into the surrounding campesino communities, Coroiqueños endured what they called "twelve years of neglect." The neglect was not total, since it was during the period 1961-63, when Eduardo Zuazo Cuenca was prefect, that the town received funds to improve the plaza and to continue the work on another, larger hydroelectric plant at nearby Huarinella. But it is true that rather little money has been forthcoming for a long time.

The past decade has been a period of deterioration. The old hydroelectric plant operates sporadically. The hospital was never opened because its foundation sank at the start. What there was of it was partially dismantled so that the materials could be used on other projects, and the building is now but a shell. The public toilets have become a public nuisance, the streets are potholes covered by the trash and the slops that are thrown from the houses that line them. So much water escapes from breaks in the water system that during the dry season water frequently must be rationed. During the rainy season there is no shortage, even with the breaks in the line, but then the system is often filled with dirt, debris, and dead animals.

After the fall of the MNR government in November of 1964, the new local FSB officials proclaimed that the era of deprivation was over and that Coroico could look forward to a renewed prosperity. In the following weeks there was considerable discussion of town problems, especially among vecinos. Alcalde Pablo Jimenez, his first deputy, Apolinar Brambila, a druggist, and the sub-prefect, Ignacio Espinosa, brought in the non-local professionals for informal talks. Among them were the dentist, Anastacio Camacho; the town's only physician, Dr. Joaquin Galarza; the administrator of the large prefectural hotel, Martin Dominguez; one of the Franciscan priests, Padre Dionicio Martinez; and the local Peace Corps Volunteer, and finally, the distinguished vecinos, mostly middle-aged or elderly men, many of them at one time officials in the local government. With the health professionals and Church seriously concerned with medical care, discussions turned to the health of the community and the run-down public facilities that threatened its health. Of particular concern were the inadequate and contaminated water system and the absence of a hospital, for La Paz is too distant for emergency medical attention. In addition, Dr. Galarza spoke of the severe problems of inadequate diet and the need for birth control.

By January of 1965 a group of approximately fifteen men, drawn from three chief categories of residents, began regular meetings to discuss possible courses of action. At a meeting on the night of January 12 it was decided to launch a community action campaign, and the repair and expansion of the water system became the first project. The construction of several latrines was second, and the rebuilding of the hospital was third. The group agreed to hold a public rally on the following evening to explain their plans to the community and seek support. Padre Dionicio took the responsibility for organizing the rally and publicizing it. The following day he used the public address system to call all residents to the plaza that evening at eight o'clock to hear an important announcement, and he and the Peace Corps Volunteer, assisted by several townspeople, made signs to be carried at the rally. "Civic Action Committee" was lettered on most of them. That was the name Padre Dionicio had given the community action group.

Typical of Coroico, there were few people in the plaza at eight o'clock, but by nine o'clock nearly 600 had assembled. To the surprise of the throng, they were treated to a parade led by a young man on a motorcycle. There was a drum corps of older school children and a campesino pipe and drum band. Padre Dionicio's "Civic Action Committee" wore arm bands with a picture of a faucet and the slogan, "Civic Action Committee, Potable Water." There were also marching groups of women and children, town campesino men and a contingent of teenagers, carrying a sign that read: "Always Friends Club: The youth of Coroico are ready to collaborate in civic action. Project number one, potable water." Bystanders cheered them on, shouting "Viva Coroico"; "Viva the people of Coroico, the vanguard of progress"; "What do we want?—Potable Water! What do we want?—Clean Water!"; "Viva civic action"; "Viva Peace Corps"; "Viva Franciscan Padres." The crowd was enjoying itself and there was even more cheering for the speeches that followed.

After the parade the civic action group assembled on the balcony of the government building. The alcalde began, emphasizing the new era that was opening for Coroico now that the MNR government had been deposed. He was followed by Dr. Galarza, who spoke of the water system and the need for a new hospital. The two main crowd pleasers were Dr. Camacho, the dentist, and especially Padre Dionicio, both skilled in the Latin American oratorical style. The padre is considered to be the best public speaker in town and was given the loudest applause of the evening. He told the crowd:

> Civic Action is not a special group, but the whole town. The aim is not just potable water, but all necessary improvements. Potable water is first because health has a basic importance. The second project will be sewage and public latrines. The third will be a hospital. There will be others, but these are plenty for now.

> If we can get aid from the prefecture, good. If we can get aid from the national government, good. If we can get aid from USAID or the Alliance for Progress, good. But we have applied for aid before, with the sad case of the Chobacollo highway, and we were ignored. This time we are ready to do what needs to be done with our own strength. Whatever aid we can get would be welcome, but I tell you, people of Coroico, the time has come for us to work on our own if necessary. As the famous Spanish philosopher said, "In unity there is strength, and in strength there is victory." The people of Coroico must unite for civic action, and win the victory of potable water, latrines and sewage and hospital. Win the victory of making our town the model city of Latin America.

The padre's speech got several minutes of shouted "vivas." He concluded by calling for money contributions to the committee, pointing out that there would be many expenses. He also sought to reassure his audience, always suspicious of corruption in the handling of public funds, by saying that he personally would handle all money received and would give a complete accounting to the community of how all donated funds were used.

On the following day Padre Dionicio organized a house-to-house collection. He assigned volunteer pairs of men to different blocks to call at each household and ask for donations. By the end of the day the several teams had collected almost one million bolivianos ($83.33).

On the following Friday night, January 15, an open meeting was held on the potable water project in the town government building. It was late starting, and most of those who came were the same persons who had been active earlier. Much of the discussion was over proposals for raising funds. It was seen that voluntary contributions would never bring in enough to cover the operating costs of the project, so it was proposed that a tax be levied on trucks coming into the town and on beer, and that stiffer fines be exacted for drinking in the cemetery and for not displaying the flag when ordered by the town government to do so. Most favored the tax on trucking, but a decision could not be taken because local officials have no authority to originate new taxes.

The meeting was sidetracked for a time by the issue of the Chobacollo road project, in which townspeople the year before had volunteered their labor to improve an old road that would bring the Caranavi bypass directly through town. A committee collected funds and materials and the volunteer force cleared several sections of the road, but then encountered areas of rock that required heavy equipment and blasting and ravines they would have had to bridge. There being neither heavy equipment nor funds, this community effort came to a dead halt. Up to now the Chobacollo Road Committee has not accounted for the monies collected, with the result that some people who were approached for water project donations refused, on the ground that it would only be another Chobacollo fiasco. It was also recalled at the meeting that the road committee received tools from the prefecture—picks, shovels, and wheelbarrows—and that these would be needed for the water project, and some people wanted the alcalde or sub-prefect to summon the Chobacollo Road Committee to the police station and there require them to give an accounting. The alcalde, however, wanted no enemies, and argued for an informal meeting with the committee to resolve the oustanding questions. Others argued that this was a matter strictly for the local officials, that the Civic Action Committee was not concerned to bring other residents to justice, that this would only cause dissension and impede their own progress.

When someone proposed that a delegation be sent to La Paz to seek aid from the national government as well as USAID, Padre Dionicio commented:

What matters is that we start work. We don't need help from the government. Nor from USAID. Nor from the Alliance for Progress. I don't know where the money is nor where it's to come from, but let's begin work so that we can go on even if they do cut us off. How many times have we waited for help from La Paz? How many times have they ignored our requests? This time it must be different. If we have already worked, we will be in a better position to get aid. We will be grateful if it is offered, but we mustn't ask for it, and then wait around for six months while they "make a study," and then find that it's been forgotten.

The final matter discussed was the fact that the prefect was coming on the following day. Padre Dionicio realized that this was an opportunity not to be lost. Plans were made for an official reception, some were designated to speak on problems in the town, and it was decided to hold a community-wide rally in the prefect's honor. Most of Saturday was spent in awaiting his arrival, no one knew when; and since there are no telephones in the area, no one could know when. As it turned out, the prefect went first to inspect the hydroelectric plant so long under construction at Huarinilla, so he arrived in town late in the afternoon. It was then decided that the prefect—an army colonel from Cochabamba— and his party would go to the hotel for an informal meeting with town officials and civic action leaders over soda and pisco sours. The alcalde opened the session with a short comment on the town's twelve years of neglect, and on its hope for improvement with the change in national government. Padre Dionicio spoke about water contamination and the need to renovate the system. The alcalde got up again to speak of the need for new public latrines. Finally, Dr. Galarza discussed the need for a new hospital. The prefect made no response to any of these appeals, saying he would reserve his answer for the rally that evening.

Everyone left then for a walking tour of the town, so the prefect and his party might see sewage flowing along in open gutters, and piles of trash and filth every few blocks, and the rundown condition of the market, and the public latrines so smelly that close inspection was inadvisable, and the government building wall, which is seriously cracked from top to bottom of its three stories, and offices without adequate furniture or supplies, and the aborted Chobacollo road which cost nearly $50,000. The prefect promised to see whether any of the road funds could be recovered.

Later that evening there was another parade, and townspeople assembled in the plaza to see and hear the prefect. He was preceded by Civic Action spokesmen who restated all their pleas all over again for the edification and stimulation of the citizens. In his turn the prefect complimented the people on their civic interest, and in quick order he gave a personal check for one million bolivianos to the work of the Civic Action Committee, tools and cement to be applied to the potable water project, one-and-a-half million bolivianos to improve the public latrines, the promise that within six months a study would be made of the hospital problem, and a statement of intent to bring suit to recover as much of the money as possible that had been squandered on the road. Even as he spoke, one truck loaded with picks, shovels and wheelbarrows was driven into the plaza, and a few minutes later another one appeared, loaded with bags of cement. Everyone was pleased, and there were many "vivas" for the prefect, for civic action, the Civic Action Committee and the town.

A few days later the alcalde levied taxes on vehicles coming into the town and on beer and liquor, beginning with the week of January 18, though he had not solicited authorization from La Paz to do so. This taxing effort lasted only a few days. Padre Dionicio had hoped that work might begin on renovating the water system during this week, but a large-scale community effort presented too many problems to permit such quick action.

On Friday, January 22, an open meeting was held, well attended by vecinos, at which Padre Dionicio announced a work plan for voluntary groups that he had already organized. He had assigned the residents of each of the eight major streets and their adjoining sections to a single work group, and appointed one or two leading vecinos in each street to be responsible for their group. To each street he assigned one of the five working days of the week, when all the able-bodied male residents were to appear for work on the water project. He suggested that men who failed to appear be fined, not the minimal 5000 bolivianos but at least 10,000 bolivianos, for otherwise everyone would pay and no one would do any work. The prefectural hotel administrator, Martin Dominguez, as head of the sports league, offered the collaboration of all soccer clubs. The meeting accepted the padre's work plan and he announced that work would begin on the following Monday, January 25. Finally, at this meeting the first steps were taken to organize the Civic Action group formally. Padre Dionicio was elected president, the alcalde was elected vice president, Apolinar Brambila, who was the deputy administrator of the town government, was elected general secretary, and Padre Evan Connors became treasurer.

Before work on the water project could begin, Coroico learned that General Barrientos, the new head of the national government, was coming for a visit. It was decided that a reception similar to that held for the prefect would be organized for the general. Unfortunately, again no one knew the hour, though he was expected in the early evening. Shortly after six o'clock the community public address system blared out a call for residents to assemble in the plaza, but by nine o'clock the general had still not appeared and many had gone home despite the exhortations of community leaders. The general's party appeared about 9:30, but having been on the road making speeches since six o'clock that morning, they were all tired and looking forward to a rest. However, the alcalde prevailed upon the general to make a brief appearance, so the group proceeded to the town hall on the plaza, followed by a crowd of townspeople.

The general and the town leaders climbed to the government building balcony and the alcalde opened with a welcoming speech, in the course of which he read a proclamation naming the general an honorary son of Coroico. He was followed by the sub-prefect, Padre Dionicio, and Dr. Camacho, and the general then spoke for fifteen minutes, emphasizing national unity, the non-partisan character of his government, the junta's concern for development, and his personal belief in civic action. This talk was greeted with applause, and the presidential party and the town officials and prominent citizens adjourned to the government meeting room.

The room was crowded with as many townspeople as could fit in, backed against the walls and standing on chairs to get a better view of the general. Padre Dionicio addressed the meeting, reiterating the determination of the community to improve the town and describing again the three initial projects of Civic Action. He ended by calling for financial contributions, pointing out that the prefect had presented the town with a million bolivianos. The general responded by giving two million, to the enthusiastic applause of those assembled, while another half-million was collected from the members of the general's party. Finally, the alcalde called the members of the Civic Action Committee to step forward and be sworn by the general "to uphold the integrity of the community and work selflessly for the improvement of the community." The meeting broke up after this ceremony, and many came forward to embrace the general.

On the Monday after the general's visit work on the water system at last began. Coroico gets its water from about five kilometers above the town, at a place where a stream leaps from the sheer mountainside in a waterfall. From a catch basin at the foot of the falls the water is carried several yards in an open ditch to a large cement pipe, and so to town. There it runs into a large brick-lined storage tank.

This water system, only thirty-five years old, has been completely neg-lected. The catch basin is full of rocks, tree branches and dirt. The filter at the mouth of the concrete conduit does not filter. At many places landslides have broken the pipe. The storage tank lacks a cover and is filled with debris, not water. Many Coroico houses are not piped, and in many of those that are, the piping has decayed beyond repair.

The first week of work was the height of the rainy season. Despite continuous downpour, groups of from thirty to sixty men regularly turned out to cut brush and dig along the water pipe. The alcalde him-self was impressed: "No one gets a cent for all this work. It's simply re-markable." Each day the public address system announced the street that was to work that day and the street that would be working on the morrow. In the evening the names of those who went out to work were broadcast, as well as the names of those who did not appear. The street leaders visited each house on their assigned streets the night before their work party was due on the job, and for doing this they themselves were exempted from the work detail. Each household was required to send one man, or, if it had no man, had to pay for a man to go. By the end of the first week of work enthusiasm was running high. Despite the cross-section of vecinos and officials represented in civic action, most towns-people believed that Padre Dionicio and the Peace Corps Volunteer were the true leaders. In this they were only partly correct, on the Peace Corps Volunteer's testimony:

I didn't have anything to do with this idea of civic action. I'm sure glad it happened, but it was all a big surprise to me. Really, it's all Padre Dionicio's doing. I just sort of got caught up in it and then swept along by it. I was looking for something and this seemed a good opportunity. So I just help any way I can.

The Peace Corps Volunteer was not being unduly modest. He was handicapped by limited Spanish and it was not very clear how he was to work in the community, a question that Civic Action answered for him. On Padre Dionicio's part, he clearly hoped that the Peace Corps Volunteer would be able to get help from United States agencies work-ing in Bolivia.

On January 31, in the midst of this developing civic action, without fair warning, without credible explanation, on only two hours' notice, Padre Dionicio left Coroico. By the following day the news had sped to every corner. Many were incredulous. The padre had been the subject of gossip, but so are most other residents; but no one offered anything like an adequate explanation. Hastily assembled prominent citizens called that same day on the bishop to request that the padre be returned. The bishop said Padre Dionicio had gone back to the United States for a vacation. He indicated that the matter was closed, that he would not discuss it further. The alcalde said, in eulogy, "What a restless man! We need such a person, one who always feels he has to be doing something. And what a speaker! He made people jump from their beds. He had force, dynamism. It is a great loss." With Padre Dionicio gone, the presidency of Civic Action passed to Padre Evan Connors. After twice postponing meetings, he presided over the civic activists on Saturday evening, February 5. By this time, the end of the second week of work, and six days after the departure of Padre Dionicio, defections from work on the water system had become a problem.

On one day a large group of men would appear, but on the next only a handful. There was talk of punishment and it was finally agreed that defaulters would be fined double the going rate of 10,000 bolivianos for a day's work. The meeting was told that the alcalde, the primary school director, and the Peace Corps Volunteer had met with the USAID director of water projects, and that USAID was not interested in patching old water systems but would participate in the construction of a completely new system. The USAID representative estimated the cost at $60,000, and said USAID would contribute up to 50 per cent of this. But the other half—$30,000—was a far cry from the $500 or so that the town had been able to raise.

To dissipate the depressing effect of this news, Padre Evan exhorted the group to maintain enthusiasm and await a technical evaluation of the system. By this date the alcalde had suspended the informally arranged taxes on vehicles and liquor, but a number of other fund-raising possibilities were presented. Among the suggestions were community dances, the sale of food and beverages, raffles, and auctions. In the following three weeks all these different suggestions were tried out, with considerable success. Meanwhile the Civic Action Committee drafted a letter to USAID on February 7, requesting a technical evaluation. Work to clear the pipeline continued through the second and third weeks of the project, but the work force fell off. At the end of the third week of work the alcalde himself, shovel on shoulder, led the town officials and employees out to join the volunteers.

By the end of the fourth week the work crews were down to fewer than twenty men. In the meantime there had been a gradual shift in leadership within the Civic Action Committee. Padre Evan had little of Padre Dionicio's intense interest in community work, and even less of his driving spirit. Besides, the negotiations with USAID required the participation of a local government official, so the alcalde increasingly became the central directing force. It was also at this time that the alcalde was having his problems with the national government.

The Civic Action Committee held another meeting at the beginning of the fifth week of work, mainly to discuss defaulters. Padre Evan noted that in the past few days not more than five men had appeared to work and that this day, the beginning of the fifth week, only one man showed up. The alcalde reported that block leaders had not even handed in the names of those who were not appearing for work, and suggested that even heavier fines be imposed, or even that the water be cut off from the households of the defectors. The dentist, on the other hand, felt that the committee itself was in part responsible for the current situation, since it was holding fewer meetings and rallies. He and others argued for more intensive work to inform the community of the water project and to persuade everyone of its importance. This point of view prevailed, and several committee members were added to the publicity subcommittee, which decided to begin a house-to-house information campaign on the following day. The meeting also decided to reject the resignation of the head of the women's subcommittee, who wrote that she could not carry on because of lack of collaboration. On the following day a special commission headed by the alcalde called on her and persuaded her to stay, promising that she would be assisted by at least a half-dozen women.

On Tuesday, February 23, several Civic Action Committee members started a door-to-door campaign to remind residents that work on the water project was continuing and that it was necessary to keep up the volunteer work. The response was generally sympathetic, most pointing out that in fact they had been participating and would continue. Some women directed the committee members to specific houses from which, they charged, there had been no collaboration.

The Civic Action meeting that was to have been held the next day was postponed because the town's electric generator failed. Despite the renewed propaganda work by the Civic Action Committee, community participation continued to decline because of the pre-Lenten carnival starting on the coming weekend. When the committee meeting took place on Friday it was devoted almost exclusively to a fund-raising program for Sunday, when booths were to be set up in the central plaza for the sale of food and drink.

Beginning on Saturday, children and young adults returned from out-of-town schools, and relatives, friends, weekend visitors, and tourists flocked into Coroico for the carnival holiday, which would continue to Ash Wednesday. The two hotels had been sold out for weeks, and every spare room in town was filled with visiting relatives, friends, or paying guests. On Sunday morning the Civic Action Committee set up booths at the four corners of the plaza, and on Monday and Tuesday the members held fund-raising dances at the alcalde's house. All of these efforts were successful, but the sums raised were not large. Over the holiday, naturally, work on the water project came to a complete halt.

Toward the end of carnival week, the sixth week of the water project, work on the pipeline began to pick up. The alcalde was especially concerned that the interest of the townspeople be revived in time to ensure that a large work party would go out on the following Monday, March 8, when the USAID engineers were to arrive. On Friday, March 5, some members of the publicity subcommittee toured the pipeline so that they would be able to report to the community the progress that had been made to date. They found that the entire length of the line had been cleared of brush and that the catch basin at the upper end, as well as the storage tank at the lower, had been cleared of debris. In addition, approximately 1700 yards of pipe had been excavated, though 2100 yards remained to be uncovered. Sixty yards of pipe that had been uncovered had been again reburied under sliding mud and dirt. Unfortunately, the publicity subcommittee was not able to present their report to the town over the public address system because the town's hydroelectric plant was again out of action as a result of a landslide, and there was a new padre in town who would not authorize use of the church's generator, Padre Evan being absent in La Paz.

Anticipating the arrival of the USAID engineers on Monday, the alcalde dispatched five employees of the town government to augment the voluntary work crew, and the administrator of the hotel, a member of the Civic Action Committee, sent six of his employees. Even with these efforts to create a better impression, there were no more than thirty-six men working that day. Padre Evan, returned from La Paz, agreed that the church generator be used to power the town public address system so that townspeople might be informed of the impending

USAID visit. He also informed the civic action group that the USAID engineers could be expected around noon, but it was one o'clock before they arrived. Most of the officials and several committee members were on hand, and the engineers were taken out to inspect the pipeline, led by the alcalde, one committee member and an employee of the Franciscan padres, who had been authorized by them to help supervise the work, although there had in fact been very little supervision. The party set out at three o'clock and did not return until seven thirty. The engineers were astonished to find that there was no supervising engineer, and they made little effort to conceal their opinion that much of the work to date was wasted.

An open meeting for civic action on the water project was called for that evening to hear a report from the engineers. It began at nine o'clock, with about twenty adults and a few teenagers present. The engineers said they had not come to make promises, nor to give anything away, but only to conduct a study that could serve as the basis for a plan for a potable water system. They pointed out that they intended to spend several days, for the plan would require census data and detailed mapping. When asked about timing, the engineers responded that it would require two months to prepare the technical report, but that by June this should be ready, and that work on the water system could begin in the latter part of the year. The engineers also discussed a number of technical matters, but the most important point was that, while voluntary labor could be counted as part of the required 50 per cent contribution from the town, no work undertaken before the technical engineering program was implemented could be counted as part of the town's 50 per cent. In short, none of the six weeks of labor that had thus far gone into clearing the pipeline would count for anything. In fact, the engineers emphasized that many of the breaks in the line were clearly caused by the workers. When asked point-blank whether the community should suspend the work, the engineers refused to take an unequivocal position, but the implication was clear.

The USAID engineers spent five days inspecting, mapping, census-taking, and interviewing officials. That done, they were skeptical. Said one:

I doubt whether all the land belongs to the municipality. Who knows what kinds of problems would arise once we started to work up there? And the matter of prefectural funds: I wonder how much they can hope to get from the prefecture. As for their own local resources, it seems they've hardly started

collecting funds. Raffles and dances are all well and good, but they need contributions—and large ones—to make up the sum they'll need. They seem to be
living in a dream, irresponsibly waiting for others to do everything for them.
Well, they have a long way to go. The problem is that they are used to having everything come from above. Now they'll want to get money from the
prefecture, and so on. They never think of their own resources. Coroico's not
that poor a town.

The engineers were finished by Friday and returned to La Paz on
Saturday. Their departure brought work to an end. It seemed clear that
the only thing to do now was to await the report of the engineers, but
some people even at this stage doubted whether any good would come
of it. On the night of their arrival the engineers had indicated that the
cost simply of laying six kilometers of pipeline would be 300 million
bolivianos, a sum many considered well out of reach of the town. In succeeding weeks there was little talk of civic action or potable water. When
asked about the project a month later, the alcalde replied:

It's latent at the moment. We're just waiting for the report of the USAID
engineers. But it looks as if it'll be extremely expensive. Maybe 300 million
bolivianos. That would mean 150 million from the town. I don't see it.
We'll have to find some other project more modest, something within our
means. But we'll see when the report is completed.

A month later, in May, a town employee said of Civic Action: "It's
dead. Completely terminated for total lack of interest among the townspeople." The alcalde, however, disagreed with him:

Ah, no, Carlos. More accurately, it's dormant. Since the visit of the USAID
engineers, no one has wanted to invest work in the water project because
we're waiting for their report. But as soon as they make their report—it should
be within a couple of weeks—you'll see that the committee regains its life.

Two weeks later, on June 1, the alcalde received a telegram from
USAID informing him that the engineers' report was completed. He left
the same afternoon for La Paz, taking in a load of his coffee in one of
his trucks. On the following afternoon he met with an official of the
Potable Water Projects office of USAID and was informed that the estimated cost of a new water system for the town was 450 million bolivianos, which meant that the town would have to contribute 225 million.
The alcalde thanked him and said that he thought the town could obtain
a loan from the National Bank on the basis of the municipal agricultural
tax, which yields one to two million bolivianos each month, and the income from the electric power that the new Huarinilla plant would pro-

duce, which should amount to nearly twenty million bolivianos each month. The USAID official agreed to prepare an official letter outlining the proposed water project collaboration between USAID and the town, which the alcalde needed to support his request for aid. After the meeting the alcalde commented that he hoped to have General Alfredo Ovando, co-President of the ruling junta with General Barrientos, authorize a loan from the state bank.

On the following Sunday, almost a week later, the alcalde called a meeting for the next day, June 7. The names of thirty-two persons were on his list, but only ten to twelve showed up. Padre Carlos, who had recently come to town from the United States, explained that by subtracting the estimated materials and manpower that the town could provide, the water project would require 150 million bolivianos in cash from the town. He also reported that donations as well as proceeds from fundraising activities thus far totaled only about twelve million bolivianos. The alcalde reported that the prefecture was unable to offer any financial aid. The state bank was prepared to make a loan, but only if the town could provide evidence of financial solvency. Since the town treasurer had only recently reported that taxes and financial receipts were not even sufficient to pay the salaries of town government employees, this was an unlikely possibility. The alcalde, however, still held out hope that General Ovando might intercede on behalf of the town. There were few even among the civic action stalwarts who shared his optimism.

This was the last meeting of the Civic Action Committee on the potable water project. Life went on as before, and so did the officials. There were other problems, other concerns. A cholo shopkeeper summed up the feelings of many with this comment:

The alcalde told us that now we would have potable water, pure and clean, without microbes, without diseases, and so on. Everybody participated and made contributions. I gave 200,000 bolivianos and several days of work, but what came of it? Nothing. At best, there is less water available to the town than before working on the pipeline. And now there is nothing but silence. No one protests, no one says anything.

WHAT MAKES CIVIC ACTION

The ultimate failure of the civic action water project was perhaps inevitable, but only perhaps. Faced with the astronomical cost of 450 million bolivianos to rebuild a new drinking water system and the slight chance that any significant part of this sum could be obtained from the national government, both the alcalde and the other members of the Civic Action Committee regarded the prospects as hopeless and let the project die. It is quite possible that Padre Dionicio would not have accepted this setback, for he had always insisted that the water project must be basically dependent on the community, not on outside persons or agencies. However, Padre Dionicio was no longer present to champion this viewpoint.

There is in Coroico a pervasive willingness to accept disagreeable conditions. This is a pronounced characteristic of the community. There is no lack of complaining about streets filled with garbage and sewage; the run-down plaza; the malodorous public latrines; the government house of the subprefecture, falling to pieces; the water shortages in the dry season; the muddy, debris-filled water during the rainy season; the lack of economic movement, and so on and on. But in the next breath, instead of proposing solutions, critics berate the townspeople and say how hopeless it is to work with them. When one vecino was asked how Coroiqueños could improve the community, he replied, "Well, there is nothing to be done now because there is no unity among the townspeople. No one is interested in improvement. At this time it is very difficult to think of this community's progressing." Added to the frequent criticism that the townspeople are uninterested, apathetic, and unwilling, if not totally incapable of sustained collaboration, is the reiterated charge that only the politicians profit from community projects:

It is all money-making, all the money they obtain is only for themselves, and they don't do anything that benefits the town. In the twenty-four years that I have lived here I have never seen them do anything with the single exception of the repaving of the streets around the central plaza. I would be pleased to pay these and other taxes in addition, if I could see money from taxes used on projects to improve the town. But up to now the story is always that there is no money, that they can't do anything because they have no funds. I ask myself, where are the millions and millions of bolivianos going that are collected as taxes, aside from those taxes that go to the national government? The fact is that these officials are shameless thieves.

Against this background of adverse criticism and distrust, the carrying out of public works depends largely on the strength of a town official's "connections," on the classic pattern of strong muñeca between governmental levels. Drinking-water systems, hydroelectric plants, hospitals, and government buildings cannot be built by local labor alone, but require substantial sums of money. The successful local politician is one who knows the right people in the national government and who can use them at the right time. Since important local officials, like alcaldes or sub-prefects, are all appointees, these men by definition have some connections at higher levels. In addition, the proximity of Coroico to the national capital, as well as the taxable agricultural riches that surround the town, give it a competitive advantage over more distant, more isolated, poorer communities.

The various public projects that have been carried out in Coroico over the years are evidence of its favorable position. No doubt the politicians have profited from these projects, but so has the town. The twelve years of neglect so often mentioned must be seen as relative neglect, for there are many communities that have never in their history profited as much from government assistance as Coroico.

Suspiciousness about motives, assumptive chicanery of fellow citizens —especially local officials—and presumptuous expectations of outside assistance make local self-help projects difficult to develop. Community projects can be got under way only by a leader who has the will and opportunity to devote considerable time to such activities, and a background and position above suspicion of private financial gain. Such persons do not happen along very often, but Padre Dionicio was one. To many people he not only stood for Civic Action, but personified it, and his associates were considered mere hangers-on. Even critics of the water project approved the central role Padre Dionicio played in Civic Action:

There was a gringo padre here who they say was Cuban. Well, one day this padre decided that he ought to work to get more water for the town. From that time he started a campaign to gain the cooperation of all the townspeople. This padre was a pretty fast worker and—whether good or bad, at times dealing admirably and at other times insulting the townspeople—he organized the work. Practically every person in town collaborated in one form or another.

He excited the townspeople with his flamboyant speeches. He was also trusted, which he recognized when he pointedly emphasized in one of his speeches to the community that he, personally, would handle the account for all monies donated to Civic Action. In contrast to the dominant political custom of seeking outside aid, Padre Dionicio impressed on everyone that the town must first depend on itself, first show by its action that it deserved outside assistance. When Padre Dionicio left the community—probably for reasons unrelated to the water project—he was replaced by another padre more in keeping with the dominant Church style. The community regards the Franciscan mission as a great asset. They have one long-established school and have started another in a near-by former hacienda, wholly supported by the Church. These activities benefit the townspeople but are completely operated by the Church. Padre Dionicio's concern had been with cooperatives, with enterprises of benefit to large numbers of people, requiring their understanding, participation and membership. His successor, Padre Evan, found many reasons to postpone Civic Action meetings and many others for absenting himself altogether. Eventually he handed the job over to another padre, whose comment on civic action in June epitomized the change that had taken place in the Church's attitude: "Our role in Civic Action is simply a vote of confidence in the community. We don't have much else to do with it."

The political style of the alcalde was early forced on Padre Dionicio and the Civic Action Committee by the unexpected visits of the prefect and the President during the early phase of civic action. Even Padre Dionicio appreciated that these were opportunities that could not be turned aside. On the other hand, they provided an excellent showcase for the new FSB alcalde, who was able to present the town as united behind him, sincerely concerned with overcoming its problems and thus deserving of aid. The distinguished and varied group of residents who spoke for Civic Action were indirectly speaking for the continued administration of the town by the Falangistas. If they had been successful in getting the support of high officials, it would have marked the alcalde as a successful politician and himself and his party as being worthy of backing by the townspeople. Since this was a period in Bolivia when military officers, for the most part without party affiliation, were holding most of the important positions, and there was as yet no clear indication how this situation was going to affect the future of the different political parties, the alcalde's actions were tactically prudent.

Local politicians are most concerned with trying to discover what higher officials want to hear. The cues may be subtle, but the alert local official readily picks them up, because he is not in a position to argue. His job depends on pleasing his superiors. If the prefect wants to build a bridge instead of a road, if an agency director wants to build a new water system instead of repairing the old, so be it. This is the successful political style of the local politician, and the alcalde could conceive of no other. That the interest of AID in the water project came to nothing was simply one of the risks of the game.

The uncertain political future of the FSB was also a factor in the death of the water project. The political neutrality of the new military rulers began to waver early in 1965, as General Barrientos sought a means of legitimating his position as the head of the government. Though it was not until many months later that his new MPC party began to organize locally in Coroico, the national political pattern had long since become clear. Some of the local FSB members hoped that General Barrientos would tolerate their continuing in power, but as 1966 came in and wore on it became more and more likely that this would not be so, and that the days of FSB control in Coroico were numbered. Thus, with the passing weeks the alcalde's hope to obtain a large loan in La Paz became increasingly unreal and his own political position increasingly insecure. The trouble lay not in his political approach—for it had succeeded in the past—but in that he was, unfortunately, a stalwart in the wrong party.

The dominant role of a politician like the alcalde in the Civic Action Committee also weakened the water project in other ways. When he approached the campesino villagers to assist the town in the work on the water system they did not refuse flatly; but they did not cooperate. Padre Dionicio might have been able to persuade them to help, but certainly the alcalde could not. This was the comment of one resident on the alcalde's part in the project:

Civic action is a farce. It was supposed to be all nonpolitical and all that. Now the alcalde's put his hand in and there will be no end to it. Now that he's started, Civic Action is dead.

V

SORATA
A Complex
Revolutionized
Community

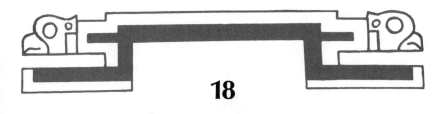

18

THE SETTING

Northwest of the Yungas there is a continuation of the complicated belt of jagged mountains and valleys that descends in a generally northeastern direction from the permanently snow-covered mountain peaks of the eastern Andes into the tropical lowland. North of Lake Titicaca a road climbs the Andes and then begins a dizzying descent. In minutes, the cold, treeless, shrubless landscape gives way to tilled land. In the distance a narrow ribbon of water gleams from the canyon thousands of feet below. At one point the road reaches the end of a mountain spur and crosses to the other side to continue its descent. This side of the mountain looks just like the other, dotted by stands of tall eucalyptus trees between which are checkered squares of farm land. The land is sharply inclined, and hundreds of feet below is the river. Directly opposite, on the edge of a similar spur that forms the other side of the valley, is a large town. On three sides of the town the land falls sharply away for hundreds of feet, while on the fourth side it rises almost as steeply and as far.

Small houses, the homes of campesinos, dot the mountain slopes on all sides. Within sight of the town are a few campesino hamlets, each with its small chapel, and occasionally a new schoolhouse. Here and there the large manor house of a former hacienda can be seen. From an airplane many more farmhouses, farm villages, and casas de hacienda are visible. Sorata commands a spectacular 270-degree view. A shallow valley and rising hillsides lie on the right, a deep valley on the left, and in front a broad valley which, in the distance, cuts through the mountains to enter the lower altitudes. In back of the town is majestic Illampu, highest mountain in Bolivia. The picturesque setting of the town

View of Sorata (Lambros Comitas)

is complemented by a mean annual temperature of 63 degrees Fahrenheit, with few extreme variations. Rains cool the hot summer days, and the winter winds, particularly in July, chill the air enough to keep most people indoors when they blow.

Despite a somewhat aerie-ish location, Sorata conforms closely to the classic Spanish town plan in the New World, with its grid pattern of streets and its two separated plazas. The cutting edge of the spur on which the town lies is only three blocks wide, but where it backs against the mountains the town is seven blocks wide. There is great variation in the size of blocks. Those sloping up from the central plaza (at the center) vary from one-half to one-quarter the size of the blocks that slope down, leaving nineteen blocks above the central plaza, though only nine in the lower half of the town, which is equal in area. The streets do not—as in Coroico—trail into the countryside, but end with the perimeter of the town.

The central plaza, filled with huge old palm trees, is walled with large buildings of two and three stories, some of which themselves enclose an entire block and have two or even three interior patios. On the plaza is a large church, and beside it the new, modern-styled quarters and offices of the resident priests. Along another side of the plaza are buildings owned by the local government, in which provincial and national agencies have their offices. The second plaza looks like the first, but is only half its size. As on the central plaza, many of the buildings here house tiendas as well as shops of various craftsmen, while in the upper stories and in the other parts of the buildings live their families and other renters.

The buildings at the center of town are large and very old, massive in construction, with walls two to three feet thick. Many need paint and extensive repair. Most are heavily decorated in stuccowork architraves, and their windows are enclosed by elaborate iron grills. Toward the edges of town the houses become somewhat smaller, but most are still very old, and two or three stories in height.

On a street off the plaza is the public market, a two-tiered area that has been carved out of the hillside and paved with concrete. The upper tier is a large, roofed, but open square, with counters at which women comerciantes sell their foodstuffs. Down below, in a larger area, women vendors sit on the concrete beside their goods. At the far end of this tier is a covered stall reserved for butchers. One block onward the street breaks at a right angle to wind down into a barranca (ravine), and then climbs the far hillside to the campesino village of Laripata; but a foot-path continues straight on from the end of the plaza street to clusters of new one-room and two-room houses built over the last ten years to accommodate the immigrants from the campo.

Also lying close by are large houses built by well-to-do townspeople who wanted a more open setting, and old casas de hacienda still main-tained as residences. On the road to Laripata is a soccer field flanked by a basketball court and a long-uncompleted swimming pool. Here and there within the town there are open lots planted with corn or fruit trees, while on the edges the continuous built-over pattern is occasionally broken where landslides have carried away walls and buildings.

THE PEOPLE

In 1965 Sorata had a population of 1774 persons, distributed in 520 households. Another sixty-eight persons (not interviewed) maintain per-manent dwellings in Sorata but do not occupy them continuously; they are mostly campesinos whose regular homes are in the countryside, but who attend the weekly market in town and stay two or three nights out of seven. Another nineteen dwellings are owned either by families who have moved away, but who return each year for vacations and fiestas, sometimes spending two or three months in town, or by men who have left temporarily to work elsewhere. Some of the large buildings at the center of town contain as many as twenty-four separate households in the space formerly occupied by a single family.

The culture and traditions of Reyes and Villa Abecia are essentially Spanish, as modified in the New World. The same is true of Coroico, despite an influx of a noticeable number of campesinos. Sorata, in con-trast, is much more Indian in character. Only 54 per cent of Sorata's residents were born in town, compared with 68 per cent in Coroico and 77 per cent in Reyes. In Sorata, 62 per cent speak only Aymara, while in Coroico the comparative proportion is 14.8 per cent. The population of Sorata is mainly cholo and indio, with only a remnant of Spanish-speaking blanco families remaining.

Sunday is the big market day in Sorata, so on Saturday and early Sun-day the campesinos for miles around come by truck and afoot over the trails, bringing agricultural and craft products to sell and to buy staples for the week. On Sunday all the tiendas and all the government offices

A tienda in Sorata (William McEwen)

are open and the streets around the two plazas are full of people. At the corners of the central plaza and at other points along its edges traveling merchants set up stalls where they sell a variety of manufactured goods. The street in front of the public market is lined solidly with campesino vendors, and from mid-morning to early afternoon the area is packed solidly with people. This occurs again on Thursdays, on a much smaller scale. Over the rest of the week there are times when the town appears almost deserted, particularly on Mondays and Tuesdays, the traditional days of rest. All stores and public offices are closed on Tuesdays and many stores shut on Monday afternoon. On these days families either stay indoors or go to the countryside for an outing. This open-shut pattern is rarely interrupted except for family fiestas and major local and national celebrations.

OUTSIDE COMMUNICATION

Sorata is the first town in the northern valleys between the Yungas and the Peruvian border that can be entered by road. Even before the turn of the century a road was completed into the Sorata valleys area from the old road running beside Lake Titicaca between the Peruvian border and La Paz. It did not reach Sorata, but only a near-by mountain ridge. A stagecoach service established at this time took three days, including two stopovers for lodging at night, to cover the distance between its local terminal, seven miles from Sorata, and La Paz. The seven miles to town had to be covered on mules or on foot. In 1920 the road was extended to the town itself, and around 1926 there came a motorized taxi service between Sorata and La Paz.

Today trucks and cars can reach Sorata by road throughout the year. It is an unimproved dirt road, wide enough in most places for only one vehicle. It twists and turns down the mountainsides, which at places are sheer drops of several thousand feet, without walls or guardrails. These heights of the road are sometimes shrouded in fog, and vehicles not infrequently go over the edge, carrying many passengers to their deaths. Once the road reaches down, most of the eighty-five-mile distance to La Paz traverses the level altiplano. The trip can be made in under five hours in a lightweight vehicle, but heavily loaded trucks take half again as long.

There is no regular motor traffic beyond Sorata, except for the trucks that go out to Laripata to pick up produce for the Sunday and Thursday markets. Nor, aside from the trucks, is there any regular motor traffic in or out of Sorata. There are no buses, no railroads, no airlines; and no one in town except the Franciscan priests possesses a private passenger vehicle. The trucks consequently enjoy a monopoly position in transport. Out of Sorata, trails radiate to the many estancias and campesino villages that cover the hillsides and valleys, and whatever is carried over them is on a person's back or on small burros. The outlying hamlets use the Sorata post and telegraph offices, but neither is very efficient. Many of the townspeople entrust their mail to truck drivers or to friends going to La Paz. Truckers returning from La Paz bring in newspapers and magazines, but illiteracy is high, so most of the population get their news by radio. Battery-operated sets are common throughout the countryside. For official communications the local government uses a bulletin board outside the alcaldia, and a town crier, a village Stentor, who roams the town, pausing at the busiest spots to bawl out his proclamations and announcements.

IN TIME

Coroico developed principally as a commercial center for an agricultural countryside. Sorata has been not only that, but also a point of embarkation for the exploitation of the metals and other raw materials in the interior lowlands. As the mountains drop away toward the northeast, the climate changes within a distance of less than twenty miles from temperate to tropical. Along this northeasterly route, approximately sixty miles from Sorata, lies Tipuani, and twenty miles farther on, Guanay. To the northeast of them is Mapiri. These are but three of the more important communities of a tropical interior for which Sorata has been a gateway, through which this interior contributed first gold, then rubber, then quinine, and today, to a limited degree, gold again.

These interior gold fields were being worked in the days of the Incas, well before the arrival of the Spaniards. Thus the Sorata area was doubly attractive to the conquistadores, to those to whom existing Indian agricultural populations in a temperate climate were ready-made for hacienda settlement, and to those who needed a jumping off place into the gold fields. It seems likely that the present town was established by the Spanish before the end of the sixteenth century.

Sorata has had periods of relatively great prosperity out of gold, cinchona bark, and rubber. In 1638 the Spanish in Peru learned of the value of cinchona bark in the treatment of malaria, a scourge throughout the tropical land then being colonized by the European powers. Demand for the bark eventually led to a ruthless exploitation which threatened to exterminate the tree in South America. In the middle of the nineteenth century several foreign firms established cinchona plantations in Sorata's tropical interior. One was that of Otto Rechter in Mapiri, a forerunner of the big commercial houses that were established in Sorata at the turn of the century to exploit natural rubber. Cinchona bark was brought out on mules to Sorata and then carried to the lake for shipment, while provisions for the plantations were brought in over the same route. Plantation cinchona production lasted for approximately half a century, but by 1902 there was a slackening of demand and Bolivian production could not compete with the large Indonesian and other Asian plantations [Pardo Valle, 1951, p. 124]. The plantations in Bolivia were abandoned and wild growth reabsorbed them.

In 1920, partly as a result of international competition in the European drug and chemical industries, the demand for cinchona bark in the world market greatly increased, and cinchona again became important to Bolivia. For example, the Casa Brandt company, one of the large foreign commercial houses of Sorata, established the Hacienda San Carlos on a tract reputed to have been more than 4,500,000 acres, on which they planted a million cinchona trees. Hacienda San Carlos produced more than 10,000 tons of dry bark each year. Despite heavy export taxes, it was a profitable business and endured for over 20 years. In 1943 a root disease appeared and quickly destroyed the plantation. At this time, also, quinine was synthesized (1944), and demand for bark fell away. The big trading houses in Sorata never recovered, and by the mid-1940's they had all departed. Their departure was hastened by protectionist economic policies of the national government, which tended to restrict international commerce, and by the reorganization and centralization of the customs offices in La Paz, which ended the flow of goods out of near-by lakeside ports and made it expedient for the trading houses to move to the capital.

In the tropical lands below Sorata wild rubber grew in abundance. At the turn of the century the rapidly increasing use of rubber drove the world price to new highs. In 1890 it was $.67 per pound. By 1903 it had risen to $1.00 per pound, and by 1910 to $2.09 per pound [Knorr, 1945]. The boom in rubber drew large numbers of investors, entrepreneurs, and adventurers to Bolivia, many of them European, and several large foreign trading houses were founded in Sorata. Prominent among these was the German Casa Brandt, the English Casa Boston, and the Spanish Casa Perez. With these firms came their top administrative and other key business personnel and their families. They brought rubber collected by local tappers out by mule train to Sorata, there prepared it for shipment, and, again by mule, sent it to one of the port towns on Lake

Titicaca for transport by boat to Peru and abroad. On the return trip the mule trains brought in goods from overseas that were consumed in the town, and in a second stage took in provisions from Sorata to the lowland interior for sale to the rubber tappers. This commerce was profitable in both directions, and the large commercial houses prospered greatly.

While Bolivian rubber production steadily increased during the decade between 1903 and 1913, it leveled off after this period. One of the causes was the introduction of an export duty on rubber in 1913, which made it a somewhat less profitable commodity. Of even greater importance was the increasingly unfavorable competitive position of wild rubber. By 1914 the more efficiently produced plantation rubber was beginning to have a significant impact on the world market. Thus, while 99.7 per cent of the world's rubber produced in 1905 was wild, the proportion had fallen to 55 per cent between 1909 and 1913, and to 5 per cent between 1925 and 1929 [Pando Gutierrez, 1947, p. 221]. That Bolivian production, which was all wild rubber, did not similarly decline, but remained practically constant until 1920, is the result of the greatly increased demand for rubber that was stimulated by World War I. However, by 1920, production of the more costly wild rubber began to decline to approximately 50 per cent of its earlier levels. With the international economic depression of the 1930's, wild rubber production sank to lows from which it never has recovered. The big commercial houses in Sorata, however, did not experience a similar decline, for, fortunately for them, the market for quinine opened again.

Throughout all of these decades gold deposits were found, were mined out, and then new ones were sought in the tropical interior below Sorata, especially around Tipuani. Up until the twentieth century most of this mining was undertaken on a small-scale by individual entrepreneurs, such as Villamil de Rada of Sorata. However, beginning in the early 1900's, most of the Tipuani gold properties were acquired by the Aramayo Company, one of the three mining firms that came to dominate the exploitation of Bolivian ores. The mining of gold, in contrast to the exploitation of rubber and cinchona, did not have as strong an impact on the town as a whole, for it did not stimulate the development of important new forms of economic activity. No large amounts of gold came into Sorata. The quantities mined were not great, and, besides, all gold was required by law to be sold only to state banks in La Paz. Sorata's trading houses benefited by selling provisions to the miners and by transporting heavy equipment into the mining areas, while some lesser merchants also profited from stolen gold brought out by miners and sold or traded in Sorata. However, much of the provisioning and transport business to the mines ended by 1947, when landing strips were built at Tipuani and Mapiri for direct flights to La Paz.

Closer to the town are rich deposits of other metals—zinc, tin, copper, tungsten, and lead. Small quantities of these ores have been taken out over the years by individual entrepreneurs, using peons from the near-by haciendas. Some of these properties have been worked by Sorateños. The outstanding large-scale mining efforts in this area are the Matilde zinc and lead mines, once owned by the Hochschild Company, one of the big Bolivian mining corporations. The chief effect of these local operations on the town was to provide jobs. One of the important vecinos in the town today is a former Matilde mine administrator who married into an important land-owning family in Sorata.

Mining, especially gold mining, has had a much stronger impact on Sorata since the Revolution of 1952. One of the first acts of the new MNR government was to nationalize the mining properties of Aramayo, Hochschild, and Patiño, the giants of Bolivian mining. While arrangements were being made for the legal transfer of these properties and the formation of a government corporation (COMIBOL) to run them, the miners in the Tipuani gold mines seized the properties and organized a cooperative. When COMIBOL officials arrived to take over in Tipuani they were met by an armed contingent of miners who forced them to return by the same plane to La Paz. By a special national government order, the Tipuani miners were permitted to retain cooperative control of the mines but were required to deliver all gold to government representatives at the official price. These mine cooperatives have provided a greatly increased source of income to the mine-workers, many of whom are campesinos from the haciendas around Sorata, and a part of this income has found its way back to Sorata.

The big mines that were taken over by COMIBOL have had a rather different history. Operations in many of these had become antiquated and COMIBOL management was often inexperienced, its personnel inadequately prepared, and, in particular, its policies designed more to benefit mining personnel than to provide government income. The Matilde mine, though reputed to contain up to three million tons of ore, closed in the turmoil of the Revolution and was never reopened. In recent years the government has sought to interest foreign mining corporations in the Matilde mine, but it would need large-scale and expensive improvement. Early in 1966 excitement was stirred in Sorata by the announcement that Japanese and American firms had made offers to lease the Matilde mine. Such a development would likely mean the construction of one or more auxiliary plants close to Sorata itself, from which the town and its economy would profit in many different ways.

Prospecting for gold (Lambros Comitas)

The Revolution of 1952 had a variety of more immediate economic, demographic, and political effects on Sorata than those that flowed from the changes in the Tipuani and other mines. Many of these paralleled developments in the Coroico region. Most of the surrounding countryside was divided into large haciendas owned by a small group of families and worked by peons tied to the haciendas by strong economic and social bonds. The Quintana family owned well over 1000 hectares. Their hacienda stretched from just outside town right to the top of the surrounding mountains and contained 120 campesino families. Another important local family, the Palacios, owned a hacienda of about 1000 hectares, worked by about fifty campesino families. The hacienda Chilcani had over 100 campesino families. As in other areas, the hacienda peons were given the right to cultivate a small plot of land for their own use in exchange for their labor, which varied from three to five days each week, depending on the hacienda. In addition, each peon was subject along with his wife to a variety of further labor and other obligations.

As in Coroico, the Revolution brought an end to the hacienda system, but the end here neither came so quickly nor was as complete. The extent of land seizure depended on the classification of property as small, medium, or large. The productivity of the land in turn determined the definitions of these three categories. Most of the haciendas in the Sorata area were classed as medium properties. While most of the haciendas were broken up, the majority of the hacendados were able to keep a portion of the land they formerly had under cultivation. But under the agrarian reform they were forced to cultivate their land either with wage labor or under a sharecropping arrangement. This the hacendados of Sorata have done, as those of Coroico have not.

At the same time, Sorata hacienda peons were organized in campesino sindicatos. Leadership in this development was taken by MNR officials from La Paz and by local campesinos who had been miners and had had experience in the mining sindicatos. Geography in these more recent political changes has been important. The road into Sorata branches off the lakeside road on the altiplano at the town of Achacachi, known as one of the two major centers of campesino political militancy in Bolivia. With the armed, belligerent, anti-patrón, anti-blanco Achacachi sindicatos sitting astride communication into Sorata, Achacachi sindicato dirigentes exerted a strong influence on the sindicatos around Sorata to arm their members and to assert their political and economic rights. One of the most important outcomes of this development was the early replacement of townspeople by campesinos in the various offices of provincial and local government in Sorata. This in turn accelerated the emigration of blanco families, who had begun to leave Sorata almost a decade earlier, when the cinchona boom ended. Over the years, they have been replaced by growing numbers of campesinos, until today town campesinos comprise close to two-thirds of the Sorata population, while most of the remainder are cholos. Only a handful of the blanco families remained; the others have long since left for La Paz, or for Argentina, Brazil, and other countries.

Many of the foreign businessmen who came in boom days married into old Spanish landowning families of the town and in this way the town's two principal forms of economic enterprise were joined together. It was international commerce that was the major source of wealth. As in other parts of the New World, many of the patróns were land-poor. This was a period when money circulated freely. It is recalled as a kind of golden age. One elderly woman who carries a distinguished family name says:

Oh, in my generation, when I was a girl, around 1906, 1910, 1915, then Sorata was a booming town. Each trade house had at least fifteen employees, foreigners and their families. From Sorata they'd ship the cargoes to La Paz. The imports came directly from Lake Titicaca, and from there to Sorata. We drank the best kind of liquors. We traded with English sterling then, it ran so freely in town. We could afford to have whatever we wanted, and parties with real orchestras all the time.

The distinguished Palacios family, who divided their time between La Paz and Sorata, used to house and entertain as many as seventy guests at a time, providing everything from linen to whisky during fiestas that lasted for as long as twenty days. Not only the once wealthy blancos, but also cholitas with their little tiendas, remember this as a period of affluence for themselves. According to one, "Once there was movement. In a little tienda just like this one, for instance, we always had lots of money on hand." And, acccording to another, "I myself notice this difference. I was left a widow, young, with lots of children. I had to work day and night. But there was selling then. I'd make a blouse one night and it would sell the next day. Now those blouses sit around."

These are only memories, but they live on to influence present outlook and action. In addition, the signs of decay on once palatial residences, the sight of a distinguished blanco couple waiting on campesinos in their tienda, and the presence of campesinos from the estancias as officials of the local government are more objective evidence of the major changes that have occurred in the town in the past twenty years, and especially in the last decade.

While for some the golden age has long been dead, replaced by a period of decay and dislocation, others have a rather different view. For these the past is seen as a burden, while the present is a time of promise.

In the following comment of a young campesino who has his home with his father and sister in Sorata, but lives and works on a near-by ex-hacienda, this view is expressed in terms of the changed relations between campesino and blancos, whom he calls vecinos:

Before 1952 the campesinos could not pass without offering a greeting to the vecinos. Even if the distance was great, one had to greet them, taking off his hat and bowing. And if the greeting was not acknowledged, my father told me to walk half-way around them, to make sure they saw the greeting. Also, there were some vecinos who did not like campesinos to walk in front of their homes or their tiendas, and always made them go around the back of their buildings. That's the way it was before. Now? Well, now you don't pay attention to those things. When a vecino says, "That stupid campesino," we ask, "What's the matter? he's no more stupid than you." Or when they walk down the road as if they own it, never greeting anyone, we say, "He's just like an animal." Or, "What's the matter with that 'misti' [vecino]?" We dress the same, our head is the same, our belly is the same, our heart is the same. We're just not going to pay any attention to him and won't greet him either.

TOWN ECONOMY

Sorata is still a town of trade and commerce. However, the large-scale international commerce of a few big trading houses has been replaced by small-scale buying and selling by a large number of merchants geared to the surrounding area. Close to one-third of the labor force in town earn at least a part of their living by buying and selling goods. About half of this number are comerciantes, and at least two-thirds of these are women, though this estimate is particularly unstable because local selling is almost invariably a family enterprise, the man directing, his wife filling in for him behind the counter, and the older children perhaps augmenting the sales staff or watching the store during slack periods.

The town is full of small retail sales establishments, not only around the central plaza, where they are traditionally located, but also in all the smallest, most peripheral streets. Around the two plazas and near the center of the town are the bigger tiendas, which carry a good stock of household necessities, like kerosene, candles, canned goods, noodles, sugar, flour, and bread; but also flashlights, one or two transistor radios, china dishes, and similar more expensive and less frequently purchased items. Many also sell at wholesale to tienda comerciantes in the more distant hamlets. Scattered throughout the town is a second level of tiendas, which restrict their goods almost completely to household neces-sities. Finally, there is a third level of tienda, much more numerous than either of the other two, in which there is specialization in the sale of one or a few articles. Some of these sell only fruit, others only bread, others only noodles, some a combination, such as fruit and pancitos. As with several other types of work in town, especially those in which women are predominant, the smallest tienda is economically marginal, viable only because the woman's time is not considered a cost.

The other half of the comerciantes in Sorata are the traveling mer-chants. While a handful of these are men operating on a large scale, buy-ing up truckloads of farm produce for sale to large retail dealers in La Paz, about 95 per cent are women doing small-scale buying and selling of agricultural products, much of which goes to La Paz. For the majority of these women the buying and selling of agricultural produce is a prime means of support. Most have one or more small children to care for, and, though in some cases they are married, the husband is frequently absent, working elsewhere, often in the Tipuani mining area. Most of these women comerciantes, but not all, belong to the Sindicato de Comerciantes Minoristas de La Paz. Non-members are required to pay a fee to the sindicato before they are permitted to travel with produce to La Paz. These minoristas, the female comerciantes, go by truck from Sorata to the near-by hacienda village of Laripata every Thursday and Sunday to buy their fruit and vegetables in wholesale quantity from the rescatadors who have brought it in by mule to the Laripata market. Working with little capital, they buy several bundles of seasonal produce and have it trucked back to Sorata.

If they are taking the produce to La Paz, they leave on trucks early Friday and Saturday mornings. The Sorata minoristas congregate on the same streets in a section of La Paz where the sidewalks are an open-air vegetable market. They sell from Thursday afternoon until Saturday morning and from Monday afternoon until Wednesday morning. Early Saturday and Wednesday the trucks pick them up again for the return trip to Sorata. If they have not sold all of their produce by departure time, many of them will leave what remains with a local minorista who receives a part of the profits for whatever she sells.

The markets in Sorata each Sunday are jammed from early morning until early afternoon. On Calle Muñecas below the central plaza is the big formal market for vegetables, meats, and fruits such as bananas and chirimoyas. Most of the vendors there and in a triangular plot across the way are comerciantes, male and female, from the altiplano, mostly from Aymara lakeside communities. Most of the comerciantes in this three-cornered marketplace sell the same staples, fish, and whatever is being harvested from their irrigated lakeside plots, such as onions or carrots. Along the street between the two markets sit sellers of a variety of other things from the altiplano Indian communities—reed flutes, leather thongs and ropes, flower and vegetable seeds, metal plow tips and other agricultural tools, and so on. From there up to the central plaza, cholo comerciantes from La Paz set up stands for the sale of manufactured clothing and derby and fedora hats.

As in the Coroico area, the hacienda system by which most of the land around Sorata was owned and worked was swept away in the early years following the Revolution, and the former peons now have their own plots of land on which they plant one or two crops for sale. In the area around Sorata the major cash crop is maize, but wheat, squash, barley, beans, peas, peaches, pears, plums, and apples are grown in small quantities. Many campesinos also raise pigs and chickens and sell eggs. A very few also have a cow or two, and at the higher altitudes some raise sheep. Potatoes are grown above Sorata, and in the lowlands the chief cash crops are tomatoes and citrus fruits.

The decline of agricultural production after the Revolution, a decline exaggerated in reports by those opposed to agrarian reform, and assessed only in very inexact terms, seems attributable in part to the dislocation in the agricultural marketing mechanism. Some of the campesino agriculturalists in the Sorata area sell to the Sorata tienda comerciantes. Apart from the sale of crops to comerciantes, there is a great deal of minuscule trade in a few eggs, a chicken, a few peppers or some wild honey, a small bundle of potatoes or beans or a squash, sold or bartered in the tiendas for kerosene, matches, or candles. Campesinos for whom Sorata is more than a day's walk are likely to make quantity sales to a campesino rescatador, who then takes his purchases once or twice each week to a market such as that in Laripata, where all will be sold in bulk to the minoristas. Sorata itself consumes but a small part of the agricultural produce of the region. But trade is active because of the emergence since the Revolution of the campesino rescatadors and wholesale agricultural produce markets like that in Laripata, and because of the minoristas who trade with the cities—a complex replacement for the hacienda marketing system, and a new and vital part of the agricultural economy.

Most crops in the Sorata area depend on rainfall alone; there is almost no irrigation. Fields are plowed and seeded in August and September to be ready for the rains that begin around November. With maize, once the plowing and seeding have been completed, there is relatively little work until the harvest, which usually begins the following April and may last until June. Some campesinos, in the free time between, work additional land in the Alto Beni colonization zone around Caranavi, and regularly move back and forth. A few of the younger men go to La Paz for some form of unskilled work, especially if they have a relative there, but the majority go to the mines, mostly to the Tipuani gold fields. In fact, mining is so prominent in the lives of both town and rural campesinos that it has become almost a symbol of a man's having come of age. Tipuani has become for the young men the exciting world beyond the familiar home and rural village, and they chafe to follow in the footsteps of their fathers and older brothers, leaving for the mines when they are fifteen or sixteen, some even at twelve.

In Tipuani there is work for all. Some of the mining is strip work, off the surface, but most of it involves tunneling, even under the river. The work is heavy, and the suffocating heat makes it even more strenuous. The shoring in the tunnels is often inadequate, and men who are not crushed in a collapse may well be drowned. Seventy men died in one tunnel disaster. In addition to such risks, the rainy season brings the threat of flooding from swollen streams, and there are disabling injuries and the chance of pulmonary disease. But beyond the hazards there are rewards. A laborer in Tipuani can earn $1.00 to $1.50 a day, almost twice what an unskilled worker receives in Sorata. Instead of wages, some laborers prefer to have a sack of tailing, which may yield up to $300 in gold for a month's work—or the yield may be very small, or nothing at all. These men are called voluntarios.

The veteran miners and the more affluent campesinos who have joined them are members of the cooperatives that run these mines for the government. A membership share in one of the cooperatives costs from $160 to $800, the price varying like corporate stock, rising and falling with the current earnings of the cooperative and with estimates of anticipated productivity. All shares are held by working members of the cooperatives, whether miners, haulers, weighers, or accountants. Members have no rights to any particular job, but rotate through all of them.

At the end of each day each cooperative exchanges its ore for currency at the local branch of the Banco Minero, the state mining bank, the national government being the only legal purchaser of gold. The cooperative deducts costs and expenses and divides the remainder in equal sums along all its members. Shares may double or triple in value, but much depends on chance, rich veins of gold becoming thinner and thinner until the daily earnings hardly pay the living expenses of the members. The campesino who joins a successful cooperative may stay for six to ten months, but almost all return by September for the fiesta patronal and the plowing and planting. While many earn little or nothing beyond their daily expenses, some come out ahead, and a few are able to amass substantial sums. In any case, they are probably not worse off than before they went, for on the estancias or in town there are few opportunities for profitable work.

Most campesino miners who are very successful leave the campo entirely and settle in town. This has been going on since 1952, until today they constitute the largest occupational group in town after the two types of comerciantes, and, if only men are considered, they are the largest group. A great many of the houses once occupied by big foreign traders and hacienda patróns, the largest and most ostentatious of which are on the central plaza, have passed into the hands of campesino miners.

Most campesinos who go to the mines hope to earn enough over a period of several years to launch a new and permanent business enterprise. One of the most desired businesses is truck transportation. The large Toyota, popular with truckers, costs about $5500, a very substantial sum even for the luckiest miners, but generally more than half of this can be borrowed. There are now fifteen trucks in town making the twice-weekly run between Sorata and La Paz, all of them owned by town campesinos or cholos, none by a vecino.

Most truck owners are also drivers. All of these owner-drivers live in Sorata, but they spend as much time on the road and in La Paz as in town. For this reason some keep their wives and children in La Paz, where school facilities are better, and rent a room for themselves in Sorata. Carrying passengers and cargo, they make $50 to $60 a week. All drivers, including owners who are drivers, are organized in a sindicato which keeps tight control on transport activities. No truck is allowed to make the run to La Paz without sindicato authorization, and the rules are that the trucks must line up in convoy order for departure on Friday and Monday mornings. Drivers are not permitted to take non-paying customers, are not allowed to compete for the minorista clients of other drivers, and must abide by a schedule of charges fixed by the sindicato.

A second occupational aspiration of the campesino miner is to become a tienda comerciante, but this is a riskier business. Miners invest in small stocks of goods and set up businesses which are operated for the most part by their wives, while they themselves continue to devote most of their time to mining. The varied buying and selling, the different conditions in the town, rural, and city markets, all require the learning of a varied set of new skills. The limited education of most campesinos has not prepared them for this type of work, but some have been quite successful. One of them operates one of the biggest tiendas in Sorata.

There are few of the old landowners left in town. Almost all have died or emigrated, but many more, as absentee owners, have the land that was left to them worked by campesinos. In the first few years following the Revolution the efforts of the MNR government to organize the rural campesinos into sindicatos, the hostility toward the patrón that was engendered in this effort, and the unsettled conditions in the countryside, resulted in the abandonment of haciendas. After this early turmoil, and especially when it became clear that the Agrarian Reform Law was going to permit the patróns to retain a part of their haciendas, they began to reassert their rights. Different patróns placed different interpretations on just what those rights were, as did the different sindicatos. Their major problem was how to get their land cultivated.

The Agrarian Reform Law permitted two arrangements. Either the patrón could pay wages or he could give up half the harvest for campesino labor. In either case he was required to supply seed and tools. The patróns rarely pay wages because they no longer have the capital, so cultivation of their small parcels is all done on shares; though there are variations from the legally prescribed arrangements. Some patróns take 60 per cent of the harvest, some take half, but do not provide seed or tools; and some take even more than 60 per cent and still provide nothing. They invest little, and certainly not for improved agricultural methods. So the land around Sorata is worked as it has been for centuries. Fields are still cleared by cutting and burning them over, and while fertilizers were introduced in 1965, their use is limited.

Over a third of the town's work force is made up of skilled workers and craftsmen who supply the variety of skills and products typical of rural central market towns, including furniture. There are substantial numbers of masons, as well as woodcutters and carpenters who utilize the trees that are abundant below Sorata—pine, cedar, myrtle, walnut, eucalyptus, and palm. There are butchers and bakers, shoemakers, tailors, and hatters in great numbers. Dressmaking is one of the important women's occupations, though it does not rank with shopkeeping or minorista trade. To eke out their income from dressmaking many women are weavers, almost as many as there are miners whose homes are in town. Some spin their own wool, others buy it ready-spun, but all do their own dyeing and designing. They all make aguayos, a vari-colored wool blanket approximately three feet by six feet, woven in a week or ten days, and used as a sleeping blanket, as a shawl, and as a bundle wrapper. Much of the produce brought up by the minoristas is carried to La Paz in aguayos.

In the early years after the Revolution many local craftsmen were organized into a sindicato de gremiales, but it was never very active and has been defunct for many years, defying efforts to reorganize it in 1966. This is rather symptomatic of the economic situation of many craft workers. The Sorata crafts market has been oversupplied for some time, so craft workers and some skilled workers have had to seek sales outlets farther afield. Most shoemakers try to sell part of their production in other communities as far off as the adjoining provinces. Many of the woodworkers spend only a part of the year in Sorata and then go to other woodcutting regions in search of temporary employment.

In addition to there being a limited market, there is marked cyclical buying. The big town fiestas are not only the recreation highpoints of the year, but also the sales highpoints for comerciantes and craft producers. During slack periods a shoemaker will run a small tienda on the side, or a carpenter will double as a mason. The situation is further aggravated by the machine-made products that are pushing hand-made articles out of the local market. Finally, there is the larger number of campesinos and sons of campesinos seeking town jobs. Around 15 per cent of the labor force is comprised of unskilled laborers, mostly town campesinos who attach themselves to skilled or craft workers for a nominal wage, and, after a year or two of apprenticeship, try to compete with their former teachers, further glutting the market.

The final occupational group of importance is that of the professionals and the empleados, the white-collar-type workers. These are the higher professionals—the doctor, the dentist, the two highest judges, the agricultural extension agent, the nurses occasionally present, the priests, the teaching nuns, and the public school teachers—all outsiders who do not expect to stay in Sorata. In some cases, though far from all, these professionals spend considerable time away from the town, either in the capital or in the towns from which they came. Then there are the quasi-professionals, the tinterillos who are self-taught lawyers, the midwives, and the curanderos, the traditional healers. Finally, there are the empleados who hold minor public jobs and clerical positions. All of the different professionals and empleados combined are less than 5 per cent of the local work force.

Local economic enterprises stay small because, perhaps, of limited capital and little credit. Many of the persons who have here been termed comerciantes are simply individuals who may sell nothing more than pancitos, small rolls set on stands in the doorway, or have a half-dozen staple foods brought in by truckers to sell to campesinos from the countryside. The working capital of such comerciantes is no more than $25. Even with ambition, and possibly talent, most would have great difficulty in raising capital, and if they could it would cost too much.

There are no banks in town. At one time there was a branch of the Banco Minero, the state bank authorized to purchase mineral ore, but it was closed in 1965. A few lend money, but interest rates are high, varying from 4 per cent to 10 per cent a month, and lenders almost always require that substantial assets be advanced as guarantees that loans will be repaid. More frequently, borrowers will go to friends or compadres who probably will not even ask for interest, but the sums that can be borrowed from friends and compadres are generally small.

With money in limited supply, some of the larger tienda comerciantes selectively sell on credit, but the small comerciantes cannot, for credit sales involve considerable risk. Even the purchaser may be the loser in credit transactions, for often the comerciante keeps no records, and the debt is what he says it is. Gregorio Vogel, who operates what is left of the Casa Brandt, now a large tienda, by keeping exact accounts and being scrupulously fair has earned so great a reputation for honesty that he is entrusted with some of the functions of a bank, cashing and holding monies for the repayment of loans. He conducts this banking business out of a huge antique safe, a remnant of the golden age of the Casa Brandt.

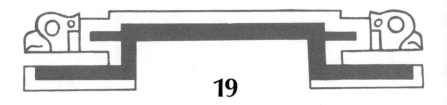

19

POWER AND
AUTHORITY

Sorata is a rural town similar to Coroico in many respects. They are the largest towns in their immediate areas, the chief marketplaces of their regions, and each is the capital of a province. They are both old Spanish towns, the commercial and administrative centers of a countryside owned and worked for generations by Spanish hacienda patróns.

There are also structural and environmental resemblances, but as a consequence of the Revolution of 1952 there are now some very striking contrasts between the two towns. The emigration of vecino mercantile and landowning families has altered the character of Sorata's population, now primarily town campesino and cholo, with all the socio-cultural changes that this implies. Other changes, political in character, have had equally profound effects. In the three towns thus far examined, each found more or less successful ways of coping with the realities of the Revolution of 1952. The impact of the Revolution was minimal on Villa Abecia, somewhat greater on Reyes, while in Coroico the impact was serious indeed, and changes there have been many and important. Nevertheless, much of the cultural and social tradition of the first two towns has been maintained in the face of radical challenges from national governmental legislation and programs, and even in Coroico a good part of it survives. Sorata is like Coroico, but unlike the other two towns, in having experienced drastic changes in the Revolution. In contrast to Coroico and the other two towns, it has been more thoroughly transformed by these changes. Very little remains of the old Spanish town of Sorata. The town has for many years now been a pawn in the campesino play for power, and the effects of this are everywhere present.

ECONOMIC POWER AND ORGANIZATIONS

In Villa Abecia wealth was grapes, in Reyes cattle, and in Coroico coffee. In Sorata the first major source of real wealth was goma (rubber), and then cinchona bark. The scale of international commerce in these products was profitable far beyond the counterpart enterprises in the other three towns, which made hacienda agriculture relatively less remunerative and less important to the wealthy families of the community. Further thrusting hacienda agriculture to secondary status was the lower productivity of the land at Sorata altitudes under dry-farming conditions.

The decline of goma and cinchona commerce has reduced the wealth of the town and the agrarian reform program has diffused it. Both of these changes have been significant in vitiating economic power in the community. From being a strategic link in a large-scale commercial chain, Sorata has become a regional market town characterized by small-scale retail trade and small-crop agricultural commerce. The few great commercial houses have been replaced by many dozens of rescatadors and negociantes, town commerciantes and the minoristas, as well as by hundreds of buying-and-selling campesinos. Instead of a few dozen patróns who sent large quantities of agricultural produce to market, there are now hundreds of campesinos who participate both directly and indirectly. The rise in the number of participants in the agricultural market is reflected in the development of new wholesale markets, like that in Laripata. The inability of the local market to absorb the greater agricultural production, as well as the inability of local producers and intermediaries to deal with distant markets, led to the development of the minorista trade.

The combined process of declining scale and growing numbers in agriculture has been paralleled in town in the tiendas and related outlets for retail trade. In Coroico, the mini-scale production which followed agrarian reform and diffused the economic power of the haciendas was stabilized with less loss in gross value by the large-scale trading function of the coffee rescatador. In that case, concentrated economic power merely shifted from the pre-Revolutionary hacendado to the post-Revolutionary rescatador. In Sorata, no such countervailing mechanism developed. The trading intermediaries, the town comerciantes and the traveling minoristas, multiplied almost as fast as the campesino agricultural producers, with the result that the economic power potential in Sorata is rather thoroughly dispersed in the whole population.

Agricultural production and distribution, as well as the buying and selling of retail goods, vary considerably, but the range is from small to minuscule. Only three or four tiendas, some of whose owners are also buying and selling agricultural produce as well as transporting these and other goods, are high on the scale. Significantly, these few important comerciantes are almost equally divided among vecinos, cholos, and town campesinos. In general, it has been the cholos and town campesinos who have inaugurated new enterprises, mainly trucking, perhaps invariably with Tipuani gold mine wages as capital.

With most vecinos either impoverished or living a marginal economic existence, with commerce dominated by cholos and town campesinos but highly fractionated, with the lowly campesino moving in increasing numbers into crafts and skilled jobs and entrepreneurial trucking and local commerce, there no longer exists an economic elite in Sorata, nor are the few outstanding entrepreneurs a socially homogeneous force. The result is that certain individuals are influential and many individual actions are influenced through economic forces, but few social relations are based on economic power. The stable economic differential on which the power relations were based between the big merchant and his employees, or the big merchant and his debtor clients, no longer exists. No group in Sorata any longer commands great economic resources, and the few individuals who have been successful in recent years are still far from establishing themselves as dominant figures.

Collectively, however, there is economic power in the town sindicatos. There are two sindicatos presently active in Sorata, those of the minoristas and the transportistas. Both are branches operating under regulations set by parent organizations in La Paz, and both are concerned almost exclusively with economic issues, in contrast to the very politically-oriented campesino sindicatos. For the most part these issues are control of access to jobs and the regulation of charges and conditions of work in each occupation. The truckers' sindicato (the Sindicato de Transportistas del Altiplano) has come to play a vital role, not only in the operation of the town's economy, but more generally in the linking of the town to the outside world, because the truckers provide the only means for moving people or things in or out of the town. In addition, the truckers are a relatively small group, which solidifies the influence of the sindicato. Finally, the sindicato's secretary general, its principal officer, is an energetic, outspoken, intelligent person, with experience as an official in the La Paz headquarters.

The truckers' sindicato has no regular schedule of meetings, but meets whenever the secretary general or one of the other members raises a problem that requires action. Technically, only members are permitted to attend these meetings, which are generally held in the early morning just before the trucks depart from Sorata, but owners who regularly accompany their drivers are permitted to attend, along with anyone connected with the topic or problem behind the meeting. At these meetings hearings are held on the violation of rules, such as driving out of turn and picking up the regular passengers of another driver.

The violation of sindicato rules is regarded as a serious matter by almost all members. The punishment meted out is strongly affirmed by most members, and the violator generally accepts his punishment without complaint. The unceremonious dispatch with which this discussion and adjudication process takes place, so different from conduct in other town associations and organizations, is due not only to the firm leadership of Eduardo Soruco, the secretary general, but also to the strong social bonds that have formed between the members of the sindicato. As one of the more prominent driver-owners says, "We must consider it a sacred duty to respect the rules because we issue them ourselves, and we must respect each other as brothers." Similarly, on the proposed construction of a religious shrine with sindicato funds along the Sorata-La Paz route, another driver said, "We do this to give us good luck on our journeys, and also as a pledge of affection and harmony among the truck drivers."

Many of the regulations of the sindicato are means for controlling potentially ruinous competition. Only members in good standing are permitted to operate along the main routes, and one of the major concerns of each branch sindicato is to prevent poaching by other sindicatos. The formal procedure for handling intrusions is to send a warning message to headquarters in La Paz, where it is forwarded to the infringing local. But this procedure is time-consuming, so most local sindicatos are likely to take direct action. For example, one day a driver from the Achacachi sindicato appeared in town and carried back to the lakeside communities near Achacachi the campesinos who had come to Sorata with their fish for the market day. A week later the same Achacachi driver appeared in Sorata and the sindicato immediately called him to a meeting. He argued that there was no law against a trucker's driving anywhere he chose, and that greater competition would result in improved transport services. The answer of the Sorata sindicato was this:

You have to take into consideration that we work permanently on this route and that we provide the service under any conditions, no matter how many passengers or how much freight there is. Furthermore, we don't invade other people's routes.

The Sorata local had no power to fine the Achacachi driver, but he was warned off in bellicose terms and did not appear again.

Competition is avoided in the minorista passengers trade because the women are understood to be clients of specific drivers, and a violator of this understanding is liable to a sindicato fine of eight pesos. Regular passengers accept the system, even though it may not always be to their advantage. If they fail to play the game according to the truckers' rules they may find themselves fighting for a bit of space on top of a truck twice a week. Such punitive pressure on the minoristas has lessened over the years as the number of trucks and the space available for transport have increased, forcing truckers to provide competitive extra services for regular clients, like waiting for them when they are not ready at the regular departure time, or accepting heavier bundles for the same transport cost, all to hold their loyalty.

The truckers are quite aware of the importance of their work to the community, but they have also developed a marked sense of public responsibility. They are generally willing participants in any effort to aid the community as a whole, and most of them take pride in their efforts to improve the public welfare. A driver commented, "We always collaborate with our trucks in all the work or needs required by the community. We also cooperate financially with the community. Each of us tries to serve according to his capabilities." When the alcalde told the sindicato that sand needed for the public swimming pool was available free near Achacachi there was unanimous agreement among the transportistas that each driver would haul three truckloads without cost. When the welfare of the truckers is threatened the political power of the sindicato becomes apparent, as when the road from Sorata to Laripata had deteriorated too far to be ignored. While the construction and maintenance of roads is entrusted to a national agency, the Servicio Nacional de Caminos, its limited resources are stretched even in maintaining the major road network in the country, let alone minor roads. One night about eight o'clock, twelve members of the truckers' sindicato, led by Eduardo Soruco, set out to find the local government official to see what could be done. In the plaza they found the sub-prefect, Fernando Campos, and the alcalde, Juan Roblis, with four important campesino sindicato leaders. Soruco greeted them and told the sub-prefect that he had a problem to discuss. He then added, "It is even better that the campesino leaders are present to hear our problem, because it concerns them also." Campos suggested that they go to his office, and he turned to the campesino dirigentes and asked them to please wait for him. At this point one of the other important figures in the truckers' sindicato interjected, "No, why should we go to your office? We can talk better right here. It will be quicker, and afterwards you can continue as before." Soruco seconded this, and immediately brought up the problem of the Laripata road, saying that the truck drivers felt it was the duty of the government to repair it. He emphasized the benefits of truck service to Sorata, Laripata, and the surrounding campesino villages, and ended by announcing that the truckers had decided to suspend service to Laripata if the road were not repaired. The response of the government officials was that the problem was beyond their control. As sub-prefect Campos put it:

I can't do anything, because the campesinos refused to obey my orders. In fact, they have already complained once to the Highway Agency of the Ministry of Communication and Public Works, saying it was not my responsibility to make them work on the road. And the ministry didn't back me up. So, in the face of this, what can I do, even if it is a question of a service that involves the province?

The truckers have developed a direct, practical style of dealing, and they were not prepared to let the problem rest because of some intragovernmental jurisdictional difficulty. First, Soruco rejected the response of the sub-prefect:

Compañeros, we cannot accept such a thing, because it is the duty of the officials to take care of the welfare of the community. It would be like denying the authority of yourselves. By that criterion, where are we to go for help? If you refuse your responsibility and at the same time are ignored by your superiors, what happens?

This brought a proposal by Ramon Sedano, one of the spokesmen of the truckers, that campesino road crews be taken on under their prestación vial obligations:

It is very easy. You just ask the campesinos to repair the worst parts of the road and in exchange you give them the ticket of the prestación vial. So we will have the road repaired and the campesinos will get their tickets, which they should have anyway.

The sub-prefect agreed. He might have suggested such a plan himself, an arrangement certainly familiar to him, but he is more concerned with building support for himself among the campesinos than he is in helping the truckers. The campesinos will not be happy at having to give time for road repair, and they represent hundreds of votes, while the truckers are only a handful. He might rather have done nothing, but the transport service to Laripata is as important to the campesinos in that area as it is to the minoristas traveling out from Sorata, something that the sub-prefect knows as well as Vicente Pelayo, the dirigente of the Laripata sindicato, who was in the company of the sub-prefect when the truckers approached. Given the propensity of the truckers for direct action, the threat of Soruco to suspend service until the road would be repaired was sufficient to impress upon the sub-prefect the logic of the truckers' solution.

POLITICAL POWER

Economic events in the recent past of Sorata, many of them associated with the Revolution, have caused a variety of important changes in the community. Equally striking, and in some ways more important, have been the many political changes brought about by the Revolution. As in Coroico, the politicization of the Indian population on the haciendas introduced a new dimension to politics and the pattern of civic power. While political awareness has grown very unevenly in the area, Sorata has witnessed the development of a much more militant campesino political style, which has also taken the form of violent sindicato factionalism.

TRADITIONAL AUTHORITY AND NEW SINDICATOS

In the past, the dominance of the town over the surrounding campesino population was based on the traditional authority of the patrón over the peon. This patrón-peon system did not differ essentially from the system that has been described for Villa Abecia and the pre-Revolutionary era around Coroico. Peons had the use of small plots of land in exchange for specified numbers of days per week of labor, plus a variety of additional services and obligations that included not only themselves, but also their wives and even their children. Further, the hacienda peon was subjected to much more than obligations of labor, for the patrón was virtually unrestricted by law. He *was* the law, as far as the peon was concerned. As one ex-peon tells it, "We always had something to do for the master, like carrying water or taking care of his animals. When the master asked you to do something you had to stop everything and obey him right away. We never had time to work our land."

The life of the peon under the autocratic authority of the patrón and his representative, the mayordomo, was hard. The profits of the haciendas depended on the driving force of the mayordomo, who not only thus secured his position but sometimes could profit personally by gouging more work from the peon. "He made us work until we dropped in our tracks from fatigue." Pushed beyond endurance, the peon might run away, but he knew only agriculture, and all the land familiar to him was already occupied. He had to take the pushing, and when he shirked his work he had to take the punishment. This was meted out by the patrón or his overseer in customary fashion.

That the patróns saw their absolute authority in a different light, in some cases as a responsibility, is revealed by the daughter of an important Sorata patrón, herself the owner of several small haciendas:

When my father was the master he was always very good with the campesinos. He used to settle their disputes. They'd come to him and say, "Patrón, you fix this, make it right, whip us." And he'd get out the little whip and lash them a bit. They'd go away happy, saying that now they had both had justice. But we were never harsh with them, never any hard lashes, no scars or sores. And every Sunday he'd call them all with the big gong we had and he'd line them all up, starting with the oldest down to the youngest, and give them some money to buy candies. Every night they would come to my father's bedroom and say, "Tata [father], we're here," and he would talk with them about the day's work and what they had to do tomorrow.

The peon was treated as a child who could distinguish right from wrong only dimly, who had to be guided, and when occasion required, punished. Even the traditional Indian vocabulary of patrón-peon relations presents the patrón as the all-powerful father. The hacienda system engendered not only an economic, but also a psychological dependence of the peon on the patrón. Some of this can still be observed in elderly campesinos who dog the footsteps of an ex-patrón who is visiting his former hacienda, who still treat him with veneration. An ex-patrón says:

I hear the old ones say they'd like to return to the times before because, you see, they didn't gain from the reform like the young ones did. They were used to having my father or my mother, and now no one is here. So when I come, they sit in the house just to be around. They miss this, and they still come to me with some of their problems.

This servility of peons was not everywhere typical. On some haciendas there was even a tradition of resistance to the authority of the patrón. Julio Martinez, campesino leader from Atahuallpani, recalls that the campesinos of Atahuallpani, who today have a formidable reputation for belligerence, resisted the tyranny of patróns before the Revolution. When the patrón brought police from the town to enforce his authority, rebel peons occasionally sought refuge in the surrounding mountains, sometimes carrying an old firearm, forbidden to them by law.

During the early stages of the Revolution of 1952, representatives of the MNR government moved quickly into the Yungas, including Coroico, to inform peons of their new economic and political rights as campesinos, and to aid them in organizing sindicatos; but MNR representatives were rather slow in reaching Sorata. Sorata is farther from La Paz than Coroico is, it is somewhat more isolated from the political center of the country, and, perhaps of greatest importance, the value of its haciendas was considerably less than those around Coroico. But news of peon uprisings in the Cochabamba valley and the northern altiplano reached Sorata by radio, newspaper, and word of mouth, and at least part of the new rural social order was initiated around Sorata by campesinos themselves.

Most of the campesinos who took a leading part in the Sorata action had come in contact with the militant miners' sindicatos. Revolt was organized, and victory was made easier as patróns and their associates abandoned the haciendas in the early days of the fighting to flee to La Paz and elsewhere. In many instances, no further change apparently was desired by peons. Freed of their labor and service obligations, the majority turned their attention to their own chacras. There was little pillaging or destruction of hacienda property. Most casas de hacienda were allowed to stand, though in time they were thoroughly stripped and allowed to deteriorate. Even the gardens, orchards, and lands of the patrón were often left undisturbed until the advent of the formal agrarian reform program. It was several years before the surveyors and agrarian judges reached Sorata, and it was not until 1956 that the legal tramites, the actions to reform the hacienda holdings, reached their peak.

As early as 1953 the campesinos on the more central haciendas organized in sindicatos, and this process spread throughout the province. Today there are about 150 campesino sindicatos in the province, grouped into twenty subcentrals linked to a single central. From among their members the campesinos elect a set of officials (secretarios), headed by a secretary general who directs all activities. Each sindicato has its secretary of agriculture, secretary of justice, secretary of education, and so on. In the early years, age and experience were important criteria for election to a sindicato office, just as they were traditionally important for selection as jilakata, a community leader, or as an important official in one of the traditional campesino fiestas; but these new sindicato men were invariably illiterate, and in most cases were unable to adapt themselves to new conditions and new duties—for example, in representing their sindicato before higher officials, or in legal actions against the former patróns—so they were soon replaced by younger, more widely traveled, better educated, and more demanding campesinos, a process which reduced the status of older males, if, indeed, they were not wholly discredited.

For an area that has been thoroughly affected by the Revolution there has been a striking amount of accommodation in relations between the hacienda campesinos and their former patróns, and in relations between the sindicato and the old patrón. In only a very few cases has there been a total abandonment of hacienda property. After a period of several years the majority of ex-patróns sought out the campesinos of their former haciendas, or, almost as often, were sought out by officials of the sindicato, to arrange for the disposition of the property. It was in the interests of both parties to get together, for both stood to profit. The campesinos could not legally take over that portion of his old holding to which the patrón had just received title, but neither could the patrón do much with this land without the assistance of the campesinos. In most cases some form of sharecropping plan has been adopted, often in violation, as described earlier, of official rules about sharecropping agreements. One patrona, faced with demands that she fulfill her obligations, weeps over ungrateful campesinos who would make such demands, then brushes aside campesino leaders to give the older, meeker campesinos an opening to side with her. In this way she has managed to avoid supplying seed and equipment for the cultivation of her land and has taken an illegally large share of the harvest. These deviations from the law are facilitated by the absence of work contracts that would specify the mutual obligations of patrón and peon, required by law but widely ignored. Another aged patrona, who rarely visits her sharecropped land except to collect the harvest, is adept in manipulating the social situation of officials of the local sindicato. She has influence over the campesinos because most of them are her ahijados, her godchildren, but this is not all, as she herself tells:

I take part from time to time in the election of campesino leaders, suggesting the names of candidates. I say, "This man is fit," or "This one is lazy and capable only of criticizing. It would be good for him to learn to be a dirigente." Furthermore, the leader of the sindicato central, who comes here for the elections, also takes into account my suggestions, which obviously are for my own advantage rather than that of the peons. The fact is that I gain his cooperation. I invite him over for lunch and I sit him down to my own table. He feels very flattered, and then is very well disposed toward me. To this I sometimes add a few bolivianos, which he accepts with pleasure, and the trick is done.

This is one side of the Sorata rural campesino situation. In the struggle to obtain the benefits from the cultivation of the former patrón's parcel of land, the campesinos do not always come off best, or even come away with their legitimate share. For their part, the old patróns and their relatives have discovered that in many cases their authority may be gone, but their influence is still considerable. However, there is another side of the local sindicato situation, the political town and regional side, in which the former patróns have been less successful against the campesinos.

SINDICATO POLTICS

The local sindicatos are the base of a pyramidal organization which is topped by the Ministerio de Asuntos Campesinos. The sindicatos, with a membership of over two million, are an important political feature of modern Bolivia. With the enfranchising of the campesinos after the Revolution of 1952, the sindicatos took a central place in the electoral dominance of the MNR, and thus had strong influence on the national government. The secretary general of each local sindicato, and lesser secretaries as well, attend meetings of the central organization, and officials at the central level attend meetings of the departmental sindicato federation. The experience and the connections, the muñeca, lead to political careers even for campesinos.

While there is some flow of sindicato officials up the hierarchy, there is domination from above, in conformity with the centralist tendency in Bolivian governmental organization. With the sindicatos organized as an important political base for the MNR party, it follows that important MNR politicians were appointed to many of the leading posts at the higher sindicato levels. At intermediate and lower levels, it is not always clear whether an official has been appointed or elected. In general, sindicato officials must be approved at some higher level, and the higher the level of the office the more likely it is that it has been filled by appointment. It is not at all unusual even for the subcentral to intervene in the local sindicato to indicate a preference for one campesino over another. But to be approved for nomination or appointment, the candidate must generally demonstrate that he has the support of the rank and file. If an official loses support his position is very likely to be in jeopardy.

While the local-to-national sindicato structure can be drawn as a neat pyramid, it is probably more accurately viewed as a series of overlapping, shifting fields of forces. Regional campesino leaders have emerged on the national scene with strong followings and have attempted to extend their influence over ever wider sectors of the total sindicato structure. The same process has occurred at lower levels, down to the local. The high stakes in this game, and the considerable power at issue, have been matched by the intensity of the struggle. One of the national centers of this struggle has been Achacachi, which has influenced the sindicato political climate of the near-by Sorata area. In the Sorata area itself, there has been a counterpart struggle between several of the individual sindicatos. One of the indicators of the intensity of the struggle is its record of violence.

In 1956 Alfredo Quintana, a Sorata vecino, but an old and prominent member of the MNR, was shot and killed on the central plaza. It was the day of the sixteenth of July national holiday, and a civic parade was under way, led by MNR officials of the town and including large contingents of armed campesinos from the surrounding sindicatos. The sindicato from Atahuallpani was heavily represented, led by Marcos Lupa, who had joined the MNR before the Revolution and was one of the founders and first secretary general of the provincial Campesino Central. It was a festive occasion, with much drinking, especially by the campesinos, and as the parade entered the plaza a group of vecinos appeared at one corner, the women dressed in their urban-style dresses and the men in their tailored trousers and clean white shirts. Unfortunately, the "camisas blancas" had become a symbol employed by the MNR to identify the Falangista opposition to the Revolution. At their sudden appearance, the "white shirts" were surrounded by the campesinos, many of whom were extremely drunk, and were forced to dance as the campesinos brandished their weapons and fired into the air and into the ground. When Quintana saw what was happening he rushed over, shouting, "Comrades, don't be foolish! They belong to our party." Before he could say more he was shot down, a casualty of the political climate, with its strong anti-vecino, anti-patrón overtones, as sindicatos competed to establish militant reputations. No campesino was ever officially identified as the man responsible for the killing, but the vecinos of the town placed the blame on the Atahuallpani sindicato.

In July, 1957, an intense struggle was going on at the national level between conservative elements seeking to re-establish Bolivia's international financial respectability and a left wing faction led by Juan Lechin of the Central Obrero Boliviano (the Bolivian national labor union), more concerned with extending the Revolution for the immediate benefit of the campesinos. Since both factions were struggling for grass roots support, clashes occurred at lower levels. In one of these clashes the Director of the Ministerio de Asuntos Campesinos, Vincentes Alvarez Plata, was shot to death in a campesino ambush. Alvarez Plata had attended a provincial meeting in Sorata at which the sindicatos of the towns of Atahuallpani and Millipaya were in opposition, the former favoring Plata's faction, the latter favoring the left wing faction headed at this provincial level by Toribio Salas of the Achacachi Central.

Late in the afternoon Alvarez Plata set out by car for La Paz, accompanied by two of his machinegun-carrying bodyguards, by Carlos Palacios, a prominent Sorata vecino who was also a prominent politician, and one or two other MNR politicians. When the group reached the campesino village of Atahuallpani, on the hillside almost directly opposite Sorata, they found the road blocked by a truck loaded with armed campesinos, including some from Achacachi. The campesinos attempted to seize Plata, but he resisted and was shot to death. In the confusion of the struggle and the failing light of sunset, the others in the car escaped down the mountainside, but the same conditions that had facilitated their escape made it difficult for them to describe exactly who had done what.

The news of the assassination naturally created a sensation, and it brought further notoriety to Achacachi, Sorata, and especially Atahuallpani. Marcos Lupa, who had supported Plata, was forced to resign as secretary general of the Sorata Central and was replaced by a supporter of the Salas faction, Santiago Romero of Millipaya. An investigation was conducted and a few arrests were made, but all suspects were soon released and no further official action was ever taken.

Local factionalism sometimes mirrored national factionalism, but at times it grew out of local competition between aspiring campesino leaders, who were just as much inclined to use national factionalism to further their own careers as national politicians were inclined to abet local factionalism in seeking support for themselves. In one of these incidents the campesinos of Atahuallpani seized Fernando Campos and beat him until he agreed to sign his resignation as alcalde of Sorata. In another incident, campesinos from Atahuallpani shot it out with others from Millipaya in an attempt to force the leaders of the latter sindicato to vacate the Sorata alcaldia.

In 1962, while Alvaro Diaz was alcalde, and his uncle, José Corona, was Jefe de Comando of the MNR in Sorata, the town was visited by an important MNR political troubleshooter. His mission was to gain support of the campesino sindicatos for President Paz Estenssoro, who was looking forward to the election of 1964, and to neutralize the support for Juan Lechin. He was assisted in his local politicking by a young Sorateño named Armando Montes, noted for his pugnaciousness and heavy drinking. While these qualities suited him for the task he was asked to perform, they did not endear him to many, and one foggy afternoon while he was walking down an apparently empty street he was shot and killed. It was rumored that the shots were meant for his boss, and even that the campesino government officials of Sorata were behind the attack, but the investigating commission from La Paz accused no one, and this, like many political murders, was left unsolved.

The decline in fortune of the patrón families of the Sorata area had been set in motion at least a decade before the Revolution, and agrarian reform only served to accelerate the trend. The town has been turned upside down by the Revolution to a degree never experienced in Coroico. The Sorata campesino sindicatos and their leaders quickly became involved in MNR politics and factionalism, which locally was focused not only on control of the provincial sindicato organization, the offices of the centrals and subcentrals, but also on control of the local government, primarily the alcaldia and the subprefecture. From 1952 until the present, the posts of sub-prefect and alcalde, as well as many minor positions, have been filled chiefly by campesino leaders from one or another of the surrounding sindicatos, though, infrequently, a vecino who has been a prominent MNR supporter has held office for short periods of time.

PARTY POLITICS AND POLITICAL CHANGE

Between the last half of 1964 and 1966, Sorata experienced a series of political events which not only polarized sindicato factionalism, but also revived the struggle between town vecinos and the campesino sindicatos. All of these events took place within local party politics. In Sorata, as in Coroico, the major political parties—which had been the Liberals and the Republicans in the 1920's and the 1930's—were the Movimientistas (MNR) and Falangistas (FSB) in the 1940's and 1950's. The MNR dominated the town from 1952 until 1964, depending in large part on the organized strength of the campesino sindicatos. MNR activists were also drawn from all social sectors of the town, and as long as the MNR controlled the national government the local party could count on the support of a large part of the community. To organize a mass party, the MNR established a hierarchical party structure, with party chiefs at the departmental, provincial, and local levels; and at each level there was also a unit of the MNR para-military command.

A majority of the politically active vecinos of Sorata have supported the FSB since before the Revolution. Not until 1964 did they have an opportunity to exercise any political power. At the end of that year the MNR government was overthrown, temporarily releasing provincial areas like Sorata from the overwhelming centralization of political power in Bolivia. This gave the various local groups an opportunity to reassert themselves, and the vecino-dominated FSB in Sorata attempted to regain control of local government from campesino sindicato leaders.

When news of the fall of the MNR came over the radio on November 4, there was a widespread impulse to prepare for civil disorder. Shopkeepers closed down, people shut themselves up in their houses and gathered with family and friends around transistor radios to learn the latest news from the capital. On the following day, when it was announced that Paz Estenssoro had fled the country and that General Barrientos had become the head of a temporary military government, the majority of the vecinos and all those who had suffered exploitation or oppression under the MNR viewed the coup with great satisfaction. Though the position of Barrientos on important national questions was unknown, it was assumed that a change in government would mean a change in national policies, and the traditional support by the army of the hacendados and the upper class reinforced the belief in all sectors of the population that many of the reform programs of the MNR would be halted or even reversed. The local MNR leaders made themselves as inconspicuous as possible.

The vecinos feared that armed contingents of the campesino sindicatos might stage a violent demonstration in protest against the overthrow of Paz Estenssoro. To consider what should be done, they called a meeting of the Junta de Vecinos, an almost moribund association that before 1952 had had a quasi-legal voice in public affairs as an advisory body to the local government. The meeting was open to all, and, besides the junta, members of the Veterans of the Chaco War Association, the Sindicato de Gremiales, the Sindicato de Transportistas, and others attended. No clear course of action was proposed, but a plan to replace campesino town officials by vecinos was agreed upon.

General Barrientos had announced that his aim was to restore the Revolution by eliminating the victimization and graft that had developed under the MNR. In line with this, the meeting of the junta decided to form a Committee for the Restoration of the Revolution, which was made up of ten vecinos, with Nicanor Hernandez, a prominent comerciante and truck owner, as chairman. The committee was authorized to guarantee the support of the town to General Barrientos and his government and to ask for replacement of campesino town officials by vecinos. At the end of the meeting some of the younger men ran through the plaza shouting, "Death to Paz Estenssoro and his collaborators! Let's take the weapons away from the campesinos! Let's destroy the sindicatos!"

While the vecinos were discussing how to reestablish their rule over the town, the sindicato campesinos were in a state of confusion and disarray. Some of their leaders went into hiding, while others tried to rally support. Alvaro Diaz locked the doors of his alcaldia on hearing that the government had fallen and fled to his home in Atahuallpani. Amid this confusion, factionalism was already developing within the new military government, a great advantage to those who had the skill to put up a convincing front. Many vecinos had such skill, but so did some campesinos at this late date after the Revolution. The campesino sub-prefect, Fernando Campos, was the first Sorateño to reach La Paz after the November coup, and on the strength of his leadership in the Sorata sindicatos and a statement of support for General Barrientos and the new government, his appointment as sub-prefect was reconfirmed. Armed with a letter of reappointment from the Ministry of Government, Campos returned to Sorata on November 15. Knowing that, in the uncertain situation, many were hoping to be able to settle old scores, and realizing that tension was high, he did not return alone, but entered town at the head of 800 campesinos who could be expected to apply convincing force against any move to question the validity of the authoritative document he carried.

Whether to avoid an outbreak of violence that he might not be able to control, or because he was uncertain of the extent to which the new government would support him, the campesino force led by Campos was unarmed. Campos asked the police to assemble a delegation of vecinos to witness his reappointment. The captain of the police sent out invitations to several leading vecinos, but none appeared. Two hours later Campos occupied his old office in the alcaldia building.

In the meantime, the vecino Committee for the Restoration of the Revolution had decided to seek the appointment of Jaime Madrigal, a marginal vecino, as alcalde. A delegation from the committee, headed by Nabor Moran, a tienda owner, landowner, and ex-patrón, and Eduardo Soruco, truck driver, head of the local truck drivers' sindicato, and a person with considerable muñeca, were sent to La Paz to call on officials of the Ministry of Government to appoint Madrigal. Soruco had to break away, however, summoned back from La Paz because of his work, and left the task of the delegation in the hands of Moran. On November 18, three days after Campos had returned to Sorata as sub-prefect, Moran rode back to town with an official appointment of a new alcalde in his pocket, naming himself to the office, not Madrigal.

Moran was not unopposed. He was suspected of having been especially corrupt when he had been alcalde many years before, and he was strongly opposed by campesino sindicato leaders. When he presented

his document of appointment to the head of the local police, prepara-
tory to his occupying the alcaldia, the police official demurred, saying
that he had received many complaints about Moran's mismanagement
of public office. Moran said he had records that would prove his innocence, but when the police official examined the documents the next
day he declared them inadequate. That the head of the local police
raised these objections suggests that he was being supported by higher
officials, most probably the sub-prefect. Not to be denied the victory
that was at hand, a group of vecinos headed by Nicanor Hernandez of
the Committee for the Restoration of the Revolution broke into the
alcaldia on a day when the sub-prefect was absent and installed Moran
in office. About a hundred townspeople assembled to hear him take the
oath of office.

But Moran had still to contend with opposition. On November 22 a
meeting was held, attended by twenty cholo comerciantes, thirty members of the Sindicato de Gremiales, and some town campesinos. Some
demanded an accounting from Moran, but there were tinterillos present
who warned this group that they were committing slander in making
unsupported charges. It was agreed that a hearing on evidence against
Moran would be held on the following day. At this confused second
meeting Moran succeeded less in proving his innocence than in having
himself certified as alcalde. To the charges of corruption his response
was a protestation of innocence and a questioning of the integrity of his
antagonists. His trump was that he had his official appointment as alcalde, and he had a bit of luck, in that an army officer had arrived in
town to enlist conscripts. With his legal notice of appointment and this
representative of higher officialdom present, Moran was able to force
the sub-prefect to recognize him as alcalde.

In gaining the initial support by the new military government the
sub-prefect risked repudiation by his campesino followers. Early in January a Sorateño worker commented:

I became a member of the MNR because my wife is from Atahuallpani and
everybody there is a member of this party. We always remember Paz Estenssoro and we hope he will soon return. In the meantime, it is convenient to
support Campos, but later when Paz Estenssoro returns we will remember
that Campos became a partisan of the military government.

In the early months after the coup the sub-prefect faced little opposition
from the campesinos or the sindicatos. Confusion was widespread

throughout the rural campesino hamlets, and the MNR party seemed to be disintegrating. There was talk of a new government party, there was even talk that the land was to be given back to the ex-patróns. There was considerable suspicion of the new government and disillusionment at the turn of events. A campesino dirigente lamented:

I am tired and disheartened. I want to forget about politics, and many other campesino leaders feel the same way. The campesinos are bitter and they are right. Shares, contributions, fines, meetings, and all this for what? For nothing!

As the months passed and ex-patróns did not return, and the agrarian reform was not repealed, the campesino sindicatos and dirigentes began to regain confidence. At the same time and for the same reasons the vecinos lost some of theirs. The chairman of their committee for the Restoration of the Revolution spoke prophetically:

In the Province of Larecaja the MNR has not disappeared with the fall of Paz Estenssoro. On the contrary, it is quite possible that it will be organized again with another name, maybe with that of the MPC.

The alcalde and sub-prefect stood as opponents at the center of political forces of change and uncertainty that dominated the last months of 1964 and the early months of 1965. Both men had to be prepared to protect their positions. In addition, the sub-prefect was faced with the complicated task of maintaining his campesino following when his very position as sub-prefect removed him from much direct contact with the campesinos, who were badly split and demoralized. A departmental congress of sindicatos was held in La Paz in February of 1966, and its deliberations showed that the recent political changes had seriously divided the campesinos. The sub-prefect summed up the meeting this way:

Frankly, the congress was a real fiasco, mainly because the campesinos split into two groups, one supporting Siles Zuazo [ex-President of Bolivia and ranking leader of the old MNR] and the other Barrientos. Of the comrades from Larecaja, only Santiago Romero betrayed us by taking the side of Siles Zuazo.

This congress was very badly organized. In fact, they should have called a provincial congress, then a departmental one, and finally one at the national level. Instead, they did the opposite, which resulted in a fight among the campesinos. It was a real fracas, with stones being thrown, and fistfights, but luckily only a few were injured.

This departmental meeting was followed by a provincial one, held in Sorata from March 13 to 16. This was to be the first test for Campos in his own bailiwick and he was determined to use it to strengthen his leadership of the provincial sindicatos. However, even within the province he faced opposition. Before the meeting took place, Santiago Romero attempted to have it nullified. He claimed that the meeting was organized without proper authorization, meaning that he as secretary general of the provincial sindicato organization had not signed any meeting announcement. Campos countered this by enlisting the participation of the national sindicato organization in the person of its executive secretary, important central government officials like the executive secretary of the Ministry of Government, and the national coordinator of the new government-sponsored MPC. It was even rumored that General Barrientos himself would be present. In the face of this array of national power Romero could not afford to be absent, and the meeting took place.

From the standpoint of the sub-prefect, the meeting itself progressed from an ominous beginning to a successful conclusion. When the officials from La Paz entered they were greeted by a forest of arms, hands making the sign of a V, the traditional salute of Paz Estenssoro and his MNR party. Then the campesinos proceeded to elect as chairman of the congress, not the executive secretary of the national campesino federation, who was being supported by Campos, but Vincente Pelayo, the dirigente of the Laripata sindicato who was playing both sides of the Campos-Romero conflict. Speeches by the visiting officials followed and these aided greatly in quieting the suspicion of the campesinos and creating support for General Barrientos. Throughout these speeches the speakers reiterated again and again that the general supported the reform program of the old MNR, that he particularly supported the agrarian reform program, that he was prepared to defend the new rights that had been given to the campesinos after the Revolution, and that there would be no return of pre-Revolution times.

This provincial campesino meeting had been instigated by the central government to enlist campesino support for General Barrientos and the new MPC party. The sub-prefect, a former MNR activist, had already declared for the MPC, and other politicians throughout the country were taking the same action. A more specific objective of the Sorata provincial meeting was to replace Santiago Romero as secretary general, for he had already reaffirmed his support for the MNR and was challenging Campos in the province. The problem was how to oust Romero without dividing the sindicatos. Campos attempted to construct a united front through the support he had from the central government. When even old enemies of Campos, José Corona and Marcos Lupa, the Atahuallpani dirigentes, sided with the sub-prefect, Romero gave in and resigned as secretary general. At an evening meeting of thirty of the most important dirigentes, Campos was then elected, and the same group also gave him a vote of support as sub-prefect.

This victory of Campos was not completely unqualified, for Santiago Romero was elected by the same group as secretary of relations, the number two position in the provincial sindicato organization. It was also apparent from discussion and comment during the meeting that the Barrientos government and the MPC party had not gained the unqualified confidence of campesino leaders.

The campesino congress renewed the conflict between the campesino sindicatos and the town vecinos. On the last day of the meeting Moran was invited to attend, but was greeted by a barrage of accusations. He was charged with not recognizing campesino rights, with being a rightist FSB militant who wanted to reverse the reform programs of the Revolution, and with being a thief in public office. He responded more or less in kind, attacking the dirigentes for political opportunism. He left the session under a barrage of invective, and the sub-prefect then promised the gathering that he would have Moran removed, along with the other vecinos who had taken office in the alcaldia. As their replacements, he promised to appoint Juan Roblis and Herminio Zepeda. Roblis was at that time the agrarian judge. A person of slight education and a sometime tailor by occupation, Roblis had served in a variety of local offices over much of the preceding decade and was known as a typical MNR politician. He was not a campesino, having been born in Sorata of a poor cholo family, but he had long been identified with campesino interests and sindicato politics. Zepeda has a similar background, except that he was better educated and his cholo family had been somewhat prominent in town. He too had a long career as a local MNR politician, and in fact was serving as deputy alcalde in Sorata when the MNR government was overthrown in 1964.

In the weeks following the campesino congress in Sorata the sub-prefect endeavored to keep his promise to return control of local government to the campesino sindicatos. He made several trips to La Paz for this purpose. Alcalde Moran, in turn, was going to the capital to keep himself in office, presenting letters of commendation and support from the Junta de Vecinos, the Veterans of the Chaco War, and other associations to Ministry of Government officials. All of these letters strongly asserted the importance of keeping Moran as alcalde, but then they all came from the vecino sector of the community. There is some indication that Moran might have continued in office if he had offered to switch from the FSB to the MPC, but more than a change of political party was involved here, for the importance of the change was to have an alcalde who could work with the sub-prefect and produce a united front within the provincial government in support of the MPC. Aside from his political sympathies and possible party allegiance, the alcalde could hardly join forces with the campesino sub-prefect and still retain his position as a leader of the vecinos, or even his social position within the community.

In the first week of July orders arrived from the central government in La Paz deposing Moran and naming the sub-prefect's candidate, Juan Roblis, as his successor. Roblis marched to the alcaldia at the head of a group of campesinos and demanded that Moran turn the office and its keys over to him, but Moran refused. Instead, he called a meeting of the Junta de Vecinos and delivered the keys to the alcaldia to the elderly president of this organization. The new alcalde and his supporters refused to accept this standoff and proceeded to break into the alcaldia and occupy it. At this point the president of the Junta de Vecinos decided there was nothing more that could be done and on the following day he delivered the keys to the head of the local police, who in turn handed them over to the new alcalde. This brought to an end the brief period of vecino control of town government in Sorata.

This rise and fall of the FSB in Sorata repeats a pattern already described in Coroico. The fall of the national government temporarily released both towns from central political control. This in turn enabled the social elite of both communities to reassert their traditional dominance of town affairs. In both towns this sector of the community was sympathetic or allied with the FSB political party, and consequently in both cases the FSB replaced the MNR officials in the local government. But as the national political scene became stabilized, and especially after a new government-supported political party was formed, central government control was reasserted over the provincial capitals and a new political allegiance was demanded. When it became clear that the new military government did not intend to repudiate the Revolution and its reform programs and, further, intended to seek campesino support, it became easier for the old MNR politicians to switch, but more difficult for those in the FSB. By the summer of 1965 the political lines were being drawn, and the old FSB militants in towns like Coroico and Sorata were losing hope and losing office. The FSB politicians in Coroico had to contend only with the central government, while those in Sorata had also to face the politicized sindicato structure, which had in fact retained its hold over the provincial government of the subprefecture throughout this entire period.

A NATIONAL ELECTION

At the campesino congress in Sorata in March 1965, sub-prefect Campos promised campesino delegates that he would see to the reassertion of campesino power in the province by having vecino officials removed from the town government. By July he had succeeded, and once more both town and provincial governments were in the hands of campesino leaders. But politicking just as intense as that of the past eight months continued as the town became embroiled in preparations for national elections. The locus of activity was the countryside, for the new MPC party looked to the campesino dirigentes to deliver a massive vote in support of General Barrientos. In the thick of it were the sub-prefect, the alcalde, and a few other local officials who by this time had become partisans of the MPC. These men felt that, despite the strong attachment of the campesinos to the MNR, at least their sindicato leaders would see advantages in supporting the party that already held national power. One of the dirigentes from Atahuallpani, even though he had long opposed Campos, said:

The obligation was assumed during the congress of March 1965, to support General Barrientos and to organize the MPC in this province, represented a big step forward as far as politics is concerned. It had great importance in keeping political power for us, and in our favor.

National elections were set for July 1966, and the organizing and maneuvering began in earnest in the spring. General Barrientos campaigned throughout the country, dramatically traveling by helicopter to many relatively inaccessible communities. On April 9 he arrived in Sorata by car, accompanied by the prefect of the department and by national officers of the MPC and the campesino confederation. The sub-prefect had notified sindicato leaders to make sure of a large turnout. Food and transportation were promised, and a fine of five bolivianos was threatened for those campesinos who would fail to appear.

The general and his party were met at the edge of town by the sub-prefect, the alcalde, the official mayor, and several campesino dirigentes. The entire group marched to the central plaza where a dense mass of people awaited them. Most, perhaps four-fifths, were campesinos whose sindicato banners identified them: "Central Campesino de la Provincia Larecaja," "Subcentral Campesino de Laripata," "Subcentral Campesino de Ylabaya," "Subcentral Campesino de Tacacoma," "Subcentral Campesino de Quiabaya," "Subcentral Campesino de Sorejaya," "Subcentral Campesino de Atahuallpani." And there were signs with political slogans: "General Barrientos, future President of Bolivia," "No more campesino demagogues with Barrientos," "With Barrientos grows the Agrarian Reform," "Barrientos, the people of Sorata salute you." Few of those present were actually people of Sorata.

The general and his entourage mounted to the second-story balconies of the alcaldia, and there for an hour made speeches typical of such occasions. The alcalde and the sub-prefect opened the series with the usual words of praise and welcome. Both appeared nervous and ill at ease, and their presentations excited no one. They were followed by an official of the national campesino confederation. He spoke in Aymara and addressed his comments strictly to the campesinos, asserting that the general was the only real friend they had and that the old MNR politicians had helped themselves much more than they had helped the campesinos. He was followed by the official mayor of Sorata, who read a proclamation which declared that the campesino sindicatos of the province had voted unanimously to support General Barrientos for the presidency and Francisco Campos as national deputy to represent the province, and, further, that all of the rest of the people of the province, including all the social classes, had resolved to support an identical resolution. This announcement was met with astonishment, since no one knew of any meeting of the provincial sindicatos that could have voted such a resolution, and the few vecinos present, who certainly were a part of "all the social classes," were even more certain that they had not assented to any such proclamation. The vecinos were incensed by this announcement that they supported Barrientos when, in fact, most of them opposed him.

General Barrientos came forward last, speaking briefly and concentrating on the evils of the old MNR rather than on promises to the campesinos. Only in his final sentences did he touch on rural problems, and then not in specific terms. He pointed out the importance of economic development, the usefulness of roads to link the internal markets of the country, and the special need to improve rural education and agricultural technology, ending with a reminder that it was a civic obligation to vote on July 3. The sub-prefect and the visiting sindicato officials from La Paz led the crowd in cheering the general during his speech. Everyone applauded when he was done, but there was no great show of enthusiasm. The ceremony over, the official party crossed the plaza to the home of a prominent vecino for a very brief reception, after which the general and his party immediately set off for La Paz.

The general did not help his cause very much in Sorata, especially among the campesinos. They were less interested in hearing about the crimes of the MNR than about the future of agrarian reform and the protection and aid they could expect from the MPC. Meantime, sindicato leaders, refraining from any attack on the MNR, were stressing that the new MPC was but a continuation of the MNR. The same programs were to continue, only some of the names were to be changed. Indeed, even the names were remaining the same, as old MNR politicians reappeared under the MPC label. The level of befuddlement among the campesinos at this time is suggested by the fact that one of them said that he had been told to come to town that day to welcome Paz Estenssoro to Sorata. This compesino, who had never seen any President of Bolivia, went back to the ex-hacienda thinking that he had in fact seen Paz Estenssoro.

The sindicato dirigentes themselves were not so easily manipulated. That the general had failed in his visit to dispel the suspicion that he might betray the Revolution became apparent on the first of May, when a meeting of dirigentes and officials was held in Sorata. It was called by the sub-prefect, as secretary general of the provincial sindicato organization. The aim of Campos in holding this meeting was to secure approval of his candidacy for the post of deputy in the national congress. It now became clear that the proclamation read during the Barrientos visit, in which the sindicatos were alleged to have declared themselves in favor of the sub-prefect as national deputy, was but a piece of political sleight-of-hand. It was, in fact, the national campesino confederation in La Paz that had picked Campos to run. But they were aware that he would have to have support of the provincial dirigentes to have any effect on the campesino vote, and the proclamation had been a dodge to give the impression that he had dirigente backing. The dirigentes, not the national campesino confederation, controlled the campesino vote, and the national government and MPC officials had to have it to legalize their regime. Campos stressed at the meeting that he was a candidate of the national campesino confederation, not of the MPC, and that his moving to higher office would be of great benefit to the campesinos of the province.

The meeting called by Campos disclosed uncertainty and dissatisfaction with him and with the MPC. It was typically chaotic. Seated at a table on one side of the patio of the alcaldia were the sub-prefect; the alcalde; the agrarian judge; the Laripata dirigente, Vicente Pelayo; and the Millipaya dirigente, Santiago Romero. Seated in groups around the courtyard were other sindicato dirigentes and delegates. The men seated at the central table successively addressed the group and a few dirigentes occasionally responded, but throughout the session there was a continuous murmur and hubbub, constant conversation and commenting, whether or not anyone had the floor.

Dirigentes from Ilabaya, Atahuallpani, and Laripata attacked the sub-prefect, complaining of the lack of visible rewards for campesino support of the government over the years. Alonso Cullco of Ilabaya summed up the criticism: "We have always given our support, but for nothing. We have not been aided in any way." One campesino said, "Well spoken. Those are true words," and another, "That's right. That and more ought to be told them."

After many variations of this theme, Campos finally responded, pleading that he had done his best but was hampered by lack of resources. "You are right to complain, but you should consider that I never abused my office, as Toribio Salas did, who filled his house with gifts. If there is no money, nothing can be done. What should I do, rob a bank to get money?"

After considerably more criticism, several of the chief dirigentes moved toward conciliation. Romero of Millipaya said, "If the confederation in La Paz has selected him for the panel of candidates, what is there for us to do?"

Another dirigente emphasized the value of having a campesino deputy. "I am not happy to deliver my body and soul to politics, but the province must have a deputy. In this, the political parties ought to reward the campesinos."

Finally it was said that Campos would have to take his obligations to the campesinos seriously, and several suggested that he be required to commit to paper that he would work for what the campesinos wanted, for more teachers, for agricultural equipment and improved communications. Some dirigentes argued that the sindicato should support Campos only if he would run under the MNR label, but the more experienced recognized that this would threaten the influence of Sorata sindicatos in the national government, and they succeeded in silencing this proposal. The agrarian judge then read a declaration giving the support of the Larecaja sindicatos to Campos. He read it in Spanish, leaving many not fully aware of what he had said. At this point it was late in the afternoon and most of the delegates were long since ready to begin their hike back to their own communities. There was no statement of opposition when the judge finished his reading, so the declaration was accepted. The dirigente from Atahuallpani expressed the viewpoint of many:

We agreed on the candidacy of Campos, but as a representative of the campesinos and not of the MPC. Once elected he will have to remain loyal to us and a firm defender of MNR ideals. We want to maintain the unity of the campesinos and take advantage of the circumstances to send to the national congress a large number of campesino delegates, since we don't know whether we will have another occasion like this one. But we are determined, also, to follow the policy of the MNR, even if it is in a concealed way.

Discussing the meeting on the following day, a dirigente from Atahuallpani, now residing in Sorata, said, "To have supported the MNR would inevitably have meant loss of the influence and power we have in the province."

In the two months between this May meeting and the national elections on July 3 the sub-prefect spent most of his time visiting the campesino sindicato communities throughout the province. Aware of the dissatisfaction, as well as the confusion caused by his having changed parties, he emphasized the continuity of the MPC with the MNR and the value of having campesino representatives in the national government. He was sometimes accompanied by the agrarian judge, who had been named the electoral judge for some of the cantons, and sometimes by the alcalde.

The law requires the registering of all adult citizens not later than thirty days before an election. An electoral judge must also be named for each province. For Larecaja, the juez instructor was named to this post, with the responsibility to uphold the electoral laws. In Sorata, 1796 persons were registered, among them all adult residents of the near-by campesino village of Laripata and campesinos on the surrounding ex-haciendas. This total included a small number of campesinos who were slipped in to register the night before the election on orders of the sub-prefect. This caused a flurry when it was discovered by MNR and FSB militants. They seized the registration book in a cloak-and-dagger operation, but agreed to turn it over to the electoral judge in exchange for a sworn statement about the events, to be used as a basis of formal complaint.

Six voting tables were set up in Sorata for the six separate lists of registered voters. The tables opened at eight thirty, each manned by eight literate residents elected at a public meeting, and voting went on for eight hours. Contrary to law, representatives of all parties—including the sub-prefect, the alcalde, and the official mayor—continued electioneering efforts among the registrants who were waiting in line to vote. At the start of the voting, soldiers of a detachment that had been sent to the town to avert violence were stationed at each of the voting tables and at the main plaza intersections. Spokesmen of the minority parties objected that this was a heavy-handed show of force, meant to intimidate the voters, especially the campesinos, so the electoral judge ordered them away from the voting lines.

The outcome of the election in Sorata approximated the outcome widely predicted at both national and local levels. The MPC coalition received 58 per cent of the votes, the MNR 24 per cent, the FSB 15 per cent. There were two other MNR groups involved in the election, one called the MRP, while the factions headed by Siles Zuazo, Lechin, and other important national MNR leaders, had asked their followers to cast a white ballot in protest. The MRP and white ballots accounted for the remaining 3 per cent. While a detailed analysis of voting patterns among Sorata residents alone is not possible, the registration of voters in sets of 300 makes it possible to contrast a town list with a Laripata campesino list. The Laripata campesinos overwhelmingly voted for the MPC, giving it 79 per cent, compared to 18 per cent for the MNR and 3 per cent for the FSB. In contrast, town voters strongly supported each of the three major local parties, giving the MPC 39 per cent, the MNR 29 per cent, and the FSB 26 per cent. While no white or MRP ballots were cast by the Laripata campesinos, 5 per cent in Sorata cast white ballots. Thus the Laripata sindicato delivered a sizeable majority vote for the new MPC party. The confusion in switching the sindicato campesinos from the MNR to a new party was successfully overcome. Even in the town itself, MPC leaders, who were also the major local government officials, were able to persuade a majority of the townsmen to vote for the new party. However, the old MNR and the FSB have strong political leadership, and both were able to obtain a substantial vote.

On the local level, the national election was a victory for the sub-prefect and his leadership of the MPC. It was also a victory for the campesinos over the vecinos of Sorata. Campos became national deputy for the province, and he was replaced as sub-prefect by a campesino dirigente from Ilabaya, one of a panel of three nominated by the May campesino meeting in Sorata. In this somewhat tortuous and uncertain transition from one national administration to another, from one government political party to a new one, the campesino dirigentes managed to maintain their political ascendancy in the province of Larecaja and continue their domination of the town.

GOVERNING THE TOWN

The formal structure of local government in Sorata, as a provincial capital, is identical to that described for Coroico and the other two communities, but some of the problems affecting the operation of local government in the other towns are even greater in Sorata. The occupancy of local government office by sindicato campesino leaders is viewed as a reward for party work. In addition, campesino sindicato influence frequently places barely literate campesinos in local government, rather than town vecinos who are educated elite of the community. Further, sindicato factionalism makes for sudden changes of officeholders.

In addition to the familiar problems of overlapping jurisdiction, lack of training, insecure tenure, underfinancing, and the self-serving of officeholders, there are special differences in Sorata that are attributable to campesino control of government. A campesino official is likely to have his residence, or at least his primary residence, in a campesino village. In addition, he generally owns land in his village. For both of these reasons campesino officials are frequently absent from the town and hence are out of touch with townspeople, many of whom already resent them as outsiders, as crude "indios." Since these officials are relatively isolated in the community, and sensitive to the sindicatos as their source of power, they are not responsive to the desires of townspeople. The campesino point of view in the conflict between townspeople, meaning the vecinos who once controlled the local government, and the new officials who represent the sindicatos, is expressed in the following comment by a campesino on the activities of the former vecino alcalde:

It is true that Moran pruned the plaza shrubs and trees and painted the alcaldia, but we campesinos don't eat better for what the alcalde did. What's the use of these works? What we need are more seeds and more tools.

The great differences in education, style of life, and social status, and therefore in social and civic interests and objectives, between town vecinos and campesino officials give rise to unremitting conflict that oscillates between outspoken recriminations and a studied ignoring of the opposition. Criticism of campesino officials by vecinos among themselves is continuous and intense, directed at incompetence, corruption, boorish manners, and drunkenness. With the lengthening of time since the vecinos were in power, a pattern of destructive criticism and general obstructionism has developed among them. They have become a passive opposition, active only to complain or ridicule. The officials are privately sensitive to vecino criticism, but in their official activities they ignore it completely, though from time to time they make overtures to vecinos to participate in civic celebrations for a show of unity. For the most part, vecinos ignore these overtures and are conspicuous by their absence. For example, on the July 16 Independence Day celebration of 1966 the alcalde, Juan Roblis, put up posters around town inviting everyone to a reception at the alcaldia. Commenting on the absence of vecinos, Campos said, "The only ones who didn't take part were the vecinos, because they don't want to get involved with 'those indios.' But we don't pay any attention. After so many years of living here, we know how they behave."

When vecinos are stimulated to act on some community issue they generally attempt to do so quite independently. When the Bolivian Automobile Club announced that one of their series of road races would be run between La Paz and Sorata, the vecinos realized that this would bring national attention to the town and perhaps result in improvement of the road, so they formed a committee to raise funds and organize a fiesta at the conclusion of the race. On the day of the race the vecino committee formed a welcoming group at the edge of town, while town officials waited at the alcaldia to greet the racers with nothing more than a brief ceremony. The big event of the day was a splendid dinner and party given by the vecinos at the large prefectural hotel. Everyone in town was invited, but while vecinos dined and danced in the hotel with the racers, the less distinguished townspeople, including government officials, drank and danced in the courtyard. Similarly, an impending visit of inspection by the prefect of the department was announced to local officials by a vecino forastero as if it were a personal visit to himself, he adding that the vecinos would hold a meeting with the prefect. The official mayor commented:

This guy would like to show the prefect that the authorities here in Sorata are asleep, while he is the only one who does anything. Imagine, when we called a meeting to organize a reception and to prepare a list of requests to submit to the prefect, this fellow called another meeting of vecinos to take place at the same time at the public school.

Since it was an official visit, the prefect attended the meeting called by the local authorities. Later in the day, while the prefect was inspecting the town, in the company of the local officials and a few prominent vecinos, Roblis, the alcalde, pointed to the community swimming pool then being completed and boasted of his initiative in this project. He had hardly closed his mouth when Soruco, the head of the truckers' sindicato and a marginal vecino, broke out with this statement:

Allow me, señor prefect, but I think that you have the right to know that the only thing that the alcalde, together with his official mayor, is able to do is drink all day long. Even in the case of the swimming pool, the truck drivers are the ones who carried the sand from Achacachi without cost, and he didn't even mention that. It would be much better if this man here were dismissed because, as an alcalde, he's no good.

There is some indication that campesino officials would like an end to this conflict, would prefer collaboration. But their wish is ignored. Though the vecinos, through their criticism and hostility, isolate themselves from the center of political power in the area, they still retain a little of their former prestige.

The formal structure of justice in Sorata is identical to that of the three provincial capitals already described. There are the two levels of judges, juez de partido and juez instructor, professional lawyers who are assisted by full-time clerks. There are also four parochial judges who certify signatures and take depositions. And there is the agrarian judge, concerned with agrarian reform and land disputes, though he was formerly a surveyor and has had no legal training. As in the other three towns, the enforcement of law is an activity of any local official. The professional law enforcers consisted until 1965 of a small unit of the national police, the Carbineros. After the coup of November 1964, the new military government reorganized the Carbineros in two separate branches, the Guardia de Seguridad Nacional and the Direccion de Investigacion Criminal, with the former responsible for law enforcement and the latter responsible for the investigation of crime. This added a second police officer to the local scene and further complicated the jurisdictional problem. Besides their having the informal and vague judicial authority that almost any local government official may assume, police officers are authorized to sit as judges in minor cases.

Aside from summary justice dispensed by local officials, there is not much judicial activity. In 1964 there were forty-one civil and criminal cases heard by the two local judges, and in 1965 they heard seventeen; but these figures may be an inexact indication of formal legal action, for there are no venue limitations on the jurisdiction of courts. A case may be taken to any part of the country. There may be advantages in this regulation. Vecinos prefer not to air their problems before local judges, and therefore they initiate legal actions in La Paz. Similarly, country campesinos avoid the courts in town whenever possible, for they suspect the quality of local justice. Further, a wide range of both civil and criminal cases are resolved in the campesino villages either by dirigentes, much as local government officials hear cases in the town, or by their sindicato's secretario de justicia.

For the most part, only town campesinos and a few cholos appear in civil and criminal courts in town. Criminal cases predominate, mostly charges of physical assault, while marital desertion and separation account for a majority of the civil cases. The participants have available as counsel only the tinterillos. There are six full-time tinterillos, all middle-aged to elderly men, plus three or four young men who occasionally take cases. Most of the tinterillos have had less than a complete primary school education and know little formal law. Instead, they depend on good personal relations with the judges. Judges and tinterillos see much of each other. They drink and dine together and pass many hours in informal chatting. Such relations make it easy to settle on procedures and reach a judgment before a case is called. The formal moves, such as the filing of a writ, are frequently not undertaken by the advocate tinterillo, but by the judge, for he is the only one who knows the proper form. Under this system it is not unusual for both plaintiff and defendant to suffer alike through informal agreements reached between the contending tinterillos on the one hand and the presiding judge on the other.

The tinterillos have no fixed fees, but charge what the client can afford or what the case appears to be worth. Actions continue for weeks, months, even years, and at each successive stage the tinterillo expects some payment. Higher payments stir his diligence and often ensure favorable decisions. The modest salaries of judges, which provide them with a very meager livelihood, make them sympathetic and persuadable.

In 1966 a small campesino merchant went to La Paz on business, leaving his tienda in charge of his two adolescent daughters. One night during the father's absence five town campesino boys got into the house, had sexual relations with the two girls and took $80 from the till when they left. On the following day the boys came back for more, but their noisy coming and going and the rumpus in the tienda aroused the suspicion of a neighbor, who blocked the doorway, forcing the boys to go out a back window. On the father's return the neighbor told him what had been going on. After questioning his daughters the father went to the police and denounced the boys for theft and sexual abuse of minors, the two girls giving evidence. The police captain arrested all five of the boys and locked them in the local jail.

The police captain turned the case over to the juez de partido for disposition. The case actually belonged to the juez instructor, but since he was absent from town the police captain decided to give it to the other judge. In the meantime, one of the tinterillos was asked to defend two of the boys, and he invited the judge and captain to his house to discuss the case. The captain brought with him the two young clients of the tinterillo. There at the house, after an hour or so of pleasant drinking, the three decided that an informal settlement out of court was the best solution, and ordered the families of the two boys to pay damages of $16 each and to return the stolen $80. The judge then persuaded the father of the two girls to drop his complaints. It is not known who received what part of the damages. When the parents of the other three boys heard of the settlement they went to the sub-prefect and alcalde and asked that their sons be released until the juez instructor could hear the case. By the time the juez instructor came back all five families had accepted the settlement and the father of the girls had dropped his complaint.

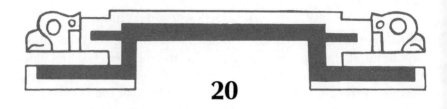

20

SOCIAL
STRATIFICATION

Until the middle of this century Sorata had a classical rural Bolivian stratification order. At the top were the gente decente, the families of European ancestry who owned or managed the large trading houses and the large haciendas. There were perhaps fifty such families in Sorata. They were somewhat more heterogeneous in terms of original nationality than their counterparts in Coroico, for not only were there families of Spanish origin, but also many who had come from Germany, England, and other European countries. These are the families who spoke Spanish, who had university educations, and who occupied the large mansions on or near the central plaza. They dressed in clothing imported from Europe, furnished their houses with articles from Europe, modeled their living and lives after European high culture and society, and were at their very best in the century between 1850 and 1950, the period of great mercantile affluence. This is how one of the elderly decentes, a woman whose family has abandoned Sorata and who now lives with her adult children in La Paz, recalls those times:

After work, around six o'clock, all the gente buena would go home and change into their summer clothes to parade around the plaza—the women with their parasols, their light cotton summer dresses down to their ankles, strolling around, the children playing in the park. There would be a band playing and everyone would be walking around. Then, after that they would go to the club to dance and drink. It had carpeted floors, not wood, and the best furniture, brought from Vienna. And grand pianos. There were people who knew how to play then. They would go there to drink and to listen to good music.

We drank the best kinds of liquors: champagne from France, wine from

Spain, whiskey from England. Anything we wanted. That whiskey cost three bolivianos and twenty centavos, a lot then. The champagne cost twelve bolivianos, also a lot. But we traded in English sterling at that time. It was used freely in town and everybody had money. In those days we could afford to have whatever we wanted, like parties with real bands all the time. The preserves and food that were brought in was another fantastic thing. No one in La Paz could get or even knew of these brands. We had smoked fish from Norway in huge cans, and olive oil from Italy. There were crackers, candies, and cheeses from Switzerland and Holland. There was everything we wanted, and the people came from La Paz to buy these things.

For the dances the women carried feathered fans for the quadrilles and wore long white gloves. They wore dresses brought from France, made from the best velvet. And they wore their hair high. It reminds me of the current pouf styles. There were tiny shoes, made of leather so fine that you could double them over, that were just for dancing, and in any color that you wanted. The men wore smoking jackets for these parties, with black tie, white gloves, also for the quadrille. And they would bring in orchestras from La Paz on mule back. People would come from La Paz just to shop in these stores. And for the fiestas, the best families would come out from La Paz and stay for weeks in the big houses like ours, or that of the Palacios, or the Gunthers. Oh, there was constant activity, and the young people could always find work and diversion.

The decentes of that time had the wealth, the power and authority. They dominated government and had authority over the campesino population. They were also the prestige elite in both town and countryside. Below the decentes were the two mixed strata, the mestizos and then the cholos, both racially mixed, the mestizos usually the offspring of decente fathers. The fourth and bottom rung of the hierarchy was occupied by the indios.

CHANGING THE STRATIFICATION ORDER

In the late 1930's and 1940's the internal and international commerce from which the decente families drew the major share of their income began to decline, and since hacienda profits could not compensate for the losses in trade, decente families sought opportunities elsewhere. This process had hardly begun when the Revolution of 1952 occurred, and that greatly accelerated the gente decente exodus. Although apparently rather little physical violence occurred on the haciendas, the anti-hacendado and pro-campesino slogans and statements of the MNR leaders, the land reform policies of the new government, and the economic and political agitation among the campesino population made it expedient for most decentes to abandon their haciendas. One of the few detentes remaining in town comments:

The hacienda is a long way from town, and for five years there was that fear of the campesinos. My mother told us to leave the haciendas alone, that running them was not worth the risk of being killed by the campesinos. We didn't come back for five whole years for fear of them. They took over the hacienda house and ruined it.

It was several years before decente families had enough confidence to assert their rights to land that remained to them, but by that time most had established themselves in the cities. One elderly decente, now a resident of La Paz, explains what happened:

Here in Sorata, this used to be my home. I had that big house that is now the public primary school. I sold that. Then we also had property way up in the mountains that we sold. And we sold our villa down at the canto to the Urtados because my children went to La Paz to be educated. Then they found work there and they no longer came back to Sorata. It's a problem to maintain the properties, and we sold the fincas to pay for the education of the children. Now there is nothing here. There are no youth because they can't find jobs here. There is no activity at all. It's vacant. I even note a difference with this generation. They don't look the same. They are all mixed now. But before, they were blancos and they were tall. That was my generation. Now I'm old and sad because I knew what Sorata was like.

When the Revolution freed the peons they went off in increasing numbers to the Tipuani and Mapiri gold fields, and the lucky ones returned to settle in the town. As one of the cholas puts it:

Today the only ones who are in a good position are these indios, who are into everything. Don't you see that they are the only ones buying houses on the plaza, trucks, houses in La Paz, with all that money that they take out of Tipuani? In contrast, the vecinos are ruined and they are behind, like the dull-witted. The reason is that they are poor and are selling everything, while the indios have money and are better off than we vecinos. There used to be gente decente of the real society here in Sorata, but now it's all these indios.

As a result of economic and political changes and subsequent demographic changes, the foundations of the traditional stratification order were largely destroyed and the means of recruitment to status radically altered; the conditions and symbols of status have changed until they conflict rather than reinforce each other. The symmetry in wealth, power, and prestige seen in a stable, little-changing stratification system like that of Villa Abecia has disappeared in Sorata. No stratum or social group has survived that can claim significant measures of the several elements of status.

While racial terms like blanco and indio are still in widespread use locally, the congruity of race and status has virtually disappeared. The European types who once constituted the vecinos are almost all gone, while those of mixed race have begun to intermarry with the remnant blancos and are moving up into the vecino stratum. There is also increasing intermarriage of former Indian peons with cholos and mestizos. Race has ceased to be an important justification for the stratification order and has become mainly a vehicle of protest utilized by those who have been threatened or who have suffered from the changes that followed the Revolution. Language, occupation, education, dress, and other cultural attributes have also become ambiguous in defining status. Whereas campesinos once received little or no education, campesino children are now required, at least under law, to attend public school. This has been an important factor in the movement of campesinos to the towns, where the schools are better than in the countryside. Today the public primary school has many more children of campesino and former campesino families in it than children of any other stratum. A prominent comerciante describes what has happened:

None of the Sorateños of my age [forty-five to fifty] knows how to read or write. I myself was unable to attend school because campesinos were prohibited from going to classes. When we would venture to enter the classrooms the school children as well as the teachers kicked us and mistreated us until we would leave. In my time hardly any campesinos could go to school, but today, thanks to God, all that has changed. In the church school and in the public school, more than four-fifths of the students are children of campesinos and cholos. If it is true that education here has not progressed much, nevertheless we can say that we now enjoy much more freedom to educate our children.

The advanced education that was taken for granted among the old decentes has become an important goal of many cholos and town campesinos. Many of the more prosperous cholo and town campesino families are sending their children to the universities in La Paz and other centers.

As a result of some exposure to formal education, greater freedom of movement, and new social contacts, the Aymara speaker in town is learning Spanish. Aymara is still widely used in the home, the marketplace and the tiendas, especially by women, but there is a growing awareness among town campesinos that their language reveals their peon origin and they have become quite intent upon the use of Spanish. For example, a town campesino came to the office of the public notary and in broken Spanish asked for a document he needed. A vecino who could speak Aymara questioned him, using Aymara; but before he could complete his sentence the town campesino interrupted to say that he could speak perfectly well and preferred to discuss his business in Spanish.

As with education and language, so with the strata distinctiveness of dress and other aspects of life style. Almost all men in town wear the same type of manufactured clothing, different only in cleanliness and condition. Western-style dress is also being adopted by the women, though it is far from having displaced the traditional pollera.

In the past decade all of the remaining decentes have suffered a decline in their standard of living. All have financial problems, though for some they are more serious than they are for others. Many have had to engage in hard physical work for the first time in their lives. As their friends have moved away or died, as their living conditions have declined and their economic problems continually press in on them, and as the town and its residents have changed, the old decentes have become resigned to a bleak future, but most have become withdrawn and bitter, an attitude well expressed in the following comment by one of them:

Look how those indios have progressed. Before they had only straw on the roofs of their houses and now they have corrugated metal. There are some indios who are good, respectful, loving, and deferential. Others think a lot of themselves, think they are señores. Imagine, they do not even greet the gente blanca. Before, the indios would affectionately greet the vecinos, but today the indios want the vecinos to greet them first. What a barbarity! How people have changed!

Look at the town, once the pride of Bolivia, now a town of indios. Most of the vecinos have died or have left it. In a little while only indios are going to own the town. Obviously, they have the money and can buy what they please. It is all right that the campesinos live in good houses, but it is painful to see the town populated by indios when before there were only caballeros, dressed in cashmere clothes and well off.

I do not believe those times will ever return. I do not believe we will see again those good days when the vecinos, cholos, and indios all kept to their own places. Today everything has changed. Vecinos, cholos, and indios are all mixed together. You have seen that vecinos have married cholos, and indios have married cholos. Yes, today there is no justice. There is no sense of responsibility. The government is against the patróns. There is no loyalty. Hate and rancor dominate the dirigentes. I do not know what is to become of Bolivia. Life is becoming more difficult because there are no guarantees for anyone.

Most of the few decentes still in town are granted vecino status, though often qualified; but this survival of status does not necessarily extend to their children. Another social type that is generally accorded vecino status is the outside professional. This would include the doctor, the dentist, the agronomist, the water resources engineer, and the judges. In communities where there is a substantial, cohesive, vecino stratum, such outsiders are generally accorded vecino status, but separate and slightly below that of the local vecino. He is the vecino forastero, and will continue to be considered an outsider no matter how long he remains in town. He is generally kept at a distance by true vecinos. Since there are so few traditional vecinos in Sorata, these outside professionals are much more readily accepted among them, though some, such as the judges, may find that their work brings them together with the local government campesinos and cholos, and this clouds their status.

In a situation where so many of the old vecinos have little money and a negative outlook, the enterprising, positive character of the successful comerciante cholos has made them prominent in the community and has earned them a measure of vecino status, even though old vecinos as well as others are apt to disparage them as "only cholos."

The same instability of status that characterizes the vecinos applies also to the other 90 per cent of the population. A large proportion of these townspeople are cholos. An even larger proportion are campesino immigrants from the surrounding countryside. Many of these families are different from the campesinos of the villages and ex-haciendas in dress, speech, and manner. Most can be readily distinguished from the rural campesino who comes to town only on market days. While some are still engaged in agriculture, the majority by far now work at town jobs, the same jobs that were once a monopoly of the cholos, such as small-scale buying and selling, craft work, and skilled labor. The female minoristas come not only from cholo families, but from former campesino families. The tailors, the shoemakers, the truck drivers, the carpenters, are not alone cholos, but former campesinos.

Many terms are current to differentiate town campesinos from the rural campesinos—campesino refinado, chuta, medio, indio, indio refinado, and mozo. However, the distinctions implied by these terms are mainly observed at the extremes. A blending of town campesino with cholo has been speeded by a decreasing distinctiveness in the cholos themselves, whose special forms of dress, forms of Spanish speech, and forms of conduct are disappearing as they adopt vecino-like ways. There are townspeople who are clearly identifiable, by their speech, dress, and manner, as having a campesino background. On the other hand, there are growing numbers of persons from both cholo and campesino families who are now indistinguishable not only from each other but also from the old vecinos. These persons are no longer cholos or campesinos, but neither are they as yet vecinos.

MOBILITY AND STATUS RELATIONS

Status change, radical social mobility, is on all sides, both up and down, blurring the concepts and assignment of position, as shown in the following question and answer discussion:

Q: I don't understand all the differences that exist. There is de pollera, de vestido, gente buena. Can you tell me what they all mean?

A: All right. I will because I know. First of all, an indio is an indio, no matter what.

Q: How can you tell?

A: By the way he looks, his face, and the way he speaks. One just knows. And you know what his background is. Then there are cholos, who are refined indios, like this one next door. She is a chola.

Q: Does she wear pollera?

A: Yes, she does, but her daughters don't. They are trying to raise themselves up, but they can't because they have a chola mother. You can't change what you are. Why, there are even cases of indias here in town trying to put on vestidos. Other indios tell them to take those clothes off and not to try to put on airs.

Q: What about this Tola family?

A: Indios. They come from the interior, and were nothing but panderos [bakers] when they first came. I saw them then, so I know how they were. But they worked hard and lifted themselves up. Now she has a tienda. But they were nothing but panderos who started out with a sack of flour and a tin of lard and worked like dogs.

Q: Now explain to me about the gente decente. Can they ever lose their position?

A: Never. Don't you see? Take the race, any race—you, for instance, are a gringo. Even if you put on Indian clothes and wore the worst poncho they would still call you a gringo. But they'd say, "oh, look at the poor gringuita." That's the way it is with the gente buena here too. They can lose all their money and not dress nicely, but you still recognize them for what they are.

Q: How?

A: Because they speak well, they act well. The people still hold a respect for them because of these qualities that one retains no matter what situation he is in. A caballero, born a caballero, is always a caballero.

Q: What if they marry an india or a chola?

A: No, they can't.

Q: But what if they do? Aren't there some cases like that?

A: Not that I know of.

[The husband of the daughter of a well-known vecino family walks by.]

Q: What about that fellow who just walked by?

A: Ah, yes. Now there is an example. That Quintana girl married him and, well, he's really not of the gente buena. His mother is nothing but an india. And the thing with the wife is that her first husband was below her too. His mother still lives down by the market, that old cholita who is in mourning all the time. I remember when the girl wanted to marry the first husband. Her family told her not to, that he was nothing more than a cholo, but she didn't listen to them. They say that the old mother ran him out of town, down to the mines. They got a divorce.

Q: What about the present marriage?

A: Well, as I said, he's below her, but you have to look at it this way. She was so thin before, poor little thing. Her waist was no bigger than a branch. Since she's married to him, she's gotten fatter and happier, you can tell. I guess it's a case of la vida buena sin orgullo. Oh, I have another example for you. You know the woman on the corner? Well, she is contrabando de la cocina. [You see, her] father was some vecino in town, but he was fooling around with the cook, a common india, in the kitchen, and she was the result. She put on polleras, then de vestidos. She couldn't make up her mind what she was.

Q: How do the people of the town refer to her?

A: Those of us who know call her the cholita! Then she married just another of her kind, some indio from the interior. They are "ordinary" people. [She sees Antonio Paso walk by.] You see him? There's another example of a cholo.

Q: How do you mean?

A: He's sort of a refined indio. He and his wife come from the interior.

This brief discussion illustrates many of the varieties of status mobility taking place in Sorata. One is the movement from campesino to cholo-like status. An example was Paso, the refined indio who is now considered a cholo. He has been successful economically, runs a small hotel, sells gasoline, and has several other commercial activities. His arrival as a cholo was symbolized when he was the preste, the formal host, a very costly and honorific role, for one of the major town fiestas. Another route to status is political. There are several men in town now who currently are or in past years have been important political figures. They came from the campesino villages but are now considered townsmen with an ambiguous cholo rather than campesino status. Most have profited economically from political success, but this prosperity has not always proved very durable.

Aside from the general decline of the old vecino stratum as a whole, there has been considerable variation in the extent of individual or family downward mobility. One or two families have survived with much of their former prestige still intact, the last survivals of the real social elite of the community, but most have had their claims to old elite status compromised in varying degrees. Such is the case of the family of Alfredo Quintana, who was shot by campesinos during a civic celebration (see Chapter 19, p. 249).

Quintana was a brother of the woman who chose "la vida buena sin orgullo." The Quintana family is a distinguished one in Sorata, but today only fragments remain, an elderly widowed mother and her three daughters, two married and one single. The mother occupies a large house at the corner of the plaza, but because she has no land and little money she rents rooms to female schoolteachers. The husbands of both of the married daughters come from cholo families, though neither is identified as a traditional cholo. However, neither are they vecinos. The marriages have been a constant source of humiliation and displeasure to the mother. One married daughter was married previously to a cholo, with the following familial effect:

In her first marriage she married a man of cholo background, son of a señora de pollera, which was the basis of constant hostility on the part of her relatives. They kept telling her, "you have married a cholo," and always referred to him as "el cholito Espinosa." Finally the husband couldn't take it any longer and deserted the family to go to Tipuani in search of his fortune, in order to bring about some change in his life. Embittered by that family, he died in the gold fields. The widow then married again, a man who was also of cholo background.

Both the mother and the single daughter are extremely outspoken in disparaging everyone who is cholo or campesino. They let pass few opportunities to criticize or demean those whom they consider their social inferiors, which is almost everyone in town. Indeed, one of the prominent features of the Sorata status order is the antagonism shown toward those of different status. One form of this is the negative stereotype. Vecinos say of campesinos that they smell bad, that they have limited abilities and are not good for much except simple agricultural work, that they are dangerous and violent, that they are like animals in their behavior. Another form of this antagonism is ridicule, making fun of campesinos who ask for letters at the post office in the name of the sender instead of the receiver. A third form is abuse. A vecino widow who has a small tienda on the plaza presents an example. The local government had undertaken to prune the large trees in the central plaza in preparation for the July 16 Independence Day celebration, and one afternoon three days before the big event several men appeared with machetes and started chopping. The widow stood at the front of her tienda on the plaza, ranting:

Indios! that's all they are. Ignorantes! Burros! Lackeys! They don't even think. Ay, we used to have a nice town of vecinos, not people from the outside. They were people who cared, and now they are nothing who are running this city. [A young man, her nephew, walks up and the widow tells him in strong, grating tones to look at the mess being made of the plaza.] The worst of them all is that guy Zepeda. He couldn't make it when we vecinos were in power, but now he's here and taking advantage of the campesinos. But I ask him who he thinks he is.

Hey you, Zepeda [said in a most offensive way], what are you doing to the plaza? A bunch of brutes you're employing to fix up those trees. You should go and see with what fondness they care for their trees in Cochabamba and La Paz. [Zepeda hears her, looks over, then turns his back again. She continues to yell at him. Everyone along the plaza can hear her yelling, but he won't turn and face her. As she calls out, he moves away and walks down through the plaza.] Che, burro! Don't go away, don't run away. He always runs whenever you confront him to his face. He's a coward. That's the way they all are, brutes, ignorantes, not a brain in their head.

Another form of antagonism is social rejection. One mobile young man from a cholo family complains sadly that he told his vecino wife before their marriage that she was not to be upset if she heard his enemies call him a cholo. Now, he says that when his young wife gets mad at him she calls him a cholo. But he also is very ambivalent about his cholo relatives. It bothers him that his mother wears pollera. In talking to his mother, he tells of her dignity and good manners and how well she wears the pollera, but in the next sentence asserts that she is too good to be wearing pollera. The traditional cholo identifies with the traditional vecino, as the following discussion indicates:

Q: Do you people ever get together with the vecinos?

A: No, we always have our reunions apart.

Q: What is the reason for that?

A: As you must know, the aristocracy are different and it is difficult for them to mix with craftsmen and workers.

Q: What about the town campesinos? Do you ever get together with them, for example, at some fiesta or social occasion?

A: Well, just as the principal vecinos don't mix with the craftsmen, neither do we mix with the town campesinos. We call them indios refinados. Since they do the same kinds of work they try to approach me. From time to time they will tell me, "Let's have a beer," but I always find some pretext to avoid them, like saying I'm not well.

Q: What would happen if you accepted such an invitation?

A: There would be a lot of talk. The other craftsmen would say to me, "What's the matter with you? You must be degenerating." Besides, I don't mix with them because they're very forward and ill-bred, and because they are always getting drunk and bothering the blancos.

In Sorata, as in Coroico, the status order has undergone a series of major changes, but in Sorata these have been more profound. This is vividly expressed in the following comment by an elderly member of an old cholo family:

We say, "The toad is on the balcony and the eagle is in the dirt." That suits them. Don't you see? This means that the people give undue importance to the lowly people, to the campesinos, and they forget the really good people, who are at the bottom now, like the eagle.

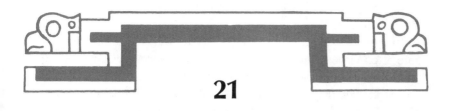

21

GROUPS AND ORGANIZATIONS

There is in Sorata the same range of groups and organizations already encountered in Reyes and Coroico. And again, most of the formal groups and organizations are of limited importance to their members and of even less importance to town affairs as a whole, though there is an exception in the sindicato de transportistas. The significant groups tend to be those formed on the basis of kinship, and secondarily, friendship. But even in these groups there is much conflict, physical violence, and rupture of relations.

FAMILY AND KIN

The strongest social bonds are those between close kin, between husband and wife and parents and their children. In this nuclear family there are the stronger and more enduring relations of affection, cooperation, and support. The tendency toward small family size observed in Coroico is even greater in Sorata. While 25.9 per cent of the households in Coroico have two or less persons and 58.8 per cent have four or less, the comparable proportions in Sorata are 36.2 per cent and 71.3 per cent, respectively.

This is in part the result of several trends in the past decade. One is the increased tendency of young adults to leave Sorata for the cities, especially La Paz, because of few job opportunities at home. Town campesino families send their daughters to La Paz to work as servants, and their brothers look for unskilled work or jobs as apprentices to skilled craftsmen. At the other end of the status scale, young vecino adults more often leave town to pursue an advanced education, but the importance of education is also widely recognized beyond the old vecino families. As one of the most successful of the town campesino merchants puts it, "In relation to the future of my children, I hope to give them a secondary education. With that they will be able to defend themselves, since I have no house or land or cattle to leave them as inheritance." The effect of the departure of young adults is a large number of two-person families, of couples ranging in age from the mid-thirties on.

Another trend affecting family size is that men seek work in the mines of the lowland interior. The single largest occupational category in town consists of miners. Boys begin work in the mines while still teenagers or even earlier, either attracted by adventure, wealth, and adult status, or sent off by their families to reduce the burdens of life. Not only young men, but men in their thirties, forties, and fifties go to the Tipuani mines. In 13 per cent of the households of the town a woman is the head of the family. This figure greatly underestimates the proportion of female-run households, for, while some husbands are absent from Sorata only two to three months of the year, others are present for only two to three months. During the peak periods of the yearly mining cycle, entire blocks are almost without adult males. Further, a high incidence of tuberculosis and fatal accidents among miners contributes to a high proportion of single-person households—15 per cent—of women alone. Many of these women take in a criado, a servant foster child, who can help around the house and run errands. Daughters place children with widowed mothers, though in several instances it was clear that the daughter gave up the child to its grandmother to relieve herself of a burden. Sometimes it is an aunt rather than a mother who is the dubious beneficiary of a criado. There were at least twenty such arrangements in Sorata, several of which were criticized by neighbors who said these stand-in parents did not properly supervise the children, but let them run wild and misbehave.

As in Coroico, many of the one-person households of men are campesinos who have recently moved to town to work, but who have wives and children in the countryside to care for their chacra. Another important stream of migrants is made up of the young men who return from the mine fields and rent a room or buy a house in town rather than go back to the ex-hacienda.

Some Sorateños who go off to the mines send money to their wives, but living costs are extremely high in Tipuani and many of the men spend heavily on alcohol, gambling, and women, and may even be robbed in the bargain. Many miners barely get by, so the consequence back in Sorata is that the mother is required to work to maintain the family. While local, small-scale retail selling and weaving are important women's occupations, more women work as minoristas, spending about half their time away from home. If there is an older child in the family, he or she takes charge; if not, the children are left with a relative or a neighborhood friend.

In families at all status levels wives are expected to assist husbands and children to assist parents. A wife may operate a small tienda while her husband is driving his truck, or wives and older daughters weave while the husbands and older sons make shoes or do carpentry. Or they all together run a family enterprise, a tienda in which husband and wife work full-time, assisted by their older children. Close cooperation in work is illustrated in the following report by one of the project workers about a relatively poor family:

At the tienda of Francisco Preciado I stopped to chat for a while. It was ten minutes after ten and I found Señora Preciado very busy at her daily work, kneading dough for the rolls they sell daily. She said to me: "You know, Pacito, every day we have to do something to earn a little money. We have to begin at three o'clock in the morning to start our work, and later go to the oven. At that hour we start the water boiling, and meanwhile Francisco goes to Alonso at the oven to get flour. Afterwards we begin to prepare the dough for the rolls. By five o'clock, or six at the latest, the rolls are ready to be taken from the oven. At that hour I open the tienda, and my customers start coming to buy rolls, sugar, coffee, or some other small thing. The people on this street know that by six o'clock in the morning we will have opened the tienda and they start coming for their purchases. At that early hour it is also time for them to start work. No? Every day it's the same for us poor ones."

In this family there are three children ranging in age from three to seven. They are no help now, but when they are older they will be put to work in the shop.

The pattern of cooperative work in families does not always end when the children grow up and move away. One elderly cholo woman has seven adult children, none at home. She lives alone and supports herself by making women's blouses, but she is in this business with two of her married daughters who live in La Paz. After the big September 14 Saint's Day Fiesta she reported:

Why, just during this fiesta I sold 450 pesos worth of blouses. A man who travels into the Yungas bought the whole lot. My older daughters and I have an arrangement in making blouses. I send the specifications of embroidering to my two daughters in La Paz and they send back the finished embroidered part of the blouse. Since most of those that I sold during the fiesta were made by my daughters, I sent them the money. Of course, that man also bought 300 pesos worth of my own blouses. Now I am sending some more specifications and we will split the profits, my daughters and I.

There are also many strains in family relations, the more likely to cause breakdown the longer the periods are when men are away from their wives and children. Men at the mines seek other women, and back in Sorata many wives behave in like manner. Ill-considered, hasty mating, as well as the form of marriage itself, are factors in the breakup of families. Ideally, most families seek sons-in-law who are hard workers, men of exemplary moral conduct. Vecinos and marginal vecinos expect a good deal in terms of education, job prospects, and good manners. Women, in turn, are expected to be accomplished homemakers and attentive to the ways of husbands. Daughters of vecino families are expected to be chaste, so their families devote considerable attention to keeping them from casual encounters with men, especially those who would not be acceptable as husbands; but town campesinos and cholos are less concerned about a girl's sexual history than with her capacity to work.

In few instances are marriages arranged by parents any more, especially in families of lower social status. Market days, weekend athletic events, and fiestas are important occasions for the meeting of the sexes, and these encounters occasionally lead to sudden marriage, as in the following case:

I had to get married when I was fourteen years old. You know how crazy young people are. I fell in love with a young boy who was nineteen and told my parents. Instead of opposing the idea and separating me until I had forgotten about him, my father with his old ideas said, "My daughter might get out with some man. It is better that she marries." And so he married me off.

Most early marriages take place in cholo and town campesino families and are all the easier because there is frequently no formal ceremony at all, nothing but agreement to live together, and possibly at some later date pay the fees of a civil marriage. Few have a religious marriage because the ceremony, the wedding fiesta, and the related celebrations are costly. In many cases marriages of this sort are quickly regretted:

We lived in the same neighborhood, and one day he said to me, "let's live together." I was just a young girl and hadn't thought much about it. My mother was opposed, and it was on a whim that I married him. I did it just to make my mother mad. It was sure bad judgment. My husband was a real rascal. He never helped out and I had to continue working. After living with him for a year I asked myself, "What have I done to be married to this man?" It seemed like a bad dream.

Among town campesinos there is also a somewhat Saturnalian way of acquiring a spouse. A young town campesino wife describes it:

Sometimes, after knowing each other for a while, a fiesta arrives, the pair get drunk, and they start living together. Sometimes the girl goes to live with the man. Other times the man gets drunk and the girl takes him to her house. Then her mother tells him, "You have been seeing to my daughter for some time and now you have placed her in a predicament." They don't let him leave, so they just start living together. After the September fiesta you are going to see a lot of marriages. Why? Because a lot of couples are going to get drunk.

Heavy drinking is prevalent throughout the population, at fiestas, parties, celebrations, and family ceremonies. One of the most distinguished families in town is notorious for continual drinking, which begins early in the morning and goes on throughout the day, day in and day out. It is said that anyone who has business with this family must see them before noon because after that they will be too far gone to think. A large proportion of the older vecino women are constant heavy drinkers, have servants to do all the work in the house and take care of them when they are drunk. Some are able to conceal the extent of their drinking, but it nevertheless causes family friction, as one of these women confessed:

That day before the baptism, the sixteenth it was, some compadres, indios from the interior and cholos, came with their cocktails and I began to drink in the kitchen with them. We had beer, which I invited them to drink, and then they invited me to drink their alcohol. It came time for my old man to come home and I went into the kitchen to be out of the way so that he wouldn't see that I was drunk. Rotten luck! I fell over backwards and passed out just as he walked in.

The little servant couldn't take care of me by herself, and there I was unconscious on the kitchen floor. That is the first time that ever happened in all of the years I have drunk until dawn—drunk, but never passed out. I was so ashamed. I don't remember anything. They tell me they tried to get me into bed, but I kept saying, "I don't want to." Somehow I got up, went into my daughter's room and slept there. Then in the morning I was so ashamed that I didn't want to leave that room. My old man didn't speak to me for three full days.

The wife of a former minor official in local government is considering leaving her husband because of his drinking.

You ought to see my husband. His drinking is like a sickness. He cannot resist it. If you just begin to get near him you can smell the alcohol. I am thinking of going with my children to Cochabamba, or to the south where my oldest daughter lives. I am sure I can find work there and will be able at least to earn enough to educate my children. I can't take any more here in Sorata. At eight o'clock in the morning the people are beginning to drink, and my husband, who never has to be asked, is there drinking right alongside all of them. Frankly, I don't know what to do about my husband. It grieves me that he is in such a state. People have suggested to me various remedies against alcohol, but none has cured him.

In one town campesino family the husband was constantly drunk, and the wife's parents took her and her four children back to live with them. Before such separations are reached there may be days or weeks of brawling. Marital conflict occurs at all status levels in the community, though its expression in violence is disproportionately associated with families of lower social status. It occurs between all of the significant pairs in the nuclear family, between couples, between siblings, between parents and children, as well as between those relatives most closely related to the nuclear family, the grandparents and grandparents-in-law. Much of the more serious conflict between couples occurs in disagreement over connubial rights and sexual duties. Husbands assert exclusive right to their wives' sexual favors. Wives make no such claim, but nevertheless resent the involvement—or even possible involvement—of their husbands with other women. There is an example in a young marginal vecino couple who have two pre-school children. The husband is a personable fellow who is not disinclined to become acquainted with young, single women —schoolteachers, for instance. That his wife is suspicious can clearly be seen in the following account of an incident described by one of the husband's unattached female friends:

One night after Ramon [the husband] had come by to visit, and Ana and I were doing our laundry under the tap in the patio, Ramon's wife came in from the street. She did not greet us—Ramon, Ana, or me—but went upstairs where Señora Peralta lives. She was there only a few minutes and then left, again without saying a word to us. Another evening several days later Ramon dropped by with some nails to help us put up curtains. He told us about a big fight he had had with his wife. He had been out until late, and when he got home his wife was still up waiting for him. She grabbed him by his clothes and tore them. She hit him and scratched him. There was a lot of commotion, neighbors came to see what was happening, and he finally got away from her and left the house. He said that his wife had become too jealous, that she was jealous if he talked to any other woman. She was always accusing him, scolding him, until he could hardly stand it.

It is not always the case of the jealous wife and the wandering husband. Wives also have affairs, more frequently among cholos than vecinos, and most frequently among town campesinos, for it is these women whose husbands—the miners and woodcutters—are absent for the longest periods of time. They take up with another man or take to prostitution.

A man who neglects his wife and family or who beats his wife is likely to find his mother-in-law and other members of his wife's family bearing down on him, and he will be the target of considerable verbal abuse. The wife who neglects her children or takes up with other men can expect similar abuse from her husband's mother and his close relatives.

Family conflict extends also to adult siblings, where the issue is frequently the apportionment of an inheritance. Dissatisfaction with the division of property, especially among town campesinos, may end in violence. Many of the issues behind family conflict culminating in violence—jealousy, extramarital affairs, inadequate economic support, heavy drinking, child neglect, and meddling in-laws—occurred over a short period in a single nuclear family. This was the family of Francisco Chambila and his wife Elba. The couple are in their mid-twenties. Their civil marriage took place five years ago and they have two children, a little girl of four years and a boy almost one. Francisco is a miner in Tipuani, where he spends most of the year, but returns to Sorata for all the big fiestas and stays home for a few weeks. Elba makes blouses for sale and also runs a small general tienda, which her husband has stocked. This sort of life is not Elba's idea of a good time. When a project field worker visited Elba she was seated on the floor, leaning against the door jamb of the entrance way, listening to a Javier Soliz record on her phonograph, and making a blouse.

Ay, señorita, when I hear this music, I become unhappy and want to travel.
But when I tell my husband, he says I must stay married to him. About my
children? The littlest one I'd leave with his grandmother, my husband's
mother. The little girl I'll take with me, and the older boy I'll leave with my
own mother. But oh, señorita, the littlest one is so sick. He's going to die, I
think. It's better that he die, isn't it? There is no one really to look after him.
I get so tired, I really do. I want to get away and have nothing to do with my
family or my children. About my husband? All he does is beat me. Really,
he's so bad. He comes at me with the bottle when he's been drinking. He
never appreciates anything I do. Do you know, in the time since we've been
married he's not bought me one little thing. I have had to use the pollera that
I had before I was married. Imagine that!

Elba greatly exaggerates lack of support from her husband. In fact,
he gives her money and jewelry, and the profits from the tienda are hers
to use. She also mentions another son, a boy about seven years old, an
illegitimate child who lives a few houses away with Elba's mother, her
father, and her unmarried younger sister. He is assumed by neighbors to
be a criado, and he has been taught to call Elba by her first name, not
"mother." She has upset her mother with her talk of wanting to be rid
of her children.

Elba stocks beer in her tienda and enjoys having a few of her chola
friends over to drink and pass the time. Neighbors say, too, that they
have seen men coming out of the tienda at late hours. Elba's extramarital activities eventually brought her into conflict with her sister. This
young girl had been keeping company with a young truck driver and
was beginning to think seriously about him when she heard rumors that
he was also acquainted with Elba—the more experienced, the more willing to please.

She spied on Elba's tienda from another shop across the street for
days, until one afternoon she saw her novio enter and go into the back
room. After several minutes she went over and caught the two of them
in bed. In the uproar that ensued the truck driver escaped, but the
neighbors were treated to an ear-splitting eruption of cursing, and bottle-
throwing and smashing, that spilled out into the street.

Less than a month after the battle between the sisters, Elba's husband
returned for the big September 14 fiesta. In the meantime, her sister had
taken her weaving to Tipuani to sell and remained there to keep house
for her father, then working in the mines. This was in part to escape
from neighborhood gossip after the fight. The embarrassment was such,
indeed, that both she and the father decided not to come back for the

big fiesta. Francisco himself heard tales in Tipuani about Elba's neglect of the children—the little boy having died—and of her affairs with men, passed on to him by friends from Sorata and in letters from relatives in town, and Elba's mother had cautioned her daughter to prepare for his arrival:

Hija, what you must do is forget the truck driver. We know that your husband has already heard the news of the death of the baby. A letter has come from Tipuani saying that he was crying and screaming and said that he had to come out of the mines to be with his wife. So, hija, things have to be in good order when he comes back. Neither your father nor I want your husband to find you with another man. He's going to arrive and you must be alone, there with your children, and working hard.

On his return, Francisco's relatives filled him with details and surmises concerning his wife's neglect of the family and her fun and games. He found the tienda almost empty of merchandise. Some of the jewelry he had given Elba was gone and there was almost no money in the house. The reunion was guardedly hostile, but on the first day of the fiesta Francisco tried to draw Elba into the dancing, drinking, and partying. Elba rejected him, and late in the afternoon, after a brief angry exchange, he went off to drink with his male friends. In the early evening he returned to the tienda drunk. He and Elba started quarreling and he gave her a vicious beating. A project field worker reported:

I was walking in front of the church in the early evening when the little daughter of Elba Chambila came running up to me and said breathlessly, "Daddy hit Mommy with a bottle right here on the front of the mouth, and she's bleeding and crying."
On the following morning I visited Elba. Where are you hurt? I asked her. "I ache all over," she said, moaning. "He hit me on the arms and legs." She removed the covers and pulled up her underslips, exposing her knees, which were all swollen and black and blue. "It hurts awfully. I'm all swollen and it hurts so much. I want to die I hurt so much."

Later that day the mother went to see the doctor and had him go to the tienda to examine Elba. He treated her and later gave the mother a signed statement about the injuries, which she thought might be useful in obtaining a divorce for her daughter, or at least as a threat to hold over Francisco, who was now contrite and keen on making amends. He promised to have the two front teeth that he had knocked loose fixed, or replaced by gold ones if necessary. He admitted being at fault, but claimed provocation:

Well, I was drunk and I beat her up. She was saying all those things to me and so I hit her. Then she hit me too. [He had a huge black eye.] Ay, I was drunk and thinking of all the things people had told me. I don't know what to believe, and when I'm like that she is a shrew. She eggs me on. Well, a man can't just stand there like a woman and take that, so I hit her. It's that everyone has been telling me that she's been mixing with other men. Then she had this fight with her sister over a man. I don't know whom to believe. I heard it down in the mines, and they even told me she was with another man who helped to kill our baby boy.

A few days after the end of the fiesta Francisco returned to Tipuani. He wanted Elba to return with him because he did not want a divorce and felt that he could not leave her alone. She promised to follow him some weeks later, but instead of that she packed her things and went to La Paz, doing what she had wanted to do for some time.

The recent history of the Chambila family exemplifies several features of family life in Sorata that are especially characteristic of town campesinos and lower cholos. Elba's behavior, however, was extreme, for few mothers appear deliberately to neglect their children, though death may be wished on a young child who is chronically ill. Even mothers without the problems and interests of Elba express this wish, conditioned as they are by a very high infant mortality rate.

EXTENDED KIN AND COMPADRAZGO

Immigration, emigration, and mobility of the town's population have greatly affected relations between kin. The moving forces behind geographic mobility for the different parts of the population in town, coupled with the widespread expectation that each nuclear family will occupy its own household, have resulted in considerable physical separation between even close kin. Vecino and cholo children tend to set up separate households in the cities, and their rural campesino counterparts have moved to Sorata. This has reduced the active membership of many of the old vecino families and has added many new, unrelated persons to the town. Nevertheless, it is still possible to find a kinship relation between almost all of the old vecinos as well as among many of the marginal vecinos who have married into the old families. Such kinship relations, however, have only slight contemporary significance, calling for little more than customary respectful behavior, and are really more strongly impelled by status than by kinship. Returning from a velorio, a wake, a member of an old vecino family revealed this type of tie:

My good friend, who died recently, was the granddaughter of this old lady that just died. In fact I am distantly related to the old lady myself. We are parientes, but remotely. We are related through great-grandfathers and are some kind of fifth cousins, something like that.

As in the towns discussed previously, there are customs of cooperation between kin, and the closer the kinship relation the greater the cooperation. In an elective situation that involves kin and non-kin, other things being equal, the kin are likely to receive preferential treatment. However, other things generally are not equal. Estrangement and hostility are found between the closest of kin, and therefore it is not surprising that relations between more distant kin are extremely variable. The extension of kinship in the form of compadrazgo appears to be a more important basis of social relations than distant kinship.

Compadres, unlike kin, are voluntarily chosen, and those who are chosen usually are persons who already have some close tie to the chooser. While impeccable moral and religious character is considered ideal, in practice a person of substance, someone with power, money, and status, is sought as a compadre. These considerations are much less obvious in the choices made by vecinos, for they select from among friends and close relatives, who are almost invariably people of substance in the community. As in Coroico, the lower strata tend to select padrinos from among persons in higher strata, but this tendency is weak here in comparison with Reyes, and especially with Villa Abecia, because it is now necessary in Sorata to ask, high in what respect? Wealth? Manners? Political power? Prestige? All these qualities are no longer held by the same persons. The chance of forming compadrazgo ties is also lessened by refusals to accept the relationship because of the financial cost, which the old vecinos in particular cannot afford, as the following exchange indicates:

Before, we never did decline to be godparents, but now we have to. Why? Money! Before, we'd accept all who came, and they were many. And my family, we had money then, we'd give each godchild a present for Christmas. We did this until they reached their tenth year. Now that's not possible, for there's no money to make those kinds of gifts. Ay, we used to have the gifts stacked up to the ceiling, but now nothing.

In addition to its reinforcing some existing significant relationships, compadrazgo in Sorata, as in the other communities, is important for the mutual aid it encourages. Hardly anyone seeks out the role and obligations of compadre. The exceptions are the rising cholo and town campesino merchants, and it is the rural campesino whom they encourage to make the request. For comerciante and rural campesino it can be mutually beneficial. Rural campesinos also seek local officials or the tinterillos for compadres, for these men can assist and protect when legal problems arise, advancing money to pay a fine or interceding with the police to keep a man out of jail. With town campesinos, however, this calculated approach to compadrazgo is not typical.

FRIENDSHIP

Friendship is an important component of highly cohesive but informal groups, several of which bring together men of the same occupation—butchers, truck drivers, etc. Other groups are of men of the same political party, such as the group made up of some local government officials. Others are not so narrowly based, but still attract persons of similar economic status and political characteristics. These congregations of men are distinguishable as friendship groups by what they do, by gathering, sometimes on a predictable schedule, and passing an hour or two, or more—sometimes a great deal more—chatting, drinking and playing such games as generala or sapo. The reigning consideration is fellowship. Those whose work and income permit considerable discretion in the use of leisure can be found in the more prominent friendship groups, those that assemble daily in one of the four better-known drinking spots on or just off the plaza.

Every day at the cocktail hour I go to the plaza to play generala and drink with my friends. They never fail to be there each day. When I was younger I used to play soccer for the Atletico Sorata sports club, but now I am not able to play, so I dedicate myself to the sport of drink and generala.

A central activity of these friendship groups is drinking. From the meeting places on the plaza it is easy to keep an eye on the arrivals and departures from the town, to keep the alcaldia and the church under observation, and to watch activity in the public market. These amusements are overlaid with a good deal of gossiping about family problems, sexual affairs, and miscellaneous crises of other people—discussed in detail. Many of the tiendas throughout the town sell beer and alcohol, and town campesino friends go to these rather than to the pensiones and bars on the plaza.

Friendships are sometimes initiated with the expectation that they will provide some advantage or assistance. A number of the friends of one of the more important comerciantes in town are rather clearly motivated by self-interest, but most friendships of this sort rarely develop to the point of real advantage. In other instances, friendship is used as a means of mutual benefit. For example, an elderly, distinguished vecino was very friendly with a young, poor, marginal vecino. The younger man was skilled in repairing machinery and found himself on constant call to repair things in the old man's house. In turn, the older man sat on a committee that employed the younger one, who could thus be more independent and do almost as he pleased with his job without fear of reprisal.

The mutual support of friends is also important in both the prevention and resolution of conflict. There is a tendency to avoid antagonizing a person who is linked through a close friend, and friends are expected to assist in a conflict problem. After Elba's fight with her sister she invited three of her friends to come to the tienda and spend the rest of the day and evening with her. They sat around drinking, listening to Elba's side of the story and saying sympathetic things. In another case, a young marginal vecino returned home drunk one night and beat his wife severely. On the following day he invited two of his best friends into his house without telling them anything of the incident. Then he called his wife into the central room and apologized to her and begged her forgiveness, asking his friends to witness his shame and contrition. Both friends gently remonstrated him and cautioned him to avoid such heavy drinking. The husband shed as many tears as penance demanded, and then poured a round of drinks for all.

There is an almost continuous series of occasions throughout the year for people to get together to drink. Some of these are quasi-religious or have a religious aspect. Others are national holidays. Some are neighborhood fiestas, like the Abaroa Day Fiesta on Calle Abaroa, or the Obispo Bosque Fiesta in the smaller plaza of that name. Other fiestas are associated with occupational groups, as is the yearly blessing of the trucks of the transportistas, which includes a procession to the Christ statue on the side of the valley opposite Sorata. Then there are marriages, birthdays, and baptisms, all celebrated with fiestas. A person's going away, or returning, or his starting a new business enterprise, are times of fiestas. Finally, parties are held just to have a party. The important community and family fiestas last two to three days, sometimes longer, and at every one the supply of liquor is adequate for even the thirstiest guest. The drinks are beer and straight alcohol, the latter usually mixed with a little fruit juice, enough to color and flavor without seriously diluting. Both men and women are expected to drink, and the combination of beer with alcohol produces a state of drunkenness while the evening is yet young.

At cholo or town campesino fiestas, women bearing pitchers of straight alcohol offer each male guest a shot glass of it. The offering cannot be refused without giving offense, and the glass must be immediately drained, for she waits to see that it is before going on to the next man. As she moves on, another comes with a similar offering. With many such women circulating at a fiesta, intoxication spreads rapidly. Friends will gather late in the morning of the day after to compare heads, stomachs, and eyes, and go to their favorite bar for a glass of the universal remedy. More friends come in, and soon a generala game is under way to see who will pay for the drinks.

FORMAL GROUPS AND ASSOCIATIONS

The range of formal associations in Sorata is not essentially different from that described in Coroico and Reyes. There are the sports clubs, the religious associations, a Padres de Familia organization for each school, the Chaco Veterans organization, art and culture groups, and civic associations, as well as the sindicatos and political parties already discussed. The major difference between these organizations and their counterparts in the other two towns is that they are even weaker and more unstable. Membership is highly variable and uncertain, interest is fragile, and leadership is often characterized by conflict and sudden change. Long periods of organizational somnolence alternate with episodes of energetic activity as a new leader or leadership group revives membership interest and develops purposeful activities. These episodes end in disagreement, resignations, and further disillusionment.

The changes in population and the other changes discussed above have all contributed to a decline in community social cohesion. Vecinos and marginal vecinos are disproportionately dominant in almost all the voluntary organizations except town sindicatos, but with the departure of many vecino families in the 1940's and 1950's, and the departure of younger vecinos since, much of the traditional base of membership and leadership in organizations has been drastically narrowed. The recent past of Sorata is littered with defunct organizations whose members moved away, who could no longer recruit socially qualified persons, whose activities had declining relevance in post-1952 Sorata. These included chess, ping-pong, and shooting clubs, as well as the more typical soccer clubs. There were also several artistic and social clubs. Today there are only a couple of sports clubs of young men, and they have a rather irregular character. There is only one Catholic women's association, in contrast to several in both Coroico and Reyes, and even this one has membership problems. The Veterans of the Chaco War are rarely heard from, except for their appearance at the major national holiday parades. Few organizations except the town sindicatos have been able to develop strong membership commitment, but even with the sindicatos this has occurred only as they have been successful as trade unions, and thus significant to the work of the members.

The problems and conditions of voluntary organizations are also applicable to the civic groups. Events subsequent to 1952 have made the Junta de Vecinos an historical relic. Its extra-legal powers as an advisory group of the leading citizens of the community have disappeared as a result of political and social stratification changes. The junta exists more as a vague memory than as a current fact, though it still occasionally meets to elect officers. Its only recent activity occurred in the aftermath of the 1964 coup, when it was used to provide a quasi-legal format for effecting a change of officials in the local government. Even this instance reveals the insignificance of the junta, for it was clearly used expediently by a small number of vecinos opposed to the MNR, and disappeared from view after that one meeting. There have been other civic groups formed more recently, similar in form to the citizens' associations in both Reyes and Coroico. These, such as the Amigos de Sorata, have followed a course more similar to that of the other voluntary organizations in Sorata than to the comparable organizations in the other two towns, as will be seen in the following chapter.

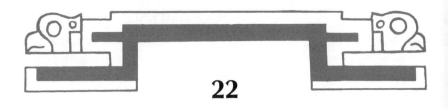

22

COMMUNITY ACTION

In November of 1964, Nabor Moran took office as a vecino alcalde, the first in many years. On the following New Year's Day he celebrated by inviting a group of vecinos and cholos to a party at the alcaldia. About fifty persons showed up for drinks and small talk, and there were several impromptu speeches. A Sorateño who teaches in the public primary school had this to say:

Señores, sometimes one must be frank. One of the greatest problems of our town is the quagmire in which we find ourselves. Why can't we all join the political party of progress? Why can't we forget the hate and rancor between brothers? Why can't we unite and work for the progress of the town? There are some persons who like to incite disorder and then step back as if they had done nothing. We must face the problem that we are not united. We want the government, local and national, to do everything for us. No, señores, we are very wrong. If we expect that, you can be sure that the town of Sorata will never progress. I ask all of you present here to get together to do something for the town. Neglect, apathy, laziness, lack of interest, irresponsibility, and lack of discipline are some of the worst traits that keep Sorata in its present diseased state. But now we have liberty, and we must fight this disease by our own actions and our own unselfish work. Thank you.

The "diseases" of the town are the many problems that affect the general health and welfare of the population. While the parochial primary school is housed in a new church building, both the public primary and public secondary schools have no quarters of their own. The public primary school occupies a big townhouse that belonged to one of the old vecino families, an old, run-down building of small, dark rooms, not conducive to teaching and learning. The public secondary school is no better off, occupying a couple of rooms in the alcaldia building.

Health and sanitation facilities are bad. For toilets and latrines, most families use a corner of the patio, the corral, or the garden. There are only two public latrines and these are in such poor condition that hardly anyone uses them, but all roads and paths leading into town are freely used and liberally contaminated with human waste. Many townspeople simply relieve themselves in a gutter or against a wall. The stench, especially on hot days, is formidable.

A hospital is needed. There has been a sanitary post in town for some years, occupying a former private home. A sanitarian is stationed there, and occasionally there are nurses posted by the Ministry of Health. Frequently, but intermittently, a young physician serves part of his año de provincia at this post. There is very little equipment, and it is likely not to be in working order. In short, there are no facilities for dealing with serious or emergency medical cases. The situation was alleviated somewhat when the Franciscans moved into a new parish house in 1966 and offered the old one as a health center. The local but temporary doctor and dentist thought that this building, which was in good condition, would not only provide adequate space for an out-patient clinic, but also enough extra rooms for in-patient beds, as well as quarters for nurses.

Beyond these problems is a series of others just as important but possibly less pressing. The water piped into town is occasionally cut off by landslides or arrives in a murky condition that suggests the possibility of contamination. Since the water is not treated, this is not an unlikely possibility. Electricity supplied by a small hydroelectric plant is both weak and irregular, and in recent years power has been fed in only from about 6 p.m. until about 11. When there is an important fiesta or some special celebration the plant is kept going for a few extra hours, but the current is generally so weak that the glow of a light bulb is considerably less than that of a match. Many householders do not bother with electricity.

These are some of the more obvious problems affecting the general welfare in Sorata. It is obvious that this town sometimes has been able to solve some of its problems, for it did build the now well-worn hydroelectric plant. But problems affecting the public well-being are solved only by following a pattern that must by now be familiar. The major form of this pattern is the attainment by a Sorateño of a high political office, which can subsequently lead to the availability of national funds for local projects. One does not necessarily follow the other, but there is a reasonably good chance that it will. The minor form is the attainment of high local office by a Sorateño who has excellent muñeca with important national officials and who is willing to use that muñeca to advance local projects. General Enrique Peñaranda, former President of Bolivia, was from the Sorata area, and during his administration provided funds for a public market and for the improvement of the central plaza, now named for him. Through other important politicians from Sorata the town built its hydroelectric plant and its water supply system, the latter largely with United States funds as part of the Inter-American Public Health Program.

Not all of the problems of Sorata are great, requiring massive resources for their solution. Many, like the problem of refuse in the street, are well within the capacity of the local population. Moreover, as seen in Villa Abecia and, more especially, Reyes, even the building of schools and roads is not beyond the capacity of a town. However, there is an especially critical difference between Sorata and the other two communities. In the effort at community action in Reyes, the organization of vecinos successfully took over certain functions of the local government. In Coroico, the reverse took place. It was the local government, the alcalde, who took over the vecino organization. In Sorata, on the other hand, there is almost continual antagonism and conflict between the local government and the vecino group. Having lost their traditional leadership role, the vecinos have lost interest in the fate of the town:

This morning the doctor came looking for me to get my help in organizing a health committee for the town. We have decided to call a meeting of the townspeople for this purpose, but I doubt whether anyone will come. How often I have called them together to select new officers of the Junta de Vecinos! But no one ever comes. This lack of meetings of the Junta de Vecinos, and the little or no interest that townspeople have in improving their welfare, means that organizations like this lose their effectiveness in promoting the progress of the community.

Vecinos are unrelenting in their criticism of local government officials. Officials are criticized for an almost endless series of faults, many having little to do with their performing their jobs, such as that they are not natives to the town or do not speak good Spanish. Other accusations, that they neglect the town's needs, for example, are to a large extent valid. Local government officials since 1952 have not exerted themselves very much, because their basic interest is not in the town.

The long period of antagonism appears to have had a marked effect on the short-lived administration of Alcalde Moran. His few months in office were devoted in large part to establishing a record of good works:

In the two months of my administration of the municipal government we have had the central plaza cleaned and the iron fence around it painted. We are repairing some of the streets. With the help of the police we are improving the organization of the market. Finally, we have just finished painting the alcaldia building. I also have pending several projects that I hope to be able to undertake. I am interested in the construction of a municipal building that would serve as a market. I also want to remodel the municipal jail, and see whether it may be possible to construct a new building for the public school.

A month later the alcalde was pointing to a newspaper reading stand that he had installed in the alcaldia for public use. He also had three masons and two helpers busily putting in steps and railings and making other repairs, some of them safety measures, in the building occupied by the public primary school. The alcalde was proud of these achievements, but he also never let pass the opportunity for invidious comparison of his few months in office with previous years of neglect:

Seven bags of cement have been used on these repairs, and all of this is paid for with money from the alcaldia. This same work could have been done by those indios who were the authorities before, but they devoted themselves exclusively to their personal interests. They have no interest at all in the town.

Moran had also had the salon in the alcaldia repaired and redecorated. His comment on this was: "In this salon are held the most important social reunions of the town, but when the indios were here it was like a pigpen."

To a degree even greater than in Coroico, the fall of the MNR government was followed in Sorata by a surge of optimism among the vecinos. At last it was to be possible to rid themselves of the hated indios in the alcaldia. However, the new era was even shorter in Sorata than in Coroico. Within a few months Moran was out of office, and campesinos and their confederates were filling the positions in local government. That neither this new alcalde nor the official mayor came from a campesino village, and that the latter belonged to a cholo family, made no difference, for both were allies of the campesino sub-prefect and associated with campesinos and sindicato politics. To vecinos, they were all "indios, no mas." Moran was not in office long enough to demonstrate whether the change that he represented would have been sufficient in itself to have altered the lack of interest and the apathy that are so much commented on in Sorata. Moran felt that he might have made a difference:

Sorata is a good town. If you understand how to treat the people it is possible to accomplish many progressive works. It is true that at this time the town is very divided by political affairs. Nevertheless, as I have just said, by organizing a good group of vecinos it is possible to work for the development of the town.

In the other towns that have been discussed, a "good group of vecinos" has in fact been a crucial element in community action. It is possible for a vecino-like group to play an even more important role than the local government, as in Reyes, but Sorata vecinos no longer respond to that type of challenge. Their ranks have been shattered by death and emigration. Many of them manage little more than to keep alive, and none has important wealth. Their political power is almost nil. Their future is not promising. It is not surprising that the formation of community action groups from among vecinos is as hazardous an enterprise as one marginal vecino notes:

Frankly, we can't do anything about health problems because there is no collaboration among vecinos. At the beginning they are enthusiastic to do something, but unfortunately they never persevere. From the experience we have, it is better not to get involved in organizing committees, or that kind of thing, because, for example, whenever you try to collect funds all the members disappear. And when they do make any contributions, then they accuse the leaders of not doing anything or of pilfering the treasury. They leave everything for the leaders to do, from contributing money to contributing time, while all the others just stand around with folded arms.

In this rather unpromising situation there still occurred an attempt by vecinos to organize to promote community projects. In November 1965, vecinos formed the Amigos de Sorata. At its founding meeting hardly more than a dozen persons were present, and two of them were cholos. It was announced as an open group, but the lower social strata were not encouraged to join. A seven-man directorate was established, in the hope that this would result in a more stable organization, less dependent on the energies of one man. Nevertheless, one person, the juez instructor, took the lead in making policy for the Amigos.

The stated purpose of the Amigos de Sorata was "to work for the good and development of Sorata." The initial project was the improvement of the central plaza, including a general cleanup and putting water and fish in an unused pond. Further projects were to be the improvement of the soccer field and the cleaning of town streets. Performance even on some of these small projects was very uneven. Most Amigos had no thought of going out to wield a pick and shovel, but rather saw themselves as promoting and then supervising. The juez instructor was in the best position to do exactly this, for he would take prisoners from the jail and put them to work.

In the early discussions among the Amigos, great emphasis was placed on the non-political character of their motives and organization. Two of the seven members of the organization directorate had well-known reputations for being apolitical, but the situation in Sorata made it impossible for the organization to maintain this position. While the Amigos told themselves that their work was above politics, local government officials, understandably, did not see it that way. Among the Amigos were several of their harshest critics, Nabor Moran for one; and many of the projects selected by the Amigos, such as the cleaning of the streets, were implicitly critical of local officials. Among some members of the Amigos there was very explicit criticism. It was proposed that educational films be obtained from foreign embassies in La Paz for showing in town. A letter of request was prepared and the members of the directorate signed it. When it was pointed out that a letter which would also bear signatures of town officials might receive a better hearing, the Amigos demurred. According to one of the directors, "It isn't a matter of being egoistic. It is that the alcalde never wants to do anything, and we want to show him what can be done for the town." The alcalde's own attitudes were harsher:

Do I have any collaboration from townspeople? Absolutely no one [helps]. With the exception of my official mayor, who is a key aide, no one wants to help. We have the Amigos de Sorata, but they also don't do anything. Instead, they are concerned with politics. It is a stupidity talking to them, and it is difficult, because there is nothing that can be done with these people. There is no unity in this town, and for that reason I have to do everything myself.

Shortly after they organized, the Amigos were forced into collaboration with town officials. An important prefectural and national political figure, the official mayor of La Paz, who also happens to be a Sorateño, came for a short visit. He was sought out by several Amigos directors and taken on a tour to discuss projects. Somewhat later he was joined by the alcalde and other local government officials. Before leaving, the visiting official mayor agreed to contribute thirty bags of cement, several meters of metal pipe, some cement pipe, and several dozen ornamental plants. These materials would come to the local government, but the alcalde was directed to collaborate with the Amigos.

Shortly after this visit, the juez instructor, who had been a prime mover among the Amigos, resigned his position and returned to La Paz. Some projects continued, but there was a gradual slackening of interest and effort. An exception was the swimming pool and near-by children's playground, but this project had become as much a project of the alcaldia as of the Amigos.

In June a leading member of the Amigos was reassigned by his superiors to another community. Toward the end of August one of the directors commented:

Is there still an Amigos de Sorata group? Yes, but it's not functioning. It more or less died when judge what's-his-name left. He was active in everything, but now I think the only ones left are the agronomist, the captain, and myself. But it's nothing any more.

By August a number of other changes had taken place in Sorata. A new sub-prefect, the successor of Campos, who had become a national deputy as a result of the July elections, designated several projects that he hoped to accomplish while in office. Among these he listed the construction of a new primary school, the construction of a road into the Mapiri gold fields (which would also go through his own home town), the construction of a hospital, and the remodeling of the alcaldia. Aware of the dissension and conflict in the town, he said:

I did not know the reason why previous officials have not gotten on well with the vecinos of this town. I think that it is time to put aside the despotism, the negligence, the concern of who is in my party and who is in some other party. I hope to get along with everybody. I think that I can get the collaboration of all the townspeople, and once that is done, whatever project we undertake will be a lot easier.

The response of the alcalde to this statement was:

It's not possible to work with these Falangistas. They are obstinate. They think that the alcaldia has a lot of money, and that all we do is spend it for our own amusement.

And the sub-prefect replied:

No, Juan, first you have to reach an understanding, leaving aside politics. When everyone is in agreement, then it is possible to think of doing something. Your problem is that your first concern is always the person's politics, and only afterwards do you ask what can be done. With that outlook you will not get anywhere.

These words of reconciliation were echoed several times by former Sub-prefect Campos, now national deputy. He too called for the people of the town to unite, to set aside political differences, to work on common problems for the good of all. Unfortunately, the conflicts are old and deep. They are not just a matter of differences in political party, even though the alcalde speaks of "those Falangistas." Rather, the conflicts reflect the fundamental social reshuffling that has occurred, in which some have experienced significant losses of prestige, power, and wealth.

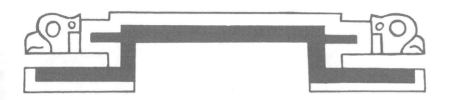

VI

SAN MIGUEL AND COMPI
One Simple Traditional
and One Simple
Radically Changed
Community

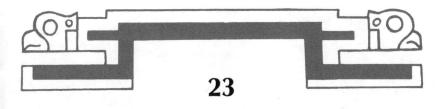

23

THE SETTING

The four communities discussed thus far differ in many ways, but despite these differences they are basically similar and represent a type of community in Bolivia, the rural town. They are all government centers, all regional market towns, in which a wide range of skills and services are to be found, and in all four there are complex social stratification orders.

The last two communities of this study, San Miguel and Compi, are a distinctly different type, the agricultural village, in which virtually the entire adult male labor force is engaged in agriculture as small-scale peasant farmers. Some of the communities of this type have public markets—San Miguel is one—but such villages are so small as to be insignificant regionally, and there are few or no specialized skills to be found among their residents. There is but one basic social stratum in each of them. A further marked contrast between the two agricultural villages and the four towns is that the villagers are Aymara-speaking Indians. The two communities differ in themselves as well, San Miguel being a free community, in the sense that its people were never in peonage, while Compi is an ex-hacienda community, a distinction of long-standing importance, in that so many of the more radical MNR reform programs were directed at the haciendas, leaving the free communities less likely to become involved in the rural politicization process. It so happens, however, that Compi, though an ex-hacienda community, has not become as highly politicized as some of the ex-haciendas in the Sorata and Cochabamba areas [Patch, 1956]. Nevertheless, Compi is an agricultural village that has, unlike San Miguel, felt the full impact of MNR

Typical houses in San Miguel (Lambros Comitas)

reform programs, and therefore it is representative of rural communities that have been strongly affected by the Revolution of 1952.

SAN MIGUEL

The Department of Oruro, which is almost square, is bounded on the west and east by Andean ranges. Much of the central section of the department is quite flat. In the southern half, there are two large shallow lakes and several dry lake beds extending over large areas. To the north, a range of hills extends from the western cordillera to the center of the department. The flat pampa is again east and north of these hills. Just off the pampa lies the community of San Miguel.

A steep dirt road rises several hundred feet to a relatively flat shelf, and there it enters the village as a narrow street. The settlement is a dense cluster of more than 250 one-story adobe houses with thatched roofs. Some have two or three very small rooms, but most have only one. There are the two separate plazas, a lesser and a greater, as is traditional to New World Spanish towns. Each is dominated by a small church. But, beyond these features, traditional pattern breaks. There are only two streets, approximately parallel, cutting through the smaller, more central plaza and forming two of its sides. Some houses are grouped in twos and threes, forming courtyards closed in by walls of free-standing stone. Especially on the eastern side of town, these compounds abut one another without any intervening streets. Within a few of them are corrals of rock walls for llamas and sheep. Surrounding the community are the small chacras, the farm plots of the villagers, separated by the free-standing walls built of stones readily available in the hills.

Although there are more than 250 dwellings of various sizes in San Miguel, rarely are more than a handful of adults seen in the village except on special occasions. Most of the dwellings are padlocked, closed for days, weeks, even months at a time, the reason being that they are second homes, the headquarters village homes of families whose working time is spent in the eleven other major and three minor settlements that constitute the whole of the San Miguelean community. A few of these settlements are on the pampa at the foot of the hills in front of San Miguel, but most of them are scattered in the hills to the sides of the central settlement. There are crude roads over open land or in temporarily dry river beds by which—with caution—motorcars can reach a few of the outer settlements, but most of them can be reached only on foot, walking time varying from about twenty minutes to upwards of three hours.

A few of the larger outer settlements have a dense arrangement of dwellings like that of San Miguel, though the number of buildings is considerably smaller. Most of these larger settlements also have a small church as well as a one-room government building, but no streets at all because the dwelling compounds are joined one to another. In the smaller settlements the dwelling compounds are dispersed, and surrounded by agricultural fields. The terrain over which the settlements are scattered varies greatly. Some are on the edge of the immense, flat pampa, which stretches north and south as far as the eye can see. Others are in small valleys in the hills, some close to streams, and still others are on the rolling puna uplands west of the main settlement. In all these different settings the vegetation is sparse, for the pampa is about 13,000 feet above sea level, and most of the settlements probably lie between 13,500 and 14,500 feet. A lone tree stands in the small central plaza of San Miguel, but the landscape beyond is treeless. Clumps of short grass make good pasture for sheep and llamas down on the sandy pampa, and though the upland puna bears only scattered clumps of thola, a low evergreen shrub, and the paja brava, a bristly knee-high grass, it also is widely used as pasture.

There are springs, streams, and wells throughout the settlement area, but water is not abundant. Most plant growth depends on the sparse rainfall which falls in the summer months from December through March. As autumn gives way to winter, the streams recede and some go dry. While the sun even during the winter months is warm, lack of sunshine even during the summer chills everything. Winter temperatures regularly drop below freezing, and few houses are very secure against the bitterly cold winds. Finally, there is snow for a few days of the year, though it generally melts quickly.

A resident of San Miguel is simultaneously a member of an estancia, of one of the four ayllus, "free" Indian communities, in which the canton of San Miguel is divided, and of the canton itself. Two of the four ayllus contain four major estancias, while each of the other two contains three. These fourteen estancias are the primary units of settlement. The population of the whole canton of San Miguel is about 1200. This figure can only be an approximation. A census cannot claim comprehensiveness for a population in which as many as 25 per cent of the male heads of households are absent from the canton with some part of their families at the height of the inactive agricultural season. Accurate census is further hindered by the complex dispersal of the population.

The estancias are not grouped in the several ayllus in an orderly fashion. Some are closer and more accessible to estancias of other ayllus, and in fact collaborate with these, isolating themselves from their own ayllu. Many families have houses, or huts, not only in their estancia settlements but also in their ayllu settlements and in the canton headquarters settlement of San Miguel village, which is in itself an estancia of one of the four ayllus. In San Miguel as well as in Compi, and perhaps in most of the highland Indian communities, this complex settlement pattern has evolved over a long period of time, the result of a continuous process of fission and amalgamation.

Although the population of San Miguel canton is as large as that of any of the towns studied, the people live in very small groups. In the three largest estancias, each in a different ayllu, there are 54, 37, and 33 households, respectively, listed as members, and in the smallest there are but four or five. Some people regarded as members of estancias have left home, but are carried on the rosters of the settlements because they still own land in them. Many members, too, are likely to be absent temporarily, either at San Miguel village, fulfilling a canton responsibility, or away at work in Oruro, Cochabamba, or La Paz. Since the only complete primary school in the canton is in the canton headquarters settlement, families in the more distant estancias often settle the mothers and children in their canton houses for the school year.

San Miguel is on the southern frontier of the Aymara-speaking region of Bolivia. Taking only adult males, all speak Aymara, 26 per cent are bilingual in Aymara and Spanish, and 47 per cent speak a third language, Quechua. Again taking only adult males, only 25 per cent have had no education at all, while 73 per cent have received some primary schooling.

Fifty miles away, on the eastern side of the pampa, is the city of Oruro. The road is unimproved, but the going can be steady on the flat pampa except for the Rio Desaguadero, which is too deep or too soft for fording, but is crossable at a number of points on barges. Only the weather may be a serious obstacle. Since the pampa is crisscrossed with truck tracks and there are no posted signs, direction is maintained by sight. In darkness or bad weather direction becomes a problem, and in a hard rain the flat pampa will disappear under water in a few minutes.

Roman Catholic Church and ancient shrine in San Miguel
(Lambros Comitas)

View of altiplano from ancient Inca road in San Miguel
(Lambros Comitas)

Crossing Río Desaguadero en route to San Miguel (Lambros Comitas)

A room in the San Miguel school (Lambros Comitas)

Not only do the road tracks disappear, but traction itself vanishes. During the dry season a truck from Oruro stops twice a week at San Miguel for goods and passengers. In the rainy season it does not come at all. Many households have bicycles, and on them the trip to Oruro can be made in about four hours—more quickly than the truck, which stops to load and unload so often that its trip may take six to seven hours.

While the city of Oruro is the most important regional community for San Miguel, there are others of some importance that are closer. Corque lies thirty miles almost due south. This is the capital of the province, with a sub-prefect and sub-prefectural government similar to that seen in the four towns already described, and with jurisdiction over the other settlements of the province, including San Miguel. Closer at hand are three other canton settlements all larger than the headquarters settlement of San Miguel. About eight miles to the southeast, on the road to Corque, is Llanquera. Six miles in the opposite direction, to the northwest, is Chuquichambi, and ten more miles in the same direction is Huayllamarca. All of these villages have markets and fiestas that residents of some of the San Miguel estancias attend from time to time. Huayllamarca is particularly important, as it is the location of the nearest provincial law official, the intendente. There, also, is a new twenty-nine-bed hospital run by a Catholic order. Finally, about fifteen miles to the northeast of Huayllamaraca, is Papelpampa, which has one of the biggest regional markets in the area, and an annual fiesta attended by numerous buyers and sellers from San Miguel.

COMPI

Lake Titicaca, 138 miles long and 70 miles wide at its widest points, covers a large part of the northwestern perimeter of the northern altiplano. Dotting the coastline are villages, small towns, and a few lake ports. Compi is one of these lakeside communities.

This part of the altiplano is quite unlike bleak San Miguel. The fresh water of the lake supports a heavy growth of totora rushes along the shallow edges. Here the land gently rises to low hills. Compi, not as high as San Miguel, is at an elevation of approximately 12,500 feet. Winter nights are freezing cold, but the slightly lower elevation and the waters of the lake are moderating influences. An abundance of water and the somewhat softer climate permit more intensive cultivation of the land

Reed boats on Lake Titicaca (Lambros Comitas)

along the lake and nurture more wild vegetation on the small amounts of land not cultivated. Groves of eucalyptus trees, more intensive planting, and greater natural vegetation impart an almost lush appearance to the otherwise harsh altiplano environment.

Like San Miguel, Compi is a community of several settlements. As an hacienda before the Revolution, it was made up of five separate estancias, comparable in many ways to the estancias of San Miguel. Just as in San Miguel, families live in compounds, usually of two or three small one-room and two-room adobe houses with thatched roofs. Since the Revolution some families have built second houses along the main road that passes near the lake, often two-story adobe buildings with corrugated tin roofs. Since the main church of Compi and the public primary school are also near this road, this recent house construction has begun to give a part of the community something of a clumpy roadside shape. But aside from this, there is even less concentration of dwellings on the former hacienda of Compi than there is on any of the San Miguel estancias. Although the very small size of farm plots frequently has resulted in compounds relatively close together, each is set in the midst of its own land and on none of the estancias is there a compact settlement.

In 1965 there were 269 households on the ex-hacienda, with a total resident population of 1404. This figure does not include the small number of families that were temporarily absent, nor the much larger proportion still considered members of the community because they have land in Compi, but actually reside elsewhere, mainly in the cities or colonization zones.

In Compi, 57 per cent of male heads of households, over twice the proportion in San Miguel, have had no education, for most of these men grew up under hacienda authority before the Revolution of 1952. There are also language differences between Compi and San Miguel. The Compi population has not had the long exposure to Quechua that the people of San Miguel have. On the other hand, it has had long exposure to Spanish, but even here it proves to be a more isolated community linguistically than San Miguel. Sixty-three per cent of the adult men in Compi speak only Aymara, while 37 per cent are bilingual in Aymara and Spanish. Since adult men are most likely to have been exposed to bilingual situations, they under-represent Compi's language conservatism. Taking the entire population, 85 per cent speak only Aymara and only 15 per cent are bilingual, despite their exposure to outside influences.

The road along the lake on which Compi's new houses are being built is a good all-weather transport route which runs easterly to Huarina, where it joins the main road out of La Paz, and northwest to Achacachi, and along the northern side of the lake to the Peruvian frontier. This road branches off at Achacachi, the provincial capital of the Compi area, and on to Sorata. To the west of the hacienda, the road continues to the mile-wide Strait of Tiquina, where large sailboat ferries carry trucks and other vehicles over to a road that traverses the peninsula to Copacabana and goes on to the Peruvian border. Since the Revolution there has been daily truck traffic over this route to La Paz and a daily bus service between Copacabana and the capital. The trip from Compi to La Paz takes from two to three hours.

Just beyond the western borders of Compi lies the village of Jank'o Amaya, once part of an hacienda but since 1965 the headquarters settlement and administrative center of the canton to which Compi belongs, and analogous to the canton headquarters settlement of San Miguel. Jank'o Amaya is Compi's nearest marketplace. Relations between Compi and Achacachi, the provincial capital, are not very close, chiefly because the most direct route to the capital is an all-day hike over the hills. Along the lake, about half-way between Compi and Huarina, is the large village of Huatajata, which has one of the largest weekly markets in the area and is only thirty minutes by bicycle from Compi. For many years Huatajata has also been an important center of Protestant missionary activity, which in this area has emphasized education and medical care. A Canadian Baptist Mission station operates an infirmary with a permanent nurse and a once-a-week physician. This is the closest facility to Compi that offers any sort of modern medical care.

Compi has no telephones or telegraph, nor does it receive magazines or periodicals regularly, but many families have transistor radios and there are regular broadcasts in Aymara. Being on a main road to the national capital, Compi is much more in the mainstream of national Bolivian life than is San Miguel. San Miguel not only lacks all the same means of emergency communication, but is also completely isolated for long periods during each year.

IN TIME

San Miguel and Compi in the past occupied very different positions in the regional socio-economic organizations of the altiplano, and have been subjected to rather different forces in their distant as well as more recent past. This is clear, even though historical data are lacking and interpretation must rely on oral testimony and tangential information. Although the age of neither community is known, it is known that the regions of both villages had been absorbed by the Inca empire well before the Spanish Conquest. From both Inca and pre-Inca periods, San Miguel and Compi derive a good many of the beliefs, action patterns, and forms of organization that they hold in common. After the Spanish Conquest both villages underwent many important changes as a result of the imposition of Spanish rule and the development of Spanish colonial society.

It seems probable that early in the post-Conquest period the estancias in the region of San Miguel were given in encomienda, royal land grant, to a shipbuilder in Spain, but there was probably little profit to be had in the form of agricultural or any other kind of tribute from the barren lands of western Oruro, and it appears that the grant was allowed to lapse. San Miguel, for the same profitless reasons, never became the object of colonial encroachment, but remained a free Indian community.

Although untouched by the continual expansion of the hacienda system on the altiplano, San Miguel has not been a static Indian community. When the Department of Oruro was created in 1826, over half the department was in a single province. The provincial capital then, as today, was Corque. At that time the estancias of San Miguel were considered to be part of a single ayllu. Toward the end of the nineteenth century, perhaps a little later, the ayllu was divided into two parts. In the early 1950's the second of the two ayllus divided itself into two ayllus, and in 1956 the first of the original two did the same. At the time of these changes in the 1950's, the four ayllus of San Miguel took their present names. This process of subdivision possibly relates to population growth, but it more likely reflects the changed political scene and a change in political awareness in San Miguel itself.

Some of the most important reforms of the MNR government had little or no effect on San Miguel. A few of San Miguel's comunarios have worked in the Oruro mines, but too few to have been of any political importance to San Miguel, and—it being a free community—the impact of the land reform program was nil. One of the most important corollaries of the land reform, the organization of the campesino sindicatos, was not restricted to the haciendas, but it was unlikely to take hold in the free communities. There is no indication that an effort to organize a sindicato was ever made in San Miguel. Even though the enfranchizing of the adult population applied to the free Indian communities just as it did to every other, and further, even though San Miguel's contact with a city like Oruro—a center of politically radical and militant trade unionism—has conveyed a certain political awareness to the community, the political impact of the MNR government could only have been slight without the organization and new leadership that the sindicatos provided on the ex-haciendas.

The one reform that seems to have aroused the greatest interest with great effect was that of education. The special interest of the new government in the education of the rural population was indicated in the separation of rural from urban education and in assigning the administration of it to the Ministerio de Asuntos Campesinos. In the years following the Revolution there occurred in the heavily populated regions an extension of formal government organization, especially on the ex-haciendas, but since the resources of the national government were—and still are—always inadequate, only the most important localities were likely to receive assistance from many of the new programs. "Important" in this sense partly means being visible from the higher levels of national government, which in turn means having a distinguished government status, such as being a canton. From this it can be seen that the sub-dividing of the San Miguel estancias into four separate ayllus is prob-ably best understood as a maneuver to attract recognition. San Miguel achieved this recognition in 1959. Its recognition as a canton enabled it to become the nucleo, the headquarters, of a school district, while the larger neighboring villages of Llanquera and Chuquichambi are only sections of school districts. The advantage to the nucleo community is that the district director spends most of his time there.

San Miguel appears, on balance, to have undergone few of the radical changes associated with the MNR government after 1952, or to have felt earlier any of the major economic changes that occurred in some of the other areas that have been discussed. As a somewhat isolated Indian vil-lage living by subsistence agriculture, it has occupied a remote position in the national economic and political system. For some of its people, however, it is important that San Miguel has long had important de-pendent relations on outside population centers like Oruro. Over the years Oruro has become an increasingly important source of short-term work and, to a much lesser extent, a place of permanent relocation. This contact with Oruro does not seem to have changed San Miguel very much, but it has changed many of the comunarios. Thus, while San Miguel appears relatively little changed in the spectrum of change oc-curring in Bolivia today, neither is it an unchanging community.

Compi, on the other hand, was subjected to different influences fol-lowing the Conquest. The greater fertility of the land and the more moderate climate of the lakeside area attracted the Spanish. Although precise historical documentation is lacking, it is probable that much of this zone was given as encomienda and later, in the seventeenth century, made the transition to hacienda-type ownership. No one can recall a time when Compi was not an hacienda, or when the haciendas of Chua on the east and of Jank'o Amaya on the west did not exist.

About the middle of the nineteenth century, Compi hacienda appears to have consisted of little more than the estancia of Compi. At that time the estancia of Capilaya was an independent hacienda, while Cawaya, Kalamaya, and Tauca were all part of the free community of Tauca, which also included a fourth estancia, Llamacachi, just west of Compi. Throughout much of the eighteenth and nineteenth centuries, and continuing into the twentieth century, a continual process of hacienda encroachment on free Indian land took place on the altiplano [Urquidi, 1966, pp. 208-9]. Toward the latter part of this period a process of hacienda consolidation also seems to have taken place. Both of these developments occurred in the Compi area.

In the late 1800's great pressure, both legal and extra-legal, was exerted by the patrón of Chua hacienda to force the comunarios of Llamacachi to sell him their land. The comunarios resisted for several years, but finally most of them sold. Nevertheless, the comunarios of Llamacachi proved so recalcitrant to hacienda exploitation that the patrón of Chua agreed nine years later to sell their land back to them, keeping only a fertile strip along the lake shore.

Apparently, during the period of the latter 1800's the Compi hacienda was expanding in a similar fashion, partly through consolidation with the adjoining Capilaya hacienda, and partly by absorbing the land of comunarios on the near-by free community estancias. As in the case of the Llamacachi estancia, this constant enroachment on free community land by the haciendas was frequently resisted, for it disrupted traditions of work, land tenure, inheritance, and basic social relations. The antagonism and deprivation that this process probably engendered is at least one of the important factors in the outbreak of widespread violence that occurred in this area in the first few years of the twentieth century.

For several years the area was plagued by pitched battles between comunarios of the free communities and colonos of the haciendas. The weapons were often only rocks, but there were wounds and even deaths. The issue at the forefront of this fighting was disputed land, but an important contributory factor was conflict among the heirs of the Compi hacienda. Some of the comunarios wanted to follow the example of Llamacachi and get back the land they had sold to the hacienda, and they were encouraged in this by dissident heirs to the Compi estancia. In the end, the comunarios were defeated, and all of the free land of the estancias between hacienda Chua and hacienda Jank'o Amaya was absorbed by Compi, except for the small free community of Llamacachi.

As an hacienda, Compi followed the classic pattern of work organization. Each colono was assigned a plot of land for his personal use, and in exchange he gave the hacienda specific quotas of general and special work. The over-all administration of work on the hacienda was in the hands of a mayordomo, while direct supervising was done by jilakatas and alcaldes on the larger estancias, and alcaldes alone on the smaller estancias. All of these officials were appointed by the patrón, who sometimes involved himself directly in the administration of the hacienda. Under the last of all the patróns, another level of hacienda supervision was instituted, the sot'a. Two sot'as served as assistants to the mayordomo and directly supervised the jilakatas and alcaldes. The importance of this in connection with hacienda work is that the labor obligations on the hacienda became increasingly burdensome for the colono. Over a period of years the obligations of each family were increased from one person for three days per week, to two persons for three days per week, to four persons for six days per week. These labor increases forced many families to accept smaller pieces of land for their own use, with correspondingly smaller labor obligations. Families that were unable to subsist emigrated permanently, either to the cities or into the near-by, less densely populated valleys.

The increasing pressure of hacienda demands on the colonos was abruptly terminated by the Revolution of 1952. Beginning in 1950, there had been a slight decrease in hacienda labor requirements when the American owner of the neighboring hacienda of Chua rented Compi and introduced agricultural machinery. He demanded as many days of work, but fewer hours. It was not until after the Revolution that really radical changes occurred.

Because of Compi's proximity to La Paz and the presence of something like an émigré colony in the federal capital, the meaning of the Revolution was quickly sensed on the hacienda. Within a few months the colonos rejected all control over their personal plots of land and denounced all labor obligations; but they did not seize the hacienda, as happened elsewhere. Arrangements were made to sharecrop the patrón's lands, but soon the colonos also initiated legal action to obtain his land for themselves. This was a slow procedure, but by 1957 the hacienda had been declared a latifundia and was divided among the working colonos and a few of the dispossessed emigrants.

Another Revolutionary change was the shift from subsistence agriculture to commercial production, which remarkably increased available quantities of food. For example, two trucks were sufficient to carry the

Scene at altiplano feria (Lambros Comitas)

patrón's hacienda produce to La Paz, but now eight trucks are necessary. The new MNR government contributed to this shift to a market orientation by setting up special markets in La Paz so that campesinos could bypass the retail middleman and sell directly to consumers. Another important change has been the replacement of the potato by the onion as the major sales commodity grown by the campesinos, the advantage being that the onion yields a continuous crop.

Paralleling the agricultural and economic changes were important

organizational changes. The responsibility given to the sindicatos in implementing agrarian reform decrees quickly established for them a central place in community affairs. Cooperative organizations were also introduced, and, in the government's anxiety to counteract any decline in
agricultural production following the disorders and uncertainties created
by the Revolution, mechanized agriculture was promoted. However, little technical support was available to assist the campesinos in the use of
the machinery. Equipment disappeared or rusted. In addition, cooperatives were mulcted and otherwise mismanaged, and most of them with-
ered away.

As in San Miguel, the Revolution brought school facilities to the hacienda community. Compi now has a public primary school, and education is one of the major concerns of the community.

These are some of the changes in Compi that have resulted from the
Revolution of 1952. It altered the economic and political organization of
the community, drew the people into a very active dependency on La
Paz, and involved the community in the national politics of the MNR
government. If Compi has not developed the political militancy associated with some of the Cochabamba campesino communities, it now
has a practical awareness of national politics that distinguishes it from
itself in the past and from more traditional communities like San Miguel
today.

ECONOMY

All male heads of households in both San Miguel and Compi are agriculturalists, but San Miguel is oriented far more strongly to subsistence
agriculture than is Compi, which directs itself to the urban market. Still,
agriculture is the sole preoccupation of both villages, giving them a uniformity of interest and activity that contrasts with the diverse economic
activities of the four towns of this study.

In San Miguel, planting time is from August to November, after
which the rains set in. The first plantings are of beans, oka, papalisa,
esaña, alberja, lettuce, and onions. In September, while there is still run-
off from melted snows, potatoes and some quinua are put in. By October
the weather is dry, ready for the planting of barley, wheat, and corn. The
most important of these crops are potatoes, wheat, beans, and oka. Very
little corn, lettuce, or onions are grown.

Beginning with the planting season in August, the family herds of sheep and llamas, and perhaps a cow, are driven to the communal pasture in the puna. Shepherding is generally the responsibility of older children. The animals are kept on the communal lands until May, when they are brought in to graze on the straw stumps in newly harvested grain fields, or they are driven to grass on the lower pampa.

During the rainy season from December to March as many as 25 per cent of the adult men leave the community for Oruro, La Paz, Cochabamba, and the former Bolivian port of Arica, in Chile, to work as assistants to masons, carpenters, and electricians—if they are lucky—and may earn from 55¢ to as much as $2.00 a day. A few go to new agricultural zones in the Yungas to work for other campesinos. Teenage boys, too, frequently seek temporary work in Oruro, some as house servants, for which they get little besides board and room—but then, their absence from home reduces family living costs. Few of these migrant workers remain away from the community for more than a few weeks at a time, though they may go away more than once in the year, and most return for the harvest.

The harvest season runs through April, May, and June. In March the rains taper off, and by late April the days are sunny and warm. In May the winds and the cold nights return, and in June the temperature drops to freezing again. During July and August snow, wind-whipped over the grazing lands, can be expected, and there is a second decline in agricultural work, during which some comunarios again go to the cities. By the end of August they are back for the planting.

Agriculture in San Miguel is family labor. Even women with small children help in the fields, carrying infants on their backs in aguayos, or they leave a small child at the edge of a field to play. Children as young as six become assistant shepherds, and the teenage boys pitch in beside their fathers in the fields. Hired labor is negligible, though there is some exchange of work service among the comunarios when a large plot is to be planted or harvested. In these instances the comunario pays no wages, but is expected to return an equal amount of labor to each of those who aided him.

The men plow with oxen, using iron-tipped wooden shares, guiding their teams by leather thongs attached to the outside horns. Wives follow behind with seed in the folds of uplifted skirts. A clump of thola shrub is tied to the lower part of the plow, and as a second parallel furrow is uncovered the shrub pushes back the soil turned up by the plow along the first furrow, covering the seed. In an observed instance, plowing and planting began about eleven a.m. and broke off at about four-thirty p.m., with about three-quarters of an hour taken for the midday meal. This was a day's work on a chacra of about one-quarter of an acre, one of the larger plots among the twenty-two separate chacras of varying size owned by one man. On smaller chacras it is not practical to use oxen, so the comunario yokes himself to the plow and his wife or older son guide and pushes.

Since no measurements of landholdings have ever been made—at least not within living memory—there are no reliable production data on the size of landholdings. The relatively large holdings in San Miguel, compared with Compi, suggest that the land is not highly productive. A comunario in estancia Gisca Llacsa estimated that he owned ten hectares, approximately twenty-five acres, divided into many small chacras. Of his ten hectares, he cultivates three each year, resting the other seven because "the land gets tired with the cold." To maximize production he plants several crops in the same field, occasionally fertilizing with sheep droppings.

The father in every landowning household is obliged to give land to his son when he marries, but ultimately all male children receive equal shares of the cultivated land through inheritance. One of the comunarios explains the system of land acquisition:

A man has three sons and fifteen chacras. When his first son is old enough to get married he must calculate how much he will give him so as to be left with enough for himself, as well as enough to give equal portions to the rest of his sons when they get married. He may give his first son two chacras. Then, when his second son is ready to marry, the father will give him land either of equal size or equal productivity, and then his third son the same. If he makes more sons after the first gets married, the father will still have enough to give them equal portions at marriage. The newly married son will find, of course, that this small portion of land is not enough to live on. But the family stays close together, so that even the married son still works with his father and gets a share of his father's harvest, while at the same time having his own land. Sometimes, if the father doesn't have enough land, the married son goes to Oruro to work, coming back only for the planting and the harvest. But still his father must give him some land, and thus the son becomes a comunario.

A few men do not marry, but may still be given a share of land and certainly will inherit a full share when the father dies. Land is also acquired through marriage, even though daughters do not directly inherit. A man may marry a widow who possesses her former husband's personal share of land, or he may marry a girl without brothers, and instead of bringing his wife home to live with his family he goes to live with hers, and receives a share of his father-in-law's land.

Some comunarios who have more land than they can work may let a chacra for one-half of the harvest, or rent on a cash basis, the amount of rent being determined by the time required to plant the chacra. If a chacra can be planted in one day, the rent is twenty pesos ($1.60) a year. Cash rent, sharecropping (partir), receiving one's own chacras, or sharing in the harvest of the father's land are the several ways of obtaining access to land. For younger men particularly, all of these possibilities are inadequate for reasonable subsistence, forcing them to seek temporary employment in the agricultural off-seasons. Some emigrate permanently, allowing their brothers to cultivate the complete set of family chacras in return for half of the harvest taken from the land to which they were entitled.

A small stream, Rio Lacamara, winds through the canton, permitting irrigation on some of the chacras. Ditches carry water from the stream to catch basins as well, holding it in reserve. Irrigation begins in June or early July and becomes unnecessary by the end of December. The maintenance of the ditches and rules for the sharing of water are the responsibility of the individual ayllus. The alcalde de campo, a canton official, is formally responsible for surveillance of the irrigation system in the canton, but his attention is rarely required, for the comunarios are extremely watchful of breaks.

Every family keeps a few chickens and guinea pigs in the house, and all have herds of llamas and sheep. Some have one or two cows and burros. All grazing animals are marked over a three-day period every year, much of the time being given to fiesta activity. The shearing of llamas and sheep is done by the women with knives made from tin cans. This knife does a less than efficient job and leaves the beast's coat in tatters, but a woman can shear twelve to fifteen animals in half a morning. In 1964 a federal program for agricultural improvement built sheep dips in three estancias of San Miguel in an effort to help the comunarios improve their herds. Now a fourth estancia has expressed interest in building a dip of its own.

While many of the adult men work in the cities during land-idle periods, many more find work at other jobs in San Miguel itself, some as

Costumed dancers at feria near Compi (Lambros Comitas)

stonecutters in a quarry near the canton settlement. Stone is used for foundations. A number of comunarios do work as masons, making the adobe as well. Unskilled labor is often provided by the owner and his family, while the construction specialist supervises and does the more skilled tasks. Many men work as tailors and weavers, and others produce stucco from material called poke lomanake, found on the surface in the hills around San Miguel. This material is easily removed by pick or dynamite, is baked in large ovens to soften it, then is ground by hand between huge stones, and finally is sifted and is ready for sale. Stucco production halts in the rainy season because the wood used in the ovens must be very dry. Six stucco ovens were in operation in 1966. Two to three men, generally members of a single family, are sufficient for all the separate operations, and produce five to ten quintales (500 to 1000 pounds) a day. Truckers from Oruro and other near-by towns buy it for about 20¢ a quintal. Carpentry is done by several comunarios. Another is able to do a bit of soldering, while two more have some skill in fixing simple household equipment. But no one makes a living or could support a family on these jobs alone.

There are six tiendas in the central canton settlement, usually open every day but frequently for only a few hours, and all deal in the same goods: matches, candles, kerosene, soap, dyes, sugar, coca leaves, bottled beer, bottled papaya juice, and cane alcohol. Sales volume is low but relatively steady. Prices are set at a meeting of the tienda owners. A few families in the central settlement, some of whom are also operators of tiendas, bake rolls for sale now and then. One reports that his profit from a day's baking is about 20¢. There are also a few tiendas out in the ayllu settlement.

There is a weekly market in the main plaza of the central settlement on every Wednesday that is not too windy, but there are not often more than twelve to fifteen vendors, men and women. Three of these are operators of local tiendas, a few are comunarios from other San Miguel ayllus, but the majority are residents of near-by cantons. This weekly market offers some of the items found in the tiendas, in addition to bananas, hot peppers, oranges, herbs and medicines, pencils and paper, and candy. The afternoon of market day is one of the few times when San Miguel appears to be a bustling settlement.

Many of the closest communities are villages like San Miguel, and though their markets are not much more ample, each also has an annual market feria, so there are many occasions throughout the year when a large, active market takes place within range of San Miguel. There are local ferias through the year, except in October and from February to May.

The biggest market of all is held at the annual fiesta patronal, the feast of Arcángel Miguel, on September 29. Buyers and sellers come from as far off as the adjoining provinces, and especially from Oruro, and every manufactured item that a comunario could possibly want is available—from clothing, cloth in bulk, hats, and shoes, to agricultural implements, cattle, and llamas.

While all the men of San Miguel depend directly on agriculture, profit varies, for some have more land or better land. In some parts of the community water is more accessible, in other parts the land is more sheltered, and some men have fewer brothers with whom they must share the land. Most of the comunarios who leave the community for temporary work do so out of necessity, and they return just as soon as they can. In short, there are material differences, but for the most part these are hardly more than slight. In dress, housing, possessions, there are many variations, but mostly minor. Even in land and animals no differences are great. San Miguel is a community with a relatively undifferentiated village economy.

Compi, too, is basically an agricultural community, sharing cultural, technological, environmental, and economic similarities with San Miguel. But there are also some important differences between the two communities, and it is these which will receive the greatest share of attention here.

The lakeside location gives Compi more productive soil and a more moderate climate, and hence longer growing seasons. Except for wheat in San Miguel, and barley and onions in Compi, the most important crops are the same. The onion, which had been a minor crop in the period before the Revolution, has come to occupy a central place in Compi agriculture because it is a major source of cash in the La Paz market. Onions may be planted at almost any time on irrigated land, yielding a continuous harvest, and most Compi families ship to La Paz once or twice a month, some more frequently.

Since the Revolution the government has permitted campesinos to sell produce on certain streets in the capital on Saturdays and Sundays without paying a fee. In addition, the more active sellers from the Compi estancias have organized a cooperative which rents space in one of the important markets in La Paz, and they permit other residents

Onion fields near Compi (Lambros Comitas)

from Compi to sell there for a small fee. Like the minoristas in Sorata, the Compi campesinos get their onions to La Paz by buying space in the large open trucks of the Achacachi Sindicato de Transportistas that serve the lakeside route. Five to eight of them regularly carry the Compi onion cargo to the city. There the campesinos unload at the tambos, large patios that have been converted into storehouses, and most of them find lodging with relatives or go to houses of their own.

The more temperate climate of the lakeside affects all crops. Growth begins a month or more before planting is possible in the San Miguel area. September through November are the important planting months, but the long slack season between December and April in San Miguel is narrowed to February and March in Compi. For some campesinos there is barley to be harvested in January, and potatoes, okas, and beans in March through April and May. Chuño is made in June, barley is planted in July, and broad beans and potatoes in August. Planting and harvesting go on throughout a good part of the year. Technology and labor are essentially the same as in San Miguel. Compi farmers also raise animals, but again with certain differences. The herds are smaller than in San Miguel, and sheep are more numerous than llamas. Another difference is that most Compi families raise pigs for sale in near-by markets. Animals are pastured on community land in the hills, tended—as in San Miguel—by women and children.

Despite a generally richer soil and a more moderate climate, and even though irrigation is possible in two of the three open valleys that constitute the Compi hinterland, and lakeside land receives an abundance of water, the campesinos of Compi are not appreciably better off than the comunarios of San Miguel. The chief reason is that few campesinos have more than one hectare (2.471 acres) of land, made up of numerous and scattered plots. Many of them hold but a series of furrows, each furrow in a different field.

The pressure of the Indian population on the land has been intense, erupting in the considerable emigration that has characterized this community for as long as residents remember. Some emigrants wanted to return to Compi when the government, in the early years following the Revolution, promised the return of land to all campesinos who had been forced off the haciendas, but when hacienda land was divided among the campesinos none was kept for any of the emigrants, and very few ever managed to re-establish themselves in Compi. Despite access to some additional land, the pressure continues unabated, aggravated by inheritance practices. Since the Revolution, inheritance of land at Compi has been according to national law, and all children, including girls, inherit equally, so the son who marries can now expect to receive no more than a few furrows from his father. As a consequence of the land squeeze few can live by agriculture alone, and three-quarters of the men have secondary occupations. Large numbers work in building construction as masons and carpenters. Another large group are merchants, some taking meat from the altiplano to the Yungas and others buying coca in the Yungas for sale in La Paz and the lakeside area. Others do weaving and tailoring. Some are musicians and a few are fishermen. For most men in Compi, secondary work is carried on more or less simultaneously with agriculture, as the demands of their patches of land permit.

Compi has a couple of tiendas, much the same as those in San Miguel, but no public market. Close by, however, the new canton settlement of Jack'o Amaya has developed rapidly in recent years as a local commercial center. It has an active weekly market and several large tiendas. On the other side of Compi, not as close, is Huatajata, which also has a large and active weekly market as well as several tiendas. These facilities not being sufficient, the campesinos of Compi also shop in the huge public markets and stores of La Paz, which stock the total range of manufactured goods available in Bolivia. Most of these goods are beyond the means of the average campesino, but there he can buy the flashlights, bicycles, and transistor radios so common in the community.

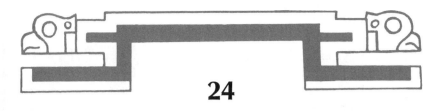

24

POLITICAL ORGANIZATION

In the communities we have studied there is similarity between town and village, between municipal and cantonal governments, in that these governments have similar sets of officials with similar prescribed duties. But this likeness is to a large extent superficial, for there are in fact very fundamental differences between town and village governments in the way officials are selected, in the way a resident qualifies for office, in the way officials carry out their offices, and in the rights and responsibilities of community members. In analyzing political organization in the towns, attention was focused on social groups and organizations that held disproportionate economic and political power. Local government in the towns was seen as an ill-defined structure with limited authority, functioning in a manner which reflects to an important extent the organization of power in these communities. In San Miguel, local government comes close to being the power organization in the community, and it is not distinct from, or a reflection of, any other power bases. This follows, in part, from the absence of significant economic differentiation and of social stratification. Further, many of the characteristics of local government stem from the distinctive cultural tradition of San Miguel as a free Indian community. Though the community has adopted some of the national forms, there has been no significant alteration of its traditional political organization.

SAN MIGUEL: GOVERNMENT OFFICIALS

In the national political structure San Miguel is a canton, the lowest level of governmental jurisdiction under national law. It is one of the several political subdivisions of the province of Carangas, which in turn is one of the several provinces of the Department of Oruro. This makes San Miguel immediately responsible to the sub-prefect in the provincial capital of Corque, and then, one step beyond, to the prefect in the department capital city of Oruro.

The chief responsibilities of the canton are the administration of law and public services within its jurisdiction. Close dependence of cantons on provincial and departmental capitals—at least under the law—is ensured by making canton offices subject to the appointive authority of the sub-prefect. This power is in fact not exercised in respect of San Miguel, an indication of the community's marginal political significance to provincial and departmental authorities. Nevertheless, its complement of officials compares very favorably to the other communities. There are ten canton offices and twenty-one officials in San Miguel. Most of the offices derive from Spanish colonial times, and a few from the period of the Incas, though some have been re-defined. At the top of this canton hierarchy is the corregidor, an office parallel in the canton with that of the sub-prefect in the province and the prefect in the department. His duties, beyond enforcement of law and collection of taxes, include supervision of the registration of births and deaths, supervision of the public market, and provision of facilities for voting in national elections. In addition, the corregidor has charge of community projects, presides over civic celebrations, and acts as a judge in local disputes from time to time. However, he has an unofficial responsibility to obtain for the canton all possible aid from both the regional and the central government. The corregidor's presence in San Miguel as a representative of national government gives the community a favorably recognized voice in appealing for a share of whatever largess the higher levels of government may be inclined to bestow. Because the hope of educational, medical, and agricultural grants-in-aid depends on his office, the community was not only willing but anxious to forgo traditional government practices and accept some reorganization of the ayllus, thereby conforming to the national pattern.

While the corregidor is officially the chief representative of the national government in a canton, to the people of the canton he is primarily the ambassador of the community to outside officials and government at all levels. He must represent the community at all meetings or in all negotiations with outside officials. His is the authority in decisions and actions that must be reported to higher officials, and his signature is required on the documents of such decisions. He must, therefore, be literate, which would disqualify for that office a good many of the older men in the community. The office of corregidor is broadly defined, not carefully delineated. The character of the incumbent shapes the conduct of the office.

Second to the corregidor in the canton is the agente municipal, a relatively new office which has been subject to various interpretations. He is officially responsible for the supervision and regulation of community conditions that are regulated under law in the public interest. This theoretically covers a wide range of matters, but in San Miguel it means his keeping the streets in a state of reasonable repair, setting hours when the tiendas must remain open, supervising the public market, issuing commercial licenses, and collecting fees. The agente municipal has his own one-room office building on the central plaza opposite the church, separate from the casa de gobierno, another one-room building, which serves the corregidor and local government as headquarters.

Outside the official hierarchy are four jilakatas, one for each of the ayllus. The jilakatas are not recognized as government officials under national law, but this has no effect on their actual authority in the community. The role of the jilakata in canton government is to represent his ayllu, meaning constituent estancias and their populations of comunarios. Jilakatas, like the other officials, are expected to reside in the canton settlement. The traditional authority of the jilakatas is greater than the official authority of the corregidor or agente municipal, and their prestige is generally considerably greater. They are the leaders of cohesive constituencies in the San Miguel ayllus, while the other officials—as canton officials—find that their positions tend to isolate them from, rather than strengthen their influence over, the comunarios.

Next in the hierarchy are the three jueces parroquiales, the parochial judges, called first, second, and third juez, but there is no other official distinction among them. They preside over all classes of civil and criminal legal proceedings within the canton, there being no recourse to higher levels of legal jurisdiction except, it would seem, in the most serious instances of criminal violence and murder.

As in the towns already described, most of the major offices in San Miguel government intrude upon the authority of the judiciary. A person seeking justice customarily appeals to a judge who is a member of his own ayllu. If none of the three judges is of his ayllu, he will address himself to any official who is; or—if there be none who is—he will seek out a judge or other high official who is not from the same ayllu as his legal opponent. The comunario assumes that social relations inevitably bias judgment, so each party to a dispute attempts to maximize the bias in his favor. However, the very suspicion that this is so has generated much cautiousness in judges and higher officials and flagrant miscarriages of justice seem to occur infrequently.

The judges are also responsible for keeping records of the participation by comunarios in canton projects. Their lists tell who has worked, when, and on which project, in compliance with community work obligations. The judges are sometimes approached to make decisions about community matters. They may be asked by local officials to select a site for a school or a sanitary post, or some such thing, a ticklish business, because there is no vacant or unused community land, and some comunario will have to give up his property and, because it will be put to community use, will get no compensation.

Rather low in the hierarchy are four other officials, two comisarios and two alcaldes de campo, adjuvants to the higher officials, especially the jueces, whose decisions it is their job to enforce. However, since the other officials above the jueces also hear disputes and pass judgments, the comisarios work just as closely with the jilakatas, the agente municipal, and the corregidor. Enforcement in San Miguel generally means bringing in a person who has ignored a court summons, or it means going out to collect a fine. The comisarios are the bailiffs, the catchpoles, and should not be mistaken for policemen. In San Miguel there are no policemen.

The alcaldes de campo are a sort of comisario. They too are responsible for enforcing the decisions of the jueces, but are in part distinguished from the comisarios in that they are concerned largely with affairs of the land. An alcalde de campo is sent by a juez to check on a complaint that a neighbor's cow is damaging crops. Later, perhaps, he summons one or both parties to appear in court. The alcalde de campo is also traditionally responsible for seeing that community land rules are obeyed, especially those concerning irrigation ditch maintenance and water rights. Finally, it is a duty of the alcaldes de campo to give notice in the ayllus of public meetings to be held in the canton settlement. Since there are no telephones, each alcalde walks to two of the ayllus, delivering his announcements in person.

The office of cacique cobrador is charged solely with the collection of the annual land tax and its delivery to Oruro. Having a limited, specific task is a common characteristic of less important offices in canton government, and officials who hold them have less prestige and are much less consulted on the broader issues of canton leadership; but the cacique cobrador differs significantly from this pattern in that he is generally a comunario of great prestige, most likely an elderly man who has already held many if not all of the offices in local government. The selection of such a person for so limited an office reflects the importance of his one task, the collection of the land tax. Though the advanced age of the cacique cobrador may prevent his active participation in government affairs, he has prestige, and occupies a position relatively high in the hierarchy.

The canton's public primary school is the specific responsibility of four alcaldes escolares, one for each of the ayllus in the canton. They are the representatives of the ayllus to the school in the headquarters settlement, representing the interests of the ayllus in how the school is run—although with no authority over it—and are responsible for aid to the school in general. The interest of the community in the school and in education can be seen in the new school building that was constructed with community labor and mostly community materials, and the construction later of a small apartment building for the teachers. The alcaldes escolares supervise planting and harvesting on the lands set aside by the community for the schools, and they are also truant officers.

Finally, on the lowest rungs of the governmental hierarchy, there are two offices of simple, limited duties. The more important of these is the notario, the compiler of the vital statistics of birth, death, and marriage, for which he is permitted to charge fees. The marriage fee is a not insubstantial forty pesos, which results in a delay of several years in the registration of most couples. The notario is also responsible for the registration of voters for national elections, for which there is no fee. The other office is that of the correo. His job is to deliver the mail—only a few pieces in a whole year.

These are the ten offices which, with twenty-one incumbents, constitute the government of the canton-wide community of San Miguel. Two of the offices, that of jilakata and alcalde de campo, are traditional in the community but are not recognized by the national government. Two other offices, the cacique cobrador and the comisario, are also traditional, but these are recognized by the national government. Many of the other posts in the canton government are not traditional, but overlap other traditional offices. This is the case of the corregidor, for example, vis-

à-vis the jilakata. The rather recent formation of a canton-type government in the community, and the consequent necessity to adapt the traditional ways of government to the requirements of national law, account
for some of the anomalies of prestige and authority in relation to the different offices.

The ambiguities of authority and the indistinctness in jurisdiction
among offices, so conspicuous in the towns, pose no serious problems in
the effective operation of San Miguel's local government because of the
transcendent traditional, collaborative concept of the nature of office.
While it is possible, in varying degrees, to specify the respective responsibilities of the different offices in accord with the way they are defined at
superior levels of government, none of the higher offices in San Miguel
in fact operates independently of the others. Instead, the conduct of offices and the actions of officials are governed by an implicit commitment
to rule by consensus. Officials do not act on their own, but only in concert, and within the group there is no fixed hierarchy of influence. Certain offices bear greater prestige than others, but incumbents at any
given time differ considerably in age, ability, experience, and established
prestige. These attributes may outweigh the authority and prestige that
a specific office confers. Regardless of their titles, the men who constitute the working local government operate as a collective unit. These
men see each other frequently, raise with each other any problems or issues that they think require their attention as authorities, and discuss all
suggested courses of action until there is agreement among them. When
referring to the local government or government acts, comunarios speak
of "the authorities" rather than "the corregidor" or any other specific
office. Indeed, this is appropriate, for—except for the conduct of routine
tasks—no official, from the highest to the lowest, has a prerogative in
raising issues, making proposals, or expressing opinions. Everyone may
speak and be heard, though in practice the lower officials speak less than
the higher.

On Wednesday of every week, in late afternoon or early evening, "the
authorities" meet at the casa de gobierno. All twenty-one officials are required to attend. He who fails is liable to a fine of four pesos, though
this does not appear ever to have been levied. Since distances between
some of the estancias and ayllus and the canton settlement are considerable for a man on foot, officials are expected to move to the canton
settlement during the year they hold office. Many of them will already

have a house in the canton settlement, and part of the family is there during the school year, so this is easy. But no one is forced to move, so there is generally some official who is absent from the weekly meeting, and the lower the rank the more likely that he is a frequent absentee. In 1966 the corregidor did not move to the canton settlement and was frequently absent. He was widely criticized.

There are no fixed agenda for the weekly meetings of the canton authorities. They discuss whatever is currently confronting the community, and any official is free to raise any topics that interest him. Two or more officials frequently will already have discussed a problem informally, and they will then present it to the group. If there is an issue of considerable importance that directly affects the comunarios, the authorities issue a call for a public assembly in the canton settlement. The alcaldes de campo carry the word to the ayllus, and all comunarios are expected to attend or pay a four-peso fine, though, again, no one appears ever to have paid it. At these assemblies every comunario has an opportunity to speak his mind.

The essential difference between political office in the towns and in San Miguel is that in the latter community official position entails obligation without privilege. The offices endow the holders with prestige and present opportunities to exercise leadership, but they also require sacrifices, particularly of time. In this community in which every man is a campesino, officials are required to devote time to political office that could be given to their agricultural work. In the towns, all officeholders, even the lowliest, expect to profit to some degree from their office. In San Miguel, one of the few certainties of officeholding is that it will be costly to the incumbent. There are no revenues available to the local government. The land tax goes to the department. The limited number of fees go to the specific offices that concern them. Since there are no funds to be disposed of, there is no budget. Money is appropriated as need arises.

If there are no funds available to the local government, what monies can be expended? This, it turns out, is one of the onerous businesses of office. Comunarios do not expect to be assessed to pay for the activities or projects of the authorities. Rather, they think the authorities should finance whatever activities they authorize. That is the way it goes, as the following exchange at a gathering of ten of the leading authorities shows:

Corregidor What should we do about money to entertain our guests at the fiesta [September 29]?

Juez Parroquial We'll have to put a levy on ourselves. [All agree.]

Several How much? Two pesos each? [All agree.]

The discussion shifts briefly to another topic and then comes back to the question of money for the fiesta, and an official of ayllu Pueblo points out that a levy of two pesos will amount to only forty-two pesos:

Corregidor That won't be enough. Let's make it three pesos each. [They all agree.]

The cost of holding office is highly variable, cannot be estimated with much certainty, but it has been put at around 500 pesos per year for each official. This is a considerable sum for most comunarios. Moreover, the cost appears to be going up. Throughout the community and especially among the authorities there are signs of a promotional zeal for progress. In the recent past, in addition to the school and housing for the teachers, they have laid a pipeline to bring water to the central plaza of the canton settlement. In 1966 there was talk of a telephone line from the canton to Oruro, among other things.

The community is able to call on its members to contribute labor to community projects, but almost all of them require some outlay of funds, so the cost of progress to those who hold office has become increasingly formidable and is forcing them to look outside the canton for assistance. For this reason there has been a drive to establish San Miguel as a second section of the province of Carangas. In 1966 the national government was considering the establishment of a second section in Carangas, and San Miguel was one of four canton communities considered as the capital. The other three communities—Chuquichambi, Huayllamarca and Llanquera—are all larger than San Miguel, but San Miguel appears to have been most eager to secure the nomination. Most of the authorities in San Miguel see increased government assistance coming from such a change, which would be of benefit not only to the community but also to themselves. Their concern to attract outside interest and support impels them to struggle through the composition of letters to the Minister of Health and the Director of the Institute of Rural Development. In these approaches they are seeking the advantages of the larger society for the community, though what these are is not clearly perceived.

The authorities of the canton are represented in miniature in each of the four ayllus. In three of these the local ayllu government has a corregidor auxiliar, an agente auxiliar, and an alcalde de campo auxiliar. The character of these offices parallels that of their counterparts on the canton level, but the scope of the office is restricted to the affairs of the ayllu. There are no regular duties for any of these officials. They act as occasion demands. There are no regular meetings of ayllu authorities, but the likelihood is that they will see each other daily in the normal course of their lives anyway.

Comunarios must collaborate on ayllu projects also, and are called out to repair the chapel and the irrigation ditches. Some ayllus, socially more cohesive than others, plan rather ambitious projects, but, again, there are no public funds available.

Though the ayllu jilakata resides in the canton settlement during his term of office, he must spend considerable time in his ayllu because his fields are there and some of his family may still be living there. His position as representative of his ayllu gives him considerably more prestige than any of the other ayllu officials has. He is "the authority" to his fellow comunarios. In short, the notion of hierarchy is much clearer and much more decisive with respect to ayllu officials than to those of the canton. For example, the agente auxiliar called a meeting of musicians in one of the ayllus, but at the last minute it was postponed for a week. Responding to questions, one of the comunarios explained:

The jilakata wants to wait until after the fiesta of San Andres. [But the agente auxiliar wanted it tonight, and didn't he advise some people to be here?] Yes, but that was before he had discussed it with the jilakata. [Why did the jilakata want to postpone it?] He said the people had just finished with one fiesta and now had to get ready for San Andres. It would be too much. Everything will be quiet next week and it would be better to do it then. [Suppose the agente auxiliar insisted that the session be held tonight?] No, he would not insist. He would not insist against the jilakata, for the jilakata has much more respect. He has had more offices and holds a position in which one receives the respect of the people.

This respect for the jilakata in his community is the basis of his traditional high rank among the canton authorities.

Ayllu Pueblo, in which the canton settlement lies, is a little different from the others in the form of its political organization. Ayllu Pueblo consists of three primary estancias, Pueblo, Condoriri, and Vilaque. In the canton government the ayllu is represented by a jilakata and by one of the alcaldes escolares. But of the usual other three ayllu authorities, not all are found in two of ayllu Pueblo's estancias, and not any in the third, estancia Pueblo, which is the canton headquarters settlement. This estancia conducts its affairs under the direction of a political society headed by a president. The reason for this arrangement in ayllu Pueblo is not at all apparent. In a community in which the equality of rights and obligations is a fundamental element of local political organization, the choice of one estancia as a headquarters has created a situation of inequality which disturbs the community as a whole. While the canton now has a complete primary school, housing for its teachers, and a new sanitary post, all of them are in one ayllu in one estancia. While many families have houses in the canton settlement and spend time there, there is no denying that those who live in estancia Pueblo and near by benefit to a greater extent from the development of the canton than those comunarios who live at a distance.

AYLLU INDEPENDENCE

The authorities of San Miguel canton, in contrast to those in towns, are not merely functionaries sent from on high to a community wherein they have but superficial relations with the people and a highly restricted formal authority over them. The authorities of the canton are all comunarios. Most comunarios will at some time be in authority, all take part in the election of canton authorities, and all are responsive to the authority of these officials. There are no policemen or soldiers in San Miguel. No official carries a gun. The authorities tend to avoid even any suggestion of force.

The ayllus are root and branch of the cantonal structure. The mita, the voluntary community work that every comunario owes to the canton, is determined on an ayllu basis. Canton authorities decide how many men are needed for how many days for any given project. A request for one-quarter of this number is then sent to each of the four ayllus, each being expected to contribute an equal number of men. Election to canton office is on an ayllu basis. All comunarios are eligible to hold office, but there is a strict cycle of rotation of offices between ayllus. Thus, in a given year, certain ayllus must supply candidates for specific offices and other ayllus candidates for other offices, the order of rotation being fixed. This does not result in an equal distribution of officeholders among the ayllus in any year. For example, in the election of 1966, Alianza, the largest ayllu, supplied only three officials; Bolivar supplied four; while Pueblo and Luzapata each supplied five, Luzapata being the smallest of the four.

The basic separateness of the ayllu in the canton is also symbolized at the weekly meetings of canton authorities. The officials from ayllus Pueblo and Luzapata sit on one side of the meeting room in the casa de gobierno, while those from ayllus Bolivar and Alianza sit on the other. The corregidor sits at a table at one end of the room, while the two sets of officials sit on benches along the two sides. Each year as offices rotate from one ayllu to another, the sitting places of officials will change in the room, but not the position of the ayllu itself. Each ayllu has its own authorities for managing itself. While each ayllu sends some of its members to serve in the canton government each year, and most of these are expected to serve the canton and not their particular ayllu, the jilakata serves in the canton solely as a representative of his ayllu. In the conduct of canton affairs, canton authorities not infrequently give way to ayllu interests. A working example of this deference to the ayllus occurred when a survey of the canton community was proposed by the research group.

The canton authorities heard the original proposal for the survey and then agreed to call an assembly of the canton comunarios to discuss it. Because survey interviews would impose on individual comunarios, canton authorities were not prepared to make a decision one way or the other without their consent. Only about thirty-five comunarios actually attended the assembly called to consider the proposal, but at this meeting the matter was thoroughly aired. Spring planting was about to begin, and long interviews with a large proportion of all comunarios loomed as a disruptive force. Characteristically, comunarios and authorities focused on the potential advantages. In the eyes of the comunarios, the research group was not distinguished clearly from government agencies or international programs; rather, it was considered to be one of the large class of "external groups" seen as sources of assistance to the community. The research group recognized the real hardships that carrying out the survey on schedule entailed and was prepared to help the community with some of its projects by supplying materials.

At the first meeting a decision was reached by the comunarios and their leaders to cooperate with the survey. Questions about what assistance should be asked of the research group, and especially how such assistance should be apportioned in the community, were difficult to resolve, so a second meeting was arranged for the following day. At this meeting the main issue was whether all assistance should go to the canton or be divided among the ayllus. This brought out the chronic complaint from the ayllus that no aid received, and no project completed by canton authorities, is ever seen in the ayllus. The comunarios and some canton authorities were opposed to having only the canton benefit from collaboration with the survey, so it was decided to accept the proposal only on condition that each ayllu negotiate directly with the survey team and make its own arrangements for the conditions of collaboration. By this arrangement the canton did not sacrifice all benefit to itself, but accepted a reduced share, since the canton settlement would profit as a part of ayllu Pueblo.

The determination to have independence of action in the ayllus has led to talk of separation from the canton in some of them, and the development of an apparently separatist policy in at least one, Bolivar. Because subdividing and regrouping have had a long history among the Aymara settlements on the altiplano, and San Miguel itself is a rather recent product of subdivisions grouped as a canton, allegiance to the community called San Miguel is too slight to be a strong cohesion factor. Further, three ayllus see ayllu Pueblo, more specifically, estancia Pueblo, the canton settlement, as benefiting much more than themselves from assistance obtained by the canton. The other ayllus, meaning the big estancias in these ayllus, would like to have schools of their very own. There is a widespread belief that more and different aid will be coming, which they too would like to get, and the way to get more for themselves—as they see it—is to have their own set of canton officials to deal directly with government agencies.

Before 1958, separatist-minded ayllu Bolivar was one of the estancias of ayllu Alianza. At that time it separated from Alianza, thinking, it is said, that it would thus be able to acquire its own school. Since then Bolivar has built a one-room school and a small chapel, and recently started construction of a central ayllu settlement to bring its widely dispersed population together.

These developments bear the marks of a thought-out plan. To become a canton, the ayllu must look as if it deserved this status. Every effort is being made to match the San Miguel canton settlement and even improve on the model; hence the school, the chapel, the new central settlement, and proposals for a sanitary post. A further preliminary part of the plan is to free Bolivar from participation in canton services that it wishes to provide for itself. The ayllu supports one teacher in its local primary school, though there are barely enough students to justify a teacher.

In its move toward independence Bolivar attempted in 1965 to seize one of the gypsum deposits used for stucco and operate it for the benefit of the ayllu. The several deposits in the hills around the canton are regulated by the canton, and the attempt was rebuffed in a physical clash between comunarios from ayllus Bolivar and Pueblo. In this and in its other moves, Bolivar has provoked considerable antagonism in the other ayllus, and when the corregidor of 1966, a man from Bolivar, continued to reside in his own ayllu instead of moving to the canton settlement, and even missed meetings of the authorities, this was interpreted as an expression of independence and he was accused of violating his responsibility as a canton official.

Bolivar, however, is not the only ayllu that apparently has aspirations for independence. Two of the other biggest estancias, Caicoma in Alianza and Condoriri in Pueblo, are reported to want independence also. They have not aroused the criticism and antagonism directed at Bolivar, for neither has taken concrete steps to bring about any change.

The weakness of some of the ties of the ayllus to the canton, as well as the pressures for independence that threaten to disrupt ayllu-canton ties, are at least partially counterbalanced by conditions that tend to weaken the position of the ayllu on the one hand, and by relations that bind the ayllu into the canton system on the other. One of the conditions unfavorable to independence is the limited social cohesion within the several ayllus. Ownership of land is the basis of membership in a specific ayllu, but ayllu landowners are not always neighbors, only sometimes, because holdings are fragmented and the settlements in which holders of adjoining lands live are often far apart. An important force for cohesion is the sharing of water, which is allotted on an ayllu basis. Only those who own land in an ayllu have any right to water there, though others may be permitted to use it. The sharing of water establishes a strong basis for collaboration among the comunarios. But it is not possible at present for all parcels of land to receive water, and therefore in all ayllus there are some comunarios to whom the sharing of it is of no concern and who do not on this account cohere.

Besides the division between those with and those without water, there is frequently another division within the ayllus between big and small estancias. Of the four main estancias in Bolivar, Llacsa contains more comunarios than all of the others combined, and Zescallacsa is much closer to ayllu Alianza than to the center of its own ayllu, and would prefer to be a part of that ayllu. The other two estancias, Piñeto and Culco-Condoriri, both small, are distant from the new Bolivar ayllu center and are estranged from ayllu leadership. The position of the smaller estancias is not enviable. Partly as a result of numbers alone, comunarios from the big estancias are more likely to supply officials for both ayllu and canton governments. In the management of ayllu affairs, even if one of the ayllu authorities is from one of the smaller estancias, the smaller estancias are frequently not consulted on ayllu matters, but merely informed of decisions that have been taken. Both physical separation and strained relations affect collaborative work within the ayllu, which in turn affects social cohesion among the comunarios of the ayllu.

The quasi-independent attitude of the ayllus is sometimes seen in interrelations. Ayllu Bolivar, for example, allows some of the comunarios of ayllu Pueblo to share Bolivar water, but only if they will send their children to the Bolivar primary school, because the school must have thirty children to qualify for a teacher, and often there are not enough first-grade Bolivar children to start. The arrangement continues until these children are graduated, then their fathers are summarily deprived of water and have no redress.

Chauvinistic feelings notwithstanding, there are factors in the canton political system that militate against independence for the ayllus. One of these is the canton's established role as the mediator in respect to the outside world, especially the government and its agencies. It has a protective function also, for the canton authorities are in a position to ward off external interference. More appreciated is the acquisition function— teachers to staff a complete primary school of six grades, having San Miguel named a school district with a director posted to the canton, and so on. Canton authorities had an important part in obtaining free food from Caritas, a Catholic aid organization operating in Bolivia, and they have other requests at government agencies for other forms of assistance.

A second link between ayllu and canton is the political "cargo," the office system. Except for the office of jilakata, which is also an ayllu office, all of the canton offices carry greater prestige than their counterparts in the ayllu. In a community with minimal social differentiation, the political office system is one of the few means to obtain distinction, and therefore the canton office system has become a strong cohesive force in the community. Every married man with land is a comunario and has a right to speak and be listened to at ayllu and canton meetings, but office holders have the prestige and influence. Every comunario will have an opportunity at some time to take at least a minor office, and there are strong incentives to do so.

The fiesta office system has a similar bonding effect. There are quasi-religious fiestas in the ayllus, and, in some estancias, national holiday celebrations and the patronal fiesta, all of them occasions for heavy drinking, music, and dancing. All have important cohesive effects.

The patronal fiesta in 1966 ran twenty-four hours a day for six continuous days, a fulfilling experience for most participants, though some said the fiesta is not what it used to be. Several bands were brought in and they played night and day. There were masses of food and even larger quantities of alcohol, all free. Many merchants and guests from other communities swelled the throng. Most families with second houses in the canton settlement were obliged to give them up to visiting relatives, compadres, or friends. For this big fiesta each ayllu strives to better the others by presenting the best band, the best costumed and most practiced dance troupe, the most appetizing food in the most generous quantities, and the greatest flow of alcohol.

The sponsors, called pasantes, bear with their relatives the cost of this celebration. For the September 29 fiesta there are eight pasantes, four of whom are mayordomos and four alferados. The pasantes are selected by the jilakatas in the four ayllus from among those comunarios who have not served. As with political offices, the pasante offices rotate among the ayllus. The pasantes have a year in which to meet their obligations to the fiesta. In this year they are supposed to meet weekly in the canton to pray together at one of the two churches, but these meetings are often skipped because they must devote their time to earning money. In ultimate costs, the burden of the mayordomos is considerably greater than that of the alferados. They are required to supply the bands and dance troupes, which are imported from Oruro at an estimated $175 for each. When the large quantities of food and alcohol are added to this, each mayordomo can expect to have to pay $300 to $400, so some men will have to work for much of the year in Oruro to accumulate the necessary cash. Also, their families give the year to handicrafts to earn ready money. Fiesta sponsorship calls for the fullest support of the family and

all close kin, and often compadres and padrinos as well. The preparation
and serving of meals and drinks frequently call for material and financial contributions.

For the larger fiestas the resources of the family may be taxed to the
limit. In such circumstances ample property and a large family are of
great value. In San Miguel a nearly blind comunario was named a pasante for a fiesta and accepted it as his obligation. Since he could not afford to be a pasante without raising additional funds, he left for Oruro
to beg in the streets, the only way of making money that his physical
condition permitted.

The reward for the great expense and effort on the part of the pasante
and his relatives is the tremendous prestige the pasante gains from the
event. Fiesta office, like political office, is obligatory for the comunario,
but if the costs are quite beyond a person's means he will not be asked
to serve. There are many other fiestas in the canton, all of them smaller
than the September 29 affair and more within the means of more comunarios. They also convey prestige, though to lesser degrees. The jilakata
of Caicoma describes the system:

All are expected to hold offices, but some cannot hold very many, while others
can. It is according to their means. Everybody wants to take many cargos, but
some are able to take more, others less. Everybody wants an office, but when
one has just had one he needs time to recuperate from his expenditures of
the year before. People know that he does not want another office right away.
He does not have to say he cannot afford it, but everybody will know and
not ask him.

The central place of the cargo, the political and religious office system,
in the life of the community is suggested by the fact that approximately
25 per cent of the comunarios in any given year hold either a political or
fiesta office. Both types of cargos confer community prestige. There is a
broad fiesta office base in the estancias and ayllus, and hence a more
pyramiding effect here than in the political office system, as a comunario
moves from holding a minor fiesta office in the estancia to an ayllu, and
finally to the big canton fiesta, each time accumulating a greater quantity of prestige. This pyramidal cargo structure in part cuts across estancia divisions, and thus acts as a cohesive intercommunity force in the
canton political system.

Within the canton the ayllu occupies a strategic but not overpowering position. The organizational form of San Miguel today is certainly not what it was many years ago, nor will it necessarily remain unchanged even in the near future. The same may be said of many of the Aymara communities on the altiplano. A major reason is the growing impact of the national society on these communities, especially since the Revolution of 1952. San Miguel lacks most of the obvious signs of change produced by the Revolution. Yet the governing authorities of the canton have progress very much on their minds, and their position between the ayllus and national agencies is a weighty element in maintaining the political system as it is. Even so, there are simultaneous tendencies, one toward increased canton centralization, and the other toward decentralization. This ambivalence is seen in the still amorphous but developing division of the more outspoken comunarios into progressive and conservative factions. The progressives see their future in terms a strong canton that will be able to deal more effectively with the national government and get a secondary school, or perhaps a hospital, for the community. They think the canton, to accomplish this, must be unified, strengthened at the expense of the independence of the ayllus and even the estancias. The progressives tend to minimize the importance of the fiesta cargo system and attempt to avoid such offices. The conservatives want the advantages of outside aid, but they want them for their own ayllus or their own estancias. They are probably less realistic. These conservatives more readily accept fiesta cargos. The conflict between these factions extends to other matters, such as the mita, the community work obligation. A progressive canton authority defines the problem:

If we were a strong central organization, the canton authorities could make more demands on the comunarios. The same people always come to the mita. Some people never come. We [the canton authorities] have the right to fine those who never come, but we never do fine them. They simply ignore it, and the ayllus and estancias do nothing about it.

This is not a problem unique to the canton. It occurs at ayllu and estancia levels, the consequence of a gradual shift from a traditional social order, in which a shared morality has been the central mechanism by which conformity to social obligations was ensured, to a secular order, in which persuasion and punishment must be applied to obtain conformity to now secular rules.

THE POSITION OF THE COMUNARIO

In the towns, the majority of men are related to the political system only marginally, as objects of aggrandizement, almost as if they were exterior to the civic body. In San Miguel, a comunario is an integral part of the political order, just as much as any of the authorities. Every comunario has a set of obligations to the canton community, as well as to ayllu and estancia sub-communities, and also has a set of rights.

Every comunario has a mita obligation, which requires him to provide his labor for community projects. There is yearly work to be done on the roads, the irrigation ditches, and the public buildings, and there are special projects. Some of these obligations arise annually in the canton and in the ayllus, while others occur intermittently on both these levels and in the estancias. Canton projects are usually organized in November and December, when there is little agricultural work, but they can come at any time. The canton authorities decide among themselves how many men will be needed for how many days, and then each ayllu is asked to supply one-quarter of the number.

The number of days of canton mita required from the comunarios varies from year to year, depending on the range of projects. Each ayllu maintains an official roster of its comunarios, and mita assignments both for the canton and for the ayllu are rotated so that each man serves an equal number of days. This equality obtains, however, only within each ayllu, for comunarios in the smaller ayllus will necessarily find their names coming up for canton work more frequently than those in the larger ones. How the mita obligation works out in practice is noted by a comunario from the estancia Caicoma in ayllu Alianza:

We had about four days' work before the twenty-first of November, fixing up the lower plaza, and about two days putting the roof on the church of the upper plaza, the church of San Miguel. I worked only about three days. I had to go to Oruro before the twenty-first. [Did anyone work in your place?] No, I have nobody that I could send. [Do you have to make up the lost three days?] No, the ayllu had many people there, more than the others. In general, I work the mita in the canton whenever there is a call. If I miss a few days, it's not important.

If a comunario is absent from the community, ill, or preoccupied, and not able to attend a mita call, it is permissible to send a replacement. Most often he is an adult son, but many comunarios have no grown sons and therefore cannot but default. Sometimes a comunario balks because he disagrees about the merits of a project. In any case, response to the mita request is not reflexive. Ayllu Bolivar, for example, has had considerable difficulty with its projects. One of the ayllu officials complained:

The comunarios have had many expenditures this year. Most of it was for the church. We get no help from anybody. The people from Culco come to work, but they do not pay the quotas. The people from Piñeto neither help with the work nor pay the quotas.

Here the problem is a compound of the ambitious course that ayllu Bolivar has set for itself and of disaffection in the smaller estancias within the ayllu. In this case there seems to be less evasion of canton mita than ayllu mita, but even for the canton some comunarios are not inclined to give. There is some indication that in such cases a fine is imposed at the end of the year, and the comunario must give a sheep or make some other contribution to the authorities. But it is clear that authorities at all levels are reluctant to punish. Authorities talk as if formal retribution always follows social deviance, but the comunarios see it rather differently:

If a man never comes to a mita call, then it is up to the authorities of the ayllu to make him aware that he has been missed. [Suppose he doesn't care. Can the ayllu authorities do anything about it?] Sometimes when they talk to a man he then starts to come. Sometimes he continues to ignore them. [Then what do they do?] Usually nothing. They could fine him, but they don't. [Why don't they?] Well, a person in the same ayllu is a neighbor, and nobody wants to start trouble.

Mita obligations are complicated by the fact that many comunarios own land in more than one estancia and some have plots in more than one ayllu. A comunario was asked about his separate obligations to two estancias:

[What obligations do you have to Condoriri?] I go there every year during the fiesta of the twenty-fifth of July. If there is some work to do, I help out. [When there is a meeting of the estancia, do you attend?] If I happen to be there I attend, but they never inform me of meetings when I'm not there. Or if there is an estancia mita, they sometimes inform me, but not always. [But do they expect you to work when there is an estancia mita?] Yes, they expect me to help. Sometimes I do and sometimes I don't.

The second important obligation of all comunarios is that of fiesta office. One generally begins to sponsor fiestas as a young man between eighteen and twenty years of age. Fathers who can afford it will sometimes offer a minor son as a fiesta sponsor to save the son the expense of this duty at a later date. In this way some comunarios hold their first fiesta office when they are only thirteen or fourteen years old. The holding of fiesta offices normally precedes political officeholding. The fiestas provide a setting in which the comunario can distinguish himself, bring himself to the attention of others beyond his own estancia and ayllu. Some offices are within the reach of all, for their cost is minimal. Others are relatively costly and the most prestigious are exceedingly costly, which eliminates the poorer comunarios from consideration. Age is not an important criterion for even the most important offices, and some occupants of these offices are quite young indeed. In a few of the canton political offices there is, however, a premium on literacy. There is concern lest a comunario be incompetent for office. This is seen in the following discussion with a comunario from Caicoma:

[If Fernando does not speak very much and he does not have good ideas, why was he elected agente auxiliar?] Because he knows what to do and he does it. That is the way with most people who are authorities. [Does that mean you don't choose persons with special qualities for certain offices?] Sometimes we do, but mostly we don't. We cannot choose somebody who cannot write for registro or corregidor. Or we cannot choose somebody who hasn't the head for an office. But otherwise, if he can do it we elect him. We are very few people. Sometimes we elect somebody who barely has the head to do a job, but he follows the others and gets by.

The principle of first among equals characterizes the San Miguel political order. The authorities are not an elite. They are the comunarios who happen to be in office that year. Next year there will be another set and in the following year another set. It is, therefore, important to keep qualification requirements within their means, and to accept authorities with mediocre abilities or worse, because to eliminate such persons would mean that a few would have community responsibilities that should be shouldered by all.

There are important differences in the ways that political and fiesta offices are filled. Responsibility for canton fiestas rotates among the four ayllus. The jilakata selects the pasantes who represent the ayllu, and does not select persons who have recently held either type of office, or who obviously cannot afford to accept an office. On the other hand, a comunario can refuse the jilakata's request that he serve as a pasante. He may give any of a variety of reasons, and his own decision is final. Political election is more complicated, more formal. Candidates are selected in the ayllus, with all comunarios participating. Just as offices rotate among ayllus, so they often rotate among estancias, so it is known from whence the candidates are to come. A comunario from Caicoma describes this process with respect to his own ayllu, Alianza:

In Alianza, for example, there will be nominations for corregidor, since it is Alianza's turn to have the corregidor this year. They will nominate three people and the canton assembly will elect one of them. The three nominations are finally made at an ayllu assembly, but it is the estancias that initially present the candidates. This year Tica Belen will present two candidates and Caicoma will present one. Next year, when the ayllu will nominate candidates for juez parroquial, Caicoma will present two candidates and Tica Belen one. After the nominations have been made in the various estancias there is an assembly of the total ayllu and they approve the nominations. The assembly never rejects the nominations of an estancia.

It is clear that by this process every comunario has a right to speak and be heard, but some are heard better than others. This is apparent in the following discussion with a young comunario:

Yes, everybody is equal in talking at the assemblies. [How about you?] Yes, I talk, but not as much as some of the older people. [Why is that?] Because they have more experience. For that reason younger people don't talk so much. Sometimes young people speak, but mostly the business of the ayllu is handled by the older people. [Is this because of respect for the older people?] It is partly out of respect, but it is also because the older people have been authorities several times and they know how to deal with problems.

In contrast to fiesta office, nomination to political office is not easy to reject. Some, it is said, escape to Oruro. If they are elected anyway, they may plead lack of funds or lack of time and ask the authorities to relieve them of office. In general, however, comunarios accept political office obligation. As one put it: "In one's lifetime one must. It is expected." A comunario who finds he cannot avoid an office he does not want may be able to make it tolerable in his own fashion. This is seen in the following discussion with a twenty-four-year-old comunario who has been elected to his first political office, that of comisario:

The comisario has very little to do. Manuel Tola, who was comisario from Caicoma this past year, rarely ever attended the meetings of the authorities and almost never went to the ceremonies. Once in a while, when there is a demand, when the accused refuses to come to the juez to be judged, the comisarios have to bring him in, but that rarely happens. [But don't you always have to go to the meetings of the authorities?] Yes, but Manuel and Diego [comisario in 1965] hardly ever went to those meetings unless there was something special to be discussed. I will go when I have the time, but I have much work to do in the house and in the fields. I have no grown sons to look after my work the way some people do. I cannot spend most of my time in the canton settlement. I will go to the meetings when I can, at least at first, to get some experience. Then I will see.

Sometime after the community elections in December of each year the sub-prefect in Corque comes to San Miguel in official recognition of the new authorities. A second and more important ratification of the new officials occurs when the old authorities meet with the new ones in a ritual celebration of the transfer of office. Old and new authorities go to the canton church for a brief prayer and then, in succession and procession, they visit the patios of the new authorities, each of whom will have slaughtered and prepared several animals, sheep or llamas. In the patios the new and old officials eat together, chew coca and drink, alcohol being essential to ritual occasions. During the coca chewing and drinking a short prayer is said again and again to the Pachamama, the Aymara earth goddess and central god in the Aymara pantheon. On this day both old and new authorities carry black silver-headed canes, the symbol of office, all much the same. These canes are not passed from old to new officials. Most families have one, kept out of sight until one of its members is elected to office.

The financial hardships associated with office have been evaded by a minority in recent years by their simply opting out of the fiesta system. The method is to embrace Protestantism, which—in the fundamentalist versions advocated in Bolivia—forbids the chewing of coca or the drinking of alcohol. Tulapugro, a small estancia of a half-dozen families down on the edge of the pampa in ayllu Luzapata, has become an adventista estancia. The pampa land is some of the poorest in the area and this is one of the poorest estancias. As adventistas these comunarios reject the fiesta system. They will not serve as pasantes or kill animals for sacrifice. On the other hand, they are willing, even eager, to accept political offices. Since these also involve the drinking and coca-chewing ceremonies as well as extensive participation in fiestas, they can serve only by significantly altering their conduct while in these offices. Since their number is so small, they have not yet posed a serious threat to the cargo system, but they have aroused much hostility and antagonism. Some have lost parcels of land that they held in other ayllus, and one family had their house in the canton settlement burned. While there is little evidence of much interest throughout the canton in the new religion, a good many other comunarios have become highly conscious of the financial cost of the fiesta system and of how the adventistas in Tulapugro are profiting by rejecting it.

The pressure of office obligations is a subtle factor in maintaining the central position of the ayllus in the political system. Marrying into families with land, and shifting estancias from one ayllu to another to form new ayllus, have created possibilities for multiple ayllu membership and the blurring of ayllu lines. However, the comunario holding land in more than one ayllu would necessarily be subject to cargo obligations of two or more ayllus, doubling his burden of offices and mita obligations. Very few comunarios in San Miguel have accepted such double obligations. Most comunarios avoid this by selling land held in other ayllus.

COMMUNITY LEADERS

While the holding of one of the more important political or fiesta offices gives prestige and more potential for influence, being an officeholder is not necessary to a man's being influential in the community. Insofar as comunarios are socially distinguished, it is just as important to have held office as to be occupying an office. One earns distinction, prestige, and the respect of the community by devoting oneself to a series of offices over the years. As a result, there exists in the community at any given time a prestige pyramid in which all comunarios have a place. At the apex of this pyramid are men who not only have had experience in many offices, but who also have leadership abilities, men who are good planners, willing to devote time to the community, intelligent, articulate, and often somewhat aggressive. No serious decisions are made in the community without consulting these men.

An influential comunario revealed how personal qualities severely condition practical chances for leadership. He considered the jilakata of Alianza to be influential in the ayllu because "the jilakata's voice carries weight," but he thought two other men in Alianza were more influ-

Community authorities of San Miguel (Lambros Comitas)

ential, though not currently occupying a political office. Of these two, one is not as influential as the other because, "he is not so able or clever as Fernando and he is a fool when he is drunk." He brushed aside the jilakata from Luzapata as "a nice little man on whom cargos are placed because he takes them and because the ayllu is very small."

The acquisition of experience, development of abilities, and accumulation of prestige through fiesta and political offices is a continual process covering a good part of the lifespan of every comunario. Therefore, it is somewhat misleading to speak of a set of leaders, for there are always some comunarios starting out on the route to leadership, as well as others who are well on their way, have not quite arrived, but are often energetic, willing to serve, and full of ideas. Some senior and junior leaders alike are outspoken in their dissatisfaction with things as they are. One of the minor canton authorities complained:

The juez parroquial does nothing as juez until a man comes to him to adjudicate a case. The corregidor does not initiate anything. He just takes care of routine business. The agente does traditional jobs. All canton political offices are traditional posts. Nothing is initiated from them.

Out of their dissatisfaction has come their first supplemental form of political organization in the community, the Junta Vecinal. The Junta Vecinal was inaugurated on August 6, 1966, during the Independence Day celebration in the canton settlement. This is an extension of the Junta de Vecinos organization we have already encountered in several of the towns. The junta is an authorized part of town government under Bolivian law, but its political status is presently ambiguous. The inauguration announcement stated that the plan to organize the junta had been approved by national government agencies in Oruro and by the prefect of the department. Three speakers described the new organization to the fiesta crowds, the previous year's corregidor, the current corregidor, and a junior leader who had been chosen as vice president of the junta.

The junta has twenty-three members, each of whom occupies an official position. In its organization it has a closer resemblance to a campesino sindicato than to a Junta de Vecinos. In addition to a president, a vice president, and a secretary general, there are secretaries of specific activities—secretaries of actas, justice, sports, public works, agriculture, cattle, music, and propaganda. Finally, there are four delegates and four vocales. Luzapata, the smallest ayllu, and near-by Pueblo have six and seven members, respectively, while Alianza has four and Bolivar has three. Currently, four members are canton authorities. Other members have held political offices as well as fiesta offices, and there are also several junior leaders.

The junta (obviously) intends to encourage community action in San Miguel. How it is to do this is not clear. Some of the barriers to action are only too evident, marked in the following comment by the junta president:

There are many things we could do, but the people don't want to spend any money. For instance, we could build a good dam on this river and have much more water, but the people do not want to pay for the cement. They don't understand yet that it would be a sacrifice for one year, but afterwards they would gain. We would also like to start a cooperative, but it is hard to get the people to understand that a cooperative would benefit them. With a cooperative, we would plant things according to the best possibilities of production and then exchange among ourselves. For instance, if in a certain place you get good potatoes, the owner should plant potatoes. If all his land is good for potatoes, he should plant only potatoes, and then he could trade with those whose land is good mostly for quinua or okas. This would immediately increase production.

Four months later, in early December, there was no sign that the junta was having any impact on the community. They had held a couple of meetings, but attendance was spotty. The inauguration speakers on August 6 said the junta was an agency to "produce well-being in the community" and promote an "advanced and prosperous community," but the comunarios either thought the junta was not doing what it had said it would do, or they had no idea even of what it was supposed to be doing:

I thought it was going to tell the comunarios how to do things with their cattle, sheep, and land. So far they have told us nothing. They were supposed to study these questions and tell us, but I don't think they are studying, I think they are sleeping. I don't know what the junta vecinal is supposed to do. It has done nothing since the inauguration on the sixth of August, so I don't know what they are doing, or what they are supposed to do. [A number of the members of the junta are on your soccer team. Do you ever discuss the activities of the junta with them?] This is the first discussion of the junta that I have had with anyone.

The new junta has no power. It cannot command the comunarios to collaborate. Its membership is composed primarily of the progressives, who favor the dominance of the canton over the ayllus. The junta is really a redundant organization, in that the affairs of the community are the responsibility of the traditional authorities. There is not a single matter raised by the junta that had not been discussed by the canton authorities. The junta has tried to distinguish itself as being more oriented to technical matters by having various specialized secretaries, but it is mainly distinguished from the traditional authorities in having declared that it favors more and faster action on already recognized community objectives. It remains to be seen whether the junta will develop support in the community or wither away like its counterparts in the towns.

PARTY POLITICS

Since the Revolution of 1952 the chief instrument for engaging the altiplano Indians in partisan political activity has been the campesino sindicato, but there are no sindicatos or political parties in San Miguel. There is not, however, a complete absence of party politics.

In the 1964 national elections 422 adults registered and, presumably, voted. In the national elections of 1966 the figure dropped to 378, but this was an unofficial tally and the official total may have been somewhat larger. Beyond this, 21 per cent of the comunarios admit to membership in one of the political parties. This is the smallest proportion encountered in any of the six communities studied, but still not an insignificant number. Forty-three per cent claim to prefer one party over all of the others, which again is the smallest proportion found among the study communities, but still indicates substantial awareness of partisan politics at the national level.

National political affairs are not as popular a subject of conversation in San Miguel as they are in certain sectors of town populations, which is probably a reflection of lower educational levels in San Miguel and of communications limitations. Very little reading matter reaches San Miguel, though many families have radios and news broadcasts are widely listened to. When the subject of national politics is raised with comunarios the most common response is a complaint about broken promises.

General Barrientos won in San Miguel in the elections of 1966. The unofficial count was 213 for Barrientos, 115 for the FSB, and 50 for the MNR. The distribution of this vote reflects the political sensitivity of the community as a canton. The comunarios, through the authorities, look increasingly to the national government for aid. This gave Barrientos an important edge over all of his competitors. The large vote for the FSB possibly reflects no more than the comunarios' political inexperience, for some were impressed when representatives of the MPC and FSB stayed longer, talked to more people, and "said some nice things."

COMMUNITY ACTION

In general, the authorities in San Miguel are more preoccupied with community welfare than are their counterparts in the four towns, one reason being that the authorities of San Miguel are much more representative of the population. Another is that the comunario has a working role in government. Then, too, the mita system is much more effective than the limited prestación vial of the towns, which can always be avoided through payment of a fee. Each town project evokes only an ad hoc effort that dies with a project's completion, though in Reyes traditional organizational forms may be applied in community action.

The authorities are now discussing seriously the redesigning of the canton settlement, because the few streets are too narrow for the trucks that come for the fiestas and many of the housing compounds are juxtaposed haphazardly. Not unexpectedly, the proposal that a large area of housing should be torn down to align a set of streets in a grid pattern met fierce opposition from property owners and was not adopted. But a compromise appears to have a better chance of success. This would enlarge the settlement in a grid pattern and open up new housing sites for many of the estancia members who want a house in the canton settlement but lack the land.

The mita system makes available a not inconsiderable though relatively unskilled labor pool. The enlargement of the atrio at the Church of the Patrocina required the removal of stone from the approach to the church, and that a stone wall be moved. For four days over a hundred men from all of the ayllus worked on this project. But when the task is a small and possibly urgent one, such as the need to repair the frozen water line coming into town, the authorities may undertake the job themselves. The repair of the water pipe required little labor. It had not been buried, but simply rested on the top of the ground, which explains why it froze. All the authorities themselves had to do was to separate the lengths of pipe so they could be soldered, and for that they imported a skilled solderer from a near-by community. He was paid by the authorities themselves as an obligation of their office. There being no government rents or salaries, costs arise almost entirely from the community projects the authorities decide to undertake. In recent years these costs have grown. The labor to construct the new primary school building was recruited entirely through the mita system, and the Ministry of Education gave some materials. But in most cases, as projects have become bigger so has their cost to the authorities, creating difficult personal problems for them and undermining their status in the community.

By tradition the authorities can assess the community only for their labor, not their cash. This tradition has occasionally been breeched, but the authorities are still far from ordering a cash levy on the population. There is no tradition for it and no mechanism for undertaking it. But if the entire community is not to pay, the small group of authorities must. This issue is far from decided, and it has raised one serious furore, this over a food gift. Gifts from outside agencies or the national government are received by canton authorities in the name of the community. Such aid may be held, used, or even sold by the authorities. Trouble occurred in 1966 in the disposition of Caritas food, mostly flour and cooking oil that the community had solicited from an international Catholic relief organization which operates in Bolivia. A first allotment had been received the year before without any complications, but in the latter part of 1966 Caritas introduced a rule requiring beneficiary communities to pay fifty pesos for each monthly shipment to offset some of the costs of transportation. In November the authorities faced a crisis. Five months of food allotments were about to arrive, for the months of December through March, since access to the community would shortly be interrupted by the rainy season, so the authorities were faced with a 250-peso bill, plus another fifty pesos due on the November shipment. The food previously received had been distributed equally among the comunarios, except for a small quantity held for community use, but when faced with the need to raise a large sum to pay shipping charges the authorities came up with a radical modification:

Corregidor: Have we still got any of the food from the shipment of this past month?

Juez: Yes, we have not yet used any of it.

Corregidor: Why not sell it to raise the 300 pesos. [No dissenters.] We will sell last month's shipment. You, Mauricio [the juez from Caicoma], advise your people. You, Santiago [juez from Luzapata], advise your people. And you, Victor [juez from Pueblo], advise your people.

All agreed with the corregidor's suggestion that they sell the food gift to raise money for the transportation charges. Only Bolivar was omitted from the corregidor's instructions, but since he himself is from that ayllu he presumably took it upon himself to inform that ayllu.

The sale of gift food to local shops to raise funds to pay transportation charges for the next several shipments denied some immediate aid to the comunarios, but was a means to continue this aid program. Certainly the authorities were not profiting from the sale, except in a negative sense. But in this sense the complaint arose two days later when the big food shipment arrived in the canton settlement from Oruro. One of the Bolivar senior leaders, who was not in office, asked the field worker what had arrived in the Caritas shipment:

Field worker: Twenty sacks of flour, ten sacks of cereal, and ten boxes of cans of cooking oil. [The Bolivar leader took out a pencil and scrap of paper and wrote the information down.] Why do you want to know such details?

Bolivar leader: Because we want the authorities to distribute it among the ayllus. We know that the authorities know how to cheat.

Field worker: Why should the authorities cheat you? You have representatives from Bolivar there to see that you are not cheated.

Bolivar leader: The authorities sell the food and keep the money for themselves.

Field worker: Have they ever cheated you before?

Bolivar leader: Yes. Last year when the Caritas things came, they sold it and put the money in their own pocket.

Field worker: Did they put the money in their own pocket or use it to do something for the community?

Bolivar leader: It is the same thing. What is the meaning of cargos if they get the money to do things from outside, from things that really belong to us? The authorities always cheat us.

Field worker: But you were an authority many times. Did the authorities then always cheat the comunarios?

Bolivar leader: We did not have things like Caritas food with which to cheat the comunarios.

Field worker: Do you think it would be proper if the authorities kept a few quintales to sell to pay for their activities?

Bolivar leader: No. They should pay for it themselves. The authorities have to do things for the community out of their own pockets.

Two changes have altered the close correspondence between fiesta offices and government offices. One is the increase in a new kind of cost arising from community improvement projects. As parts of the community and parts of its leadership press forward to obtain new benefits within reach, these involve the community, and especially its officials, in unprecedented demands for money. A second change was the incorporation of new kinds of governmental offices (corregidor and agente) into the traditional system. The necessity to deal with outside officials, to write and interpret official documents, has frequently drawn into these positions young men who are not senior leaders in the community. These men are more sensitive to the cost of the office and less moved by the traditional obligation of the officeholder to pay all the costs of his office. Some of the authorities today would never reach canton political office under this requirement, just as they will never reach the pinnacle of the fiesta hierarchy, for they do not have adequate economic resources. These changes seem to have convinced at least some authorities that traditional arrangements are no longer appropriate.

Since the mita project at the Church of the Patrocina was under way when the big Caritas shipment arrived, a large proportion of the comunarios of all ayllus not only knew of the arrival, but of the contents of the shipment as well. This was very opportune for those who were opposed to what the authorities planned to do with the food shipment, and it put the authorities in a rather difficult position. They held several meetings in an attempt to reach a decision. One of them described the deliberations:

We are still talking about the way the Caritas food should be distributed, but we haven't solved the problem. Since we expect to distribute the food tomorrow, we will meet again tomorrow morning. [What is the problem?] Some of the authorities feel that the food should be used by the authorities for the canton. Others want to distribute it among the comunarios. It is mainly the people from Bolivar who want to distribute it among the comunarios. They say that some of their comunarios have threatened to denounce the canton to Caritas for selling the food if it is not distributed among them. For the most part it is the Bolivar authorities who want to distribute it among the comunarios, but practically everybody else wants to use the food for something in the canton. [What do you think the outcome will be?] We will distribute the food to the comunarios through their ayllus. We know how many comunarios there are in each ayllu and we will give each ayllu a portion of the food that corresponds to the number of comunarios they have. Then the ayllu will decide for itself whether to distribute it or use it for some ayllu project. I want the authorities to have it. After all, we asked to get it, not the comunarios.

Later in the day the corregidor gave the same story, but he—being from Bolivar—was happier with what appeared to be the probable outcome. He added that the authorities were going to withhold two quintales of flour, one quintal of the food, and one box of cooking oil, which would be used by the authorities to cover their heavy expenses during the year for trips to La Paz.

As the community follows its new course of promoting improvement projects, as it pursues outside assistance to promote internal development, it risks new problems. The financial responsibility of the political offices may be one of these. There is already some resistance to the financial cost of fiesta office. Any change in the financial responsibility of the political offices would probably also have some effect on the fiesta offices.

CONFLICT, VIOLENCE, AND JUSTICE

Minor damage claims are generally settled by direct agreement between the comunarios involved. For example, if animals of one comunario get into the fields of another and eat the crops, the two will get together and negotiate. A comunario from Bolivar describes such a case:

When I see some of my neighbor's animals around, I will look over my chacras in the morning to see if any of his animals got into them. Today I found a couple of burros got into my field of alfalfa. I took the animals out, considered the damage, and reported it to my neighbor. He acknowledged that he owes me two nights of feeding for two of my animals. We write this out on paper in two copies, which both of us sign. He keeps one and I keep the other. If a couple of my animals get into his pasture some night, then we are even. If this happens many times, then I take it to the authorities and he has to pay, and maybe pay a fine too.

If an offense exceeds minor proportions it will be taken to the authorities for judgment. There are three judges, and the selection of any one is a matter of personal preference and social calculation. One selects a judge who will be sympathetic, perhaps a relative, or one who belongs to the same estancia or ayllu. If disputing comunarios cannot agree on a settlement, or if the complaint is sufficiently serious but not too serious, it will probably be taken to an ayllu official. Only if a problem is very serious will it be taken to canton officials.

Property damage, conflict over land rights, and interpersonal difficulties are three of the problems that frequently come before canton officials, and many of them are heard by the three judges. For example, a wife caught her husband visiting a widow and brought her complaint to one of the judges. He called in the husband and fined him fifty pesos after he admitted consorting with the widow.

In all of these cases there is great concern not to antagonize other people, not to make them angry. Comunarios will not press a complaint if they think it may arouse hostility. This is not to say that there is not a great deal of hostility in the community, but its appearance is almost ritualistic in character. There is little evidence of hostility in the form of gossip, criticism, or arguing. The exceptions are the arguments and fights that take place during fiestas.

Fiestas are times of eating and dancing to exhaustion and drinking to a state of unconsciousness. There is no fiesta without alcohol, no fiesta without fighting. This occurs almost always between men. Only their poor coordination while drunk and the pacification efforts of relatives and friends saves some of these fights from a very destructive end. As it is, the post-fiesta headache frequently hurts less than bruised limbs, blackened eyes and torn faces.

The fiesta over, little is ever said about this fighting. The sobered battlers carry on as if nothing at all had happened. Rarely are there consequences, though there are, occasionally, exceptions. The one exception encountered during the period of this study concerns Fernando Quispe, who got into a fight with two comunarios at a fiesta. Unfortunately for Quispe, one of the men he assaulted was a canton judge with whom Quispe had had a disagreement. Sometime before, Quispe accused a comunario of stealing from him, but the judge found the man innocent. Quispe charged the judge with unfairness, with deciding against him because the other man was from the judge's ayllu. Then the fiesta took place, and Quispe attacked the judge.

Quispe was summoned to appear before canton authorities but he ignored them. The comisarios, who had the job of informing Quispe that he was to appear, had the right to force him to come in, but they were reluctant to attempt it because Quispe had a reputation as a fighter. Canton authorities then decided to seek help from the intendente in Huayllamarca. The judge and the man Quispe had accused of theft went there to request police aid to bring Quispe to justice. The intendente listened and agreed to send his sergeant. On the way back the judge told the sergeant the type of man he had to deal with:

He has no kids, but he has many cattle. Normally, he does not work, for he has other people herd his cattle and do his work for him. But he is always hitting people and claiming afterwards that he has been insulted. There is no way to make this man a good comunario. He takes no post as an authority, nor does he help with the mita either in his ayllu or in the canton. He is a real savage.

The sergeant asked the judge what it was that the authorities now wanted him to do. Was he to apprehend Quispe and take him to jail in

Huayllamarca, or just what? The judge said that they hoped to settle the case themselves in San Miguel. They would like the sergeant to be on hand so that if Quispe refused to accept the judgment of the authorities the sergeant could then take him away to jail. The sergeant and the two comisarios set out to apprehend Quispe, but they found no one at his house. However, they seized two of Quispe's sheep and delivered them to the authorities back in the canton settlement.

The end of the case was something of a surprise. About a week later Quispe turned himself in to the police in Corque, the provincial capital. San Miguel was notified, and one of the authorities was sent to help dispose of the case. The Corque intendente fined Quispe 150 pesos. San Miguel had to pay Corque fifty pesos for the cost of the action and had to pay one sheep to the intendente in Huayllamarca. A San Miguel official who witnessed the proceeding in Corque suggested that Quispe must have given the intendente a bribe of at least 500 pesos to have got off so lightly. Since the canton had seized two of Quispe's sheep, in effect it broke even, and while there was some muttering among the canton officials about the outcome, most were satisfied that Quispe had been sufficiently punished.

Quispe's offense was not fighting, for that is a common fiesta occurrence. Quispe's crime was partly that of impugning the integrity of the judge and then in physically attacking him, an official of the community. Most importantly, Quispe had avoided or refused his obligations as a comunario. It was Quispe's social irresponsibility that brought the authorities to move against him. One of the community leaders made the point:

We want to shame the person who is troublesome to the community, but we also want the community to gain. What is the use of only punishing without the community's gaining? Let people know that such and such an article in the government house was purchased with the money from the person's fine, and he is constantly reminded of his shame. [How often do people repeat offenses?] Very rarely. Quispe has never before been called to account for his offenses. After this I do not think he will repeat them.

Most of the residents of the community who are called before one of the judges or some other official appear promptly, and accept the decision handed down. The punishment almost always is a fine of some sort, generally paid in sheep or llamas. The authorities infrequently resort to outside agencies in these cases, but even when they do they attempt to keep them in the background. The only exceptions would be truly serious crimes of violence, in which canton authorities would hand over the persons involved to higher authorities for hearing and judgment. Otherwise, San Miguel is still so isolated that national law agencies have very little bearing on the community.

COMPI

The political organization of San Miguel has been seen as an essentially traditional authority system which, presumably, has existed for centuries. The strength of this traditional system is shown in its having adapted to the imposed pattern of canton status with but slight alteration of established patterns.

For Compi, on the other hand, the years since 1952 have been a decisive break with the past. Much of the political organization of the hacienda has been swept away, and the part that remains has been extensively changed. Compi's status as an hacienda exposed the community to the full effect of the reform programs of the MNR, and the location of Compi, just a few hours out of La Paz and even closer to the militant campesino center of Achacachi, exposed her colonos to changes introduced by the Revolutionary government in ways and measures to degrees unknown to the comunarios of San Miguel. Since the range of change has been so much greater in Compi, it is necessary to an understanding of the present system there that the community's politics be examined over different time periods.

HACIENDA POLITICAL ORGANIZATION

Before 1952 hacienda Compi was governed by a small hierarchy of officials whose positions and activities did not differ in any important ways from activities of hacienda officials discussed in relation to two of the towns. At the top of the hierarchy was the patrón, below him the mayordomo, and below these two were the jilakatas and other lesser officials drawn from the ranks of the peons.

The legal authority of the patrón covered only the economic arrangements and activities under which the colonos received land from the hacienda and gave labor. In fact, however, the authority of the patrón was by tradition much broader. The economic, social, and personal lives of the colonos were traditionally his to determine. Family problems, disputes between neighbors, crime and punishment—all were legitimate concerns of the patrón. That his authority was perhaps as often appealed to by the colono as it was asserted by the patrón is an indication of the rootedness of this tradition.

The mayordomo, chief assistant to the patrón, represented him in his absence. The position and role of the mayordomo varied considerably, depending on whether the patrón was always on hand or was almost always absent. Compi knew both of these types, as well as variations between. Both the patrón and the mayordomo had force behind their authority. Refractory colonos often were flogged. Flight was their only recourse in the face of harsh treatment on the hacienda. A considerable number fled, having found themselves hopelessly in debt, with no chance to balance their hacienda obligations against their need to eat to survive. The possible loss of colonos by flight was sometimes and in some places a restraint on the temper of the patrón, but more in areas of lower population density, like the Yungas. Compi seems never to have suffered in the slightest from labor shortage.

The patróns were decentes, and the mayordomos were mestizos or cholos from the towns. Only the jilakata was locally recruited, and he occupied an ambiguous position. In such a free community as San Miguel the jilakata is himself an authority. He has a voice in the community, has judicial powers, makes decisions, and is under no man's orders; but on the hacienda he was very much an instrument of control. The patrón or the mayordomo gave orders to the jilakata, and the jilakata saw to it that the colonos carried them out. He was the whip in the hierarchy of hacienda officials. That his authority was drawn from the patrón rather than from the colonos—in contrast to the situation in the traditional communities—explains his disappearance from so many ex-hacienda communities after the Revolution.

There is some evidence that at Compi, up to a few decades before the Revolution, the position of the jilakata was strongly anchored in the community traditions of the peon population. The dual fiesta and political office system existed there, in which men earned honor and prestige by accepting obligations of community status. There also appears to have been a rotation pattern, such as that described for the ayllus in San Miguel, in which each of five subcommunities on hacienda Compi supplied the jilakata in a fixed order.

The feudalistic development of haciendas in the immediate Compi area was marked by increasing pressure on free landowning comunarios and, eventually, at Compi particularly, exploitative rationalization of hacienda administration. Both developments disrupted traditional patterns of comunario political organization. In the years just prior to the Revolution the highest colono officials at Compi were the jilakatas, one from each of the two largest subcommunities, the estancias Compi and Capilaya. Five alcaldes were assistants to the jilakatas, one in each of the full five estancias. A third type of official was the alcalde de campo, much lower and most numerous, there being as many as there were fields to inspect, cattle to keep from straying, and offenses to report.

It was to the special interest of the patrón that the jilakata was the assigner and superviser of daily work, but to the colonos he was also a traditional judge in minor offenses and a leader of ritual ceremonies. A colono generally advanced through each of the three offices in a fixed order of succession. Immediately below the jilakata was another supervisory office, that of the aljiri, who supervised other colonos when they were sent to work on another hacienda owned by the patrón. It was traditional for an aljiri of one year to become the jilakata of the next.

Paralleling these political offices was a fiesta office hierarchy, differing only in minor details from that in San Miguel. The holding of fiesta offices here, as there, was an essential condition for attaining honor and prestige in the community.

In this early period there were probably the same pressures of obligation to accept fiesta and political offices that are still present in San Miguel, and the selection of candidates was probably made by the colonos themselves. In later years, approaching the Revolution, patróns increasingly intervened in the selection of colono officials. Tradition was ignored, and colono officials came to be appointed strictly on the basis of whether they pleased the patrón. Even tenure periods came to be disregarded. If the patrón was dissatisfied for any reason with the performance of a jilakata he would replace him then and there. Age, prestige, and reputation among the colonos came to count for nothing, and such officials as pleased the patrón held their positions for years at a time.

Finally, the last of the patróns at Compi created a new position in the political organization, that of the sot'a, whose place in the hacienda hierarchy lay between the mayordomo and the jilakata. There were two sot'as, and they held their office at the pleasure of the patrón. One was closely connected to the patrón as his utawawa, his adopted child. The other was a colono who had ingratiated himself with the patrón by showing him how he could increase his profits at the expense of the colonos. One advised both the patrón and mayordomo on when certain work should be done as well as how it should be done, and also directly supervised field work. The other sot'a was something of an hacienda bookkeeper and supply clerk. He distributed the seed and received the harvest, keeping records of both outgoing and incoming materials. Though the colonos apparently regarded the sot'as suspiciously, one who still lives in Compi estancia today, now an old man, is treated with great respect.

In contrast to the organization of San Miguel, that of Compi hacienda was truly hierarchic in its strict levels of authoritative command and in a certain amount of job specialization, bearing some resemblance to an industrial hierarchy. In the free community, on the other hand, there is rather little specialization of activity and nothing of an appointive authority system at the discretion of a single ruler. The main governing positions were quite out of reach of colonos at Compi, and all of the self-governing power of a San Miguel political system was quite erased.

Before the Revolution, hacienda Compi was a part of the canton of Santiago de Huata, which covered much of the peninsula west of Achacachi. The chief official of the canton was the corregidor, who was responsible under the law for the application of national laws throughout the canton, including the haciendas. In actuality, the corregidor did not concern himself with the haciendas except at the request of a patrón—who might, for example, want a show of official force in laying heavier burdens on the colonos. Otherwise, only major crimes on the hacienda brought in the corregidor to sit and judge. In the daily life of the colono and the normal activities of the hacienda the corregidor and the canton played little or no part.

POLITICAL ORGANIZATION FOLLOWING THE REVOLUTION

The early years following the Revolution were a period of confusion, rapid change, and developing conflict over land. News of agrarian reform under the MNR government reached Compi quickly and led to prompt revolt against the hacienda obligatory labor system. Now began a struggle of several years' duration over ownership of colono land parcels and the remaining hacienda land, but there was no seizure of hacienda property by the ex-colonos. The patrón adapted to the new situation by hiring ex-colonos to work the more fertile fields beside the lake and by arranging with other ex-colonos to sharecrop the less fertile land away from the lake. Sharecroppers took 60 per cent of the harvest when they supplied their own tools and 50 per cent later on, when the patrón supplied the tools. In 1957, five years after the Revolution, the sharecropping arrangement came to an end when hacienda lands away from the lakeside were classed as latifundia and were given to the ex-colonos.

The best land along the lake was declared a "medium property," was not expropriated, and was inherited by the children of the patrón, who had died. It became increasingly difficult for them to get workers, however, because they could not always meet the wages they had now to pay, so they organized a cooperative with a group of ex-colonos. This arrangement proved less than satisfactory, and in 1961 they sold their remaining property to comunarios from the small adjoining free community of Llamacachi.

Though all of the land that had been worked for the patrón eventually was divided among campesinos, the results were not at all simple. Under agrarian reform the government had announced that all dispossessed colonos would have a share of land, so many émigrés returned to Compi, only to find that land they supposed would be theirs had long since been assigned to others and that none was available. This gave rise to conflicts that continue to the present day. Some of these émigrés had strong influence on the character of the campesino sindicato established in Compi under the Revolutionary regime.

The sindicato that took over governing authority on the hacienda only a few months after the Revolution had been organized in La Paz by colonos who had fled from the hacienda, men who were activists, now motivated by the government's announcement that dispossessed colonos would be given land on the haciendas where they had once resided. The emigrants went so far as to select the officers of the sindicato, though they exercised a certain prudence in deciding to apportion half of the posts among hacienda residents and half among themselves. In carefully planned strategy, they gave a resident of the hacienda the central office of secretary general, but this man was a colono who had several relatives in the emigrant colony.

In prescribed form, every local sindicato has thirteen officials, the most important being the secretary general, who was the head, the chief spokesman, the one official generally responsible for all sindicato activities. Depending on the person as well as the situation, the secretary general may run the sindicato like a dictator, perform as first among equals with his fellow officials, or find a workable style somewhere between these extremes. Four of the other officials are concerned with organizational tasks. These are the secretary of relations, who is a kind of assistant to the secretary general, and the secretaries of finance, of justice, and of records. The remaining secretaries specialize in important community activities, as the secretaries of agriculture, of livestock, of education, of health, of roads, and so on. From just this listing of officials it is apparent that the campesino sindicato was intended to be more than simply the legal instrument of the colonos in their obtaining land titles, though this was initially the sindicato's stated concern. In practice it provided a relatively comprehensive framework for community government.

In assuming a position as litigant for the colonos in their claims to land, the sindicato quickly became the public forum for the discussion of hacienda-wide issues, and sindicato officials became the central figures of authority on the ex-hacienda. Because very few of the returning emigrants obtained land parcels, most of them eventually returned to the city, and with their departure sindicato offices passed to residents of the estancias. These men reverted to traditional ways of selecting leaders, and soon all five estancias were fairly represented in the distribution of sindicato offices, though not in the rotation pattern of San Miguel.

Emphasis in the early years had been placed on literacy and fluency in Spanish as essential requirements for sindicato office because a primary responsibility of the leaders was to deal with mestizo and blanco outsiders from the government and its agencies. This had put many young men in important offices, especially men who had been educated during years in La Paz, but who otherwise would never have qualified. But after the agrarian court's decisions on land claims had been handed down and the sindicato had turned to the parochial routine functions of the estancias, there was less need for officials with the skills of a mestizo, of men who, for that very reason, were different from the rest of the community. The selection of new sindicato officials was made on the basis of prestige, by popular vote in open meeting. As in San Miguel, prestige comes from holding community office. Increasingly, the important secretarios are now chosen from among men who have held fiesta and political offices, though wealth, education, and facility in Spanish are qualifications recognized in Compi as they have never been in San Miguel.

When the sindicato's land reform work was completed in 1957 its unifying element disappeared. Even before this the sindicato had begun to divide because of inter-estancia competition and conflict. An ex-colono from estancia Tauca had held the position of secretary general since 1952, and the other estancias felt that he was favoring his estancia over the others. By 1956 feelings were so high that the two biggest estancias, Compi and Capilaya, decided to form a separate sindicato, but within two years they were squabbling between themselves, and in 1958 they broke up. The two small estancias, Cawaya and Kalamaya, continued with estancia Tauca for several more years. However, the same kind of dissatisfaction bothered these ex-colonos, and in 1963 Cawaya left Tauca to form a separate sindicato, and shortly after Cawaya also broke away. With the exception of Kalamaya, each of the other four estancias now has its own secretary general.

With the divisions of the original sindicato over a period of years, the estancias have moved a long way toward independence of each other. The set of local officials that was described earlier now exists on each separate estancia. The different sets are not identical, but each estancia has some sindicato officials, some of the earlier traditional officials, and some of the newer officials. On all of the estancias except Kalamaya the secretary general of the sindicato is the leading official. Election takes place within each estancia and candidates are drawn from married men with property, as in San Miguel. The usual tenure is one year, but there are some variations.

There has been a steady decline in the vitality of most sindicato offices in Compi. Today only the positions of the secretaries general and the secretaries of education and sports are significantly active. All of the others have become empty of meaning and without functional importance. They carry no responsibilities, are difficult to fill, have no prestige value. The secretaries of education and sports have survived because they represent areas of community activity that have developed since the Revolution, activity greatly promoted by these offices. Formal education, nonexistent on the hacienda before the Revolution, is now a major preoccupation of Compi campesinos, and sports are the center of leisure interest. The Compi estancias field a soccer team for which the sindicato sports secretary supervises training and even arranges matches —even with teams from La Paz.

The chief sindicato office has not merely survived. The secretary general still occupies the central position of authority among the ex-colonos. He calls public meetings and is a key spokesman for the community. His job is that of adviser, promoter, conciliator, judge, and central ceremonial figure in fiestas and on such ritual occasions as weddings and funerals. The office has the same diffuse character that the major political offices in San Miguel have collectively. He is not, however, a village Cromwell, for the traditional colono offices of jilakata, alcalde, and alcalde de campo have all continued to the present day, an indication of a weaker impact of the sindicato form of organization in Compi than in other places, where strong sindicatos have tended to pale or even obliterate traditional offices. In Compi the jilakata is clearly subordinate to the secretary general, but he ranks as the number two official in the community and sometimes replaces the secretary general in most of the latter's community activities, having a special role in religious rituals. Though the offices of alcalde and alcalde de campo are distinctly minor, they have become, as in San Miguel, nearly irrelevant, except that they help to qualify a person for senior office.

New offices of the post-Revolution period are those of the alcalde escolar, the president of the Junta Vecinal, and the president of the Junta Auxiliar. A public primary school has been built on the hacienda, and all five estancias send their children to it and work to support it. Interestingly, the job of the president of the Junta Vecinal corresponds almost exactly to that of the alcalde escolar in San Miguel, while alcaldes escolares, one from each of the five estancias, assist him in rounding up truants and in notifying families of meetings. The president is the link between the school and its teachers and the campesino families. He is responsible for attendance and for agricultural work on the lands set aside for the school. Both the Junta Vecinal and the Junta Auxiliar are rather nebulous organizations in which younger, energetic men attempt to play a leadership role in the community.

It should be mentioned here that sindicato authority might have diminished less in Compi if the effort of the national government to organize cooperatives on the ex-haciendas as a means of stimulating agricultural production in the face of a possibly disastrous decline during the confusion and chaos of the Revolution had been successful. At

Compi, a buyers' cooperative was organized for the community's five estancias and for Llamacachi on the east and peons from hacienda Jank'o Amaya on the west. Residents bought shares and were permitted to make purchases through the cooperative according to the number of their shares. The cooperative in turn was assisted by the government to buy staple articles at low cost. Since few residents had any managerial skills, La Paz emigrants played a crucial role in the cooperative's enterprises. These early years were a period of runaway inflation in Bolivia, and the cooperative was soon involved in one of the biggest money-making activities of the time, smuggling goods to Peru. Ex-colonos also found themselves being cheated on their purchases, and officers of the cooperative developed the suspicious habit of leaving office without accounting for receipts. When inflation was halted and the government discontinued its purchase support program the cooperative collapsed.

Initially, after the expropriation of the patrón's hacienda land, each of the five estancias farmed its share of the land in cooperative enterprises. After sale of the harvest, each ex-colono was paid by estancia officials in proportion to the number of days worked, and the money left over was pooled by all estancias for the building of a primary school and a church. All of these estancia cooperatives also ran into troubles which forced most of them to allot their land to member families for farming, but even then there were problems in collecting rent and the cooperative's share of the harvest. These cooperatives contributed nothing to community cohesion; rather, they created problems, provoked conflict, and in general operated as divisive forces.

As in San Miguel, an informal group of leaders has grown up in each of the estancias. Again, these men have reached their positions through having held fiesta and political offices. They, together with current officials, canvass the estancia for eligible and willing men to be candidates for office, and those men's names are then put forward at an open assembly. This system operates less smoothly than in San Miguel, for there is often a reluctance to accept nomination, a sign of declining social cohesion as a result of gradually broadening interests, such as the strong ties among the members of many split families—some of whom live on the estancias, while their relatives live in La Paz—and the many exterior commercial relationships of the ex-colonos. A more positive political effect of the city upon Compi has been the appearance of leaders with new and useful experience and skills gained from life in La Paz.

The financial burden of political office is considerably less on the

Compi estancias than in San Miguel, there being no obligation on officials to finance their activities out of their own pockets. They are the leaders, but all important matters are submitted to the ex-colonos for discussion and decision at meetings of the male heads of households. Women are permitted to act in place of absent husbands. These assemblies are held in each estancia, but there are also occasions when the estancias are called together for a collective meeting. All household heads are expected to be present, but not all ever are. They straggle in a few at a time, and at some point the secretary general decides that there are enough to begin. Men of little prestige hardly talk at all at these assemblies, but traditional rule requires consensus for any decision. There is a pattern of discussion. Positions are taken on an issue, alternatives are offered, and the various possibilities are sifted. If no agreement is reached, the issue is shelved for later consideration.

The reaching for consensus at these meetings is not so much a strain for unanimity as an effort to choke open opposition. Some may not agree with a proposal, but it may be adopted if they agree not to disagree. Obstruction of community action by minorities plagues several of the estancias. Some ex-colonos have become avocational oppositionists. They speak out against almost any proposal made by the authorities, and they are adamant, nurturing dissension, forcing issues to be dropped, greatly reducing the effectiveness of the assemblies.

Some ex-colonos on the several estancias never attend any assemblies and ignore all rulings with apparent impunity. Such rogues in San Miguel are eventually brought before the authorities and punished, and public ridicule follows, putting the comunario effectively on notice that his transgressions will not be tolerated. The looser and more open community organization of the Compi estancias is not able to exert this kind of social pressure, but neither has the community modified its traditional search for decisions by consensus.

Land reform is no longer an issue, but land rights litigations continue. One of the most recent and most serious was a dispute between estancia Compi and the neighboring free community of Llamacachi over lakeside land the patrón had sold to comunarios in Llamacachi and to some of the few comunarios left on the hacienda estancias. In 1965 some of the ex-colonos of estancia Compi, where much of this land was located, decided to contest this sale and demand the return of the hacienda land to the ex-colonos.

Both sides argued that law was on their side. The land had been assigned by the agrarian court to the patrón, and he had, therefore, a right to dispose of it. That comunarios, rather than colonos, had bought it, was in one sense irrelevant, for they had acquired good legal title. On the other hand, it was hacienda land, and under the law the ex-colonos should have been given first option to purchase. It is quite possible that the ex-colonos had had an opportunity to buy the land, but ignored it for reasons of cost. However, they now charged that they were not given an opportunity to buy. The conflict dragged on. Fistfights occurred and a house was burned. Urgent assemblies were held on the estancias. National agencies in La Paz and provincial athorities in Achacachi became involved. No end to this problem is in sight, and it is possible that there is no satisfactory solution. In the meantime, the resources and energies of the estancias and ex-colonos are being drained.

On the Compi estancias, as in so many Indian communities on the altiplano and in the valleys, introduction of an education program by the MNR was received with enthusiasm, but it was not until 1958 that the five estancias, together with Llamacachi, were able to build a public primary school. Great energy was expended in this enterprise, but the resources proved insufficient. One of the estancia leaders obtained the promise of aid from a Catholic organization, but this was unsatisfactory to Protestant families and even to the head of the province sindicato organization in Achacachi. Nevertheless, a complete primary school was opened, though the building is still not finished. The estancias are divided over which among themselves should aid most, and over whose outside aid they would be willing to accept.

For most small communities the higher levels of national government were always physically distant, and their activities had little bearing on day-to-day life. This situation was rather thoroughly shaken by the Revolution of 1952. The new MNR government, as no government before it in independent Bolivia, attempted to reach local populations with its programs and involve them in the larger plans for national development. As part of this effort, the national government broke up the large cantons, the basic unit of local government, into smaller and more functional units. This effort was especially pronounced on the altiplano, where the largest proportion of isolated local communities lay.

By a realignment of estancias and ayllus, San Miguel was able to transform itself into a canton and achieve a recognizable political position within the nation. Subsequently, the community has attempted to utilize this position to obtain a variety of benefits, such as schools. In the process, San Miguel has become, at least for the present, several communities in one. There is a real if limited canton community, which is a face-to-face interacting network of comunarios with reciprocal obligations. There is a similar ayllu community, also limited but real, made up of sets of estancias. Then there are the estancias themselves, the only neighborhood-like communities, also limited, in lacking formal offices for the exercise of leadership and responsibility. In San Miguel these communities within communities exist in a state of rather tense balance that could shift in the near future and probably will. Such a shift would increase the cohesion of each of these communities at the expense of the larger community.

In Compi, it was possible before the Revolution to distinguish three levels of organization—canton, hacienda, and estancia. Since the Revolution the hacienda community has in part disappeared and has in part been severely weakened. Today the estancias constitute the primary community for the ex-colonos, while the collective set of the five ex-hacienda estancias has lost much of its cohesiveness as a community. It has only limited influence on its members, exerted mainly through the fiesta system and the school.

While there is little balance between the Compi communities comparable to that between San Miguel communities, change since the Revolution has not all been in the direction of division and toward the weakening of the larger community. The major change in the strengthening direction has been the establishment of a new canton, paralleling what took place in San Miguel. Both the form and the consequences of this development differ, however, from what occurred in San Miguel.

The pre-Revolution canton of Santiago de Huata contained numerous haciendas and free communities. As the possibilities for canton status were expanded by the MNR government in the later years of the reform period, many of these populations sought canton status. All three of the adjoining haciendas in the Compi area—Jank'o Amaya, Compi, and Chua—sought to qualify by designating a central settlement and then building such a settlement along town lines, with a market plaza, parallel streets, and one or more buildings for government offices. Compi designated a part of its expropriated land for such a settlement. Characteristically, there was disagreement among the ex-colonos over this project, and it faltered for want of consensus. Meanwhile, the other two ex-haciendas went ahead with their projects. Jank'o Amaya ex-colonos, in particular, devoted themselves to qualifying for canton status. They established their central settlement as early as 1955 and laid it out along the classic grid pattern with the help of a professional topographer. House plots in the new settlement were allotted to all ex-colonos of each of the hacienda estancias who could be expected to have the funds to construct a house. A weekly market was established in the new settlement, attracting merchants from La Paz, many of whom were emigrants from Jank'o Amaya. Then, in 1960, the former hacienda was strategically successful in having the MNR presidential candidate appear for the inauguration of the new market. Before this, Jank'o Amaya leaders engaged the services of a tinterillo from La Paz, who had many compadres on the hacienda, to help them secure canton status. At the inauguration of the market the community leaders petitioned the presidential candidate to grant them local governmental status, and shortly afterward Jank'o Amaya was designated as capital of a canton, which included not only its own hacienda estancias, but also those of Compi, Chua, Llamacachi, and others.

The officials of the new canton are fewer and somewhat differently ordered than those in San Miguel. In Jank'o Amaya the officials, in order, are the intendente, the corregidor, the notario, and the jueces parroquiales. The notario and jueces have the same functions in Jank'o Amaya as in San Miguel. The intendente, who is head of local law enforcement, has no counterpart in San Miguel. The intendente in Jank'o Amaya completely overshadows the corregidor, whose job has been reduced largely to being his assistant, and the intendente has expanded his office beyond law enforcement to include his performing as a judge and playing a leading role in canton affairs.

This local government variation follows from a lack of governmental training in the local population, even among its most experienced members, and a related lack of information, attention, and responsibility at higher governmental levels. None of the offices is very strictly defined in the canton, so much official action depends on the person and the situation, but there are some specific rules that govern the intendente's conduct. Serious crimes and land actions are handled by other government jurisdictions, and the intendente would normally only pass these on to other officials. A very important restriction on his authority is the principle of multiple jurisdictions in Bolivian government, permitting legal problems to be taken to other localities at the discretion of the interested parties. Since Jank'o Amaya and its component communities are on a main transportation route, they have alternatives to the local intendente.

At first, all of the offices of the canton government were filled with men from Jank'o Amaya. The tinterillo who had aided the ex-hacienda in becoming a canton center was elected intendente and was given a parcel of land. This monopoly of the offices not unexpectedly provoked an outcry from the leaders of the other communities, Chua going so far as to blockade the road to the canton settlement on market day in retaliation. The tinterillo held office for the first two years and was succeeded by a police official appointed from La Paz. Then a comunario from Llamacachi was elected. In 1964 another resident of Jank'o Amaya was elected intendente, but his selection was protested by some of the other communities and the matter was taken to the provincial capital. The dispute dragged on for several weeks until a leader from Compi appeared in the canton capital with a document from the La Paz police naming him to the office. He was finally accepted by the authorities of all the communities. In 1965 a resident of Jank'o Amaya was again in the intendente's office, a young leader from Compi was elected corregidor, and the post of notario went to a resident of Chua.

The holding of canton office in Jank'o Amaya is not the community-wide responsibility that it is in San Miguel; neither is there the same degree of participation by heads of families, nor any kind of canton development program or work obligations or fiesta pattern to link the component communities. The canton is just another settlement and market village, a place where certain limited governmental activities take place, and a stage for some of the politically ambitious.

There is some indication that the rather moderate involvement of Compi in national politics is the result of hostility between the people of the ex-hacienda and the provincial sindicato leadership. For several years the provincial sindicato organization was led by Toribio Salas, whose influence covered the entire northern lake and valleys area and who was a major figure on the national scene. Salas is reported to have thought that the people of several of the lakeside communities, including Compi, had smeared him as a Communist and he threatened to invade the communities with his militia. Since Salas had such power, the threat created great fear and consternation and poisoned relations between Compi and the provincial political leadership until the coup of 1964 and Salas's flight from the country.

Despite Compi's partial estrangement from national politics, the ex-colonos were nevertheless in a better position to be politically informed and active than the comunarios of San Miguel. For example, during the final days of Paz Estenssoro the Compi sindicatos were asked to send their members to aid in the defense of the government. Most of the sindicatos ignored the request, but a few campesinos went and were caught in the fighting in the capital. These experiences are evident in the current national political attachments of the ex-colonos. While 57 per cent of the comunarios in San Miguel and 47 per cent of the residents of Coroico have no party preference, only 38 per cent of the ex-colonos in Compi expressed no preference for a political party. Similarly, 83 per cent of the comunarios and 77 per cent of the Coroiqueños say they have never been a member of a political party, but only 58 per cent of Compeños indicate this.

Some Compeños are closely involved with national political matters. Several were stalwarts of the MNR, were given jobs as local or regional representatives of national agencies from which they could profit financially, and for a time exerted great influence over ex-colonos by virtue of their national political connections. As an index of their national political sophistication, some switched to the FSB when the MNR fell from power, and then signed on with the MPC as soon as that party was formed. One of these men is said to have in his house the literature, posters, and membership cards of all the major parties, which presumably provide him with protection against any unforeseen political development.

There are supporters of all of the major parties among the ex-colonos. Some actively work at promoting their party and in enlisting new members. The more ambitious, like the young Compi leader who was elected canton corregidor for 1966, hold a party appointment as local or regional organizer. While the comunarios of San Miguel have become very much aware of the importance of the national government in their lives, they have considerably less appreciation than their Compi counterparts do of the role that partisan politics plays in the government, and of the now strategic position of the campesino in party politics.

Party politics, which does cut across estancia social boundaries, is not a cohesive force comparable to the system of mutual community obligations to which the comunarios of San Miguel are still committed. Such a system is largely absent from the hacienda community, and most of the developments since the Revolution have tended to weaken the few remaining ties to it. Within the estancias, largely traditional social mechanisms produce a set of community authorities, some traditional and some modern, but the authority of these officials has been weakened considerably. Increasing involvement of the ex-colonos in the urban political world of La Paz and, secondarily, in the new canton, has also weakened local ties. While the campesinos of Compi still have a considerable distance to go, they have already gone far toward eliminating their traditional political organization in favor of a national version.

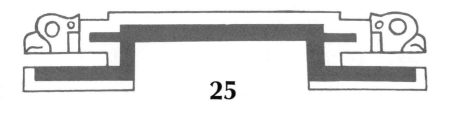

25

GROUPS AND
SOCIAL RELATIONS

The multiplicity of family relations, the strength of bonds that these establish, and their everyday value in meeting the problems of living, establish the family as the preeminent social group for both comunario and ex-colono. Despite the many and important differences between the free community and the ex-hacienda, differences which have increased since the Revolution, the family continues as the central group in both Compi and San Miguel, and even most of the important characteristics of family relations are shared between the two contrasting Indian communities. In view of this, the present discussion of the family, kinship, and certain other social relations will not distinguish between San Miguel and Compi except where important differences do in fact occur.

FAMILY AND KINSHIP

As in the towns, there is a distinction between close and distant kin. The family consists of parents, children, spouses of children, and grandchildren. Collateral and affinal relatives are counted as distant kin, not as members of the family. Family members generally have free access to one another's possessions and may freely call upon one another for assistance. Distant kin have no such license, but do join with the family on ceremonial occasions and are expected to aid in fiesta sponsorship.

Families live in compounds consisting of two or more one-room buildings clustered around a patio otherwise closed in by sheep or llama pens and rock walls. The enclosure of windowless adobe buildings with their single small door, and with various rock walls and animal pens, effectively isolates these compounds from casual intrusion. Ideally, they are occupied by parents and their children alone. One building may serve as dormitory, another as a kitchen, a third for storage. If the family has a large number of children, two buildings may be used as dormitories. Most of the daily activities of family life take place out of doors, in the patio. When children marry, girls leave their family compounds for those of their husbands, and wives of sons move in. By the time the parents die the occupants of a compound are likely to consist of male siblings and their wives and children, and the compound is sometimes rather crowded. In San Miguel, for example, a father and mother live in one house of a compound, three unmarried daughters and a son live in a second, and a married son, his wife, and two children in a third. In another three-house compound are a man and his wife and five children, the man's brother, and the wife and five children of a third brother, who has recently died.

In many parts of the northern altiplano, especially near Lake Titicaca, there is much new housing, not the small, one-room, thatched-roof variety of older campesino housing. These new houses are larger, some having even a second story topped by a corrugated metal roof, evidence of increasing commerce and greater agricultural prosperity with the disappearance of serf labor.

In Compi the new house style is having an effect on compound life. Married sons still bring their wives home, but even before the arrival of a child they may move into their own new house, perhaps beside the road, convenient for keeping an eye on bundles of produce piled there awaiting truck transport to the La Paz market. More than this, the new house is becoming a standard for younger campesinos. It is now considered demeaning for a married couple to have to live with the husband's parents.

Daughters are undeniably members of the family and close kin, but the residence rule tends to transform them into distant kin and may even eliminate them from the family. The rule is that wives be taken into their husband's families, and many married daughters live fairly far from their parents' compound, often in a different estancia. A young wife may have relatively little communication with her own parents except on a few special occasions during the year. There is one common exception to this gradual estrangement of daughters from their original family group. Sons of poorer families look for wives who have no brothers, so that they may inherit land. These men leave their families to live with their in-laws.

The son who marries receives land, but not enough to support him, and therefore he must continue to help with his father's agricultural work. Even then, he is not guaranteed a share of the harvest, but gets what his father chooses to give him. If he gets what he considers to be too little he has no legitimate grounds for complaint or any means of redress. The position is clear in the statement, by a comunario from ayllu Bolivar in San Miguel:

My father has given my brother land and he has given me land. Each of us works his own land and then we help my father with his land. Now my father doesn't do much work on his land because he is old, and also because he is the jilakata and spends much of his time in the canton settlement. My brother and I divide the work on our father's land. Sometimes, if the field is big, we work together. If the field is small, either he does it or I do it. We do an equal amount. From the land that my father gave me when I got married I will take all the harvest. From my father's land which I help work he will give me a part of the harvest. How much, I don't know. It depends on him. Last year he gave me a few quintales and he gave my brother the same.

In San Miguel the only significant property inherited by daughters is a share of the sheep and llama herds. In Compi, on the other hand, daughters also inherit land, though not as much, usually, as sons receive, and it is conditional upon their providing some help to the parents each year. If a daughter's obligations after she has married do not permit this, then the furrows she received will again be farmed by the father or allotted to someone else. Likewise, an emigrant married son loses his share if he does not from time to time aid the family.

Permanent emigration from Compi has a long history, in contrast to temporary migration from San Miguel. The main stimulus behind emigration from Compi was the shortage of land, but there were also the increasing hardships of hacienda labor. The main refuge of the migrants was La Paz, and over the years a permanent colony of ex-Compeños has grown up in that city. Since the Revolution, the ties between ex-hacienda estancias and La Paz have been greatly extended and strengthened with the shift to cash crop production and its sale in La Paz. Today most Compi men know the city, and many of the women have also traveled to La Paz to sell in the market. Among the younger people of Compi a strong attraction for the city and its ways has developed, contributing to the weakening of the family. While the old land and work arrangements still bind parents and their married sons, some of the changes produced by the Revolution are beginning to weaken the family unit seriously.

The demands of agricultural work impose cohesion on the family through the daily round of activities. They get up around five o'clock, have a quick breakfast, and set to work. The men go immediately to the fields, while their wives first do household chores. The older children take the herds to pasture and the younger leave for school. Pre-school children are taken to the fields, where the women work beside the men.

In San Miguel it is extremely difficult for a single unassisted man to exist. There was only one bachelor in the entire community. Without someone to prepare meals, weave, make clothes, and assist with the agricultural work and the herding—in which children are an important aid —the solitary male is hard pressed to survive.

Work in the fields continues until twelve or one o'clock, when all sit for an hour or so to eat the meal that the wife has brought along. Work is then resumed until about four o'clock, when all return to their compound. While the wife prepares dinner the husband tends to the animals. Dinner is eaten around six, and unless a visitor arrives or there is some special occasion, the family is off to bed about seven.

In this daily routine the members of a San Miguel family are frequently separated. Older children may be sent to the puna or pampa with the sheep and llama herds for a few days, to live by themselves in a crude shelter. If there are no older children for this task, the wife may be sent to do it. Adult men, while holding political office, spend time at meetings and on community projects, and they live in the family's ayllu or canton house, the rest of the family remaining at the estancia compound. In both communities, but especially San Miguel, the family compound constitutes a separate and private world. Outside of the special occasions that bring people together, there is often little contact between non-relatives.

A very different, very important family activity is religious ritual. The Catholic church in Compi is quite new, those in San Miguel are old, but in none is there a resident priest. San Miguel is visited but once or twice a year by a priest from one of the near-by cantons. In his absence the two churches are under the care of capileros, appointed for life, who have no special religious training though they occasionally preside over ceremonial activities. Most religious activity in San Miguel and Compi takes place outside the Catholic church, Christianity being but an aspect of religious belief among these people.

Religion in both San Miguel and Compi is a complex blend of Catholicism and Aymara beliefs. The figures of saints are worshipped alongside a set of nature spirits. Preeminent among all, and a central figure in ritual, is Pachamama, goddess of the earth, who provides for man and punishes him. Ritual supplication of Pachamama takes place prior to all major community activities, such as mita work on a canton project, at the start of the planting season, at marriages, baptisms, and funerals, and with the beginning of the day's agricultural work. Ritual supplication of Pachamama is a characteristic part of every fiesta, even though it be a feast of the Roman Church.

The ritual is simple. A short prayer is addressed to Pachamama, followed by the supplicant's chewing of coca leaves. Prayer is repeated, a bit of alcohol is poured on the ground and a bit of it is drunk. That is all, except that in some cases prayer is offered also to the one God of Christians as well as to Pachamama. A comunario of San Miguel describes the ritual start of his day:

I got up at six o'clock in the morning, stirred the fire for my wife and went out for water. Afterwards I got my tools ready for the work in the fields. In the meantime my wife was preparing breakfast as well as getting a dry meal ready to take to the fields. We ate breakfast and then I watered the bull. The field was a quarter of a legua from the house and it was nine-thirty before we began to work. Before starting the work, as is the custom, I served myself a little coca and a little alcohol and prayed that God aid us and that the Pachamama of the earth receive our niggardly offering, that our work would go well and that the seed would not dry out.

Much religious ritual activity centers on the family. In San Miguel, the larger kinship unit that includes both close and distant kin has a family saint chosen from the Christian calendar. On the saint's day all relatives at a compound with a household chapel celebrate the occasion. In the household, ritual ceremonies, primarily devoted to Pachamama, are also held from time to time. Added to the standard ritual in these cases is the burning of copal, which serves as a form of incense. At marriages, baptisms, and funerals, and on birthdays, especially plentiful meals are prepared and larger quantities of alcohol are drunk than on simpler occasions.

Ritual observances are directed at a variety of immediate ends, ranging from supplications for a good harvest, to protection of the health of a child, to honoring the dead. Bonds of family affection, cooperation, and obligation are constantly being strengthened by these observances, while those that bring together non-kin tend to strengthen bonds between members of the estancia, between the authorities, between the ayllus and the canton.

Almost all couples are under twenty-five when they marry, and many are under twenty. Men are increasingly concerned with compatibility, while their parents are more concerned with a wife's capacity for work. In the ordinary course of life in the community young men and women have numerous opportunities to become acquainted. Fiestas are important occasions for encounters, and there is hardly a month without a fiesta somewhere. Boy meets girl going for water, going to the tienda, going on an errand, or going to the fields. Many young persons become acquainted while they are out herding the family's sheep and llamas.

Marriage is generally an after-the-fact formalization of a couple's status as husband and wife. Being an expensive affair, it is often postponed for years. A civil ceremony, which is the formal arrangement accepted by most couples when they accept any, costs from forty to fifty pesos and consists simply in being registered by the notario of the canton in his marriage records. Few choose a church ceremony, for, though the fee is not greater than that required by the notario, the fiesta celebration is often an intolerable financial burden. Agreement to marry is generally the business of the young man and his girl, but this is not always the case in San Miguel. There the parents tend to influence the selection of marital partners, as a comunario somewhat ruefully describes in the following passage:

I married very young, about eight years ago, when I was seventeen years old. I hardly knew my wife, though I had seen her around many times. I was more or less forced to marry her. My father and her father were good friends. They made arrangements during carnival when they were both drunk. I was not even asked for my opinion. I did not want to marry her. I wanted to marry somebody else. I told my father this, but he said I was too young to understand about marriage. He said that both my wife and I were too young to make such an important decision, so they made it for us.

It is not typical that the interests and wishes of the young people are completely disregarded. However, the interests and wishes of the parents are still an important factor, though decreasingly so in Compi. In most cases, parents will try to cooperate with the young couple. After a young man persuades a girl to accept him, they then inform their parents and the parents get together and discuss the matter. A comunario from ayllu Bolivar in San Miguel describes what happened in his case:

About a year ago I married a girl from Bolivar. I have known her all my life. One day we decided to tell our parents that we wanted to get married. Of course, everyone knew that we were going to get married eventually, for we had been close for a long time. We told our parents and then her father visited my father. They talked it over and were in agreement. My father was asked how much land he was going to give me after the marriage, how many animals I had, and how I was going to support his daughter. We knew that she wasn't going to bring in land, but it was a question of the animals she had. My father asked how many animals she would bring. It really wouldn't have made any difference if she didn't bring any, although she did bring some sheep, because I wanted to marry her. Her father insisted that within three months we should actually get married. Everything was agreed to and then my wife came to live with me. This was about a year ago and we haven't gotten married yet. It costs a lot of money to get married, but we will do it someday soon. Her father has not complained, for he can see that we are going to stay together.

Most young men are eager to marry. They will have no land of their own, no independence, until they do. However, alternate possibilities are opening up for the young men and women of Compi. Routes to greater independence are now available through enlistment in the army or by going to live with a relative in La Paz.

COMPADRAZGO AND FRIENDSHIP

There are two other types of social relations in the two communities, but neither is the basis for significant grouping. The one is compadrazgo and the other is friendship. Compadrazgo has the same basis in Catholic doctrine in these two communities as it does in the four towns. In the towns, compadrazgo relations have become increasingly secularized and socially important beyond their religious intent, but this is much less the case in San Miguel and Compi.

As in the towns, the primary compadrazgo relations are those based on baptism and marriage, but because formal marriage and even baptisms are often long delayed, ceremonies may never take place, so no ties of compadrazgo are established. Compadrazgo ties between padrino and ahijado are the most important. A padrino must accept real responsibility to aid his ahijado, which may mean assisting him in sponsoring a fiesta or even in serving as pasante for a fiesta at the estancia of the ahijado. A compadre may be asked to supply similar assistance, but the obligation is less intense.

The relative weakness of formal Catholicism in San Miguel and Compi may account in part for there being a less prominent position for compadrazgo in these communities than in the towns. On the other hand, the continued strength and importance of the family and the resulting dominance of kinship relations also suggest why compadrazgo in these communities has not become the kinship substitute it is in the towns.

Friendship has no special importance as a social relation in San Miguel and Compi. Too many important activities are organized around other relations, mainly kinship, which leaves rather little room for friendship. This is not to say that friendships do not occur. Compi is becoming an exception in this respect. As family members are exposed to more non-kin, friendship relations begin to have a new importance, especially among the young adults.

Friends among the young men are usually companions in recreation. In Compi in particular, friends are the men a man drinks with—outside of ritual drinking. Young Compeños have begun to adopt the urban practice of gathering at a local tienda or cantina to drink, and they also travel frequently to the near-by towns in search of excitement. Such adventures are generally taken with friends, for it is not unlikely that they will receive an unfriendly or even hostile reception from the local young men. In such situations it is unwise and even dangerous to be alone.

The friendships established in youth and young adulthood may continue throughout a man's life, but there are no strong obligations between friends. They may occasionally help out in an emergency, as much as their means allow. Such cooperation is quite voluntary and without obligation, and is not within the deeper meaning of friendship as it is understood in some of the towns.

In both San Miguel and Compi the nets of social relations are both fewer and simpler than they are in the towns. Excepting political relations, kinship dominates, and the family is the only significant social group. This dominance is being strained in Compi, but it continues unabated in San Miguel. In both cases the Revolution of 1952 has had little direct effect, although indirectly it is responsible for much of the change in family and kinship ties that is now taking place.

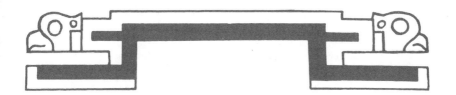

VII

CONCLUSION

Promoting cooperation (Lambros Comitas)

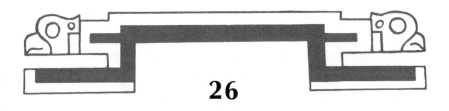

26

Function and Change
in Rural Communities

San Miguel and Compi, Villa Abecia and Reyes, Coroico and Sorata—
each of these rural communities reveals a distinctive pattern of reaction
and accommodation to the forces and trends set in motion by the social
and political Revolution of 1952. The character of this pattern in each
community as it took shape over the succeeding decade has been the
focus of the preceding sections. If San Miguel is compared with Compi,
on the one hand, or with Villa Abecia, on the other, similarities as well
as differences in the community pattern become apparent. Such comparisons establish trends and suggest implications that are not visible
in the description of a single community, but they also require a more
analytical view of the communities. The descriptions presented earlier
of each community are organized in terms of analytical topics such as
power and status, but the emphasis has been on the descriptive details
that make meaningful the complex pattern of each distinctive community. A comprehensive analytical comparison of the six communities
will not be presented here; instead, two topics have been selected for
comparative treatment as specially pertinent to the focus of this study.
The first is community function, or how the communities compare as
functioning small-scale social systems in the light of the changes or lack
of changes they have undergone since the Revolution. The second is the
matter of community change itself.

Bolivian rural communities, like others in many parts of the world,
are confronted by certain basic problems, and vary widely in how well
they perform in this regard. To sustain their members they must cope
with a common set of needs: physical and health, economic, educa-

tional, recreational-aesthetic, and administrative-regulatory [adapted from Nadel, 1951: 35]. These are the broad, basic demands that a community must satisfy if it is to thrive. The way each community is organized is a key factor in how it performs to meet community needs. From this perspective each community represents a problem-solving system. Clark [1968] has outlined and diagrammed the essential elements of such a system (see Figure 1). It provides a useful way of comparing the six Bolivian communities as functioning local social systems.

INPUTS

Inputs concern what comes into the community from the outside. They can be goods, people, money, or orders—in short, all the variety of forces emanating from the external environment to which the community reacts. This is another way of putting the question of independence versus dependence of the local community. Especially relevant to Bolivia's rural communities are existing barriers to inputs. These can be best appreciated if inputs are conceived of as a form of communication. Viewed this way, the barriers are of variable significance for the different communities. This variation follows from differences in environmental topography, distances from other places, and position within the national system. These variables determine whether there may be planes, trains, vehicles, roads, and telegraph and postal services by which inputs can enter a community. In these terms, Reyes and San Miguel have the highest barriers, while Coroico and Compi tend toward the lower, with Sorata and Villa Abecia in the intermediate range. Communities with high barriers necessarily function more independently. They are less subject to outside pressures, but so are they restricted from outside support.

All the communities studied, and probably all rural communities, receive external inputs that affect the internal organization. Inputs come by routes that are a form of supra-community organization. One set of routes is formally organized. These carry the governmental inputs, the laws, the orders for tax collection, and the appointments and dismissals of local government officials. Also included here are the educational inputs (provision of financial support for local public schools, edicts concerning curricula, and the appointing of local school personnel) and religious inputs (assigning of personnel, transmission of edicts on mat-

Figure 1
THE COMMUNITY AS A FUNCTIONING SOCIAL SYSTEM
(Adapted from Clark, 1968)

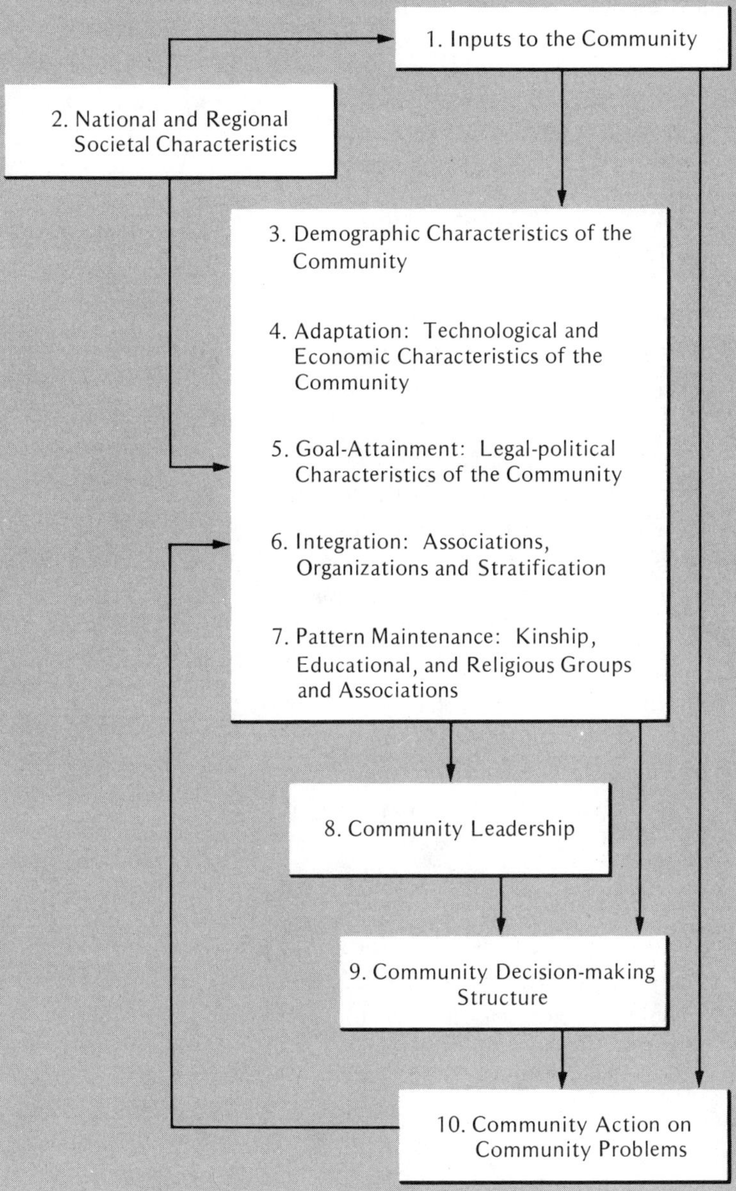

1. Inputs to the Community

2. National and Regional Societal Characteristics

3. Demographic Characteristics of the Community

4. Adaptation: Technological and Economic Characteristics of the Community

5. Goal-Attainment: Legal-political Characteristics of the Community

6. Integration: Associations, Organizations and Stratification

7. Pattern Maintenance: Kinship, Educational, and Religious Groups and Associations

8. Community Leadership

9. Community Decision-making Structure

10. Community Action on Community Problems

ters of religious belief and practice). Another set of inputs, equally important, is informally organized. These are the economic inputs, such as the provision of capital, trade relations, the hiring of local residents and the setting up of local economic enterprises by external capital. Then there are the political inputs, primarily those of influence through muñeca networks, and social inputs that enter through the kin and friendship networks.

This sketch of the input factor draws attention to the dependence of these communities to forces external to them. This conditioning is most marked for the four towns. This follows from their administrative importance, because of which they receive a generally larger share of formal inputs, but since the formal input support of community functioning is rarely decisive, and because the magnitude of community problems is often greater in the towns, there is no consistent relation between inputs and community performance. On the other hand, the presence of these inputs consistently subjects the towns to greater external influence. Coroico, for example, is a town with low barriers to inputs and a dense organization of input routes into the community. Consequently, little of importance concerning major community functions occurs that is not affected by external inputs. The potable water project was started as a local effort, but immediately became subject to external forces—the visit of General Barrientos, the visit of the sub-prefect, the soliciting of funds from AID, and support from General Ovando. Community interest, organization, and activity around the potable water project were very considerable. Yet most of this internal output was marginal; the decisive forces were all external to the community.

Towns like Reyes and Villa Abecia, but especially Reyes, though they may have high input barriers, are likely to receive more inputs than the administratively less important villages. But the organization of inputs that connects these towns to the outside is less dense and more fragile. Reyes is generally completely cut off from the outside intermittently throughout the rainy season of each year, and at such times all inputs cease. Such towns tend to be less dependent on external forces, though not less subject to them in the long run. For example, in towns like Coroico and Sorata, which initiated changes in local government officials internally after the coup of 1964, the new officials immediately sought confirmation from La Paz. In Reyes, on the other hand, the local decentes met in open meeting and chose a new set of officials who immediately took office with only the local mandate. The Reyesanos were aware that the central government eventually would have to pass on such action, but that might take place in the distant future, and in the meantime the community had to function.

The two villages of Compi and San Miguel contrast strikingly in this comparison. Although lacking the political importance of the four towns, Compi is much closer to them on this critical feature than it is to San Miguel. The reasons are Compi's proximity to a major urban center, good roads to this center, near-by regional political and marketing towns, accessible and dependable truck and bus transport, and the steady movement of Compeños back and forth. If these and other inputs are not qualitatively and quantitatively the equal of those for the four towns, they do establish the close interdependence of Compi and the larger contexts of this community. In contrast, San Miguel is more distant, more physically isolated, and less involved in intercommunications of all sorts. Yet these differences, too, are relative, for San Miguel, as earlier described, is far from totally insulated in its own immediate setting and region. And this is the case despite the continuing effort by this community to maintain its tradition of independence from external influences. While San Miguel is at one extreme in the matter of inputs, and emphasizes the important differences between the communities in this respect, it is clear that all six communities are significantly affected by the input factor.

NATIONAL AND REGIONAL SOCIETAL CHARACTERISTICS

Inputs are penetrating external forces. The source of these forces is the national society and its regional subdivisions. The term "societal characteristics" refers to pervasive elements common to the whole society that act to define or condition local community action. They do not enter the local community, as inputs do, but are already and invariably present as part of the local community. They are what makes these communities Bolivian rather than Brazilian or Indonesian. An adequate appraisal of societal characteristics as a factor would require comparison of Bolivia with other societies, to isolate the features specific to Bolivia. Nevertheless, some of the features of the large society that stand out are the low levels of education; extreme governmental centralization, often coupled with ineffective control; governmental instability; low integration of much of the population into the larger society; the marginal efficiency of the economy; very limited industrial development; the precarious economic situation of much of the population; and the modest importance of organized religion. These are some of the general features of Bolivian society that are reflected in local communities. They can be seen in lack of work skills, the constant changing of government officials, the lack of responsiveness to appeals to community self-interest, and the impoverished condition of much of the local population.

In most societies, and certainly in Bolivia, there are regional subdivisions, and these add further conditioning elements to the local community. The regional subdivision known as the Bolivian oriente is vast, low in population density, and poorly provided with means of communication. Its population is primarily mestizo and monolingual. Except for the newly formed area of western Santa Cruz, the regional economy is poorly developed and there is widespread poverty. Reyes, a prominent regional center, reflects all of these characteristics.

The altiplano; the northern valleys, in which the Yungas is a zone of sufficient individuality to be considered a separate sub-region; and the southern valleys are other major regions. We have studied at least one community in each of these four regions. Each region has a set of characteristics which distinguishes it from the others, and which gives its communities a shared character. This is not to suggest that all communities in any one region are alike, or even almost alike, but only that they all have some identical or similar characteristics.

Most, if not all, of these national and regional characteristics of Bolivian society are subject to change. Since the special importance of these characteristics is their pervasiveness, any such change is likely to be far-reaching in its implications. This point has a very special importance for Bolivia, as well as for other nations attempting to alter basic features of the national society. The Revolution of 1952 represented the beginning of a program of national change. The character of this program has been outlined earlier. Emphasis was placed there on the political, economic, and educational reforms introduced by the MNR. In varying degrees, often depending on regional characteristics, such as the population density and the predominantly Indian character of the altiplano, these reforms have altered some of the over-all features of Bolivian society.

The single most dramatic effect of the reform program has been to alter the position of the Indian in Bolivian national society. In varying degrees, the Indian has been freed of earlier restraints that assigned him to a servile position. This fundamental change has had extensive repercussions. It has brought the Indian more into contact with the larger society, has given him a position of some political importance, has provided him with more time that is his own to dispose of, and has opened new areas of economic activity for him. These changes in the position of the Indian have had an inevitable impact on the position of the blanco and the cholo. While the reforms intended to improve the position of the Indian have not solved all or even most of the special problems of the Indian communities, they have created a new set of national conditions which cannot but affect their solution. In addition, the reforms have created a greater receptivity to change in the nation. As old interests, alliances, and relations have disappeared under the impact of reform measures, new ones must be formed.

The two communities that best illustrate the impact of these national changes are Compi and Sorata, the one an Indian village of a former hacienda and the other a former mestizo town. At Compi the hacienda is gone, along with the hacendados, for the Compeños now own the former hacienda land. Gone also is a good part of the traditional Indian government of Compi. In its place is the sindicato, the new political organization which not only has replaced local Indian government in many areas, but also is a major new link between the local Indian community and the national society. Gone too are the rigid limitations of subsistence agriculture. Instead, the entrepreneurial function of the hacienda has been adopted by the individual Indian, and he has become involved with the urban markets of La Paz. Changing economy, changing government, and changing society are everywhere visible in Compi [cf. Buechler and Buechler, 1971]. In all these respects, Compi contrasts markedly with San Miguel. The program of national reform has not been very relevant to San Miguel, has not had much effect, so this is still a very traditional Indian village. Nevertheless, the national momentum of change created in 1952 has had some effect even on San Miguel, which eagerly seeks certain kinds of change, such as improved and expanded public education, but only within the framework of its traditional community organization.

The impact of national change on Sorata presents a very different picture. The kinds of changes which have taken place in Compi have also occurred on the haciendas that surround Sorata. Sorata, however, was not Indian, but a mestizo and cholo town. It therefore reveals a different part of the effect of national change on the Indian—namely, the consequences for him vis-à-vis blancos and cholos. Equally important, it reveals something of the fate of the blancos and cholos themselves in the rural communities of Bolivia. One striking change is demographic. The majority of the town population is now Indian, the town campesino. Most are immigrants from the surrounding haciendas. Many of these move to Sorata only after a transitional period in the Tipuani mines. Now that the Indian is freed of hacienda labor obligations, the near-by mines offer him quick and occasionally very large financial gains. Those who do modestly are likely to move to town, and from there commute to the mines for the season. Those who do well buy property in town and start new business enterprises, such as trucking or retail commerce. Since the Revolution, a large new agricultural middleman enterprise has developed to move products from the now numerous small producers. Rugged terrain, transport problems, and the small scale of agricultural and related enterprises have resulted in the development of several stages of middlemen who move produce from outlying parts of the Sorata valleys region to La Paz. Indians, especially Indian women, have entered these wholesaling occupations in large numbers. In all of these economic activities the Indians have become rivals of town cholos, who formerly dominated small-scale trade, transport, and skilled jobs in the region. However, the distinction between indios and cholos is rapidly blurring.

The cholos as well as the indios have been presented with their own new economic opportunities by the disappearance of blanco monopoly of large-scale commerce and land ownership. In fact, large-scale commerce and land ownership have both almost disappeared, and this decline in blanco economic dominance has enabled some cholos to enlarge their commercial activities and to buy agricultural land. The economic decline of the blancos, which began before the Revolution, but which was accelerated and brought to a climax by national reform, is best seen in the virtual disappearance of the town's blanco population. Now scattered to the cities of Bolivia and beyond, only a small, not very visible, and generally dispirited remnant remains. Perhaps the most radical change has occurred in local government, where the position of indio and blanco is now completely reversed. It is the former indio, now campesino, who occupies the government building and fills the local government offices of Sorata, while the blancos remain on the outside, subject to orders. This situation can be contrasted with that in Villa Abecia, a mestizo town little affected by the Revolution. There the patróns, the landowning elite, continue their total and rigid control of the town in all respects, and the peons who work the vineyards, though they are not Indians, are no less servile toward the patróns than the pre-Revolutionary hacienda Indians of the altiplano.

Comparison of the communities shows the range and depth of the changes wrought by the national reform program in some parts of Bolivia. It also shows the great variation in the impact of these reforms. This reflects the intent of the laws; accessibility of an area; regional differences, such as the small proportion of Indians in the oriente; the turmoil and conflict engendered by swift radical change; and other factors. Now, more than a decade later, continuing reform trends are still strongly evident. One reason is that the changes that were begun have not been completed: there still exist illegal haciendas, though far fewer than might be expected; and there also still exist many former hacienda peons without legal title to their land. Another reason is that the planned changes set in motion many unplanned changes. The classic, traditional social order of the rural town, such as can be seen in Villa Abecia, has been completely overturned in Sorata. However, the situation there is still clearly transitional, as seen in the extensive disagreement and inconsistency in how members of the community view and understand the new status order.

Change is itself a particularly relevant feature of communities with respect to planned community action. Such communities are likely to be more open to innovation, more receptive to continued change. But this statement too can be over-generalized. Both Compi and Sorata, as greatly changed and still changing communities, exhibit continued interest in change. However, the internal factionalism in Compi severely compromises this potential. In Sorata, with its disaffected, declining, former elite, its large, new, and relatively mobile campesino population, and its community government leaders embroiled in campesino sindicato, the promise is even less. Such limits point up the importance of structural elements internal to the community that affect community actions.

DEMOGRAPHIC CHARACTERISTICS OF THE COMMUNITY

This factor—plus four other factors: adaptation, goal attainment, integration, and pattern maintenance—constitute a set. They are the central organizational processes necessary for the functioning of these community social systems [Parsons, 1961: pp. 30-79]. Each defines a process critical to the continued functioning of the community, and together they constitute an integrated set that accounts for the system-like nature of the community organization. Comparison of these five internal factors brings out the similarities as well as differences in the major organizational properties of the communities.

The term "demographic characteristics" refers to the features that define the population of each community. Despite the considerable differences in size of the six communities, all are small. Size itself affects both community organization and functioning. While the lines of demarcation are difficult to draw, it is clear enough that communities of a few hundred differ from those of several thousand, which differ from those of hundreds of thousands. The physical possibilities for contact, and, therefore, of direct interpersonal communication, influence, and exchange, are drastically affected by size increases. This is likely to lead to a very different structure of community decision-making and action. Thus the various arrangements for open participation in decision-making which exist in theory, if not practice, in most of these communities—such as the open community meeting—cannot work in far larger societies except under conditions of extreme selectivity. That such selectivity also occurs in many of these small communities is a reflection of other parts of the community organization, not size.

Other demographic characteristics of general importance are growth, mobility, origin, sex and age distribution, and ethnic and educational character. Communities experiencing rapid growth are likely to encounter problems of integration, which then require some redirection of community action and resources, and may impair community functioning. Rapid growth does not appear to be taking place in any of the six communities, but extensive mobility has the same effect, and this has occurred. The major case is Sorata, in which as much as two-thirds of the population has been replaced. Population change is only one form of mobility. Sorata also illustrates two others. One is the continual export of a particular segment of the population, in this case young men, many of whom are going away for advanced education. Few of them will return. This represents a specially critical problem with respect to community problem-solving action, for it drains off some of the most promising manpower. Emigration is occurring in all of the four towns. It can also be seen in the Indian village of Compi as this community becomes more closely linked to the larger society. Another form of mobility is the seasonal migration to the mines which occurs in Sorata and its surrounding villages. This has extensive effects on the community, such as decreasing family integration, as discussed in the analysis of Sorata. On a smaller scale it also occurs in Villa Abecia, but has considerably less effect on that community because of the small numbers involved and the fact that they are of marginal importance to community functioning.

ADAPTATION

"Adaptation" refers primarily to the economic organization of the community and its arrangements for the production and distribution of goods and services. Comparison of the communities indicates considerable variation in this factor. A general distinction has been drawn between the towns and the two agricultural villages. The towns have been pictured as marketing centers with populations organized around trade and the related services. Villa Abecia is a partial exception to this generalization. It is a market center for its region, but most of its population is directly involved in grape and wine production, either as owner-managers or as workers. As marketing centers, the towns generally command greater financial resources and are better able to deal with community problems requiring financial investment. Marketing centers are also characterized by considerable work differentiation, which becomes the basis for special groups which attempt to influence community functioning in their own interests. The organized truckers in Sorata who threaten to refuse transport unless certain roads are repaired are an example. In this case the interests of the truckers may coincide with the interests of the community, enhancing community functioning rather than distorting it. The distorting effect is better seen in Villa Abecia, where the small group of patróns tend to resist community efforts to improve functional performance—as in the attempts to better the physical environment of the town—because they already enjoy a more favorable environment and the benefits would go mainly to other members of the community.

Another important characterstic of rural economic organization is its marginal productivity, which provides meager livelihoods and severely constrains community functioning. In this and in other characteristics each of the communities reveals its own special features, though it shares others with one or more of the six communities. Compi and San

Miguel are communities of agriculturalists, but Compi has shifted away from mainly subsistence production to market production, which brings more money into the community, makes the younger men more independent at an earlier age, and creates a new network of external relations to the outside society, all of which have effects on the internal community organization. One effect is an increased individualism; another, a greater dependence on outside authority. Neither of these effects is pronounced in San Miguel.

GOAL ATTAINMENT

This factor concerns the organization of collective effort for community goals. It is the formal framework within which community problem-solving takes place. The framework of goal attainment consists primarily in the community governmental and legal organization.

Governmental performance in many rural communities is so low that it often impairs community functioning. Problems of wide range and severity in the governmental and legal structures of the four towns have been catalogued in detail in earlier chapters. There is great uniformity among the towns. In all of them, problems of organization, personnel, and financing tend to subvert the purposes of these structures. They verge on being irrelevant to their formal functions. Instead, they have frequently become vehicles mainly for asserting special interests, even private individual interests; for developing and sustaining political factionalism and for diverting community resources into individual hands.

Community government cannot be held solely responsible for deficiencies in community action. Local government, as planner, initiator, organizer, supervisor, evaluator, stimulator, and supporter in community problem-solving, is severely affected by the interacting peculiarities of its own structure. The two Indian villages provide an instructive contrast. Compi is exceptional because of the strains and antagonisms engendered by the land reform, which has seriously affected government, but San Miguel has a governmental structure that is functioning effectively in community problem-solving. It is a highly integrated community with a traditional authority system, an absence of power inequalities, high community participation in governmental decision-making, and wide community responsibility for such decisions. But even in San

Miguel there are signs of problems, these arising primarily from competition among its four ayllus. In Compi, in contrast, other community structures exercise the goal attainment function and provide a viable alternative to a traditional system. One such structure is the sindicato, which in Compi has almost replaced traditional government. The truckers' sindicato in Sorata also serves this purpose. Another structure is the Civic Association. When a strong Civic Association develops, as in Reyes, it parallels the sindicato in influencing, even absorbing, governmental responsibility.

INTEGRATION

A key element in the community organization system is that of integration, which serves to link individual and small social units through participation and membership into larger, community-wide units. The effect of this is the mobilization of commitment to the community social system. The units that carry this function can assume a variety of forms. They have in common this: they identify community interests as *their* interests, and the loyalty they build tends to accrue to the larger community organization. However, it not infrequently develops that the relation of the unit to community goals is reversed, and those of the unit are taken to be those of the community. As a result, integrative structures may divide the community when they should be uniting it.

Typical integrative structures are voluntary associations, political parties, and social strata. All of these types of structures are found in the four towns, few of them in the two villages. Yet one of the most striking contrasts is how poorly integrated, in comparison with the villages, the towns generally are. The reason is not difficult to locate. While all of these integrating structures are well-represented in the towns, they have a minimal effect on community integration. As can be seen in the preceding analyses, they tend to have low attraction for their members and for others in the community, demonstrate little sense of purpose, show little activity, are often strongly divided internally, and, consequently, have little visible impact on the community. This describes most of the voluntary associations and also the political parties.

The formal organization of associations, including political parties, distinguishes them sharply from social strata, which are generally not formally organized at all. However, the sense of identification with a given stratum, allegiance to a stratum code, and the sharing of interests that produce an integrative effect are lacking in the towns, though for given strata it may be less pronounced. In Sorata and Coroico, especially Sorata, this condition is a result of the changed situation of the social strata and the widespread instability that has followed. The one major exception to this generalization concerning the towns is Villa Abecia. The major factor in the integration of that community is the persistence of the old, traditional, cohesive stratification. In Villa Abecia, all members of the community know their position, which is defined and legitimized by the stratification code. In the villages, a single cohesive stratum of small size strongly contributes to community integration.

Integration has a major effect on community problem-solving. Low integration impedes the mobilization of the community, and it tends to reduce the effectiveness of all the other parts of the organization. As integration decreases, adaptation, goal attainment, and pattern maintenance are likely to decrease, and these developments in turn will reduce or disrupt community decision-making.

PATTERN MAINTENANCE

The major institutions responsible for pattern maintenance are the family, school, and church. They inculcate values, beliefs, and norms which cover a very great range of topics, even in a small community. Many of these are of limited relevance to community problem-solving. However, values, beliefs, and norms will determine the attention given to the various community problems, as well as to the means which will be acceptable in any effort to solve problems.

Poor attendance at regular church activities, lack of responsiveness to appeals from religious authorities, and difficulty in recruiting members for the various religious associations are some of the problems of church organization in the towns. In the two villages, which have almost no church organization, religious belief and practice are considerably stronger, carried mainly through the family structure. Again, family structure in the towns is weaker and less influential. The contrast between town and village, however, should not be over-stressed, and a further comparison should be made between towns. For many contrasts there is a consistent trend running from Villa Abecia, the most traditional town, to Reyes as an intermediate town, then to Coroico and, finally, Sorata, as radically changed towns.

The pattern maintenance function of the church and school is circumscribed within the community because both of these institutions are local extensions of society-wide organizations. There is considerable variation in their range of independence, but both are subject to external direction that can and does ignore the local community. This limits their potential for performing strictly community-relevant functions. Relation to the community is further strained in the case of the church, in that most local priests are foreigners, mainly North American and European. As a result, the local church is apt to introduce and support values that are quite inconsistent or even antagonistic to those of the local community. In Sorata, a priest has waged a campaign for several years to eliminate the lavish community drinking and dancing parties that are traditional in the observance of religious festivals. He has succeeded in part, but at the cost of antagonizing a large part of the community and dividing the town against itself. In education there is a similar problem, one of the many that plague the public schools and greatly compromise their effectiveness. Most local teachers come from the urban centers, find little that attracts them in the small communities, and spend much of their time traveling to and from the city. Many are novice teachers. Their salaries are meager, they are provided limited and often inadequate materials and aids for their teaching, and the physical plant they must deal with is often a makeshift affair. Nation-wide teachers' strikes are one response. Whether teachers or students are worse off in contemporary rural Bolivia may be a moot question. There is no doubt at all that the pattern maintenance function for the community is severely weakened.

COMMUNITY LEADERSHIP

This and the following factor, community decision-making structure, are the most immediately relevant to community problem-solving and action. All of the previously discussed factors, as shown in Figure 1, can be viewed as ultimately conditioning the exercise of leadership and decision-making. Here is the point where an idea for solving a community problem or for initiating a course of action on a community problem will either stop or go forward. The leadership function in the community organization consists in orienting the community to appropriate system goals, which, of course, will derive in large part from the basic community functions. In a well-functioning community the leadership mechanism performs as a kind of system governor. It identifies potential or developing problems, alerts the community to these, and attempts to mobilize community resources to meet these problems. In poorly functioning communities the leadership mechanism is likely to be disoriented and press for irrelevant or damaging goals. Furthermore, in such communities its effectiveness is often greatly impaired.

While the leadership function is carried by community groups and organizations, it is also a peculiarly individual activity. One of the few shared characteristics of the six communities is the limited extent to which any community groups or formal organizations exercise this function. By default, it falls on individual community members, generally only members of certain classes. Once again, the organization of the towns is so different from that of the two villages that they must be separately discussed. In the towns the exercise of community leadership by individuals is greatly affected by social status. While community deficiencies may bear heaviest on those of low status, their lowly position disqualifies them from speaking out, from suggesting remedies, and from trying to stimulate community action. This is most true of Villa Abecia and least true of Sorata, but even in the latter town, barring certain exceptions, it is largely the case. In the same social terms, women and young people are generally disqualified. A partial exception is the social category of young men, the coming generation of leaders. In anticipation of their future prominence, young men are frequently extremely sensitive to possibilities for exercising leadership and very active in promoting such activities. Their zeal is often recognized by their being allowed to act with senior leaders in the community. However, this potential is seriously weakened in most of the towns by the continual emigration of the young men, generally those most qualified for leadership activity. Still, this is a specially strategic category of community members, for it is generally the most responsive to appeals for assistance in community action.

In the towns that have experienced great change, one of the important changes has been the general decline in social status of the former elite. Their position has been generally threatened and even destroyed. The remnants of this social category, once the primary source of leadership activity, now tend to withdraw from community activities or greatly restrict their participation. Their place has not been filled yet, though the situation is now more open for leadership participation by prominent cholos, as in Coroico and Sorata, as well as by persons moving up from cholo and indio status positions. The disruption of the status order in these communities, and the weakening of the effect of status on leadership, give exceptional opportunity and prominence to forastero professionals in town. These are the doctors, dentists, lawyers, and engineers, many serving in the towns as representatives of national agencies. Though their position as outsiders would normally restrict opportunity for leadership, this limitation ceases to carry much importance in relation to the many other changes occurring in these towns, and they are in fact very active in both Coroico and Sorata. In Coroico it was the dentist, rather than any of the remaining social elite, who regularly made speeches on behalf of the community. It was the foreign priest who stood out in organizing the potable water project. In Sorata it was the agronomist, the young judge, and one of the schoolteachers. Reyes occupies an intermediate position. A few outside professionals, the first doctor, for instance, were prominent in leadership activities, but they did not overshadow local leaders, as was the case in Coroico and Sorata. In Villa Abecia it is still clearly the local status elite, the local patróns, who provide community leadership.

The difference between leading and deciding, between influence and power, is much less sharp in the two villages than in the towns. The absence of fixed status distinctions that make some persons more important members of the community than others contributes to this. Other differences are the form of village organization, which enjoins all members, specifically adult males, to take part in important decisions, and the acceptance by village officials that they are not to hinder this responsibility. Nevertheless, the villages, too, exhibit status differentiation in the cargo system of the fiestas and political offices, but it is not an exclusive system, such as occurs in the towns, because it applies to all men in the community, and most will take part in it. One of the effects of cargo is to distinguish those of higher and lower prestige. And it is those of high prestige, who have filled many cargos, who are expected to provide more leadership, but it is not an exclusive mandate, as in the towns. This system works most effectively in San Miguel, but even here the national processes of change are having some effect by introducing new ideas, mainly through the younger men, who are beginning to develop as an alternative source of leadership in the community. In Compi, so changed by the Revolution, other changes in the leadership structure have occurred. New leadership requirements, such as literacy, force the community to turn to young men and to bypass older men, the once acknowledged leaders. New occasions and new structures of leadership have intruded into the community. An example is the national political party organization, which seeks local representatives and supports them in ways that are vague or little understood in the community. This support is really quite minimal, but its vagueness can be exploited by the local citizen to gain attention and influence. Sindicato offices have been incorporated into the cargo system, adding new offices, while some of the old ones have disappeared. Formal separation of some of the hacienda settlements has resulted in their retaining only part of the complete set of traditional political offices. National requirements of political officeholders not infrequently resulted in propelling men low in the office system into high offices. All of these symptoms of the changing organization of Compi are reflected in the disaffection of some community members from leadership responsibility, and in a decline in the social control of leadership, which now permits young and old, insiders and outsiders, more leadership opportunity than they ever had before. This has both benefited and damaged the community problem-solving capacity.

In general, community responsibility for exercising leadership is strongest in the traditional communities, San Miguel and Villa Abecia, and, to a somewhat lesser extent, in Reyes. But even in these communities it is doubtful whether such leadership is very effective. Certainly it has not led to solutions to community problems. Frequently, it does not even lead to recognition of problems. The first doctor in Reyes was strongly oriented to community improvement, but he was relieved of his post without a word of protest from the community. The doctor in Villa Abecia provides minimal services, and the local hospital is quite inadequate. This arouses no concern. Only in San Miguel does community leadership appear to benefit the community consistently. In the rapidly changing communities the situation is generally worse, though more easily understood. Changing population, changing restraints on leadership, changing social relations, increasing apathy, estrangement, and friction, make the exercise of leadership increasingly difficult, and erratic with respect to community problems.

COMMUNITY DECISION-MAKING STRUCTURE

If leadership is a mechanism for alerting the community system, decision-making controls the system. Decision-making is another way, a more dynamic way, of referring to power. The more traditional communities reveal a greater centralization of decision-making. In Villa Abecia there are virtually no alternatives to the power of the patróns. Other groups and organizations, local government, law agencies, the church, the schools, national agency representatives, are weak. The patróns are few, homogeneous, cohesive. They think they *are* the community, despite their small numbers, and from the standpoint of power they are. Only in a crisis situation, when the patróns were divided among themselves, as in the case of the hail disaster and the pipe repair effort, were other members of the community allowed to participate in a community decision. This, however, was a very unusual situation, and it has not altered the traditional structure. In Reyes there is somewhat less centralization. The ganaderos there are comparable to the patróns in Villa Abecia, but they must share their power with the large merchants. In addition, the national CBF agency is a powerful organization in the community. The policy of the CBF, however, is to stay out of community affairs as much as possible, and it is therefore not as prominent in community decision-making as it might be. When its own interests are involved, though, it is an important element in the community power structure, as seen in its central role in the community project to rebuild the road from the town to the Rio Beni. In San Miguel, power is spread because of the basic political equality of all adult males and their equal access to forms of power. Those who temporarily hold political office make decisions as a group on behalf of the community, but most of these decisions are limited. Important considerations are submitted to the entire community for decision.

In the two radically changed towns the major concentrations of wealth have been greatly reduced and new centers of power have developed. Professionals, such as the lawyers and tinterillos, once mere appendages of the powerful hacendados, are now independent sources of power in the community scene. These changes have introduced persons from a variety of social backgrounds and with varied interests. Thus, while power is still differentially held by members of the community, those with greater power are a heterogeneous class, and, not infrequently, in conflict. The most extreme example is the intense hostility and continual conflict between the old vecinos and the new politicos of Sorata, the latter mainly campesinos. This conflict is symbolic of changing power conditions brought about by the Revolution. Specifically, the organizing of the Indian peasants into campesino sindicatos tied to regional and national federations, and the use of the sindicato as a device for mobilizing electoral strength, have politicized the campesinos and provided them with means for challenging local power structures. Coroico has been spared the intra-community conflict because of the preoccupation of Yungas sindicatos with the new campesino communities, but the sindicatos are an ever-present consideration in Coroico decision-making. In Compi, the local sindicato has virtually become the decision-making structure; but the uncertainty, the changing economic conditions, the struggles and conflict over land redistribution have all worked against stabilization of that new structure. Further, as in San Miguel, the basic equalitarian rights of all Compi community members further diffuse decision-making.

The confused power structure in the changing communities causes greater dispersion of decision-making. That those with power are sometimes also in conflict, or at least not in agreement, aggravates the difficulties in undertaking effective decision-making in these communities. A proposal from one sector is automatically suspected by another. Every decision is an opportunity to score on an opponent. Every decision is a test of power relations. In Sorata, a public schoolteacher criticized his colleagues, including the school director, for taking unauthorized holidays. Such criticism would have meant nothing in local conversation, but he had it written up in a newspaper in the national capital. He was immediately suspended by the director for unprofessional conduct. Some residents of the town, mainly prominent vecinos, rallied to his support. Local government officials responded by denouncing the teacher and complimenting the director. The local priest was asked to announce his support of the teacher, and he did. Meetings were called by both sides to enlist support throughout the community. Under these circumstances no satisfactory outcome was possible. The Ministry of Education eventually intervened, for the problem was their formal responsibility. The Ministry attempted to mollify tempers. However, the issue had gone far beyond the two immediate antagonists and had become a test between campesino politicos and old vecinos, between whom lies a virtually unbridgeable gulf. In the end, both director and teacher were removed from the community. This ended the immediate problem, but pleased no one and left matters much as they were. The case illustrates the difficulties that community decision-making faces in such a setting.

COMMUNITY ACTION ON COMMUNITY PROBLEMS

This factor concerns the problem-solving activities of the community, on which the other factors bear and which in turn strongly affects the central set of community processes. What actually happens in community problem-solving? Each community report discusses this, but the springs of community action are often hidden and could not always be observed. The existence of problems that require attention is clear, but the magnitude of these problems and the very great limitations on local resources often prevent effective action. There are real constraints that are beyond the control of the local community, and these must be kept in mind when limited performance is considered. The death of the Coroico project to reconstruct its water supply system illustrates the problem. Only after a considerable expenditure of work by the community did project officials face the fact that extensive financing would have to come from the community, at which point the project died.

In many of the problem-solving efforts examined there is a serious lack of planning. Often the major emphasis is only on setting the action in motion. What will be required, how things should be done, what consequences may develop, are often given little or no attention. Admittedly, some of the requirements and likely consequences are not within the range of local skills and knowledge. The Reyes road, the rebuilding to end the annual rebuilding, is a good example. The consulting engineers who arrived in the midst of the effort quickly observed that the reconstruction, under the supervision of a road-grader driver, only amounted to moving dirt around. When the rains came the road would again be washed out and become rutted beyond use. Interestingly, San Miguel, with its many successful projects, appears to have little planning trouble; but their projects tend to be less technically complex, reflecting the more rudimentary technological level of this community.

The more traditional communities generally produced better problem-solving performances. They undertook more community projects and completed more of them. The projects also tended to be more relevant to community problems. Roads and schools were built in Reyes, for example; but a swimming pool was left uncompleted in Sorata. In none of the communities is there a well-focused, well-organized, well-functioning way of dealing with basic community problems. Earlier chapters have delineated the limitations of the local economy, the local government, the educational system, the health maintenance system, and the recreational-aesthetic dimension of community life. For example, lack of job opportunities, underemployment, lack of capital resources, low agricultural productivity, and inefficient land allotments are some of the more severe economic problems. Such a list calls attention to one difficulty for a community grappling with these problems. The problems extend in scope far beyond the local community and often do not have their roots in the local situation. In addition, the tools and materials for resolving problems are often unavailable to the local community. But those problems not falling under one or both of these limitations may still prove intractable. In the communities whose social orders have been seriously altered, conflict and factionalism makes coherent community action hazardous and uncertain. Basic problems are likely to polarize different interests in a population already considerably polarized, as occurred in Sorata. This leaves neutral, general problems, such as drinking water in Coroico, or very marginal problems, such as plaza maintenance in Sorata, as safe targets for community action. That these projects do not deal with the range of issues confronting these communities, whether greatly changed or little changed by the Revolution, suggests the limitations of these local social systems in general and how local problem-solving depends often on specific national developments and trends. Thus, the campesino population has for the most part experienced improved conditions both directly, through national programs, as in Compi, and indirectly, through national programs and consequent changes that affected market towns and opened opportunities to them, as in Sorata. Consequently, how these communities function and deal with community problems varies not only with type of community (market town or peasant village), cohesion of community (low conflict vs. high conflict), and stability of community (traditional vs. highly changed or changing), but also with how local individuals and groups are affected directly by national programs as well as how these programs may directly bear on the community social system. These national programs are likely to affect socially differentiated members in different ways. In addition, sub-groups in the complex communities not infrequently attempt to deal with problems affecting their interests by working independently or going outside the local community framework, as seen in the case of the Sorata transportistas, as well as by working within it. In short, community problem-solving is a highly complex and variable function in all the communities. Its workings are clearest in the more traditional communities, San Miguel and Villa Abecia, but as the communities have undergone changes, beginning with Reyes and ending with Sorata, this function is increasingly entangled in shifting attachments, interests, and conflicts, and as a consequence becomes increasingly problematical and not infrequently restricted to problems of marginal importance.

In considering the six communities as local social systems, and how they differ from and resemble each other in this respect, a central issue is community change. Here, too, the social system perspective can be useful. Considering the elements of that system as diagrammed in Figure 1, the processes of change engendered by the Revolution of 1952 worked in these communities by altering, consecutively and selectively, key community functions. First, the Revolution and its programs significantly changed element 2, Societal Characteristics. This led to changes primarily in elements 4 and 5, the Adaptation and Goal Attainment functions. These changes in turn produced changes in element 6, the Integration function, and to a lesser degree elements 7 and 3, the Pattern Maintenance and Demographic functions. The changes in element 6 then resulted in changes in elements 8 and 9, Community Leadership and Decision-making. Finally, all these changes in varying degrees altered element 10, Community Action. Where this process was not initiated, or where it was constrained at some point in this sequence, as Villa Abecia and San Miguel, in particular, illustrate, the stipulated changes either did not take place or occurred only to limited degree. None of the six communities is unchanging, but changes in national and regional societal characteristics following the Revolution of 1952 produced visible changes in some and drastic changes in others. The scope and depth of these changes across the six communities is extremely varied. The sources of these changes in national programs has been described, as well as some of the important historical, environmental, and economic features of each community that influenced its reaction to these national changes. The remaining discussion will center on the key changes in the social system elements that have taken place when the six communities are compared to each other.

Comparing the more with the less revolutionized communities establishes the great number and variety of changes that have taken place. The crucial set of social and political changes constitutes a much smaller set, and, in fact, there is one change that underlies or links most of these other key changes. This is the changed status of the campesino vis-à-vis the decente patróns. No single factor has brought this about; rather it is the consequence of a combination of economic, political, and organizational changes. The most important effect of these changes was to weaken, in some cases destroy, the ties of subordination under which campesinos labored. While most of them still occupy the lowest rung in local stratification orders, their position on that rung has greatly altered. No longer do they owe labor or service obligations to a patrón. No longer can they be required legally by a patrón to work off debts. Most important, the plot of land they have worked over the years, even over the generations, is theirs, and they no longer work it on sufferance. Although the issuing of land titles has been uneven [Clark, 1968] and is an important consideration in the eyes of most campesinos, de facto control of their personal land parcels passed to the campesinos in the highly changed communities, like Compi and the villages around Sorata and Coroico.

Accompanying the change from peon to landowner and free laborer was the development of a sense and style of independence. In the highly impacted areas the etiquette of submission and of public deference rapidly declined, especially among the younger campesinos. Campesinos also became much more visible. Not only were more of them coming to town, some to live, but their behavior in town reflected more a sense of independence than one of dependence or submissiveness. Almost fifteen years after the Revolution old decentes in Coroico and Sorata are still sensitive to this change. Certainly political effects of the Revolution are important in this change of campesino outlook and deportment, as well as economic ones. Granting full rights of citizenship to campesinos could have been merely a legal change without substantial consequences. That it was not, and instead resulted in strongly politicizing the campesino population, is an important result of organizational innovation, the development of the campesino sindicatos. The promotion of sindicatos in the rural zones offered clear advantages to the central MNR government. It was not only a means for effecting the land reform program. More importantly, it provided a way of organizing the campesino population to support the new government, even as armed paramilitary units. However, these arrangements to benefit the central government also had important consequences for the campesino population. The sindicato as a political organization carrying out political activities became a training ground in some of the rudiments of citizen politics. The new legislation created a full national political role for campesinos, in contrast to their lack of such a role before the Revolution, but without the sindicato, the lack of necessary education and experience would have greatly limited the impact of such legislation. In addition, the sindicato provided a training ground for campesino politicians. Traditional opportunities for this training were not lacking, but experience in traditional campesino government was not very useful in helping them assume leadership in local and regional politics. A related change is that the sindicatos were linked to regional and national bodies, and thus local campesino groups found themselves integrated into the national society as they never had been before. In fact, all of these implications of sindicato organization reinforce this integrating effect, which is one of the more profound changes wrought by the Revolution.

The traditional status of the campesino was inextricably linked to that of the decente. As a consequence, changes in campesino status are often accompanied by reciprocal changes in decente status. In the high impact areas the decentes lost their haciendas, their monopoly of local commerce and finance, and their dominance of local politics and government. This economic and political decline produced a flight from the rural areas and their communities, as seen in both Coroico and Sorata as well as in Compi. The remnant that stayed has generally experienced greatly reduced living conditions. Their decaying and shabby homes in the two impacted towns make this starkly clear. Just as the improved status of the campesinos does not mean that their position has shifted in the hierarchy, so the loss of status by decentes has not in general resulted in a shift in their position. But the privileges of the position are largely gone; they no longer enjoy their former influence in community affairs, the deference once shown them, their old prestige as the leading citizens. It is likely that this is a transitional situation. In a few more generations a group like the rescatadors of Coroico may coalesce into the dominant stratum, with the prestige and influence that accompanies such status, while the old decentes will have disappeared altogether.

In the complexly stratified communities most influenced by the Revolution those decentes who chose not to leave for the cities or even for another country have frequently accommodated to their reduced status position by retreating from community participation. While the campesinos have become more visible, the decentes have become less visible. Their former prominence in community affairs has been replaced by an almost total concern with private affairs. Community participation and leadership in the past was an obligation of their status. Today such participation is much more a matter of politics, and, in these communities, an arena in which campesino sindicatos and their leaders, cholo merchants, and mestizo politicians who sought their fortune in MNR reform politics either ignore or challenge decente residents. This present situation so contrasts with their privileged position of the past that it is not surprising that for many decentes the past seems more real than the present. Their home surroundings frequently contain many reminders of their former local eminence, and their conversation in those settings easily turns to the past when, they say, everyone, including campesinos, enjoyed a more orderly, just, and prosperous life. Many of these elderly decentes still do not fully recognize the sources of protest that were present in the campesino population.

Paralleling these changes in particular social strata are changes in the over-all stratification system. Most prominent of these is the increasing amount of disorder, which has been described in Coroico and Sorata. The former coalescence of power, wealth, and prestige and their symbols which once defined an unambiguous stratification order has largely disappeared under the impact of the Revolution of 1952. Rich Indians, impoverished decentes, influential cholo politicians, decente girls married to cholos whose families are Indian, campesino sindicato leaders presenting visiting national government dignitaries to the community —these, and more, are the status anomalies that abound in Sorata as well as Coroico. The traditional, well-defined, unambiguous status hierarchy of these communities has been replaced by a system characterized by considerable dissonance and ambiguity. While probably a temporary phenomenon which will eventually disappear, this is a prominent characteristic of the heavily impacted communities and one which affects much that occurs in these communities.

There are two other, related changes in the stratification systems of the greatly changed communities. One is the increase in social mobility. From closed, highly stable systems they have become relatively open, relatively changing ones. Part of this mobility is adding new components to the community through residential change. These are the campesinos who rent or buy a house in town. For some their change of residence is barely noticed by the community, for they continue to maintain a house in the country by their fields and may in fact live there most of the time. Others, however, make the town their primary place of residence and often enter a town occupation. Thus communities like Sorata have experienced a dramatic increase in town campesinos. A much smaller increase is represented by the influx of educated technicians, many from humble backgrounds who are starting careers in the national agencies and must begin in the hinterland communities where some are destined to remain. The more dramatic mobility is the movement between strata within the community. Earlier we noted the cases of the young man whose campesino father bought him a truck in order that the son would not remain a campesino, and another campesino who acquired considerable property and runs a local store. Both are no longer considered campesinos, but rather cholos. They illustrate the status mobility that has occurred both within and between generations. But all the movement is not up. An important part of it has been down, while the fate of those leaving the community is largely unknown.

The second linked stratification change of importance is the increase in inter-strata hostility and conflict. There appears a general antagonism toward other strata in communities like Sorata, but it is the old decentes especially who speak out continually against the unprincipled local politicians, irresponsible professionals, pushy cholos, but, in particular, upstart campesinos. It is those former indios who do not know their place, or how to behave properly. They and their political allies have brought the town to its present low state. Such criticism is heard constantly in the homes of these families and wherever they gather together in public. Town campesinos are generally less outspoken, but when encouraged to talk they will describe instances of continued discrimination, cheating, or abuse that they or their acquaintances experience from vecinos. It is the sindicato leaders who are more open and expressive in criticizing and denouncing decente attitudes and conduct of the past as well as the present. For these men expressions of this sort may or may not be personal beliefs, but they are almost always a part of sindicato political rhetoric whose aim is to orient and politicize campesino members. Legal conflict over former hacienda land rights is another element in this pattern. Of physical conflict, however, there is relatively little, with the exception of a few well-known political assassinations.

If these are the major changes in local community status brought about by the Revolution, the examples of Reyes, and especially Villa Abecia, should also be kept in mind. It is unnecessary to recount the various circumstances in these two communities that account for the preservation of their status orders in the face of the pressures for change unleashed by the Revolution. However, there is one point worth emphasizing in this connection, and that is the adaptive capacity shown by the various decente groups when the basis of their wealth and power has not shattered. Thus even in Villa Abecia they lost large tracks of land but retained the really productive and valuable irrigated parcels. From this position of strength they exerted themselves successfully to dominate the local campesino sindicato, the local MNR party, and with it the local government. Thus even though some groups of campesinos, like the upland arrenderos, have been able to move out from under the control of local patrons, and the local stratification system has been opened up somewhat, it basically retains its traditional form. Decentes and campesinos remain basically in their traditional relation of dominance-submission. In Reyes the traditional stratification system was not so closed and rigid and, again, while the Revolution has altered it somewhat, especially with respect to campesino rights and obligations, the form of the stratification order has emerged largely intact. Even in Coroico, whose strata have been so changed, one can see in the developing relations between rescatador and campesino the old dominance-submission pattern. However, the rescatadors are socially a very mixed set and include only a small fraction of the old decentes, while the campesinos are generally participants in highly politicized sindicatos. If not always an active force in rescatador-campesino relations, the sindicato remains a powerful potential force that cannot be ignored.

The element of power is inextricably intertwined with that of status. It has been implicit throughout this discussion, as well as quite explicit at a number of points. Yet power, like status, has undergone its own particular transformations in these communities, and there are several essential points that emerge from a comparison of the six communities. Running through the discussion of all of them is evidence of the decisive power of the central government. This occurs not in the abstract sense of comparing the weight of centralized national resources against those of a small rural community, but in the very immediate sense of both active intervention and the expectations of intervention in the local community. Even San Miguel, whose special status as a free Indian community has kept it outside the mainstream of post-Revolutionary change and whose own tenacious traditions emphasize the spirit and practice of independence, is not unaffected. Its efforts to achieve regional governmental status and to obtain the benefits of national programs are drawing it increasingly into the orbit of the national government, whose power to give and withhold programs and aid is frequently crucial to coping with local community problems. Compi, with its extensive contact with La Paz and greater involvement in national politics, is even more enmeshed in this nexus. It is the four towns, as local branches of national government, that most clearly reflect the dominance of "center over periphery" [Shills, 1961]. The parade of local delegations to the center (La Paz) in search of support and aid, the local turnouts and celebrations to honor visiting dignitaries from the center, and the turnover of local officials on orders from the center are some of the more visible signs of the intrusion of the political center into local affairs. Its ramified powers over governmental affairs, political affairs, national programs, and special forms of aid, plus its behind-the-scenes connections and influence means that the central government is a most palpable factor in town affairs.

The reciprocal of the dominating position of the central government is the generally weakened condition of community government. This is least true of the campesino villages, especially San Miguel, where the traditional form of community government is largely intact and whose performance is generally effective. But in the towns the situation varies from poor to calamitous. The character of this problem has been detailed in earlier chapters. Lacking adequate resources, competent personnel, independent authority, and clear responsibilities, these local governments cannot be expected to perform adequately. These key weaknesses are interrelated and, in turn, have developed out of the relations of local to central government in Bolivia. This deficiency makes it extremely difficult for the towns to cope with their problems.

Paralleling the weakness in local government, though not directly related to it, is the generally weak condition of most community organizations or associations. In the past such organizations have been prominent in community affairs and have operated in concert with the local government, assuming quasi-governmental responsibilities. Here the Revolution appears to have made some difference. While both little and greatly changed towns have equally weak local governments, the community associations and interest groups are weakest in the impacted towns. There they tend to be plagued by internal conflict, low morale, and high member turnover. The major exceptions are some of the sindicatos, especially the campesino sindicatos. These tend to be weak or not influential in the more traditional, less changed towns, but in the impacted towns they have become an important new influence. In some areas this influence is concentrated in the former hacienda zones and their populations where they are even responsible for the appearance of new campesino communities. This is the case around Coroico and its Yungas environs [Heath, 1969; Leons and Leons, 1971]. The campesino sindicatos as new influential associations not only flourish in the ex-hacienda zones around Sorata, they also play an important role in town affairs. These campesino sindicatos, as new sources of power in the rural scene, represent one of the most important, most basic changes brought about by the Revolution of 1952. Their importance can hardly be overestimated, even though it is clear from the earlier descriptions that they vary considerably in their organization, their activities, their effectiveness, and their power. They have played a key part in politicizing the campesinos, in preparing and enabling them to play an active role in national politics, in defending and advocating their interests, and in providing a vital link between campesinos and the national center. The political role of the new campesino sindicatos, plus the transformed status relations between campesinos and decentes are probably the two most important changes coming out of the Revolution and redefining the character of rural society in Bolivia.

In the earlier chapters we have noted the many other changes, large and small, as well as the continuities in the six communities. Many of these changes are important in their own context, and some even have a wider significance. But in comparing the communities, the elements of change just enumerated stand out as those key changes in the status and power dimensions of the community social systems that are most responsible for the differences in form as well as function of those systems. For such complex phenomena they best define the essential impact of the Revolution on the six communities. This last is important. Each community as described here represents its own reality, and the collective set of six provide evidence of similarity and variation in the community change process. These six communities, however, cannot be understood as representing all rural Bolivia. In fact, many areas of Bolivia remain largely unstudied, or at least unreported—the southern highlands of Potosi; the frontier tropical lowlands of Pando, Beni, and Santa Cruz; the chaco zone of eastern Tarija. Geography does not necessarily produce social and political variation, but it is quite likely that rather different community situations can be encountered in these less central areas. In addition, some critically important communities which are more centrally located, among them the mining communities of Oruro and Potosi and the early politicized campesino communities of Cochabamba, have not been sufficiently reported. Research in these and other areas is likely to reveal additional important variations in rural communities. An example is a brief report of a recent study made in northern Chuquisaca. It suggests that most campesinos on the hacienda studied were peons of other peons and therefore profited little, if at all, from the agrarian reform [Heyduk, 1973-74]. Until a larger series of local studies has been carried out, the wider significance beyond the situations studied and the validity of making generalizations from the research reported here will remain unclear. The complementary nature of much recent and current research in Bolivia should clarify this question.

The developments that have occurred in the highly impacted communities suggest several more general implications for rural change. One is the considerable potential for change that exists among peasant populations. This idea is not new, or even unfamiliar, but merits reaffirming. Much of the literature concerned with peasants, especially when the focus is change, has emphasized the opposite: peasant resistance to change, irrational clinging to outmoded ways, apathetic or hostile responses to innovations [Arensberg and Niehoff, 1964, pp. 139-42; Wagley, 1964]. Behind some of these conclusions lurks premature generalization. Comparison of the six communities indicates the very wide range of variation in peasant change that took place, and also the considerable range in kinds of change. Both are important qualifications, but they do not diminish the fact that profound changes in peasant life have occurred without a total reconstruction of the national society. A second and related implication is how peasant confidence has been enhanced as their power has increased. This is visible in its traditional form in a community like San Miguel, where the comuneros have long had considerable power over their own internal affairs within an otherwise peasant-dominated society. It is visible in its new post-Revolutionary form in the new campesino communities surrounding Coroico and in Sorata. The new form is an enlarged confidence, for these peasants are able to influence not only their own lives but important non-campesino individuals and groups at regional and national levels. The local campesino in Sorata who became head of the provincial government as sub-prefect and later a national deputy from the province in the election of 1966 is a symbol of this contrast. This same phenomenon has been observed on a smaller scale as a result of political and other changes on Hacienda Vicos in highland Peru [Doughty, 1964-65; Vazquez, 1964-65]. A final implication concerns the necessity of altering stratification relations. In rural societies dominated by rigid stratification hierarchies, are basic changes in these hierarchies necessary to achieve such goals as developing a sense of national citizenship and promoting economic and technological innovation? These objectives of national modernization programs may not be achievable through improved communication and education [Rogers, 1969]. In this connection, the examples of Reyes, and, especially, Villa Abecia, suggest how the elite members of intact community stratification orders, even in the face of threat of radical change, are concerned and work primarily to maintain those orders rather than change them in the slightest to accommodate sources of disaffection and protest. Rigid rural stratification orders such as these may well prevent successful accommodation of the rural sector to the changing needs and demands of the larger society.

Two decades have now passed since the Revolution, and the past decade has seen several new governments come and go. None has had the potential or concern to promote as well as accept and guide societal change that the MNR of 1952 had. Future research will establish what the long-term trends will be of rural change and continuity in Bolivia. Meanwhile, the descriptions of these six communities which reacted so differently to that Revolution reveal some of the major consequences that have developed up to 1966. The Bolivian case ranks as one of the major national experiments in socio-political change in Latin America. One of the few modern revolutions to occur in this region, it represents a significant variation on the more well-known Mexican and Cuban cases. As such it commands our attention.

Appendix 1

BOLIVIA PROJECT PERSONNEL

The following list, cited alphabetically, includes all staff members who participated in the various aspects of the project. The specific functions of each group are spelled out in the Preface, which also acknowledges the contributions of the individuals involved in field work, data organization, and analysis.

Administration and Coordination
 Vera Rubin, Director
 Lambros Comitas, Associate Director
Research and Analysis
 William McEwen, Research Director
 Abdel Omran, M.D., Director of Epidemiological Studies

ANTHROPOLOGICAL FIELD STAFF

COMPI: Hans Buechler, Pascual Nacho. *COROICO:* Alfredo Antezana, Katherine Barnes, Dwight Heath, Felix Mangudo, Eloy Robalino S. *REYES:* Alejandro Madde, Said Madde, Victor Novick, Gwen Novick, Gerardo Pereira, Julio Roca. *SAN MIGUEL:* Lauren Klein, Marcos Mamani, Solomon Miller. *SORATA:* Katherine Barnes, Eustequo Condori, Beverly Holcombe, Mauricio Mamani, William McEwen, Paz Mejia, Eloy Robalino S., Fernando Varela, Jaime Varela, Fredy Peñalosa. *VILLA ABECIA:* Katherine Barnes, Carlos Avila, Rosa Avila, Said Madde, Victor Novick.

SURVEY INTERVIEWERS

Carlos Avila, Rosa Avila, Katherine Barnes, Fernando Choque, Raul Delgado, Julio Roca Iriarte, Willy Kustermans, Dionisio Laura, Jorge Lopez, Said Madde, Armando Medrano, Paz Mejia, Blanca Muratorio, Pascual Nacho, Sergio Ossio, Benjamin Ruiz Pereyra, Michael A. Pettitt, Carlos Antonio Ptaires, Vicente Quispe, Mario Ralde, Weymar Rios, German Salinas, Humberto Schmidt, Fernando Varela, Efrain Vasquez, Jorge Vasquez, Jaime Vilela.

DATA CODERS AND ANALYSTS

Adrienne Aron, Cristina Baños, Mercedes Baños, Richard Borevitz, Martha Burela, Martha Callejo, Ines Gomez Clark, Isabella Conti, Ana Dickman, Max Dickman, Lee Dumont, Elida Fernandez, Susana Friedmann, Cata Garcia, Hector Garcia, Brunilda Velez Heilbrun, Norita S. Jones, Greta Kaninen, Joyce Kelly, Carol Mackey, Francis Many, Robert Mates, Joan Medlin, Nicola Miller, Wendie Miller, Velma Morgan, Blanca Muratorio, Michael Newman, Michael Pettitt, George F. Ray, Inti Sternback, Nydia Willbanks.

EPIDEMIOLOGY STAFF

Abdel Omran, M.D.; K. Y. Fawzy, M.D.; Mahfouz Zaki, M.D.; Franz Ressel, Elli Ressel, Catherine Champeau, Phyllis Fischer.

PROJECT ASSOCIATES

COLUMBIA–CORNELL–HARVARD–ILLINOIS FIELD PROGRAM IN LATIN AMERICA: Lambros Comitas, Director; Bambi Bernhardt, William Mitchell, Roger Newman, Susan Scrimshaw.
UNIVERSITY OF KENTUCKY MEDICAL SCHOOL INTERNATIONAL INTERNSHIP PROGRAM: Kurt Deuschle, M.D.; Hugh Fulmer, M.D.; Rachel Eubank, William Lawrence, Rice Leach, Edward Nighbert, Paul Wright.
FILMSTRIP EDITOR: Jane Gregory.

OFFICE AND CLERICAL STAFF

Carol Dickert, Dena Hirsch, Miyuki Iida, Ranko Morishige, June Murray, Andrea Talbutt, Eugene Tsujimoto.

Appendix 2

COMMUNITY STUDY OUTLINE

The following outline, based on the project research design, was developed to coordinate the collection of field data from the various community study sites in Bolivia. Based on this outline, a data-classifying system was generated in order to process field notes and to provide ongoing categorization by topic and by community.

1. Description of the geographic environment, including territorial location, accessibility, climate, physical lay-out and structure of the community.
2. Population demography (restricted to Cédula A operations).
3. History and development (collection of information relevant to the developmental history of the community, roughly before 1950).
   30. Significant historical developments (changes in one or more of the major community institutions, e.g., change in governmental status, economic crisis, basic communication change like a road, etc.).
   31. Position of the community in the region over time, especially in relation to neighboring communities and centers of power.
4. Background institutional systems
   40. Economics
      400. Major and minor material resources of the community plus limitations.
      401. Principal economic activities (production, distribution, consumption).
      402. Economic organizations and their operations.
      403. Social organization of economic enterprises.
      404. General profile of the economically active population.
      405. Meaning of work to the different segments of the community.
      406. Temporary work groups (how they are formed, how they operate, what goals).
      407. Levels of remuneration plus differentiation of economic activity, e.g., wages, profit in terms of time and labor.
      408. Labor organizations, e.g., sindicatos, protective associations.
      409. Labor conflict and mechanisms for resolving such conflict.

4010. Seasonal fluctuation in economic activity and its effects on economic organization as well as the social structure, e.g., weekly market day, planting and harvest periods, etc.

4011. Organization of finance (who loans money, to whom, what obligations are incurred, the flow of money in and out of town as well as within it).

41. Education (formal systems and types of vocational training).

410. General characteristics of formal instruction (objectives, curricula, organization of formal education).

411. Educational differences characteristic of the different segments of the community (e.g., level of education, choice of school and reason for choice).

412. Material aspects of teaching (e.g., physical plant, endowment and support, educational aids).

413. Attitudes of students, teachers and the different segments of the community toward education and the school system.

42. Religion

420. The system of religious ideas and their variation in relation to the different segments of the community.

421. Social organization of the church (ecclesiastical organization and jurisdiction, religious and community service and activity).

422. Social organization of the fiesta complex.

423. Religious participation and roles in ceremonies, services, and ritual.

424. Differences in religious attitudes in relation to the social structure.

425. Concepts of morality, philosophy, values.

43. Recreation

430. Types of recreation and entertainment; recreational facilities.

431. Culture of recreation, their patterned occasions and cycle of development.

432. Use of free time and related sociocultural norms.

433. Commercial and professional recreation-entertainment and its organization.

5. The sociopolitical system

50. The structure of the system (identification of the stable sets of more and less differentiated social relations).

500. Describing group structure.

5000. What are the groups (the distinctive relational sets, e.g., kin and fictive kin groups, age-sex groups, various interest groups—sports, religious, political as well as more complex and formalized structures like parents' educational associations, political parties, etc.)?

5001. Position structure.

50010. The "parts" of the group structure are here represented by a series of positions, which can be described in terms of distinctive sets of expected, permitted and prohibited behaviors. Of special interest are the types of power and communication positions.

50011. The positions of a group are in turn linked by several types of "bonds" (which may be more or less interrelated):

500110. authority: recognized rights to command, which may be hierarchical, equalitarian, anarchical, etc.

500111. communication: flow of information, which may be open, one-way, distorted, etc.

500112. prestige: degree of importance assigned a position, e.g., commands deference, permits certain license, etc.

500113. mobility: movement between positions, which may be open, closed, partial, etc.

5002. Interpersonal relations. (Instead of describing positions and their relations, the approach here is to describe the relations between pairs or sets of individuals. This approach is especially suited to less formalized groups where clearly identifiable positions are lacking, but it also applies to more formal types.)

50020. What are the types of attraction-repulsion patterns characteristic of the group (e.g., patterns of play, helping, discussing, avoiding, arguing, etc.)?

50021. What is the communication network, i.e., who can communicate to whom, when, what, under what conditions?

50022. What is the power structure, i.e., who has power (actually orders, commands) over whom, when, to do what, under what conditions?

50023. What other social relations exist (kinship, sexual, political friendship, exchange, etc.) that are important in organizing interpersonal behavior, how strong are they, how stable are they?

5003. Ranking within group structure

50030. What are the attributes by which group members are ranked, or assigned a standing in the group (e.g., degree of control over other persons, degree of access to important resources, degree of identification with the group, degree to which a person possesses prestige or other sociocultural traits)?

50031. How stable is the ranking process, how does ranking operate (what are the mechanisms, the symbols, e.g., titles, special privileges), what are its effects on social relations?

501. What is the degree of formalization of group structure, i.e., the explicitness of definition (e.g., written regulations, explicit sanctions, commonly known prescriptions, etc.)?

5010. What kinds of informal structures develop alongside the formal ones, what organizational problems or limitations have stimulated their development?

5011. How much tension or conflict is generated by the juxtaposition of formal and informal structures, what forms does it take, how is it resolved, how does such juxtaposition affect the functioning of the group?

502. What are the factors promoting and diminishing structure (i.e., what organizes regularity in social relations)?

5020. Efficiency of group operation (e.g., division of work, regularity of assignments and responsibilities, regular means of internal communication).

5021. Use of differential abilities and experiences.

5022. Physical and sociocultural environment (e.g., physical distance or proximity, physical problems of communication, social stratification).

503. Effects of group structure. What consequences appear to follow from occupying one position rather than another or being linked in one form rather than another (e.g., degree of activity, interest in change, mobility efforts, etc.)? (Thus solidarity of the individual to the group appears to be a function of occupying a more central position in the communication structure of the group.)

504. Further queries on structural bonds.

5040. Authority

50400. How is authority defined, and how much variation in definition occurs?

50401. How is authority achieved, augmented, diminished?

50402. What are the instruments of authority?

50403. What are the restraints on the exercise of authority?

5041. Communication

50410. What are the forms of communication within the community (e.g., radio, rumor, grapevine)?

50411. How much specialization of forms in terms of content is there, and how much do forms differ in their effectiveness and their accessibility?

50412. Who has access to, who controls the instruments of, communication and the channels of communication (including both informal means plus formal roles, e.g., gatekeepers)?

5042. Prestige

50420. How is prestige defined by different segments of the community, and how stable are the definitions?

50421. How much agreement exists on ascribing prestige?

50422. How is prestige acquired and lost?

5043. Power

50430. What are the different bases of power in the social

structure (e.g., reward power, coercive power, legitimate power, referent power, expert power)?

50431. How stable are positions of power?

50432. How much concentration of power exists, what trends can be observed, what are the forces behind the concentration and the trends?

50433. How is power amassed, applied and with what kinds of effects, lost and with what resulting consequences for groups?

505. Intergroup relations and strata

5050. How are intergroup relations defined? (Apply the same scheme described in section 500.)

5051. Social strata. (Of special interest are social strata or horizontal segments, which are not groups, though often termed "reference groups," but social categories with no social structure whose possession of common attributes serves to define expected, permitted, or proscribed behavior for members of the strata and/or members of other groups or strata, e.g., the elite, the disenfranchised, the business interests, the poor, etc.) How are such strata defined, what patterns of behavior are characteristic of strata members?

50510. How is membership in different strata defined (e.g., cultural differences, status prerogatives, group affiliation, etc.)?

50511. How much opportunity for mobility in or out is present, and what are the pressures for such mobility?

50512. Are the strata expanding, contracting, stable?

50513. What relative importance does strata membership have in relation to group membership?

50514. What are the relations between strata?

50515. What are the bases of the social strata (e.g., race, occupation, religion, etc.), how stable are they, how have they changed, how does the base affect the position of the strata in the social structure?

50516. What belief systems are associated with different strata?

51. Working of the system

510. Group action

5100. What manifest objectives are associated with different groups, and what latent objectives can be discovered?

5101. What forms and systems of action are associated with different groups and with different objectives, how much internal differentiation of action is there within groups, how much formalization?

5102. What is the impact of different group activities on the structure and working of the other groups?

5103. What systems of belief are associated with different group action systems, how much tension, how much disparity is there between belief and action?

511. Group cohesion

5110. The significance of group cohesion is its importance in the influence a group has on its members as well as its relevance to maintaining the personnel of a group and thus the group itself. Group attraction can be viewed as a function of two sets of conditions:

    51100. Properties of the group: its goals, program, size, type of structure, rank in the community, etc.

    51101. Needs of the individual: affiliation, recognition, security, etc.

5111. What are the sources of attraction of the different groups in the community?

    51110. Within the group itself as well as the group viewed as a means?

    51111. How do changing group properties, changing individual needs (e.g., with age), and changing environmental conditions alter group attraction and with what consequences?

    51112. What are the consequences of different sources of attraction for group structure, group action, group continuity?

    51113. How do groups attempt to enhance their cohesion? What factors enhance group attraction or reduce it (e.g., size, type of activity, rank)?

    51114. How do differences in group attraction affect member participation, pressures for conformity, maleability of members' behavior?

5112. What are the qualifications for membership in different groups? How do qualifications for membership differ from qualifications for continued participation? Do these qualifications vary with different positions in the group?

5113. What are the mechanisms and rituals for inducting members, what ideas are expressed in these activities, what is the impact on participants, what is the social significance of these ceremonies?

5114. Exactly how are new groups formed (e.g., families, fictive kin, recreational groups, work groups, political groups, etc.), which requires detailed decision-making data?

5115. How stable is membership in different groups? What factors account for differences in membership stability (e.g., a transitional group, a declining group, an embattled group, etc., specifying the conditions operating in each case)?

5116. How much movement is there between groups, how does it differ for different groups, what are the apparent causes of such movement?

5117. How much multiple-group membership is there, what groups are linked in this manner, what are the consequences for the groups as well as the members?

512. Group norms and pressures

5120. What are the social effects of maintaining uniformity of group norms (or standards) (e.g., helps the group accomplish its goals, helps the group maintain itself, helps define social and cultural reality for group members)?

5121. What factors affect group pressure to maintain its norms (e.g., salience of the group, achievement of the group, cohesion of the group, certainty of group sanctions, degree of individual self-confidence)?

5122. What happens when members begin to deviate from the norms? Which positions or persons with what combinations of relations, seem more prone to deviate and which are more disposed to conform?

5123. What are the incentives to conform (e.g., rewards, reciprocity, punishment—here and now, future, material or supernatural, etc.)?

5124. What are the techniques used to induce conformity (e.g., precept, praise, warnings, threats, sorcery) as well as more informal procedures (ridicule, gossip, ostracism)? Are there specialists in such techniques, under what conditions are which techniques used, how effective are they, what conditions diminish their effectiveness?

5125. What happens when deviants do not respond to pressure? What kinds of reactions occur in different groups and segments of the community, with what social effects?

5126. Under what conditions does continued deviancy result in:
    51260. Redefinition of the deviant behavior as non-deviant?
    51261. Change in the norm?
    51262. Ejection of the deviant from the group?

5127. How do pressures for uniformity differ between groups of voluntary and non-voluntary membership?

5128. What are the different forms of deviant behavior, including crimes, under what circumstances do they occur, how are they defined and popularly regarded, what are their social effects?

513. Leading and influencing
(Section 50 includes a description of the formal positions of authority as well as the more informal network of power relations that characterizes the community social structure. In this section the emphasis shifts to the more amorphous dynamic aspect of power and authority, i.e., how people are led and influenced in a given situation. Power implies the threat of sanctions and authority the recognized right to command, while influence implies willing compliance, which may have other bases than power or authority.)

5130. What bases of influence can be detected in different types of groups, within social strata, within the larger community social structure?
    51300. Personal characteristics (e.g., empathy; or the suggestion that leaders are persons with qualities needed to solve whatever problems the group is confronting).

51301. Social characteristics (e.g., prestige; or the idea that leaders are persons most representative of group norms, or perhaps are extremely accurate in judging group opinion).

51302. Cultural characteristics (e.g., possession of symbols of importance or value, possession of characteristics culturally defined as requisite of leadership, e.g., age, physical prowess, oratorical skill, etc.).

5131. How do persons acquire influence (the cultural symbols, the social perceptiveness and knowledge), how formalized are the procedures for acquiring influence, how available are they, how are they obtained?

5132. Are the different bases of influence compatible, do they engender antagonism and conflict, do they provide equally strong and stable sources of influence?

5133. What kinds of competition, antagonism, conflict occur in the community (not necessarily restricted to leading and influencing), what social positions are involved, to what extent do groups and strata become involved, what are the issues (both manifest and latent), what are the social consequences of these divisive tendencies?

5134. Can influence be transformed into authority, how, with what effects on group structure and intergroup relations?

5135. How much of the leader's influence is dependent on a network of supporters who facilitate his influencing through their own social behavior (e.g., spreading information favorable to the leader or his proposals, criticizing and otherwise undermining the position of his opponents)?

5136. How much are leadership and influence efforts affected by cultural climates of different groups (e.g., a climate of spontaneity, of free or open participation, of a spirit of competition, of an atmosphere of hostility, etc.)?

5137. What is the effect on influence efforts of multiple-group membership and multiple reference group identification? How much conflicting allegiance is thus created and how is such conflict resolved in responding to influence efforts.

5138. How do leaders use the existing communication structure, authority structure, power structure, prestige structure to influence the community?

5139. How much concentration of influence is there in given persons or given positions (e.g., some evidence indicates that persons are influenced by different people depending on the problem or interest at hand as in voting, making a purchase, selecting a form of entertainment. Another kind of differentiation to document occurs in a stratified system, where each stratum and each vertical segment may have its own leaders who act as gate-keepers between strata, seriously attenuating pyramiding tendencies)?

5140. How is influence characteristically exercised, what forms does it take in different groups and segments of the community, how much influence is self-fulfilling (people attribute great influence to X and so look to X for guides to action though X has no substantial base of power), how stable is influence (or is the leader just one of many persons trying to influence action, but his attempts are more often successful for a given situation only)?

5141. Can a secondary influence structure be discerned, i.e., persons who take cues from a leader and are themselves the instruments of influencing the wider public or members of a group? (In analyzing influence attempts, it is probably necessary to note what kind of objective is in view for influencing and then note who originates the idea, who sanctions it or places a stamp of approval on it, and who carries the idea through by suggesting, advising, telling others what to do.)

5142. What are the discernible aspects of group structure that promote or permit influence efforts (e.g., position of contact between groups and mobility between strata, centrality in the communication network or peripherality in linking the group to other groups or the group's environment)?

52. Some institutional components of the sociopolitical system.

520. Family

5200. Types of families (in numerical composition, social structure, culture).

5201. Family differences that reflect community stratification and segmentation.

5202. Family material culture (housing, budget and income, food consumption, dress, etc.).

5203. Family cultures (characteristic habits, customs, norms that predominate and distinguish).

5204. Family education activities.

5205. How are families established: marriage rules and rituals.

52050. What are the rules, or norms, governing the selection of partners, as well as the contact of sexes, restrictions of possible partners, etc.?

52051. How are the rules applied, what are the exceptions, what conditions are associated with exceptions, what reactions are produced by stretching the rules or trying to evade them?

52052. How are marriages arranged, what factors are taken into account, what persons figure in the arrangements (and what positions do they occupy in the social structure)?

52053. What kinds of social bonds are involved in marriage, what bonds are created beyond the couple to other groups, segments, strata, and what is the consequent impact of a marriage on these other social units?

52054. What factors promote the dissolution of marriages, what counteractions are set in motion by dissolving marriages, what social accommodations are required by broken marriages?

5206. Family group

52060. What kinds of social relations characterize family members, how much differentiation and formalization is there, how do these relations change over time (in relation to increasing age, growing number of children, changing position of the family in the community social structure, etc.)?

52061. What are the characteristic activities of the family group, how much specialization is there, what are the changes over time?

52062. What is the influence of the family in defining a member's social position in the larger social structure, and how influential is family membership in influencing member's behavior in other groups or social settings?

521. Kin and kinship plus fictive kin groups

5210. How is kinship defined, what are the bases for kin designations, and what is the vocabulary of kinship?

5211. What are the local kinship positions and relations, how important are they in local belief, what kinds of behaviors do they define (and in what terms: permissive, expected, required, prohibited), and how much allegiance do they actually command, especially in relation to competing demands or interests?

5212. What kinds of social groups, networks, cliques, cabals are based on or influenced importantly by kinship?

5213. In what areas of community activity are kinship considerations important, and in what areas have they little importance?

5214. What changes in the importance of kinship can be seen in comparing generations?

522. Local government and public administration.

5220. Local offices of the state (alcaldia, registro civil, etc.), their organization, jurisdiction and functions.

52200. What are the official objectives; what are the actual as well as latent objectives?

52201. What is the personnel complement and organization of work?

52202. How does the public participate and to what degree in these agencies, what are the public attitudes of different groups and strata?

52203. What is the official morality of office-holder, as well as private venality?

52204. What is the relation (formal and informal, legal and

extra-legal) of local offices and government to the national government and its agencies?

5221. What is the social position of local government officials, how is it influenced by their official positions (and vice versa)?

5222. How are government positions obtained, how much interest and competition is there, what are the job qualifications and how flexible are they, how much control is exerted over local government positions by community political and social groups?

5223. Taxation, sources of public income, and governmental regulation.

52230. What are the types of taxes levied locally by different governmental agencies?

52231. What kinds of exemptions can be obtained, how much differential application of both taxes and regulations exists, how much evasion occurs, what are the differential public attitudes toward taxation, regulation, evasion, etc.?

52232. How much governmental regulation is there, what spheres of activity does it cover (geographic movement, marriage, business activity, political activity, etc.)?

52233. What methods of evading taxation and regulation are employed, who is able to employ them, what is the effect on public morality, governmental morality, social positions?

52234. What fines (multas) are levied by local offices of the state, what is their size and range of application, the use to which they are put (e.g., supplement a government official's income, finance local public programs, etc.), what is the differential application of fines to groups and strata?

5224. Public works and programs

52240. What kinds of public programs are operating on the local scene (construction, sanitation, civic betterment, special training, etc.)?

52241. What is their personnel, activities, organization?

52242. What is the differential public attitude, and more generally what is the public sense of community problems and needs in relation to public enterprise?

52243. What are the social effects of these programs?

5225. Citizenship

52250. What is the public image of the rights and duties of citizenship; how does it differ between different groups and strata?

52251. What is the actual definition of citizenship rights and duties that follows from one's position in the community power and prestige structure?

5226. What are the instruments of governmental power?

52260. What are the formal law enforcement and/or informal

para-military groups, how are they organized, how are they commanded, who are their personnel and how are they recruited, how are they used—especially in relation to the law?

52261. What are the relations of these groups to the community social structure, what are public attitudes toward them, what parts of the community are they supposed to represent and what parts do they represent, and whose interests do they protect, with what consequences for the social structure?

52262. How stable are these groups, where is their allegiance, how rapid is personnel turnover, how dependent are they on changing political fortunes, how politicized are they as opposed to being professional?

5227. Justice

52270. What are the community concepts of justice: formal and informal, ideal and real?

52271. What are the formal agencies of justice, how are they organized, how do they operate, how are they influenced, how are they connected to the community social structure, over what spheres of action do they have jurisdiction?

52272. What are the informal means of securing justice, what is the degree of their elaboration and systematization, for what kinds of problems are they applied, are they more distinctive of some groups than others, what is their position re: the formal legal structures (feuds, assassinations, mediation, negotiation)?

52273. What groups or relations are most often involved in legal action, what are the most frequent or typical litigations, and what social effects do legal controversies have?

523. Political parties and movements

5230. What are the local political parties, what are the objectives of these parties (stated and unstated), how are they organized locally, what do they do, how are they connected to national parties, on the one hand, and the community social structure, on the other, how much interest, support and allegiance do they command, what are their extra-community connections (especially informal types), what influence do they have on community life, affairs and government?

5231. How much political factionalism is there, is it abetted by other tensions or rifts in the local social structure, what forms does this conflict take, what is its impact on the community social structure and its functioning?

5232. What other kinds of political groups are encountered (clubs, cabals, cliques), what are their idea or ideological orientations, how are they organized, what parts of the community do they represent, how stable are they, what influence do they have on community affairs?

5233. How much political awareness is characteristic of different parts of the social structure, what are the formal information media and how do they operate in relation to forming public opinion, how much centralization and governmental control is there of information sources and the spread of information, what kinds of socio-political ideologies are found and in what groups and/or strata?

5234. What is the relation of local political groups to the agencies of local as well as national government?

5235. What form does the political struggle for power take, what parts of the community are involved, how intense is the group struggle or competition, what limits are set by community-wide understandings and values, by the differential availability of resources, by the application and control of police-military force?

54. The external environment of the community

540. What have been the effects of wider economic, political, religious and social forces (throughout the province, the department, the nation) on local community affairs and social structure, currently as well as since about 1950?

541. What has been the significance of this larger environment not only as a source of external pressures producing local effects and reactions, but also as an outlet for internal pressures and contradictions, both currently as well as since 1950?

6. Community and private health

60. Concepts of health and illness.

600. How is illness defined by persons in different groups and strata?

601. How is illness explained (e.g., material, supernatural or psychological reasons; why this person at this time)?

602. What are the complementary ideas and standards of health?

603. What are the attitudes toward illness?

6030. What value is placed on health?

6031. Is there a moral component to illness and health?

6032. What is the range of attitudes toward sick people and kinds of illness (e.g., pity, fear, awe, contempt, anger, repulsion, etc.)?

61. How do attitudes toward illness affect the social position, social expectations, social relations and activities of the sick person and those related to him (brings into action different expectations, alters usual expectations, intensifies some relations and attenuates others, etc.)?

62. Treatment of illness

620. What is the range of treatments for the most important health problems (e.g., home remedies, informal treatment, traditional practitioners, etc.)?

621. How is a given form of treatment selected, who is involved in

the selection, what factors are taken into consideration, and how do they differ for persons in different social positions.

622. What is the ritual and magic component of treatment?

623. What beliefs are associated with different illnesses and their treatments?

63. What concepts and techniques of prevention are encountered and how are they distributed throughout the community?

64. Organization of medical care

640. What kinds of formal positions are found that either specialize or relate importantly to the treatment of illness, and how are they defined culturally and socially?

641. How are persons recruited to "medical" positions, what are the requirements, what are the rewards and costs, what are the social characteristics of these positions, especially in the wider arena of community influence and prestige?

642. How are "medical" positions interrelated, what kinds of social relations bind them, what are the effects of these relations on their use by the public?

65. Environmental health conditions (e.g., information on sanitation, animal vectors, housing conditions, etc.).

66. Types and prevalence of disease (both individual as well as community-wide, such as descriptions of an individual's health problems, course of disease, symptoms, or information on numbers of cases, impressions of prevalence of diseases).

7. The Peace Corps program

70. What has been the history of PC activity, community participation in PC work, and community understanding of and attitudes toward the program and its personnel?

71. Who are the present Volunteers, what has been their education and training, what Latin American experiences have they had, how long have they been in the community, what is their orientation to the community and its members, the different groups and strata?

72. PC program

720. What are the Volunteers trying to do?

721. How are they trying to accomplish their goals, what is the program of work?

722. What kinds of activities are they typically involved in, how is their activity organized?

73. Community connections

730. What parts of the community are involved with the PC program, and in what ways?

731. What kinds of attitudes are held by different parts of the community toward the Volunteers and their work?

732. What are the attitudes of the Volunteers toward different parts of the community, community problems, community affairs?

733. What kinds of relations do Volunteers have with different parts of the community social structure, what are the consequences for PC work, what effects do Volunteers have on community affairs and social life, how do Volunteer social relations affect their participation in the community, their social activities, their outlook on the PC program and the community?

GLOSSARY

actas: "Acts," generally referring to any official governmental or legal action.

adventista: An Adventist, a member of one of the Protestant religious denominations in Bolivia.

agente auxiliar: One of two chief officials in San Miguel ayllus.

agente municipal: A canton official in San Miguel.

aguayos: Woven woollen cloths made by both Indians and cholitas and used to enwrap a small child, or farm produce; a bundle wrap.

ahijado: Godchild.

alberja: A variety of bean.

alcalde: Mayor of a town.

alcalde de campo: The inspector of fields in San Miguel, also assistant to the judge.

alcalde de campo auxiliar: San Miguel ayllu official.

alcalde escolar: The inspector of schools, San Miguel.

alcaldia: City hall.

alferado: One of the two most important sponsors of fiestas in San Miguel.

aljiri: A supervisory position of obligatory labor service for peons on hacienda Compi.

altiplano: High plateau; the high basin area of western Bolivia in which the population is concentrated.

amañarse: Trial marriage among peasants.

amigos de confianza: Confidential friend; friend who can be trusted.

a partir: By shares, sharecropping.

arrendero: "Renter," a peasant who pays money in rent for land; part may also be paid in labor.

arroba: Unit of weight, equivalent to 25 pounds.

atrio: Enclosed terrace in front of a building.

ayllu: Quechua word for freehold Indian communities.

barranca: Ditch, gully.

blanco: "White"; a man of highest status in provincial society, claiming direct descent from the Spanish.

boliviano: Old monetary unit of Bolivia. One was equivalent to .008 cents; one thousand have become the new Bolivian peso, worth eight cents, U.S.

caballero: Gentleman, one of the highest social stratum of provincial society.

cacique cobrador: Canton tax collector, San Miguel.

campesino: Rural dweller, a peasant, used since 1952 for all Indians.

campesino dirigente: Leader of peasant union, often the top official.

canton: The lowest unit of regional government in the Bolivian national system.

capilero: San Miguel church servant.

cargo: A traditional Indian office, in either the political system or the fiesta system.

chacra: From the Spanish "chacara," farm, meaning a small piece of land or cultivated peasant parcel.

chacrita: Diminutive of chacra, "little parcel."

chicha: Indian beer made from masticated, maize flour which is fermented and boiled.

cholo: One who had a social status between mestizos and Indians in pre-1952 Bolivia.

chuño: Dehydrated form of potato, prepared by Aymara and Quechua Indians.

coca: The boxwood-like bush from which cocaine is derived; the leaf, which is chewed.

colono: Hacienda peon.

comando: The militia arm of the MNR.

comerciantes: Merchants of all kinds.

comisario: Aide to judges in San Miguel.

compadrazgo: Godparenthood.

compadre: Kinship term used by parents of a child to refer to his godfather; term of respect and endearment in widespread use.

comunario: Indian community peasant.

copal: Resin used for incense.

corregidor: One of the main government officials in canton San Miguel; a minor official in canton Jank'o Amaya.

corregidor auxiliar: Ayllu corregidor in San Miguel.

correo: San Miguel mailman.

criado: Foster child who may act as house servant.

de vestido: "Of dress," meaning European dress; i.e. not native costume.

empleados: Employees.

encomienda: Royal land grant of the Spanish period.

esaña: A small edible tuber.

estancia: Ranch, in Reyes comparable to hacienda, and in Coroico and Sorata, a finca; also, a farm. In San Miguel, a populated area with a given name. In Sorata and Villa Abecia, the upper, marginal lands, usually in desert or high mountain country, previously attached to the haciendas.

faena: A traditional agricultural work obligation.

feria: Fair.

fiesta patronal: Saint's Day celebration of the patron saint of an hacienda or town.

finca: Hacienda, farm, or ranch (estancia).

flotas: Buses and bus lines.

forastero: "Foreigner"; any outsider or person who, living in a provincial town, is not native to that town.

ganadero: Cattle rancher.

generala: A dice game commonly played in the cantinas of the towns.

gente decente: "Decent people"; refers to the highest stratum of provincial society—the vecinos, blancos, patróns, caballeros, and proprietarios.

gremiales: Semiskilled workers and artisans, including carpenters, metalsmiths, shoemakers, tailors, etc.

hacendado: The owner of an hacienda, the patrón. Synonymous with caballero, gente decente, propietario, and, prior to 1952, vecino.

hacienda: An agricultural property of the feudalistic system which prevailed in Bolivia until 1952.

hectare: A measure of land equivalent to 2.4 acres.

hijo: "Son," a term of endearment (slang, used familiarly).

hijo de crianza: Adopted child.

imillas: "Young girl"; also written *emillas*.

indio: Substitute term for Indian, now pejorative.

intendente: Police official.

intendente municipal: Supervisor of municipal services.

jilakata: Aymara term for chief, the highest traditional official of Indian communities.

juez parroquial: The major judicial post in San Miguel.

junta de vecinos: A survival of colonial town government, consisting of the leading citizens of the town; an advisory body to officials.

latifundia: Large feudalistic agricultural estate in pre-1952 Bolivia; now, unused estate: so used in law.

llocallas: "Youth" in Quechua, generally used by a person of a higher social class to demean a cholo peasant.

madrina: Godmother.

maestro: "Teacher," also a term of respect for an artisan, or skilled worker.

mayordomo: In pre-Revolutionary period, an overseer of peons. In the areas studied, invariably a mestizo or blanco.

mestizo: One of "mixed" blood, or of Spanish and Indian ancestry. Also, a social status between blancos and cholos in pre-1952 Bolivia.

minoristas: "Small-timers," petty merchants.

mita: Colonial obligation of Bolivian Indians to work in the mines, later extended to agricultural service.

mozo: Term for male servant, but also applied by townspeople to demean cholos or refined peasants.

muñeca: Influence with public officials.

negociantes: Traders in small wares, clothing, and staples.

notario: Registrar of vital statistics.

novio: Sweetheart, fiancé.

oficial mayor: Deputy mayor.

oka: An edible tuber.

padrino: Godfather.

pagos: Payments.

paja brava: Coarse grass used for pasture.

pampa: Grassy plain.

pandero: Baker.

papalisa: A small, sweet, edible tuber.

parientes: Relatives.

pasante: Traditional sponsor of fiestas.

patrón: Landlord.

peon: Semi-serf on the haciendas who, for usufruct rights to a small parcel was obligated to provide three days of labor a week for the patrón and perform other personal services.

peso: Unit of Bolivian currency, equal to eight cents, U.S.

puna: Bleak, arid highland of the Andes.

poke lomanake: Gypsum, used to make stucco.

pollera: The full, colorful skirt of chola women.

prestación vial: The obligation of male citizens to contribute three days a year to public works.

propietario: "Proprietor"; in provincial Bolivia, synonymous with patrón.

quina: Cinchona bark.

quintal: Unit of weight, one hundred pounds.

quinua: An edible grain.

rescatador: Middleman trader in coffee, coca, and fruits.

sapo: "Toad," a game similar to ski-ball.

sindicato: Peasant or labor union.

Sindicato Central: The major regional sindicato organization, made up of affiliated local unions and union centrals.

singani: Distillation from grapes.

sot'a: A supervisory post at hacienda Compi.

sub-central: The first grouping of local peasant or labor unions.

tambo: Unloading place in La Paz markets.

thola: Evergreen shrub.

tienda: General store.

tinterillo: Street-corner lawyers, untrained.

totora: Water reed.

tramites: Legal paperwork.

transportistas: Transporters, usually with trucks.

turno: Turn, the order of turns to be taken in receiving irrigation water.

utawawa: A foster child.

vecino: "Neighbor"; in Spanish, a citizen of the town, those able to vote and participate in civic life; also used to distinguish townspeople from campesinos.

viñatero: A peasant who works in the vineyards.

Vitichis: People from the town of Vitichi.

zafra: Sugarcane harvest or field.

zafreros: Workers in the zafra.

BIBLIOGRAPHY

Alexander, Robert J. *The Bolivian National Revolution*. New Brunswick, N.J.: Rutgers University Press, 1958.

Appelbaum, Richard P. *Theories of Social Change*. Chicago: Markham, 1970.

Arensberg, Conrad M., and Arthur H. Niehoff. *Introducing Social Change*. Chicago: Aldine, 1964.

Baudin, Louis. *A Socialist Empire: The Incas of Peru*. Princeton, N.J.: Van Nostrand, 1961.

Bell, Colin, and Howard Newby. *Community Studies: An Introduction to the Sociology of the Local Community*. New York: Praeger, 1972.

Bendix, Reinhard. *Embattled Reason: Essays on Social Knowledge*. New York: Oxford University Press, 1970.

Blasier, Cole. "Studies of Social Revolution: Origins in Mexico, Bolivia, and Cuba." *Latin American Research Review*, 2:28-64, 1966-67.

Bonfil Batalla, Guillermo. *Diagnostico sobre el Hambre en Sudzal, Yucatán*. Instituto Nacional de Antropología e Historia, Mexico, 1962.

Buechler, H., and J.-M. Buechler. *The Bolivian Tymara*. New York: Holt, Rinehart & Winston, 1971.

Carter, William E. *Aymara Communities and the Bolivian Agrarian Reform*. University of Florida Monographs, Social Sciences No. 24. Gainesville: University of Florida Press, 1964.

Chevalier, François. *Land and Society in Colonial Mexico: The Great Hacienda*. Berkeley: University of California Press, 1963.

Clark, Terry N. (ed.). *Community Structure and Decision-making: Comparative Analyses*. San Francisco: Chandler, 1968.

Clark, Ronald J. "Problems and Conflicts over Land Ownership in Bolivia." *Inter-American Economic Affairs*, 22:3-18, 1968-69.

Comitas, Lambros. "Educación y estratificación social en Bolivia." *América Indígena*, 28:631-51, 1968.

Cotler, Julio. "The Mechanics of Internal Domination and Social Change in Peru." In Irving Louis Horowitz (ed.), *Masses in Latin America* (New York: Oxford University Press, 1970), pp. 407-44.

452   Bibliography

Daniel, Thomas M. "Report of an Evaluation of the Peace Corps Tuberculosis Control Program in the Yungas Area of Bolivia." Unpublished, 1968.

Doughty, Paul L. "The Interrelationships of Power, Respect, Affection and Rectitude in Vicos." *The American Behavioral Scientist*, 8:13-17, 1964-65.

ECLA (Economic Commission for Latin America). *Social Change and Social Development Policy in Latin America*. New York: United Nations, 1970.

García, Antonio. "La reforma agraria y el desarrollo social de Bolivia." *El Trimestre Económico*, 31:339-87, 1964.

Goodenough, Ward H. *Cooperation in Change*. New York: Russell Sage Foundation, 1963.

Heath, Dwight B. "Land Reform in Bolivia." *Inter-American Economic Affairs*, 12:3-27, 1958-59.

————. "Bolivia: Peasant Syndicates among the Aymara of the Yungas—a View from the Grass Roots." In Henry A. Landsberger (ed.), *Latin American Peasant Movements* (Ithaca, N.Y.: Cornell University Press, 1969), pp. 170-209.

Heyduk, Daniel. "Bolivia's Land Reform Hacendados." *Inter-American Economic Affairs*, 27:87-96, 1973-74.

Hobsbawm, E. J. "Peasants and Rural Migrants in Politics." In Claudio Veliz (ed.), *The Politics of Conformity in Latin America* (New York: Oxford University Press, 1967), pp. 43-65.

Huntington, Samuel P. *Political Order in Changing Societies*. New Haven: Yale University Press, 1968.

Ilchman, Warren F., and Norman Thomas Uphoff. *The Political Economy of Change*. Berkeley: University of California Press, 1969.

Junta Nacional de Planeamiento. "Plan de desarrollo económico y social, 1962-1971." *Planeamiento* (September 1961), No. 3-4-5.

Kahl, Joseph. *The American Class Structure*. New York: Rinehart, 1957.

Kelly, Isabel. *Anthropology, Culture, and Public Health*. La Paz, Bolivia, n.d.

Kling, Merle. "Toward a Theory of Power and Political Instability in Latin America." In James Petras and Maurice Zeitlin (eds.), *Latin America, Reform or Revolution?* (New York: Fawcett World Library, 1968), pp. 76-93.

Knorr, K. E. *World Rubber and Its Regulation*. Stanford: Stanford University Press, 1945.

Lambert, Jacques. *Latin America: Social Structures and Political Institutions*. Berkeley: University of California Press, 1969.

Legters, Lyman H., and Wendell Blanchard (eds.), *U.S. Army Area Handbook for Bolivia*. Washington, D.C.: Special Operations Research Office, American University, 1963.

Leonard, Olen E. *Bolivia: Land, Peoples, and Institutions*. Washington, D.C.: Scarecrow Press, 1952.

Leons, Madeline B., and William Leons. "Land Reform and Economic Change in the Yungas." In James M. Malloy and Richard S. Thorn (eds.),

Beyond the Revolution: Bolivia Since 1952 (Pittsburgh: University of Pittsburgh Press, 1971), pp. 269-99.

Lyle, Norris B., and Richard A. Calman (eds.). *Statistical Abstract of Latin America*. Los Angeles: Latin American Research Center, University of California at Los Angeles, 1965.

Malloy, James M. "Revolution and Development in Bolivia." In Cole Blasier (ed.), *Constructive Change in Latin America* (Pittsburgh: University of Pittsburgh Press, 1968), pp. 177-232.

————. "Revolutionary Politics." In James M. Malloy and Richard S. Thorn (eds.), *Beyond the Revolution: Bolivia Since 1952* (Pittsburgh: University of Pittsburgh Press, 1971), pp. 111-56.

McEwen, William J. "Forms and Problems of Validation in Social Anthropology." *Current Anthropology*, 4:155-83, 1963.

Myrdal, Gunnar. *Beyond the Welfare State*. New Haven: Yale University Press, 1960; New York: Bantam Books, 1967.

Nadel, S. F. *The Foundations of Social Anthropology*. Glencoe: The Free Press, 1951.

Omran, Abdel R., William J. McEwen, and Mahfouz H. Zaki. *Epidemiological Studies in Bolivia*. New York: Research Institute for the Study of Man, 1967.

Osborne, Harold. *Bolivia: A Land Divided*. 3rd ed. London: Oxford University Press, 1964.

Pando Gutierrez, Jorge. *Bolivia y el Mundo*. La Paz, 1947.

Pardo Valle, Nazario. *Cinchona Versus Malaria: Historia, Economía, Ciencia*. La Paz: Empresa Editora Universa, 1951.

Parsons, Talcott. "An Outline of the Social System." In Talcott Parsons *et al.* (eds.), *Theories of Society*, I (Glencoe: The Free Press, 1961), pp. 30-79.

————. *Societies: Evolutionary and Comparative Perspectives*. Englewood Cliffs, N.J.: Prentice-Hall, 1966.

Patch, Richard W. "Social Implications of the Bolivian Agrarian Reform." Unpublished Ph.D. dissertation, Cornell University, 1956.

————. "Peasantry and National Revolution: Bolivia." In K. H. Silvert (ed.), *Expectant Peoples* (New York: Vintage Books, 1963), pp. 95-126.

Pike, Fredrick B. *Spanish America, 1900-1970: Tradition and Social Innovation*. New York: Norton, 1973.

Rogers, Everett M. *Modernization among Peasants*. New York: Holt, Rinehart & Winston, 1969.

Scrimshaw, Nevin S., and Taylor Gordon. *Interactions of Nutrition and Infection*. World Health Organization, Monograph No. 57, 1968.

Shills, E. A. "Center and Periphery." In *The Logic of Personal Knowledge: Essays Presented to Michael Polanyi on His Seventieth Birthday* (London: Routledge & Kegan Paul, 1961), pp. 117-31.

Strickon, Arnold. "Anthropology in Latin America." In Charles Wagley (ed.), *Social Science Research on Latin America* (New York: Columbia University Press, 1964), pp. 125-67.

Tumin, Melvin M. *Social Stratification: The Forms and Functions of Inequality*. Englewood Cliffs, N.J.: Prentice-Hall, 1967.

Urquidi, Arturo. *El Feudalismo en América y la Reforma Agraria Boliviana*. Cochabamba: Imprenta Universitaria, 1966.

Vasquez, Mario C. "The Interplay between Power and Wealth." *The American Behavioral Scientist*, 8:9-12, 1964-65.

Veliz, Claudio (ed.). *The Politics of Conformity in Latin America*. New York: Oxford University Press, 1967.

Wagley, Charles. "The Peasant." In John J. Johnson (ed.). *Continuity and Change in Latin America* (Stanford: Stanford University Press, 1964), pp. 21-48.

Whitehead, Laurence. "Bolivia Swings Right." *Current History*, 62:86-90, 117, 1972.

Zondag, Cornelius H. *The Bolivian Economy, 1952-1965: The Revolution and Its Aftermath*. New York: Praeger, 1966.

INDEX